FABRICATING HOM

SOUTH ASIA IN MOTION

FABRICATING HOMELAND SECURITY

Police Entanglements across India and Palestine/Israel

RHYS MACHOLD

STANFORD UNIVERSITY PRESS
STANFORD, CALIFORNIA

Stanford University Press
Stanford, California

Printed and bound by CPI Group (UK) Ltd, Croydon, CR0 4YY

Library of Congress Cataloging-in-Publication Data

Names: Machold, Rhys, author.
Title: Fabricating homeland security : police entanglements across India and Palestine/Israel / Rhys Machold.
Other titles: South Asia in motion.
Description: Stanford, California : Stanford University Press, 2024. | Series: South Asia in motion | Includes bibliographical references and index.
Identifiers: LCCN 2024003647 (print) | LCCN 2024003648 (ebook) | ISBN 9781503639690 (cloth) | ISBN 9781503640719 (paperback) | ISBN 9781503640726 (ebook)
Subjects: LCSH: Internal security—India. | Terrorism—India—Prevention. | Police training—India. | Security systems industry—Israel. | Private security services—Israel. | India—Relations—Israel. | Israel—Relations—India.
Classification: LCC HV8247 .M323 2024 (print) | LCC HV8247 (ebook) | DDC 363.20954—dc23/eng/20240405
LC record available at https://lccn.loc.gov/2024003647
LC ebook record available at https://lccn.loc.gov/2024003648

Cover design: Michele Wetherbee
Cover photograph: Paramita Nath
Typeset by Newgen in Adobe Caslon Pro 10.5/15

For my parents

TABLE OF CONTENTS

List of Illustrations ix

Acknowledgments xi

Abbreviations xvii

Map of Mumbai xix

Introduction 1

1 Comparative Geopolitics 32

2 Homeland Security Pioneers 58

Interlude—A Reticent Embrace 93

3 Aftermaths 98

4 The Changing Same 131

5 Encountering Difference 165

6 Educating a Market 197

Conclusion 232

Epilogue 245

Notes 249

Bibliography 291

Index 317

LIST OF ILLUSTRATIONS

3.1: Image from *The Mumbai Protector: A Magazine for the Mumbai Police* 116

3.2: Image from *The Mumbai Protector: A Magazine for the Mumbai Police* 117

3.3: Image from *The Mumbai Protector: A Magazine for the Mumbai Police* 118

3.4: Image from *The Mumbai Protector: A Magazine for the Mumbai Police* 119

4.1: Blast site inside Nariman House 132

4.2: Police standing guard outside of CST 136

4.3: EL-GO Team anti-crash bollards installed at Taj Hotel 136

4.4: BGI anti-crash bollards and security gate 137

4.5: BGI anti-crash bollards and security gate 138

4.6: Scanners at entrance of CST 139

4.7: Sandbag Bunker 140

4.8: Line of barriers 141

4.9: Line of barriers 142

4.10: Nakabandi 143

4.11: ATS Wanted Poster 144

4.12: Image featuring officer holding M82/M107 .50-caliber anti-materiel rifle 147

4.13: Posters on suburban trains 158

4.14: Poster on suburban train 159

4.15A AND B: BGI bollards being modified 164

6.1: Screenshot from SWI website 203

6.2: Entrance to IFSEC and Homeland Security India 206

6.3: BGI Engitech Pvt. Ltd. booth at IFSEC and Homeland Security India 207

6.4: BGI Engitech Pvt. Ltd. booth at IFSEC and Homeland Security India 208

6.5: Ashok Leyland police vehicle on display at IFSEC and Homeland Security India 208

6.6: Diagram from Securing Asia 2012 212

6.7: Image from "Guiding India to a Secure Future" 215

6.8: "Catalyst for Thought Leadership" 217

6.9: List of participating companies at previous SWI events 218

ACKNOWLEDGMENTS

FOR MANY YEARS I sincerely doubted that this book would ever come to fruition. That it has is due in large measure to the support, kindness, and patience of many people. While I cannot name all the people who have supported this project, as it may endanger them, I owe an enormous debt and gratitude to all.

This book has followed me around across a number of places for over a decade. It began at the Balsillie School of International Affairs in Waterloo, Canada. Faculty and colleagues there, including Kim Rygiel, Rianne Mahon, Alison Mountz, Simon Dalby, Sarah Martin, Antulio Rosales, Masaya Llavaneras Blanco, Tracey Wagner-Rizvi, Crystal Ennis, Adam Malloy, Anton Malkin, Veronica Kitchen, and Sara Koopman all nurtured my thinking immeasurably as I began on this scholarly journey. Deb Cowen has also consistently pushed my thinking and politics from its very early stages and onward.

This book would not have been possible without many formative conversations with a wide range of interlocutors who I met as I traveled across and between Canada, the U.K., Palestine/Israel, and India. I also wish to thank the many people who shared their reflections on and experiences of policing, homeland security, violence and various forms of repression, surveillance, and displacement. Some of you did so at considerable risk to yourself. I have learned things from you that I am forever grateful for. In many cases our political commitments were and continue to be directly at odds, but I sincerely appreciate that you were willing to engage with my work. A special thanks to the librarians and other staff members at the United Services Institution Library and the Institute for Defence Studies and Analyses in New Delhi, which graciously assisted me in my archival fieldwork over a number of months during two visits.

As I have carried out my fieldwork in India and Palestine/Israel, I have been nurtured by the tremendous hospitality, friendship, and assistance of many. Thanks to the people who welcomed me during my time as a visiting researcher at the Tata Institute for Social Sciences between 2012–2013 as well as on subsequent visits to Mumbai and Delhi: Swapna Banerjee-Guha, Dilnaz Boga, Abdul Shaban, Suraj Gogoi, Sanober Keshwar, Rupesh Kumar, Nilesh Kumar, Sharib Ali, Aiman Khan, Shailza Singh, Sudhir Kumar, Santana Khanikar, Surya Ghildiyal, Nikita Sonavane, Atul Bharadwaj, and Gagan Preet Singh. Special thanks to Paramita Nath for sharing many good meals, for accompanying me on walks around Mumbai, and for sharing her photos of the city's security infrastructure, some of which are reproduced in this book. During my time in Palestine/Israel, Aviad, Alma, and Timna kindly hosted me in their lovely home, and Neve Gordon and Yotam Feldman provided vital guidance and research support. Thank you.

As a visiting researcher at the Danish Institute for International Studies (DIIS), I found a warm and welcoming community. There I also benefited from formative discussions with a number of colleagues: Rens van Munster, Peer Schouten, Jessica Larsen, Finn Stepputat, Johannes Lang, Manni Crone, Stefano Guzzini, Peter Albrecht, Rose Loevgren, and Kasper Hoffman. Special thanks to Lars Erslev Anderson for organizing a DIIS research seminar to present some very early chapters together with Leila Stockmarr. After returning to Canada, a number of colleagues at York University also provided me with vital support, mentorship, and friendship: Jakeet Singh, Liz Dauphinee, James Sheptycki, Anna Agathangelou, Robert Latham, David Mutimer, Sarah Naumes, Corey Robinson, and Derek Verbakel.

The majority of the writing of my manuscript has taken place at the University of Glasgow where I have benefited immeasurably from many thoughtful and supportive colleagues and comrades: Mo Hume, Naomi Head, Alister Wedderburn, Rhys Crilley, Ty Solomon, Jane Duckett, Allan Gillies, Andy Judge, Cian O'Driscoll, Katherine Alison, Sophia Dingli, Georgios Karyotis, Kelly Kollman, Karen Wright, Diarmaid

Kelliher, Dave Featherstone, Emma Laurie, Sarah Armstrong, Oli Charbonneau, Toni Marzal, Guillem Colom-Montero, Ben Rosher, Alistair Fraser, Jay Sarkar, Ian Paterson, Jenny Morrison, Matthew Waites, Dania Thomas, Ophira Gamliel, Tim Peace, Maurizio Carbone, Petar Bankov, Sergi Pardos-Prado, Patrick Bayer, Vladimir Unkovski-Korica, Ana Langer, Rachel McLellan, Maha Rafi Atal, Marco Goldoni, Vera Pavlou, Corey Robinson, Kirsteen Paton, and Giovanni Picker. My students have also nurtured my thinking and politics: Nicole Printy Currie, James Barlow, Janica Ezzeldien, Saba Ameer, and Min Young Park.

As I began pitching the book, Somdeep Sen has been a source of endless insight and guidance throughout. Particularly at times when I faced serious doubts, he has always given me much-needed strength and inspiration to see this project through. For commenting on earlier chapter and book proposal drafts, I wish to also thank: Pete Adey, Cian O'Driscoll, Ty Solomon, Alister Wedderburn, Rhys Crilley, Jessa Loomis, Dave Featherstone, Joe Getzoff, Rebecca Jarman, Nivi Manchanda, Catherine Charrett, Corey Robinson, and Marita Murphy. Alongside three incredibly generous anonymous reviewers at Stanford University Press, these critiques and suggestions continuously pushed the depth of the writing and book's core conceptualizations and sustained my energy to continue on with it. From the outset Dylan Kyung-Lim White has helped me navigate the review process at Stanford always with great care and generosity. I am ever grateful to him as well as Austin Michael Araujo for editorial support as well as South Asia in Motion series editor Thomas Blom Hansen for believing in this project at a very early stage. In crafting the final manuscript, Abigail Rosenthal's editorial brilliance has been vital in helping me to sharpen the writing and weave the different threads together more coherently. I also wish to thank Alex Tarr for crafting the beautiful map that appears in the book and to Sarahh Scher for her work developing the index. Abha Joshi also provided crucial research assistance. A number of people have also helped me greatly with questions about Hindi translations and etymology: Ali Taqi, Gagan Preet Singh, Ophira Gamliel, and Shailza Singh. I also wish to thank Ali Taqi for his endless patience as my Hindi teacher and for his friendship.

Over the years, I have been fortunate to present earlier versions of parts of this book at a number of workshops, conference panels, and speaking invitations. Two sessions on Israel and global militarism organized by James Eastwood and Leila Stockmarr at the International Conference on Critical Geographies in Ramallah and the British International Studies Association in London helped me deepen my engagements and settler colonial studies. A subsequent roundtable session organized by Micol Seigel at the American Studies Association annual meeting in Denver as well as panels organized with Lisa Bhungalia, Andy Clarno, Sara Salazar Hughes, and Stepha Velednitsky at the American Association of Geographers as well as a session at the International Conference on Critical Geographies in Athens organized with Craig Jones further sharpened my thinking on these issues and helped to deepen my engagement with histories of empire and race-making. Special thanks to Goldie Osuri's invitation to the University of Warwick and to Santana Khanikar and Sudhir Kumar for the invitations to share my work at Jawaharlal Nehru University. Further thanks to Ali Ali for the invitation to present parts of the book at the University of Helsinki. My thinking on police power has also been nurtured by many years of collective thinking with members of the anti-security collective including: Brendan McQuade, Mark Neocleous, Catherine Charrett, Tyler Wall, Tia Dafnos, Aaron Henry, George Rigakos, Guillermina Seri, Georgios Papanicolaou, Deniz Özçetin, and Will Jackson.

This project has received support from a number of institutions over the years. Funding for the research and writing of this book was generously provided by a combination of grants and fellowships from the Balsillie School of International Affairs, Wilfrid Laurier University, the Ontario Graduate Scholarship, the Indian Commonwealth Scholarship, the Shastri Indo-Canadian Institute, and the University of Glasgow. I also wish to thank New Media for allowing me to reproduce images from the Mumbai *Protector* in this book. Chapters 2 and 3 are adapted from two articles previously published in *Environment and Planning A: Economy and Space* and *Security Dialogue*, respectively. Thanks to SAGE Publications for their willingness to allow sections of these articles to be reproduced here.

In addition to those already named, many people have supported me with their inspiration, camaraderie, mentorship, and kindness: Sara Salazar Hughes, Stepha Velednitsky, Lisa Bhungalia, Emily Gilbert, Stuart Schrader, Zoha Waseem, Deniz Yonucu, Wassim Ghantous, Mark Griffiths, Mikko Joronen, Craig Jones, Micol Seigel, Goldie Osuri, Andy Clarno, Alison Howell, Colleen Bell, Nivi Manchanda, Sharri Plonski, Kyle Grayson, Jemima Repo, Deana Heath, Majed Abulsalama, Desirée Poets, Arlene Tickner, Debbie Lisle, Jennifer Lynn Kelly, Manisha Sethi, Nisha Shah, Jess Linz, Carrie Mott, Jasbinder Nijjar, James Eastwood, Meha Priyadarshini, Una McGahern, Sabrien Amrov, Sigrid Vertommen, Jineee Lokaneeta, Rupal Oza, Camel Burak Tansel, Ajay Pasaram, Cetta Mainwaring, Muhannad Ayyash, Chris Rossdale, Heba Youssef, Jenna Marshall, Lisa Tilley, Ted Rutland, Anna Feigenbaum, Kali Rubaii, Debangana Bose, Lianne Hartnett, Olivia Mason, Rosa Maryon, Heather McLean, Olivia Rutazibwa, Kristina Hinds, Ghada Sasa, Martha O'Carroll, Mat Coleman, Jenna Loyd, Anne Bonds, Helen Berents, Marshall Beier, Lou Pingeot, Mark Salter, Ida Danewid, Phil Thomas, and Kate Hall.

My family has been by my side throughout my academic journey, and this book owes much to all of them: Rita, Clea, Ed, Findlay, Felix, Julie, and Aurora. My late father, Rainer, sadly was not able to see the final version of this book, but right to his final days he was enthusiastically supportive. It saddened me that he was unable to see it in print, but his iron will has inspired me to press on with the writing through some challenging times.

My work has also been nurtured in countless ways by a wider family and the love of many who have kept me going all these years: Nathaniel, Illyes, Shabab, Mike, Rosie, Dave, Galen, Thomas, Lori, Dunja, Taylor, Ella, Victoria, Chris, Paul, and Pawel. Without you I would not be who I am. My Danish family has also been by my side throughout with their boundless love, humor, and generosity. I hope you will all be pleased to know that the question "So, *when* will your book be done?" is now no longer relevant.

While I had already begun the work that became this book some time before we met, it is impossible to imagine it coming into being in its present form without Malene Jacobsen's unwavering love, compassion, and support. Throughout you also brought a sharp critical eye and passionate creativity that pushed me to develop my thinking very far beyond what I would have been capable of alone. I remain endlessly grateful to you for all of that and the life we share. And last but not least, thanks to Sally who has kept me sane through some very long days.

ABBREVIATIONS

ASSOCHAM	Associated Chambers of Commerce and Industry of India
ATS	Anti-Terror Squad
BGI	BG Ilanit Gates and Urban Elements Ltd.
BJP	Bharatiya Janata Party
CST	Chhatrapati Shivaji Terminus
DHS	Department of Homeland Security
FICCI	Federation of Indian Chambers of Commerce
HLEC	High Level Commission of Enquiry
IB	Intelligence Bureau
ICAO	International Civil Aviation Association
IDR	Indian Defence Review
IDSA	Institute for Defence Studies and Analyses
IED	improvised explosive device
IEICI	Israel Export and International Cooperation Institute
IFSEC	International Fire and Security Exhibition and Conference
IMOD	International Defense Cooperation Directorate of the Israeli Ministry of Defense
INSAS	Indian Small Arms System
IOF	Israel Occupation Forces
IPS	Indian Police Service
ISDS	International Security and Defense Systems Ltd.
ISI	Inter-Services Intelligence
LeT	Lashkar-e-Taiba

MARCOS	Marine commandos
MCOCA	Maharashtra Control of Organised Crime Act
MDA	Magen David Adom
MFG	Modernisation of Police Force Scheme
MHA	Ministry of Home Affairs
MKISC	MK International Security Consulting Ltd.
NADGRID	National Intelligence Grid
NCTC	National Counter Terrorism Centre
NIA	National Investigative Agency
NSG	National Security Guard
NYPD	New York Police Department
PFLP	Popular Front for the Liberation of Palestine
PLO	Palestine Liberation Organization
POTA	Prevention of Terrorism Act
QRTs	quick response teams
RAW	Research and Analysis Wing
RTI	right to information
SIMI	Students' Islamic Movement of India
SOP	standard operating procedures
SWI	Security Watch India
SWUK	Security Watch UK
TADA	Terrorist and Disruptive Activities Prevention Act
UKTI-DSO	UK Security Trade Commission
USI	United Services Institution
VT	Victoria Terminus
ZAKA	*Zihuy Korbanot Ason* (disaster victim identification)

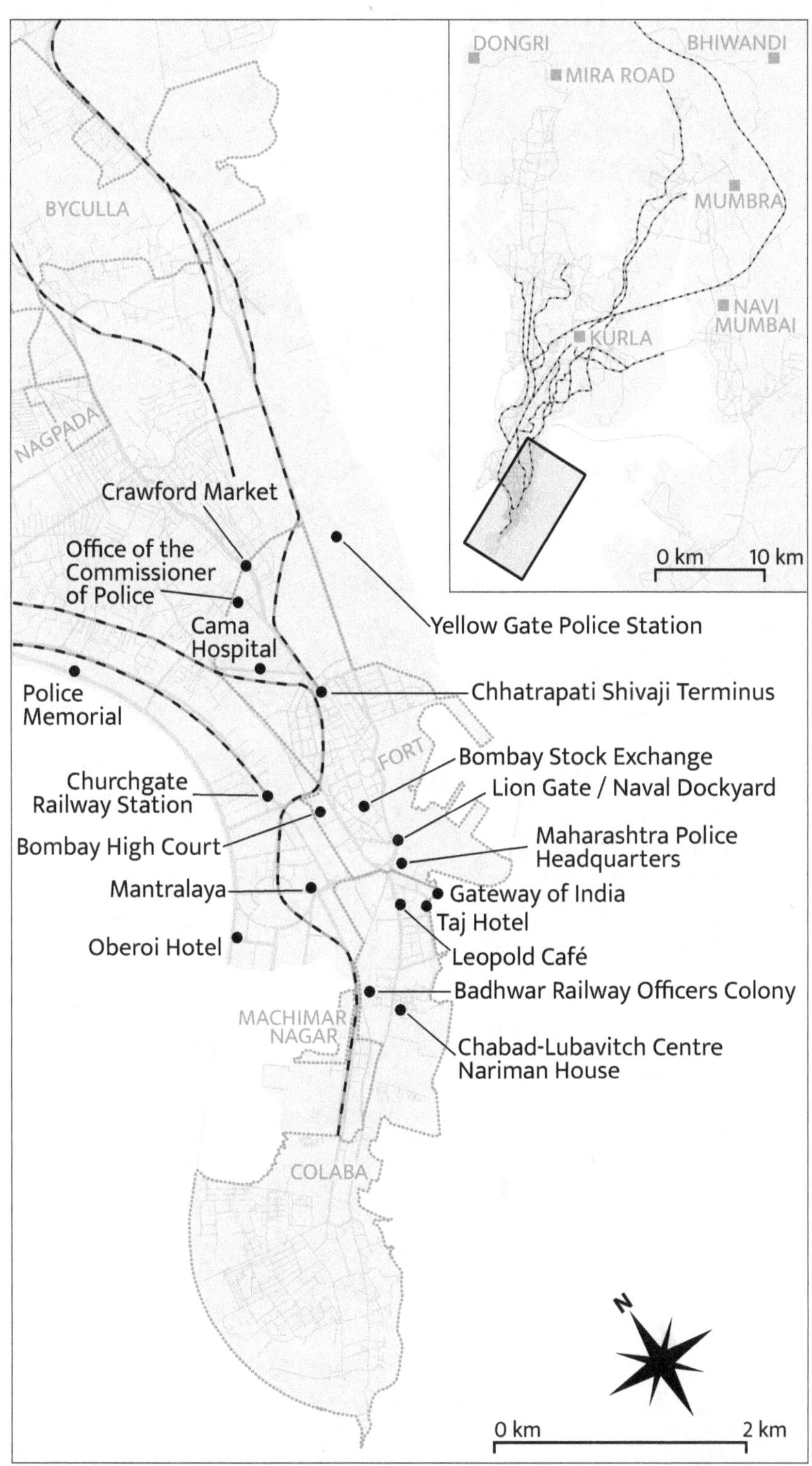

Map of Mumbai (Alex Tarr, 2023)

FABRICATING HOMELAND SECURITY

INTRODUCTION

HOMELAND SECURITY IS RARELY *just* a matter of the homeland. It involves the circulation and multiplication of policing practices across borders. In early efforts to make sense of the September 11 attacks, state officials, policy experts, and media commentators looked for parallels and connections to past events elsewhere. In a CNN segment aired on September 26, 2001, host Greta van Susteren noted: "Some aspects of the September 11 hijackings were not unique." The segment focused on the 1999 hijacking of Indian Airlines flight IC-814 en route from Kathmandu to New Delhi. With approximately 180 passengers and crew on board, five hijackers forced Flight 814's pilot to fly to Amritsar, Lahore, then on to Dubai and ultimately Kandahar, at the time under Taliban control. In order to release the passengers and crew upon arrival in Kandahar, the hijackers demanded that Indian authorities free three Muslim men imprisoned in India on terrorism charges, a request that was met by the Indian government.

In its discussion of the potential connections between the hijacking of Flight 814 and the September 11 attacks, the CNN segment featured three Indian officials: Indian government spokesperson Nirupama Rao; Captain Devi Sharan, pilot of Flight IC-814; and Kanwar Pal Singh (K.P.S.) Gill, the former director general of police in the Indian state of Punjab who had since become a security expert. Rao noted that one of the hijackers of Flight 814 was a member of the Mujahideen, which she reminded viewers was "part of Al-Qaeda." Gill further argued that there was good reason to believe that "both sets of hijackers [in 1999 and 2001] had similar training and may have shared techniques," asserting that the "experience of Kandahar [in 1999] came in very handy to plan and train those people in the USA," that is, to carry out the September 11 attacks. The segment concluded with Sharan, who stressed that India's experience with Flight 814 would be crucial to U.S. investigators in their attempts to piece together the September 11 attacks and develop a response.[1]

In carrying out the research for this book, I found some evidence of U.S. officials visiting India during their investigations and attempts to develop policy responses to September 11.[2]

Yet, Indian officials' early attempts to position the hijacking of Flight 814 as a precursor to September 11 and a lesson to be learned from were drowned out by similar efforts of other states. By the time the CNN segment aired, Israeli officials had been busy making the case that Israelis were the first to have experienced so-called "global," "Islamic" terrorism. Israel, they further claimed, had a demonstrated record of successfully fighting it. On September 13, 2001, former Israeli diplomat David Rubin was quoted in a *Washington Post* article arguing that "[t]his question of hijacking of a civilian plane that could cause damage to civilian infrastructure is something that our [Israeli] security establishment is very aware of and has thought about for many years." The tenor of Rubin's claims was also more brazenly self-promoting than those made by the Indian officials. Rubin not only praised Israel as an exemplar of security preparedness; he disparagingly contrasted this to the *lack* of imagination seen in the United States. In the same article Rubin noted, "In the U.S., this isn't even in their briefings. I don't think anyone thought about this [the use of airliners as missiles] happening in a serious way, except for Tom Clancy in his books."[3]

This strategy to position Israel as a pioneer of domestic security preparedness worked. During the days and weeks after September 11, a range of American state officials and media pundits repeated Rubin's and similar claims as gospel.[4] In the months and years thereafter, this praise of Israel materialized into policy. U.S. officials gravitated to Israel as a "model" for fighting their counterinsurgency campaigns in Afghanistan and Iraq.[5] In Israel, they also saw an inspiration for the emergent architecture of domestic surveillance, fortification, and intelligence-sharing in the United States. Indeed, Israel has been credited with developing the "all-encompassing approach" to domestic surveillance and territorial control associated with the term "homeland security" well before the term was coined by the Bush administration with the creation of the U.S. Department of Homeland Security (DHS) in November 2002.[6] As the emergent homeland security state solidified in the course of the U.S.-led global war on terror, it quickly became coterminous with a sprawling global homeland security industry that advises and supplies governments and police forces across the world. While the United States remains by far the single biggest player in this industry, Israel has emerged as a particularly influential node of influence[7] as an exemplar of homeland security to be emulated by others, including India.[8]

This book engages with the emergence of homeland security as a new state form and "model" of policing to be emulated and reproduced around the world. The book does so by tracing Indian and international state and corporate actors' attempts to remake India in the image of homeland security in the decade after the 2008 Mumbai attacks, known in India simply as "26/11." 26/11 sparked a major public backlash against the Indian political class and generated pressure to adopt "modern" homeland security approaches from the Global North. The event is widely seen as a turning point in the ways that matters of security have been imagined and governed in India ever since. This book traces the actually-existing connections forged between India and other places under the banner of homeland security in the immediate aftermath of 26/11 and the years that followed.

Bringing together insights from science and technology studies (STS) and actor-network theory (ANT) with those from decolonial and postcolonial theory, the book locates homeland security as a universalizing transnational project staged through ongoing practices and encounters across time and space. However, the book argues that the origins, directions of travel, and trajectories of homeland security are rather less self-assured and all-encompassing than they might first appear. Furthermore, this approach makes visible the multiple forms of politics, contestations, and struggles at play within this project of world-making. That is to say, following Sanjay Seth, in this project (western) knowledges of homeland security "do not merely cognize a world external to them but serve to constitute that world."[9]

From the outset, homeland security has been framed by its architects as domestically oriented yet transnational in nature. For instance, the U.S. National Strategy for Homeland Security of 2002 declared the mandate of DHS as "an exceedingly complex mission" necessarily based on carrying out activities "both at home *and* abroad."[10] In the practitioner volume *Comparative Homeland Security: Global Lessons,* Professor Nadav Morag, an Israeli-trained faculty member of the Center for Homeland Defense and Security at the Naval Postgraduate School in Monterey, California, made similar claims. While presenting homeland security as a "*Uniquely American* concept" he reminds readers that "[t]he homeland security mission is [. . .] a global one", stressing that a "homeland security approach that ends at a nation's borders *is not a homeland security approach at all.*"[11] In other words, while Morag frames the *concept* of homeland security as radically exceptional and national (i.e., "uniquely American"), he argues that the practice of homeland security is necessarily *trans*national. Morag employs a comparative case study methodology, which focuses on the United States, Israel, the U.K., France, Germany, Canada, Australia, Japan, the Netherlands, and Italy to extract and share its "global lessons." Morag's claims speak to a recurring dynamic in the fabrication of homeland security, that is, claiming it as part of particular *national* history (much like the Indian and Israeli officials above) while simultaneously mobilizing this same national branding to forge new *trans*national relations.

Morag also anticipates readers' concern about homeland security's actually-existing geography. Given "that homeland security is a concept and discipline that is of American origin," Morag notes, readers might "inquire as to the utility of a book that focuses on *international* homeland security policies."[12] Morag answers his own question, stating that although homeland security still remains "alien to other countries, there is a wealth of experience and tested policies and approaches employed overseas in the various areas that constitute homeland security."[13] Thus, despite homeland security's self-consciously world-making ambitions, Morag and other advocates cite tensions in its universal pretenses.

Through a focus on the often unseen and overlooked political struggles at work in homeland security's global mission, *Fabricating Homeland Security* tells the story of how claims to global authority are assembled, travel, and are put to work. Contra commonsense associations with global policing and security models as freestanding, coherent entities, it argues that models are better grasped as sets of contested transnational relations in-the-making that are constituted through encounters across time and space. As the examples of Indian and Israeli attempts to position their counterterrorist "experience" as instructive demonstrate, the authority that particular claims to expertise command emerges out of sustained work and struggles to gain visibility and recognition. As the CNN segment and the pages of *Comparative Homeland Security* further allude to, the question of *where* exactly other countries sit vis-à-vis the global mission of homeland security is less straightforward than it might appear. Indeed, rather than taking the geography of homeland security as given, *Fabricating Homeland Security* is concerned with state- and corporate-led efforts to stage and organize the world in the image of homeland security alongside the violence of contemporary empire.[14] Indeed, I argue that homeland security—as an idea, a set of practices, and the basis for substantial transnational commerce—is in a constant state of what I call *fabrication*. More specifically, homeland security is not only literally *made* but also *made up* and *woven together* across time and space as it seeks to fabricate social orders.

This book develops these claims through focus on Israel's homeland security industry and its engagements with India. India formally recognized the state of Israel in 1950, and the two countries began to develop ties, most of which remained informal and covert for many years thereafter. As Azad Essa notes, the first forty years of Indo-Israeli relations were marked by "ambivalence, indifference and most crucially, the struggle of perceptions," owing in large measure to India's "self-image as a leader of the colonized and a buffer against Western imperialism."[15] While there were no formalized ties during this period, some Indian politicians, ideologues, and military and police officials expressed their admiration for Zionism and

Israel's martial prowess. These desires yielded interaction between Israeli and Indian actors, albeit on a limited scale.[16]

Under the tenure of P. V. Narasimha Rao's premiership from 1991–96, rapprochement between India and Israel made significant strides, with the two countries establishing formal diplomatic relations and opening embassies in 1992. That year, Indian Minister of Defence Sharad Pawar also acknowledged the existence of bilateral counterterrorism cooperation between the two countries.[17] Since then, Israel and India have continued to forge a close bilateral alliance, which has been founded on weapons sales and India's retreat from its historic pro-Palestinian stance.[18]

In the course of the war on terror, these linkages have been deepened and consolidated. India has become more fully imbricated into the orbit of U.S. empire, forming a triad with Israel in these states' battles against the common enemy of so-called "global," "Islamic" terrorism.[19] By the early 2000s, Israel was India's second largest supplier of conventional weapons (after Russia), and other strategic ties were beginning to emerge, including on counterterrorism.[20] Yet efforts to collaborate on counterterrorism have been haunted by the historic ambivalence and struggles over perceptions referenced by Essa above. More specifically, within Indian strategic circles the prospect of emulating Israeli policing practices, technologies, and logics *at home* in India has been represented as tentative and questionable. For example, in 2000 K.P.S. Gill lauded Israel's "clear and utterly unambiguous statement of a national policy perspective on terrorism" as an inspiration for India.[21] While celebrating a number of foreign counterterrorism models (including those of Israel and the United States) and suggesting that they might advance India's own counterterrorism thinking, Gill stressed that "it is not sufficient simply to imitate these [models] or to adopt them verbatim from some other country."[22] Efforts to bring homeland security to India have proven similarly fraught and elusive.

INDIA AND HOMELAND SECURITY

Throughout the early and mid-2000s, India faced persistent bombings. Indian politicians and institutions often blamed Muslims for such events. However, the September 11 attacks were a game changer in this longer-standing demonization of Muslims in India and their representation as quintessential "terrorists." As the global war on terror began to take shape, Indian state actors took a series of measures to codify this prejudice into law. By September 27, 2001, the Students' Islamic Movement of India (SIMI) was officially declared a banned organization and on October 21, 2001, the governments of the United States and India signed the Mutual Assistance on Criminal Matters Treaty, which expressed its determination "eradicate the scourge of terrorism" through bilateral collaboration.[23]

Following the attacks on the Indian parliament on December 13, 2001, the Bharatiya Janata Party (BJP)–led National Democratic Alliance (NDA) introduced the notoriously draconian antiterrorism legislation known as the Prevention of Terrorism Act (POTA).[24] POTA was passed into law in March 2002 but was surrounded by intense controversy and political opposition. Commentators and scholars often drew parallels between POTA and the U.S. PATRIOT Act, claiming that POTA justified state-sponsored violence against minorities and leftist groups in India but Muslims in particular. POTA came with a list of "terrorist" or otherwise threatening organizations including and beyond SIMI, while crucially leaving out right-wing organizations such as Bajrang Dal, a militant Hindutva group that routinely incites violence against Muslims. In a way "unabashedly against Muslims," Rupal Oza argues that POTA "became a legislative sanction for state-sponsored terror."[25] On December 9, 2004, POTA was repealed in a parliamentary vote, following the electoral defeat of the BJP and the formation of the Congress-led United Progressive Alliance (UPA) government. Yet, crucially, many of the most problematic elements of POTA, particularly its prejudicial treatment of Muslims, were shifted into India's criminal code through the revision of the 1976 Unlawful Activities Prevention Act (UAPA) in 2004.[26]

During these political struggles surrounding legal reforms to India's domestic counterterrorism infrastructure in the early 2000s, some began to suggest that India's *lack* of an analogous institution to DHS made it increasingly—and unnecessarily—vulnerable to militant attacks. In a news article published in 2004, former Indian high-level civil servant and strategic affairs analyst K. Subrahmanyam lamented Indian politicians' apparent lack of interest in building a robust security and intelligence coordination infrastructure, in contrast to the alleged success of DHS.[27]

Four years later, Ajit Doval, a former high-ranking Indian intelligence official who, among other assignments in his career, negotiated the release of Flight 814's crew and passengers, made a similar critique of India's lack of security preparedness through a comparison to DHS. Writing in the Indian national daily *The Hindu,* Doval lamented the thousands of Indian deaths unfolding at "the hands of terrorists."[28] According to Doval, however, what was most "tragic" about this state of affairs was not the deaths alone. Rather, it was the endurance of a political status quo under which Indians continued to be

> governed by the same laws, same change-resisting bureaucratic procedures, same misplaced priorities where internal security is a low priority item in the budget, same selection procedures laced by corruption and caste politics, and same training which was designed to keep colonial masters in power. We take the losses in our stride—nobody's blood boils, no one's conscience is pricked and nothing changes.[29]

Like Subrahmanyam, Doval contrasted this lack of political commitment to deep internal security reform in India with the U.S. response to September 11, as exemplified by the creation of DHS. As Doval stressed, the "secret of success" of the ability of the United States to prevent domestic attacks post-9/11 "lies in lowering our tolerance threshold for all that which fails to deliver, changing fast and constantly, and taking the changes to the last beat constable on the road."[30] Such calls for India to replicate the U.S. homeland security state thus reflect a core desire to overcome India's colonial policing infrastructure and "backward" approach to security by emulating "modern" models from the Global North.

In the early 2000s, the global homeland security industry took note of such aspirations. It began to position itself to Indian state clientele. Although its activities remained obscure at the time, some were mentioned in Indian English-language media. For instance, an *Assam Tribune* article published on October 14, 2006, documenting an Israeli trade delegation visit to the Indian city of Shillong began: "Israel is willing to share its technology on Homeland security system [*sic*] with its 'friend' India." The article noted that Israel "takes pride in developing some of the most sophisticated gadgets pertaining to homeland security," suggesting that these were of growing relevance to India. "With terrorists striking India with increased frequency" the article noted, "New Delhi is believed to have started window-shopping for high-tech homeland security systems."[31] In October 2008, an article noted that the U.S.-based weapons firm Raytheon had its eye on India as a major new growth market for new "homeland security solutions," projecting business growth of USD $1 billion over the next five to ten years.[32]

These proposals for homeland security were pitched as a solution to India's vulnerabilities. However, the project of bringing homeland security to India appeared to be going nowhere fast. For instance, a January 2008 *Hindustan Times* article noted that despite some enthusiasm for it, "the idea of a national body to tackle terrorism—like the US Department of Homeland Security—remains bogged down by political concerns."[33] Another article later the same year reflected on some of the potential basis of such concerns. It reported that senior Indian officials had just concluded "extensive discussions" with DHS officials in New York alongside Indian Prime Minister Manmohan Singh's recent official visit to the United States. The article cited an unnamed senior Indian official who noted that members of the Indian delegation "wanted to learn from their [U.S.] experience" in preventing terror attacks on domestic soil post–September 11. But after the discussions in New York, the official claimed that he and his colleagues remained unconvinced that this experience was replicable in India.[34] Another article published the same day quoted an unnamed source who similarly attributed the success of DHS to its "draconian provisions," which he argued were ill suited for India. Despite the Americans' unambiguously "impressive success in tackling terror," the official stressed that "many of their measures cannot be implemented in India."[35] In short, despite expressing their desire to emulate DHS, Indian officials cited intractable structural impasses preventing them from doing so.

Flash forward two months, and a significant shift was afoot. As a series of brazen attacks began across the city of Mumbai on the evening of November 26, 2008, homeland security was catapulted from relative obscurity to center stage in India. Quickly dubbed "India's 9/11" or simply "26/11," the parallels to September 11 became hard to ignore. 26/11 unleashed a jingoistic fervor and an unprecedented tide of public anger over India's perceived incompetence in preventing the attacks as well as calls for a major institutional overhaul of its domestic security architecture. Critiques of the authoritarian and communal tendencies, corruption, lack of professionalism, and politicization of the Indian police apparatus were themselves nothing new. Nor were proposals to overcome such deficiencies by replicating the supposed successes of powerful western states.[36]

Yet, in the aftermath of 26/11, concerns about the corruption of Indian politicians and the lack of professionalization of the police suddenly rose in prominence and shifted in character. The systemic corruption and the adhoc, patchy nature of India's domestic security infrastructure were widely attributed as the root causes of India's "softness" in the face of "global," "Islamic" terrorism.

At this historical juncture, India's lack of homeland security became a central reference point through explicit comparisons to foreign models. For instance, a *Hindustan Times* article of November 28 lamented that India's "anachronistic" approach to fighting terrorism was out of step with the modern policies of the United States and the U.K., noting that a "department of homeland security is still shockingly a non-concept here [in India]."[37] These references to India's lack of homeland security in late 2008 were framed as the principal cause of a failure to prevent the Mumbai attacks as well as their broadly perceived (mis)handling. As a December 3 headline asked: "Homeland Security: Who Is in Charge Here?"[38] Thus, in the space of a week, the previously marginal claim that India's absence of homeland security was *the* central national problem had become conventional wisdom. Ajit Doval, it seemed, had finally gotten his wish.

Within this sudden focus on India's lack of homeland security as a national problem, references to the United States were unavoidable. The juxtaposition of the DHS and India's lack of preparedness renewed interest in building new Indian state bureaucracies modeled on those in the United States.[39] As a result, the following institutions were proposed: the National Investigative Agency (NIA), the National Counter Terrorism Centre (NCTC), and the National Intelligence Grid (NADGRID). The NIA came into existence with the enactment of the National Investigation Agency Act of 2008, passed by the Indian Parliament on December 31,

2008, and accompanied by other significant legal changes, including major amendments to UAPA.[40]

Within these efforts to refashion the Indian security state, however, the United States was not the only point of comparison or source of inspiration. Mirroring dynamics in the aftermath of September 11, Israeli actors began to position themselves as a solution to the crisis, and they were taken seriously by Indian state officials and media voices alike. In the immediate aftermath of 26/11, Israeli Prime Minister Ehud Olmert and Indian Prime Minister Manmohan Singh both made public statements pledging increased counterterrorism coordination.[41] And Indian news agencies positioned Israel's homeland security credentials as unparalleled, outstripping even those of DHS. A *Hindustan Times* article published on December 19, 2008, noted: "We are aware that post 9/11 the United States quickly created its homeland security agency and has since thwarted any attempt to attack that country. [But] Israel is a class by itself."[42] Thus, as media references to homeland security spiked in the aftermath of 26/11, Israel was positioned as the exemplar of homeland security *par excellence* that India should emulate. Thus, 26/11 emerged as what Veena Das calls a "critical event" through which a "new reality" emerged, whereby Israeli homeland security came to be seen as the solution to the crisis, an issue to be explored in greater depth in chapter 1.[43]

A WORLD-MAKING PROJECT

When the term *homeland security* emerged in the early 2000s, it was greeted with broad concern from a range of critical scholars. It became a metonym for the boundless sense of fear and *in*security characteristic of the "post-9/11" world.[44] It also functioned as a "a stand-in for a series of inchoate anxieties associated with the rapid intensification and integration of information and communication technologies and the globalized economy."[45] The paradigm of homeland security further became associated with an unprecedented acceleration in the "militarization" and "securitization" of everyday domestic spaces, particularly cities, on a planetary scale and a rescaling of security per se.[46] Some read the growing salience of homeland security as evidence that security was "coming home."[47] More recently, others have called attention to how the "homeland security model [. . .] is being replicated" around the world, including in India and other countries in the Global South.[48]

There were and remain good reasons to be alarmed by the emergence of homeland security and its transnational multiplication. Homeland security needs to be taken seriously if for no other reason than the sheer rapidity of its rise and the size of the political economy that has come to operate in its name. Although no field called homeland security existed before 2001, within just a few years it became a multi-billion-dollar industry and motivation for governments to undertake sweeping policy reforms. Between the fiscal years 2001–2020, the total outlay for DHS amounted to USD $1 trillion, representing a sixfold increase in analogous expenditures in the twenty years before.[49] Its growth as a global market has been similarly noteworthy, reaching an estimated USD $355 billion in 2020.[50] While the size of this industry and the scale of its global remit did shift after 2001, the terminology of homeland security and its associated world-making ambitions are not altogether unprecedented.[51] Rather, the homeland security state and homeland security's global mission need to be situated within the long histories of (settler-)colonialism, capitalism, and police power[52] and their civilizing missions of global counterinsurgency.[53]

The appeal of homeland security—and its cousins counterterrorism, antiterrorism, and counterinsurgency—draw on and nurture imperial discourses and logics of exceptionalism, race-making, and anti-Indigenous erasure.[54] As Amy Kaplan noted in her account of homeland security, while the term *homeland* represented a "jarringly unfamiliar way of referring to the *American* nation," it had long been referenced by aspiring nations and settler colonies such as the Zionist movement and Apartheid-era South Africa as part of their efforts to enforce racial purity.[55] For Kaplan, the central question about the newfound appreciation for the term "homeland" in the aftermath of September 11 was how it could give rise to new forms of state power and justify the United States' violation of other nations' sovereignty. In the intervening decades, Kaplan's concern became all too prescient as the "forever wars" took hold.[56] But ambitions to "export" homeland security abroad also point to a slightly different dimension of contemporary empire and sovereignty. For instance, U.S. and Israeli homeland security firms' efforts to position themselves in India evidence broader strategies to forge new geopolitical and economic ties justified under the banner of homeland security cooperation. I will return to these issues throughout the book. But first, a word on how homeland security is linked to police power.

Homeland Security: Police Power and Pacification

I understand homeland security as a form of police power, not in the narrow institutional sense of "the police" but more expansively as a technology of governance aimed at regulating social order.[57] Originating from the Latin term *securitas,* the notion of security can be traced as far back as the Roman Republic, though has its modern roots in liberal thought and the emergence of capitalism[58] as well as broader efforts to dominate the planet through an unending program of global counterinsurgency.[59] Security justifies the operation of police powers in the service of accumulation. As Karl Marx astutely noted:

> Security is the highest concept of civil society, the concept of the police. The whole of society is merely there to guarantee to each of its members the preservation of his person, rights and property. [. . .] The concept of security does not allow civil society to raise itself above its egoism. Security is more the assurance of egoism.[60]

In other words, as Mark Neocleous stresses, security "*is* the concept of police," representing a key aspect of "the rationale for the fabrication of order."[61]

"Fabrication," in this Marxian account, concerns how "the police power" works to produce social orders under capitalism as well as the ideological, euphemistic, and illusory dimensions of the work that references to security perform.[62] As such, thinking about security means thinking about state power and how it works to administrate social order in the service of property relations. When situated in this long history, the imbrication of the homeland security state with a homeland security industry is thus a variation on a broader theme, namely the collusion of the security state and capital. Rather than representing a universal value, a human need, or a public good, (homeland) security represents a modality of governing and political technology that works to colonize categories, places, spaces, and people in the service of capital.[63]

Because capitalism's roots are inextricably entwined with empire and race-making, critically interrogating police power and hence security should never focus on state power or class formation alone.[64] Rather, we also need to understand the police mandate as formative to conceptions of sovereignty and foundationally tied to the prevention of insurrection.[65] Security needs to be understood as a political technology of liberal order-making, civilization, and pacification imbricated with colonization and race-making.[66] The concept of pacification helps to theorize particular kinds of activities that take place under the banner of security politics like self-declared counterinsurgency campaigns, but it is more expansive.[67] Crucially, it enables us to apprehend how histories of imperial and colonial wars of conquest and primitive accumulation continue to inform the present.[68] Thinking about security-as-pacification further challenges any suggestion that the blurring of the domestic/foreign and police/military is in any way specific to the war on terror or paradigm of homeland security. In contrast to other influential critical theorizations of security,[69] the analytic of pacification shows their imbrication to be long-standing and foundational to security projects per se.[70] As Stuart Schrader argues, rather than representing ontologies, "foreign" and "domestic" should be approached as "contested outcomes of social, political, and economic processes" that need to be held "together in a single analytic frame."[71] Thus, situating homeland security as a form of pacification fundamentally complicates prevailing critical readings of its spatialities and colonizing ambitions as unprecedented breaks with the past. As such, this conceptualization poses new questions about the universal pretenses and world-making ambitions of (homeland) security projects.

Indian Policing

The emergence of police power in India represents a crucial part of this long transnational history of pacification projects and their legitimating discourses, or what Ranajit Guha calls the "prose of counterinsurgency."[72] These texts and their associated logics, practices, and infrastructures of repression drew inspiration, personnel, and experience from other British counterinsurgency theaters and in turn nurtured others, not least of all in Palestine under British rule in the twentieth century. Building directly on its prior counterinsurgency campaigns across the planet, the British presence in Palestine proved instrumental in developing the Israeli state's repressive security apparatus and surrounding administrative and legal architectures, a story I return to in chapter 2.

Britain's global counterinsurgency campaigns relied on the constant circulation of personnel, practices, and logics across time and space and nurtured common repertoires of violence, which endure in the present. Yet the British colonial system of administration in India was not a straightforward replica of colonial policing models supposedly "imported" from other British colonial spaces like Ireland.[73] British officials did not encounter India as some blank canvas waiting to be remade in its image. Instead, the British found in India complex and entrenched systems of hierarchy and accumulation already in place, which they sought to overlay and repurpose in the service of control, commerce, and accumulation. In the course of these efforts, British colonial practices, ideas, and techniques merged with aspects of precolonial systems of accumulation, law, and social and territorial control in India,[74] with the British mobilizing caste among other signifiers to categorize and objectify their Indian subjects.[75] As Radhika Singha's account of the British Thuggee campaign of the 1830s points out, it was always easier to prosecute prisoners "on a charge of belonging to some ill-defined criminal collectivity than to establish individual responsibility for a specific criminal offence."[76] It is out of such colonial campaigns that many contemporary stereotypes and mythologies of fanaticism and criminality like "thugs" and their surrounding infrastructures of repression have emerged. Furthermore, contemporary colloquial terms for police stations (*kotwal, chowki*), officers (*dorogha, sepoy*), and village watchman (*chowkidar*) reflect how precolonial influences lived on in India's imperial and colonial eras and continue to be part of the contemporary prose, practices, and infrastructures of Indian policing.[77]

This hybrid form of police power in colonial India was extraordinarily violent.[78] Yet the colonial processes of pacification aimed at making Indian imperial subjects empire taxable and "policeable" in Singha's terms was no easy task.[79] This owed to a combination of structural weaknesses of the Indian colonial police and uncertain relations between its personnel and target populations. According to David Arnold, this meant that "India's colonial regime fell short of being a police state in the conventional sense," stressing that "India's colonial police were often ill-informed, ineffective and at times frankly amateurish."[80] Radha Kumar has recently challenged and qualified such claims, showing that police presence in rural areas of colonial India was much more far-reaching than previously thought.[81] Nevertheless, many ordinary people in colonial India harbored a deep distrust of the police and avoided it. These communities developed alternative strategies to protect and recover their property, at times subverting the police's scope and authority.[82] And in a more overtly political register, charges of a "Police Raj" played formative roles in mobilizing Indian masses to undertake anticolonial struggles for independence.[83]

However, the organizational structure, hierarchy, and extrajudicial violence of the colonial police in India endured after Independence and remain largely intact in our time. The extent of popular legitimacy commanded by the Indian police today is founded on the extrajudicial violence that it metes out on dangerous Others through routinized torture, unlawful detention, and extrajudicial killings, known in India by the police euphemism of "encounters."[84] The endurance of this violent structure has further created a tension at the core of India's bourgeois democracy, which Achin Vanaik calls a "paradox of sorts."[85] If we understand police power in terms of fabricating social order for capital, one might anticipate that Indian state leaders and elites would have direct material and political incentives to increase its repressive capacity through forms of professionalization. As Vanaik points out, however, the Indian political class and elites have historically preferred the status quo.

Such observations should not compel us to resort to typical formulations of postcolonial states like India's as "weak" or even refer to "the postcolonial state" as an essential *type* of state.[86] Nor should we resort to traditional juxtapositions of the extraordinary violence of police power in the Global South as the antithesis of the supposedly "normal," just, and lawful functioning of police and security projects in the Global North. Violence always has been and remains foundational to police work across the planet even though this work cannot be reduced to the mere exercise of violence. Accordingly, I argue that we should focus on the complex transnational entanglements and enduring institutional legacies that colonial forms of sovereignty, control, and violence have given rise to and their effects on contemporary efforts to fabricate homeland security. Thus, engaging with police power as a transnational project should be explored through distinct but "connected histories" of empire and capital across time and space, yet with a keen eye on the tensions and impasses at work among its constituent actors, materials, orders and forms of relationality.[87]

FABRICATING HOMELAND SECURITY

This book approaches homeland security as one part of historical pacification infrastructures. Since the September 11 attacks, homeland security has come into being as an abstract idea and universal category of practice that all modern democratic nations can and should enact. Relatedly, scholars have taken the paradigm of homeland security as a given. In contrast, this book interrogates *how* homeland security has emerged as a thing in the world, distinct from other kinds of police power. I draw on insights from STS and ANT as they offer important critical sensibilities for denaturalizing and reversing the taken-for-granted assumptions about what homeland security is and how it operates in the world. More specifically, I theorize homeland security's essence as something that is (re)produced in and through relations between different entities.[88] In other words, homeland security is invented[89] and becomes a thing in the world as it is practiced by actors (state officials, security purveyors, policy and media writers, etc.) and achieves its particular form as a consequence of the relationships in which it is located. My theorization of homeland security thus enables us to understand how homeland security has come to be seen as a *thing* at all.

Furthermore, ANT complicates how we understand the terms of reality and ontology. Against the commonsense notions that reality is stable, given, universal, and external—i.e., "out there"—ANT suggests that realities are historically, culturally, and materially *located* and relationally *practiced* through what Annemarie Mol calls "ontological politics," that is, the ways in which "'the real' is implicated in the 'political' and *vice versa.*"[90] If we take seriously that reality is *done,* that is, historically and culturally located and practiced, the corollary is that reality becomes *multiple.* Some realities may clash and others may be co-constitutive. Following these insights, I show how homeland security has become a cornerstone of the "new" era of the global war on terror.

I capture this relational (re)making of homeland security as a politically contested and geographic process under the banner of what I call *fabrication*. Indeed, I argue that homeland security has been actively fabricated over decades and stitched together across borders. It remains in-the-making. I speak of the fabrication of homeland security in three senses. First is the literal *making* of the homeland security state and its surrounding global industry (its technologies, logics, weapons, and expertise). Second is the *making up* of "homeland security" as a new category, form of security, and "model" of governance in the sense of its illusory, mythical, and ideological dimensions. Third is the *weaving together* of the various threads that come to constitute homeland security. Despite the wide-ranging critical debates on the emergence and multiplication of homeland security, there remains much more to be said about how its global mission has attempted to remake the world in its image.

The fabrication of homeland security in the sense of *making* centers the often-overlooked work and forms of struggle involved in the literal manufacture of homeland security as a commodity fetish to be bought and sold. Here I am concerned with the literal manufacture of the homeland security state and its supporting industries; *what* they are, *where* they come from, and *how* they emerge as ideas and things to be traded in market transactions. This includes the production and circulation of security infrastructures, like small arms, fences, sensors, CCTV cameras, police uniforms, protective equipment, and vehicles as well as various forms of security training related to threat "awareness raising," linguistic and cultural "expertise," martial arts, bomb disposal, intelligence-gathering, target practice, surveillance, and racial categorization. Homeland security is also constructed out of more diffuse and less visible transnational linkages, which connect different people, cities, and countries through the travels of knowledges and personnel. Under the rubric of the *making* of homeland security, I am particularly concerned with what these connections are made *of* but also the routine and often unseen forms of everyday labor and hustling that go into creating and maintaining homeland security projects across space and time. As I will show in this book, the *making of* homeland security is always already transnational and needs to be understood historically.

My use of the term *fabrication* also signifies how homeland security is *made up*. Here I am not primarily concerned with fabrication of false or misleading evidence, even though such fabrication is indeed a central aspect of police work.[91] Rather, my emphasis is on how homeland security has come to be seen as a new category and way of organizing security in the war on terror. Here I am particularly concerned with the illusory, mythical, and ideological dimensions of homeland security as a global mission in the world.

This includes the *staging* and *picturing* of particular ideas about security as global forms of knowledge for others elsewhere to emulate.[92] For instance, the making up of homeland security requires the cultivation of new desires for homeland security within media and state bureaucracies and among publics. It also involves the fabrication of models of homeland security through which the global mission of homeland security attempts to remake the world in Seth's sense above. This process of making up homeland security often takes place through comparison and the negotiation of difference, issues I return to throughout the book. Focusing on the making up importantly reveals how homeland security as a world-making project needs to displace and paper over nondominant reals and disavow the violences (epistemic and material) that are foundational to homeland security.[93]

My third sense of fabrication concerns how the different elements, i.e., *threads* of homeland security, are *woven together*, forming the *fabrics* of homeland security. More specifically, when I speak of the *fabrics* of homeland security, I refer to how its constituent material and immaterial threads are woven together. One can notice the fabrics of homeland security in the urban landscape as they become visible through installations of high-tech surveillance equipment as well as more banal objects, such as warning signs, concrete blocks, sandbags, and razor wire that turn pedestrian streets, private businesses, and residences into fortresses. In some instances, homeland security products may be woven together into a particular system such as a Safe City project monitored by a central control room, whereas in others they may be more dispersed and cobbled together in patchy ways. Following Ann Laura Stoler's notion of "imperial durabilities," I foreground the ways in which this weaving involves a melding and layering of new policing instruments on top of older forms of police power across time and space.[94] It makes visible the highly contingent, fraught, and uncertain attempts to bring diverse elements from different places and histories together, some of which may seem wildly incommensurable in order to fabricate homeland security. As such, the fabrication of homeland security underscores the chronotropic nature of pacification projects in the sense of the intrinsic connection between the spatial and the temporal.[95]

While *making, making up,* and *weaving together* can be distinguished conceptually, in practice the fabrication of homeland security melds them together. Tim Mitchell's account of how the economy was *made* provides a useful point of reference. As Mitchell argues, the economy was the set of practices through which the bifurcation of the world into the real and the abstract was produced: "the economy [. . .] was both a method of staging the world as though it were divided in this way into two, and a means of overlooking the staging, and taking the division for granted."[96] Following Mitchell, making sense of the fabrication of homeland security as state and global projects is to grasp its "artifactual" nature.[97] Although homeland security is made out of processes, which are simultaneously cultural, material, ideational, real, and abstract, we must refuse to abide by any categorical distinction between such divisions.

The fabrication of homeland security, like the making of the economy, is not a smooth, straightforward, or self-assured process—indeed, quite the opposite. To center the *making, making up,* and *weaving together* of homeland security as a world-making project is precisely to recover its contingencies and conditions of possibility, particularly the vast material and symbolic resources mobilized to make these projects look smooth, whole, and inevitable. As I will show in this book, homeland security becomes a thing in the world as various actors paper over the cracks, gaps, impasses, and tensions involved in this fabrication. Paying attention to these sites of friction, dissonance, and disconnection makes visible the multiple forms of politics involved in fabricating homeland security.

To be clear, to speak of the fabrication of homeland security is *not* to suggest that homeland security is unreal. Nor is it to say that homeland security is simultaneously made up *and* real. Rather, to borrow from Bruno Latour, it is because homeland security has been "artificially made up" that it is able to "gain a complete autonomy from any sort of production, construction, or fabrication."[98] While scholars often overlook the work involved in global security projects, I suggest that attention to fabrication provides a more robust and textured accounting of homeland security in its actually-existing forms.[99] This account stands in contrast to the imaginaries and abstractions that shape most popular and scholarly understandings of what homeland security *is* and *does* in the world. As this book will show, moreover, there are a variety of practices and strategies through which homeland security is fabricated, some more stable and durable than others.

A STORY IN FRAGMENTS

This book approaches homeland security as a thing that is fabricated in a mythic and relational sense, i.e., *made*, *made up*, and *woven together*. Methodologically, this means tracing how homeland security is constituted (or impeded) relationally through particular transnational relations and encounters by *following* the involved actors.[100] Between 2012 and 2022, I lived in and traveled across Palestine/Israel, India, and the U.K., conducting multi-sited ethnographic research for this book.

The scope of my research and my research methods reflects the multiple actors and scales of engagement at play in the fabrication of homeland security. During my two months living in Jaffa in 2012, for instance, I conducted in-depth interviews and had informal conversations with trade officials, contractors, small arms dealers, fencing manufacturers, police trainers, a weapons scientist, and a number of scholars and journalists. Some of these actors had direct knowledge and experiences of working in India and promoting Indo-Israeli ties. I returned in 2019 to conduct follow-up interviews with some of these interlocutors and others. Between 2012 and 2013, I was based in Mumbai for seven months. In India, I conducted interviews with local politicians, bureaucrats, and police officials from the city of Mumbai and the state government of Maharashtra. I also conducted interviews and informal conversations with Mumbai-based human rights activists, journalists, scholars, lawyers, journalists, diplomats, security purveyors, and other businesspeople. I returned to India in

2019 and again in 2022 and 2023 to conduct archival analysis and follow-up observations and meetings with some interlocutors.

I also draw on observations from attending homeland security trade shows and policy conferences held across India and the U.K.[101] I collected information about the circulation of homeland security ideologies through a collection of diverse textual sources, including corporate websites, promotional materials, pamphlets, police magazines, consultancy reports, and government documents. I also engage with public media and strategic studies archives such as Indian professional military and counterinsurgency journals. Furthermore, during my time in Palestine/Israel and India my daily routines and travels to interview locations and industry events allowed me to observe and document the fabric of homeland security as it materialized in place.

Although comprehensive, my data did not provide me with a complete or definitive story of how homeland security is fabricated once and for all. Rather, I came to see my data as a collection of empirical fragments, which itself reflects how homeland security comes to be fabricated: in pieces, in secret, and often in a series of unfinished fits and starts, unplanned failures, and unexpected successes. In part, I ended up with fragments because of access and secrecy. When I first arrived in Tel Aviv in 2012, certain firms refused to speak with me altogether. Others initially agreed but later ceased communication without explanation. When I traveled to Mumbai later that year, I encountered even sharper barriers of access to key informants within the local state. I found a directory of telephone numbers on the Mumbai police's website that included the numbers of many officials whom I planned to speak to, but not a single one of them was active. Once I managed to get the correct numbers, many officers explained that they were not authorized to speak to me, sometimes citing national security concerns. For instance, when I called one commander of a special unit in the Maharashtra police on his personal cell phone, he explained that his unit was a "closed" organization, indicating that the same logic applied to the Maharashtra police more broadly. I twisted his arm a little, but he refused to budge and abruptly hung up the phone.

Through a combination of persistence, luck, and the contingency of ethnographic encounters, I was ultimately able to engage with the majority of Israeli and Indian officials whom I initially had set out to speak to, albeit with important exceptions. Informal encounters and conversations at industry events, parties, and private gatherings proved crucial to building trust and gaining access. During a tea break at a closed-door policy conference held on the rooftop of a luxury hotel in Mumbai, I commenced casual conversation with a conference participant. I quickly realized that he was the commander whom I had contacted by phone just a week before to arrange an interview. While he had refused during our phone conversation, over a cup of tea at the Mumbai event he warmly invited me to visit his office a week later, without any apparent hesitation. It was unclear whether he ever made the connection to our previous phone conversation, but I saw no reason to bring it up. Even once access opened, it could just as easily be withdrawn. In a few instances when I asked informants questions that they deemed out of bounds, some responded tersely and withdrew future access. Others treated me with suspicion and asked me to demonstrate that I was not myself a terrorist sympathizer or collaborator, an impossible task. Here the figure of David Headley loomed large.[102] While such constraints no doubt circumscribed the scope of my research, such encounters functioned as unexpected meetings and formative moments in my research process, in some instances enabling me to gain access to new informants and in other instances shifting the focus and scope of my research.

Yet, access and secrecy, important as they are in analysis of security projects, were hardly the only reason why I ended up with a collection of fragments.[103] Moreover, some of the stories about the fabrication of homeland security related in this book turned out to be fragmentary. During my time in Palestine/Israel and India, I found numerous examples of impasses or even failures in the conduct of homeland security's global mission. These included deals that fell through, connections that could not be sustained, incompatibility of policing technologies, and regimes of governance across different sites and locations. During a meeting at a café in central Tel Aviv, a well-known Israeli journalist told me that almost all the previously announced Israeli homeland security ventures in India had since fallen through and that there was no point in me visiting India at all as there would be nothing to find about Israeli homeland security there. That this journalist was in the know was affirmed to me a few weeks later at a barbeque on a *moshav* outside of Tel Aviv owned by the notorious Israeli-Argentinian arms dealer and security contractor Leo Gleser, whom we will meet in chapter 2. A guest there asked me if I had met this same journalist, noting that the journalist was a frequent guest at similar networking events for security industry insiders. Needless to say, I did not take the journalist's advice to abandon my travel plans to India. But crucially, these encounters began to attune me to cracks in the reach of Israel's homeland security authority and its geographically variegated nature early on in the course of my research. Such encounters also poked holes in the grand narrative of homeland security as a complete, all-encompassing project.

The fragments that I gathered varied in character and origin. One set of fragments consists of various representations and accounts of homeland security (what it is and how it circulates). I accessed some of these through publicly available marketing materials, and others were made available to me by the industry actors, journalists, and state officials with whom I engaged. They provided me with their own testimonies as well as photos, videos, state documents, classified reports, emails, and other records of personal correspondences. These fragments did not always sit comfortably alongside one another and in some cases proved directly contradictory. For instance, Israeli homeland security purveyors and trade officials cited a range of reasons as to why their self-described efforts to "penetrate" India and train Indian police forces were constrained, sometimes resorting to highly gendered, classed, and blatantly racist and self-serving caricatures of Indians as backward and unwilling to become modern, rational security subjects. The Maharashtra state officials whom I engaged with offered rather different accounts of what took place and why. However, within these partial, self-interested, and situated narratives, I found considerable overlaps as well. Rather than trying to shoehorn these competing, inconsistent accounts into a single, authoritative story of homeland security's global mission, I grapple with such tensions as part and parcel of theorizing *what* homeland security is and the work it does in the world (see chapters 5 and 6).

I also gathered ethnographic fragments of the machinery through which homeland security ideas and technologies are made up and move around the world. This included me being hustled in various ways. Alongside interviews, I was often given sales presentations about various products and services offered by homeland security purveyors. Some explicitly asked me to represent their companies favorably and a few even proposed that I go into business with them, offers I always politely declined. Others seemed to view me as a potential competitor or even a threat to their bottom line. In one such case I was first given a sales presentation on roadblock and anti-crash bollard technologies. After completing his presentation, the Israeli homeland security marketing director abruptly asked me to sign a nondisclosure statement, expressing concern that I might attempt to steal his firm's designs and have them manufactured as knockoffs in India (this was after I had inquired about his firm's activities there). These encounters began to give me a sense of the marketing tropes and strategies involved in selling homeland security to global clientele.

As I traveled across Palestine/Israel and India, I documented the ways that homeland security is materialized within the physical landscapes of cities and territories. I have come to think about these impressions as fragments of the material fabrics of homeland security in its actually-existing forms. During my time in Palestine/Israel I moved by bus, train, and rental car to meet interlocutors at industrial parks, corporate offices, cafes, bars, malls, and private residences. Through these travels, I encountered checkpoints, surveillance systems, and border walls where I observed Israeli homeland security infrastructures in place. I also attended weekly Friday demonstrations in West Bank villages, which were invariably met with violent repression from the Israel Occupation Forces (IOF), including the use of live and rubber-coated bullets, tear gas, "skunk water," beatings, and arrests.[104] These experiences enabled me to reflect on the everyday violent conditions and circumstances of life out of which security technologies emerge and to ensure that they are not abstracted from the stories that we tell about them, an issue I explore in chapter 2.

While based in Mumbai, I lived in a rented apartment in *Navi* (New) Mumbai, which required daily bus and train journeys across the river and into Mumbai proper on the city's suburban rail network for meetings in corporate offices, hotels, police stations, embassies, public venues, and private residences. Through these travels across the city and occasionally to other cities like Pune and New Delhi, I collected additional observations of security infrastructure like roadblocks, surveillance cameras, and anti-terrorism police units stationed at key locations. These travels also became opportunities to collect additional fragments such as photos of these infrastructures in action as well as security messaging like signs, designed to alert local residents to potential risks and report persons or behavior deemed to be dangerous or illegal (chapter 4).

This book is an attempt to stitch these fragments together to tell a different story of how homeland security has been assembled within and across different sites and locations. As will become clear in the following chapters, this story is not a neat or straightforward one. It is in itself a fragmented story of fabricating homeland security. I am inspired by others who have embraced fragments and fragmentary analysis to better understand imperial, nationalist, and capitalist projects. In *Friction,* Anna Tsing makes a particularly compelling case for the virtues of a fragmentary perspective in telling different stories of global connection from those we are most familiar with. She notes: "Global connections are made in fragments. [. . .] Some fragments are able to make themselves look whole. Honoring the fragment means acknowledging this power but not accepting it as a done deal."[105] Indeed, "staying with" the fragments out of which the fabric of homeland security is made and made up, we can grasp its aspirations but also chart the edges and limits of its universalist, world-making power.[106]

My approach similarly seeks to honor the various fragments that I collected. We might think of these fragments as that which makes up the fabric of homeland security and plays key roles in its fabrication. Yet it is a fabric that has layers and holes and at times can be made out of weak and questionable elements.[107] Through the painstaking work of gathering competing, partial, and sometimes less than fully forthcoming accounts of homeland security and how it travels across borders, I embrace the messiness of these accounts, including their limits and contradictions rather than treating these as tangential, anomalous, or necessarily reducible to my failures as a researcher to transcend the boundaries of secrecy imposed by security states and security industries, real and significant as they are.[108] Inspired by invitations to tell different stories about global power and planetary crisis, I recover the suppressed, overlooked, and forgotten stories of how the fabrication of homeland security takes place and comes to exist as a hegemonic, world-making project. To be clear, however, my embrace of fragmentary analysis and fragments of evidence should not be read as implying that the story I tell about homeland security is incoherent, thin, or otherwise wanting. As the analysis will show, however, this approach yields a different understanding of what homeland security *is* and *does* in the world, which reconsiders existing orthodoxies and proposes alternatives in their place.

As alluded to in my comments above, the story of fabricating homeland security in India is necessarily entwined with a longer-standing and wider story, namely the bilateral relations between India and Palestine/Israel. These stories overlap but are not reducible to one another. As such, it is crucial to spell out the specific temporal and topical parameters of this book. *Fabricating Homeland Security* is chiefly concerned with the geopolitical origins and repercussions of the event of 26/11 in India and other locations. As a result, it focuses on the immediate years that followed this event, during which the majority of its source material was collected. Since then, however, another pivotal political event in Indian politics occurred, namely the rise of Narendra Modi within Indian national politics and the coming to power of his Hindu authoritarian—BJP-led governments with overwhelming electoral victories beginning in 2014. I make reference to this in subsequent chapters and return to it in the book's epilogue. However, this book is primarily focused on developments before 2014 and is based on materials produced and gathered prior to this time. The focus on the immediate post-26/11 period is deliberate: it was during this period that the longer-standing imperative to bring homeland security to India took on a sudden and unprecedented urgency and, at least for a time, gained significant momentum. As such it represents fertile ground to investigate the fabrication of homeland security in India.

A NOTE ON "TERRORISM"

Any book concerned with homeland security necessarily requires engagement with "terrorism." The challenges of engaging with terrorism critically have been elaborated at length by others and are especially pertinent in the Indian context.[109] This is because many of the contemporary connotations of "terrorism" find their earliest articulations within colonial law, with the context of British India being particularly formative in colonial legal reasoning.[110] While I will not rehearse the wide-ranging critical debates about how to approach terrorism here, suffice it to say that what matters most about the term, politically speaking, is that it serves as a delegitimizing and depoliticizing function. To label someone a "terrorist" is to strip their violence of any political character, in part by governing it through the moralistic, technocratic languages of "counterterrorism," "antiterrorism," and "fighting pure evil."[111] Relatedly, knowledge *about* terrorism is monopolized by state actors and their allies such as experts and media pundits.[112] This does not mean that all knowledge about terrorism is necessarily inaccurate but rather that we have little possibility of ascertaining whether such claims are false or true and must therefore rely on faith.[113]

It must also be stressed, however, that such analytical challenges are hardly specific to terrorism. In their classic *Policing the Crisis*, Stuart Hall et al. noted an analogous challenge in writing about the book's focus, namely the purported rise of a new type of violent crime called "mugging" in the 1970s. As Hall et al. point out, even though we might prefer to abolish the label "mugging" altogether and refuse to employ it, it is not possible to "resolve a social contradiction by abolishing the label that has been attached to it."[114] Rather, they propose "to go behind the label to the contradictory social content which is mystifyingly reflected in it."[115] Following this insight, although this book makes repeated references to terrorism, it does not accept the label as a natural object and phenomenon to be studied. Instead, it is concerned with the political work that the term performs in the fabrication of social orders within particular places and transnationally. In light of these considerations, I concur with Darryl Li that the most apt way to study terrorism is to "refuse to take for granted the globalized order of racial violence that the national security state aims to protect."[116] Put slightly differently, the focus should not be on what defines *terrorism* but rather what terrorism *defines* in ways that render certain activities and bodies out of place.[117]

THE ORGANIZATION OF THE BOOK

This book tells the story of efforts to fabricate homeland security in India post-26/11. Through ethnographic engagements with fragments collected over more than a decade, I trace the activities of particular actors and knowledges as well as their trajectories over time. Rather than providing a genealogical or chronological account of this story, I move back and forth between different locations, actors, histories, and fragments in order to account for how fabrication of homeland security takes place across multiple geographies and histories and in relation to particular events. I do so through six substantive chapters and a conclusion and an epilogue.

Chapter 1 grapples with how 26/11 became a historical juncture through which a *new reality* emerged, a reality in which India had become a victim of "global," "Islamic" terrorism, a problem to which western and even specifically *Israeli* homeland security offered a "solution" to India's vulnerabilities. Tracing the roles of Israeli interventions into the event day by day, I show how Israel's long-standing claims about its exceptionality as *the* global innovator in counterterrorism and homeland security began to cultivate broader resonance in India. In doing so, I situate the "politics of response" as part and parcel of the event of 26/11 itself, rather than that which came *after* it. I further develop the notion of *comparative geopolitics* in order to theorize the politicking, spin, and labor mobilized to generate knowledge *about* given events (where they emerge, what they signify as well as the existence, plausibility, and desirability of solutions to them).

In Chapter 2, I shift the focus to the origins of Israel's contemporary homeland security industry and status as a pioneer or model thereof. Rather than approaching the Israeli pacification model as a thing unto itself, I situate it as a universalist project and "idea of Israel," fabricated over time through transnational encounters. Locating these processes in histories of empire and their forms of governance in Palestine and beyond, I concentrate on a number of broad historical moments and banal practices through which the Zionist settler-colonial "experience" of domination has been performatively *staged* and *pictured* as a source of global lessons for others to emulate elsewhere.

Chapter 3 returns to India to examine the aftermaths of 26/11 and the crisis of legitimacy to which the event gave rise. Focusing on how the Maharashtra government attempted to police this security crisis, I show how state actors sought to pacify the local anti-politician backlash under the banner of police modernization, while keeping the local policing infrastructure firmly in place. I argue that the government's response to the attacks is both an expression of authoritarian populism and a politics of truth, which attempted to enact and thereby police the ontological terms of reality itself.

Chapter 4 examines how the Maharashtra government's policy responses to 26/11 materialized in the everyday built environment of Mumbai. On the face of it, the Maharashtra government's focus on police modernization post-26/11 appears as an almost textbook case of the militarization of urban and domestic spaces. Drawing on photographs of the police infrastructure in Mumbai gathered by walking the city, I provide an alternative interpretation, documenting how new technologies were grafted onto preexisting policing infrastructures, in patchy, ad-hoc, and fleeting ways. Mobilizing the notion of "the changing same," I trace how the fabrication of homeland security in the city of Mumbai leveraged military aesthetics as semiotic markers of swift and far-reaching change.

Chapter 5 relates stories about what happened when Israeli and Indian actors encountered one another through the official Maharashtra delegation visit to Palestine/Israel in 2009 as well as through the Israeli police trainings and demonstrations that took place thereafter. I pay particular attention to these encounters' contingencies, including their indeterminate and unpredictable nature and the kinds of conflict and struggle at work therein. In doing so, I write difference back into the story of homeland security in a way that unsettles the terms through which we think about the power that Israel's homeland security industry commands.

Chapter 6 zooms in on the efforts by Indian capital to build a new Indian homeland security market and "sector" after 2008. Drawing on participant observations at five Indian homeland security trade shows and conferences and analysis of industry texts like risk surveys and consultancy reports, I examine the attempts to *educate* an Indian homeland security market, build greater "awareness" *of* and investment *in* homeland security across the country, and create a new Indian security subject. I argue that educating a homeland security market in India should be understood as an attempt not merely to bring homeland security *to* India but also to *secure* the western bourgeois conception of Man-as-human.

The conclusion situates the book's broader significance vis-à-vis critical research on security, policing, violence, and empire. It returns to early critiques of equivocations between "9/11" and "26/11." Despite all the efforts to develop equivalences between "9/11" and "26/11" in ways that actively forget history and elide difference, I suggest that the actually-existing connections between different actors, sites, and events are in many respects more fragile, fraught, and tentative than much critical literature on the global war on terror and empire would have us believe. This in turn prompts questions about the universality of homeland security and security per se.

ONE

COMPARATIVE GEOPOLITICS

> Solutions are here to fix whatever needs fixing; a solution, by definition, requires a problem.
>
> John Patrick Leary, *Keywords: The New Language of Capitalism*

INTRODUCTION

The Mumbai attacks began on the evening of Wednesday, November 26, 2008, when ten assailants who had allegedly traveled from Pakistan by sea entered Mumbai. According to media reports and police investigations, the sequence of events unfolded as follows. The assailants evaded attention of the Indian Coast Guard by hijacking the Indian fishing trawler *M. V. Kuber* a few days prior, murdering its four crew and later beheading its captain once close to Mumbai. They then abandoned the vessel at sea and entered Mumbai in an inflatable boat, landing around 8:30 p.m. at Machimar Nagar opposite Badhwar Railway Officers Colony. They came heavily armed with automatic assault rifles, pistols, grenades, and improvised explosive devices (IEDs) and carrying GPS devices and cell phones. Upon disembarking from their vessel, the group divided into five teams that dispersed around the city and attacked multiple sites simultaneously.

The ensuing siege of the city unfolded over the course of the next sixty-eight hours. The assailants attacked police and railway stations, hospitals, luxury hotels, the popular tourist hangout Leopold Café, and the Jewish cultural Chabad-Lubavitch community center, also known as Nariman

House. In carrying out these attacks, they combined a range of tactics including carjackings and drive-by shootings and later seized buildings, where they barricaded rooms, held victims hostage, and set fires. Police and locally stationed Marine Commandos (MARCOS) from the Indian Navy, the first to respond to these operations, were assisted by a contingent of the National Security Guard (NSG) from New Delhi, which arrived after some delay on the morning of November 27. By November 29, nine of the ten alleged assailants were declared killed, and the lone survivor, Ajmal Mohammed Amir Kasab, was captured by local authorities. The attacks wounded approximately 300 people and killed at least 172 others: 126 Indian civilians, 15 Indian police officers, one member of the NSG and 31 foreign nationals, including two Israelis and two Israeli-Americans.[1]

As the assailants carried out the attacks, national and international media covered the event in real time, quickly turning it into an intense national and global media spectacle. This coverage dominated television programming in India and around the world. For three days, publics were glued to their screens, following the unfolding developments minute by minute. In the course of this spectacle, the term "homeland security" quickly emerged as a central reference point. Numerous actors, including media commentators, state officials, security experts, and politicians, began to suggest that India's response to the attacks signified the country's *lack* of a sufficiently "modern" approach to domestic security and policing. For instance, a November 28 *Hindustan Times* article lamented that India's "anachronistic" approach to fighting terrorism was out of step with modern homeland security approaches.[2] Others made explicit references to western homeland security models as solutions to India's apparent deficiencies in modern security preparedness, highlighting the United States and its DHS as well as security approaches in the U.K. and Israel as exemplars.

The sudden ubiquity of references to homeland security in India was new. As I elaborated in the introduction to this book, although 26/11 was hardly India's first experience with large-scale attacks on major cities, homeland security and its associated technologies remained fairly peripheral in discussions about potential "solutions" to political violence in the country prior to 26/11. When journalists and state officials did discuss homeland security and foreign models of counterterrorism, they typically framed them as quintessentially foreign and out of place in India. Yet, in the aftermath of 26/11, Indian officials' historic reticence to embrace Israeli approaches to counterterrorism were eclipsed by widespread calls for India to "wake up" and embrace the paradigm of homeland security.

In this chapter, I argue that 26/11 became a historical juncture through which a *new reality* emerged. When I speak of a *new reality*, as *new* and as a *reality*, I am referring to how 26/11 solidified the notion that India had become a victim of "global" terrorism (i.e., that the Mumbai attacks were a "repeat" of similar attacks against "the West") and that homeland security offered *a solution* to India's lack of modern (homeland) security preparedness. Particularly, I show how Israeli homeland security was represented across a range of media as a solution to India's terrorism "problem," resulting in new business opportunities and governmental collaboration, to which I return in later chapters.

This chapter explores one aspect of fabrication of homeland security, namely the *making* of this new reality as the attacks were still ongoing. Israeli actors played key roles in redefining India's terrorism "problem." More specifically, Israeli state officials, security experts, lobbyists, industry boosters, emergency response personnel, religious figures, journalists, and op-ed columnists commented on India's response to the attacks as they unfolded in real time, making parallels and comparisons to the so-called "Israeli experience" of fighting terrorism.[3] Israeli state officials also offered various forms of assistance to India during the attacks such as hostage rescue and emergency management expertise. After the attacks had come to an end, Israeli actors proposed Israeli homeland security expertise and technologies as a solution to India's lack of modern security preparedness. Carefully tracing these interventions chronologically day by day and documenting how they were picked up by Indian English-language media and international news outlets, I show how Israel's long-standing claims about its exceptionality as *the* global innovator in counterterrorism and homeland security started to gain wider traction in India.

Scholars have written extensively about the ways that political responses to militant attacks and other catastrophes give rise to new forms of sovereign politics[4] and new market opportunities for expansion of the global (homeland) security industry.[5] Contributing to this body of work, this chapter unearths the often-overlooked fabrication of *how* instances of militant violence become moments of political crisis and "critical events" through which certain national and foreign actors gain influence and authority.[6] Methodologically, I follow the involved actors and trace how they took part in the fabrication of the event through the production of knowledge, controversies, conflicts, and negotiations. By wading into the texture of the event in all of its messiness and constituent fragments, I trace how actors were *enrolled* and their authorities relationally assembled. Drawn from ANT, "enrollment" concerns the processes through which "a set of interrelated roles is defined and attributed to actors who accept them."[7] Crucially, enrollment neither precludes nor implies a set of predefined roles but helps to convey how negotiations between actors are worked out and their roles become stabilized in a given situation. As such, it has some important overlaps with and distinctions from Louis Althusser's account of subject-formation through *interpellation*, which I examine in chapters 3 and 6.

I argue that we need to think about the "politics of response" as part and parcel of the event itself, rather than that which comes after the event.[8] Doing so necessarily requires close attention to comparison—both as a form of politics and as an analytic. Bringing together Andrew Barry's work on "political situations"[9] and Walter Mignolo's notions of the "geopolitics of knowledge" and the "coloniality of power,"[10] I develop the concept of *comparative geopolitics*.[11] In this chapter, I mobilize this concept to capture the politicking, spin, and work mobilized to generate knowledge about given events (their origins, meanings, handlings, and significance as well as the existence, plausibility, and desirability of solutions) out of which new realities emerge. More broadly, as subsequent chapters elaborate, comparative geopolitics helps to theorize the entanglements of geopolitics with knowledge production, approaching comparison not as a method but as a subject in its own right.[12] More specifically, I understand comparison in Ann Laura Stoler and Carole McGranahan's terms "as an *active political verb*," which draws its force from colonial and imperial grammars, politics, and forms of governance across time and space.[13]

ISRAELI INTERVENTIONS

In this section, I focus on how Israel and references to Israeli approaches to counterterrorism and homeland security became part of the event of 26/11. I survey Israeli interventions chronologically day by day and how they were picked up by Indian and international media. Doing so enables us to situate how certain figures and forms of knowledge became part of the event and how they gained traction, momentum and resonance over time. I begin on November 27, the day that references to Israel began appearing in the media archive.

Thursday, November 27

As the violence and chaos engulfed Mumbai, the 26/11 attacks became an object of live commentary in India and around the world. By November 27, domestic and international newspapers and TV stations covered the event by focusing on key details about the violence and its handling on the ground. There was also coverage of the emerging response to the attacks from foreign governments, some of which was conciliatory. An article headlined "World Rallies Behind India in Anti-Terror Fight" gave an overview of statements from foreign government officials, who roundly condemned the violence, expressed their commitment to fighting "global" terror, and pledged assistance of various kinds.[14]

As part of this wave of international support, Israeli officials voiced sympathy with the attacks' victims and proclaimed their unity in the face of "global," "Islamic" terror. Israeli President Shimon Peres stated: "The terror attacks in India are a clear warning sign to all countries in the world that terror poses a danger to all our children's welfare."[15] Alongside their expressions of support, Israeli state officials began threading their own foreign policy concerns into their remarks and insinuated that they, as Israelis, had unique insights into the nature and origins of the violence. As Peres emphasized: "We must take the war on global terror seriously and act decisively and firmly against terror centers spread across the globe, headed by the center of terror in Iran."[16] Likewise, Israeli Defense Minister Ehud Barak argued that "[t]he attacks are part of a global wave of terror, which Israel is quite familiar with" and offered to send India any help it might require, such as humanitarian and other professional expertise.[17]

This international attention, however, soon became rather less conciliatory. Similar to other foreign governments whose citizens were killed in the attacks, Israeli officials expressed concern about their handling by Indian authorities.[18] Israeli diplomatic and defense officials further suggested that Indian authorities had prematurely stormed the Taj and Oberoi luxury hotels and Nariman House. A *Jerusalem Post* article quoted a former Israeli Shin Bet official: "In hostage situations, the first thing the forces are supposed to do is assemble at the scene and begin collecting intelligence," whereas "it appears that the [Indian] forces showed up at the scene and immediately began exchanging fire with the terrorists instead of first taking control of the area."[19] These criticisms, though first published in Israeli media, were immediately picked up and amplified by non-Israeli newspapers. Quoting the statements from the Shin Bet official in the *Jerusalem Post* article, a *Hindustan Times* article's headline read, "India's Rescue Efforts 'Premature and Badly Planned', says Israel."[20]

As Israeli officials criticized India's handling of the attacks and offered assistance, they also dispatched personnel to Mumbai. There were reports as early as November 27 that Israel had sent intelligence officers to Mumbai to assist in analyzing the unfolding events on the ground.[21] While other states like the United States and the U.K. also sent intelligence personnel during the attacks, Israeli assistance went considerably further. The Israeli organization Magen David Adom (MDA) sent a paramedic team to assist with rescue efforts in Mumbai in coordination with the Israeli Foreign Ministry.[22] They were accompanied by another team of Israeli reservists as well as two additional ZAKA paramedics and six volunteers.[23] ZAKA chairman and founder Yehuda Meshi-Zahav claimed that after consulting with the Israeli Foreign Ministry "it became apparent that ZAKA must immediately send a delegation from its international response team to deal with the unfolding situation in Mumbai," stating that the team would be "carrying all the advanced medical equipment necessary to deal with any eventuality."[24]

Through these activities, Israeli officials began to gain visibility in the emerging event as experts by drawing parallels and comparisons to the "Israeli experience" with terrorism. They made a range of conciliatory and critical statements, which were picked up and reiterated in the Indian,

Israeli, and international press. These statements attempted to put an Israeli perspective on the violence and to suggest that Israelis' experiences with "global," "Islamic" terror gave them unique insights into what was unfolding and its origins. Israeli officials also suggested that India's response on the ground was incompetent and imperiled Israelis and Jews, therefore requiring that Israeli authorities dispatch their personnel to the scene in Mumbai. In doing so, these practices introduced contrasts between "Israeli" and "Indian" approaches to emergency response and counterterrorism into the emerging coverage of the attacks.

Friday, November 28

The siege on Mumbai continued through November 28. Various Mumbai police and NSG-led operations attacked assailants holed up in buildings and attempted to rescue hostages. Meanwhile, Israelis and other Jewish representatives continued to weigh in on the attacks' geopolitical significance, foregrounding "western" perspectives and explaining the violence through the lens of the Israeli experience. Israeli Foreign Minister Tzipi Livni emphasized: "*Our* world is under attack, and it doesn't matter if it's in India or somewhere else. Only when things like this happen do we understand that we are partners in the same battle."[25] Livni further stated: "We are the target, and it's not just Israel but the whole Western world."[26] Likewise, Jennifer Laszlo Mizrahi, founder and president of the U.S.-based lobby group The Israel Project argued: "Just like the [2002] Passover Massacre in Netanya, Israel, this attack [in Mumbai] was by Muslim extremists who are targeting those who love freedom, tolerance and peace."[27] These figures suggested that from Israel's vantage point, what was taking place in Mumbai was not, in fact, *new*; it was a repeat of the same kind of violence Israelis and Jews had suffered for decades.

Throughout the day, Israeli criticisms of Indian authorities multiplied and intensified, with Israeli officials employing ever more abrasive language while reiterating their offers of assistance to India. Israeli officials expressed particular outrage over the NSG-led commando raid of Nariman House, where the assailants held and later killed Israeli, Israeli-American, and Mexican hostages including Orthodox rabbi Gavriel Holtzberg and his wife, Rivka Holtzberg. Focusing on the Nariman raid, a range of Israeli,

Indian, and international media stories amplified Israeli officials' criticisms of how Indian forces immediately began firing at the assailants rather than first gathering intelligence and/or trying to negotiate with them. A story from the website for *Time* noted that Israeli officials "are waiting to hear if the Jewish hostages were killed when commandos stormed the building [Nariman House] or whether they had been slain earlier by their captors," raising questions about whether the NSG operation had unnecessarily contributed to their deaths.[28] Such Israeli criticisms were again repeated in Indian media, featuring headlines like "Israel Calls Indian Troops Handling of Mumbai Terror Siege "Risky and Premature," thereby reinforcing Israeli authority over attacks.[29]

Alongside these renewed criticisms, Israeli state officials continued their offers of assistance. A spokesperson from Israel's Foreign Ministry stated: "The Indian government knows that if there is anything they need and that we can do we will do it," stressing that Israel's offers to assist were "still on the table."[30] Meanwhile, rumors circulated that Israelis had indeed been involved in rescue operations.[31] Despite these overtures, Indian authorities showed little interest. A *Financial Times* article noted: "so far [Israeli] officials say their offer has been 'politely turned down.'"[32] This was not, apparently, well received by Israeli officials. Citing "reliable sources," one Indian news article suggested that "Tel Aviv is not happy with New Delhi's rejection of its offer to send its elite commando force to rescue hostages trapped in Mumbai's luxury hotels and in Nariman House."[33] Israeli officials also suggested that India's rebuff was reckless. An Israeli source told the *Jerusalem Post* that "India's refusal of its offer to send commandos had put the lives of a rabbi and his family in danger."[34]After these efforts to pressure Indian authorities did little to force capitulation to their offers, Israelis then made statements suggesting that Israel had halted such efforts.[35]

In concert with their ongoing criticisms, Israeli actors continued to perform their expert credentials within the unfolding event. Additional reports emerged that Foreign Minister Livni and Defense Minister Barak had dispatched an Israeli Air Force plane with teams of forensic and medical experts to Mumbai in order to help identify victims so that they could be returned to Israel.[36] Other stories noted that Israel was considering sending a group of New Delhi-based Israeli doctors to Mumbai to assist with these efforts.[37] After the NSG commando operation at Nariman House had concluded on November 28, Israeli officials appeared at the scene. Yochi Turgeman, the Israeli embassy's defense attaché, and six ZAKA team members entered the facility and later reemerged carrying body bags.[38]

After gaining access to the Nariman House victims, Israeli officials continued weighing in on the handling of the attacks and redoubling their criticisms of Indian authorities. Barak gave an interview to Israel's Channel 1 television station, confirming that bodies of Israelis and other Jews had been found at Nariman House and providing details about their condition as well as speculation on how and when they died.[39] While acknowledging the challenging nature of the multiple attacks carried out across Mumbai, Barak called the handling of the Nariman operation "a difficult spectacle," stressing that "I'm not sure it had to last three days."[40] He then repeated that Israel had offered a wide range of assistance "that is inappropriate to detail here" and claimed that the attacks originated in both Pakistan and Afghanistan, rather than just in Pakistan, as Indian state officials were asserting.[41]

Israeli and Jewish actors thus continued to impose their authority over the attacks by reiterating earlier claims and criticisms but also adapting their assertions in light of unfolding developments. Given that previous Israeli offers of assistance were rebuffed by the Indian state, Israeli officials asserted that while Israel *had* offered various forms of assistance to India, it was no longer interested. And while ZAKA and diplomatic officials continued to recover Israeli and Jewish victims from Nariman House, Israeli officials added new layers to their previous narratives. Their criticisms were considerably more inflammatory and speculative than Israeli statements from earlier days; they renewed questions about how and when Israeli and Jewish victims were killed, implying that Indian tactical incompetence was to blame.

Saturday, November 29

Indian authorities declared the siege officially over when all the alleged assailants were killed or captured in the early hours of the morning of November 29. As operations to put out fires at the Taj Hotel continued and victims were still being recovered and identified, Indian and international news stories again featured Israeli officials who centered Israeli perspectives, concerns, and criticisms of Indian officials. One Indian news article quoted Livni: "There is no doubt, we know, that the targets the terrorists singled out were Jewish, Israeli targets and targets identified with the West, Americans and Britons." Livni further attributed the attacks to "Islamic extremists who don't accept our existence or Western values."[42] A *Financial Times* article noted Israeli state officials' "displeasure" at how the government of Manmohan Singh had handled the attacks.[43] Barak's comments were again reported, suggesting that Israel had rescinded its prior offers to send a military unit to Mumbai.[44]

Statements from ZAKA members also continued to be featured in articles published that day. They revealed details and photos of the horrific scene inside Nariman House and noted that the ZAKA team had had tense negotiations with Indian officials to ensure that Indian authorities did not touch or perform autopsies on Jewish victims' bodies.[45] Thus, even as the attacks were officially declared over, Israeli efforts to center "western" and Israeli concerns continued, repeating their earlier suggestions that the Mumbai attacks were somehow *like* previous attacks against Israel as well as continuing to critique their handling by Indian authorities. In short, by asserting Israeli primacy over the attacks' meaning and critiquing Indian authorities as inept, Israeli leaders continued to interject their concerns and perspectives into the event.

Sunday, November 30

On November 30, newspaper stories continued to foreground Israeli perspectives, bringing in new Israeli analysis about what (allegedly) went wrong during the previous days. Some attempted to temper their criticisms of Indian authorities. Nitzan Nurieli, head of Israel's counterterrorism department, stressed that the Mumbai attacks were the result of a catastrophic Indian intelligence failure but also noted Israel's own lack of intelligence on the attacks: "We have to acknowledge that in the Mumbai case our [Israeli] intelligence services [also] did not have adequate advance knowledge."[46] A *Haaretz* article quoted David Tzur, a retired major general and a former commander of the Israeli police's counterterror unit

Yamam and head of a private consultancy firm, who further acknowledged that the simultaneous attacks on several different sites were "very hard to handle."[47] He emphasized that this challenge was compounded by a lack of intelligence, "which is the colossal failure in this story." "To the Indians' credit," Tzur emphasized, "they were determined and sought contact [with the enemy] all the time," adding that the taking over of a hotel is "the nightmare of every counterterrorism unit."[48] As Tzur continued, however, this complicating factor did not apply to Nariman House. He maintained that the twelve-hour operation there was unreasonable given that "there's no chance in the world that captives will survive an incident that doesn't end within minutes of the break-in."[49] Lior Lotan, a former senior officer with Israel's elite Sayeret Matkal unit, was similarly critical of India's response, claiming that "[w]hen you're rescuing captives, you enter fast, with maximum force, and try to reach the hostages as quickly as possible, even at the price of casualties."[50]

ZAKA team members who had traveled to Mumbai added additional fuel to these criticisms. A *Jerusalem Post* article headlined "Zaka Head: Indian Forces May Have Killed Some Hostages" quoted Haim Weingarten, the head of the ZAKA team on the ground in Mumbai: "Based on what I saw, [although] I can't identify the type of bullets in the bodies [of the victims], I don't think the terrorists killed all the hostages, to put it gently."[51] These claims expanded the tactical critiques of Indian responses from previous days and pushed them further. They did not merely ridicule the Nariman operation as incompetent in its execution but also insinuated that the NSG had Israeli and Jewish blood on its hands.

As in previous days, these Israeli statements and analyses from ZAKA and other Jewish community representatives were picked up and repeated in Indian news articles. One, headlined "Hatred of Jews Spurred Nariman House Attack: Israel," quoted Olmert's statements in Israeli media that "[t]he hatred of Jews, the state of Israel and Jewish symbols are still a factor that spurs and encourages such murderous acts."[52] This article cited Olmert, who stressed that images from Nariman House "are shocking and take us back to events that we pray never recur."[53] It also quoted an interview from Israeli public radio with former head of Israel's Mossad, Danny Yatom, who similarly argued that the attacks had exposed serious failures in Indian intelligence, noting that such attacks must have "involved dozens of terrorists enjoying the support of numerous sympathizers" in Mumbai.[54] Yatom further stressed, "It is vital that the Indian security services draw the necessary lessons," implying that as an Israeli security expert he had a unique perspective on what these were.[55] Another Indian news story noted that "[t]elevision pictures from Nariman House [. . .] raised questions about the professionalism of the Indian forces."[56]

Others took the comparisons implicit in Israeli criticisms further, juxtaposing India's ineptitude in responding to Israel's uncompromising approach to counterterrorism. One commentary by an Indian security expert noted that as they watched,

> the handful of 20-somethings, holding the nation to ransom for over 60 hours [. . .] some of those Indians [. . .] aware of global anti-terror folklore might have desired belligerence from the Indian state on the lines of those made famous by the *Sayaret Matkal*—Israel's counter-terror unit which has relentlessly pursued and annihilated Israel's enemies in Munich, Beirut and Entebbe.[57]

The emerging criticism of the handling of the attacks from within Indian media contributed to the resignation of India's home minister, Shivraj Patil, on November 30.

Israeli officials thereby continued to assert Israeli primacy over the attacks. These claims were in turn reiterated and extended by Indian media commentators who argued that Israeli authorities had unique insights on what had taken place and that the Mumbai attacks were not, in fact, new or even specific to India but merely a repeat of Israel's traumas. In addition, they articulated some of the implications of Israeli criticisms of India's handling of the attacks, namely that Indians should aspire to be more like Israel. While ZAKA representatives intensified the tenor of their denunciations and speculation, other Israeli officials began to tamp down their criticism and shift to a more conciliatory posture. Olmert, stating that he was "pleased" with the cooperation and coordination with India throughout the attacks, thanked the Indian government "for deciding to keep us updated throughout the events." He repeated that Israel "would be happy to provide any and all information or specific assistance that we might be asked to give."[58] However, Olmert also suggested that Israel had never actually considered dispatching Israeli forces to Mumbai in the previous days.

December 1 . . . and After

By early December, criticism of the attacks' handling had begun to translate into acute public pressure against India's political establishment in New Delhi as well as the state of Maharashtra, an issue I return to in chapter 3. In response to mounting domestic anger, Maharashtra's deputy chief minister, R. R. Patil, followed Shivraj Patil's lead and resigned on December 1.[59] The political pressure arising from the Mumbai attacks, however, did not exclusively come from Indian publics. Israeli officials also began to take note of a growing bilateral rift between the two allies. One Israeli news story commented that Israeli criticism of India's handling of rescue operations "has caused a certain amount of diplomatic tension."[60] Building on Olmert's example from the previous day, other high-level Israeli state officials similarly distanced themselves from previous Israeli criticisms and heaped praise on the Indian response. Israel's ambassador to India, Mark Sofer, disavowed Israeli press reports critical of India's response to 26/11 and attempted to shift to a more conciliatory tone: "We have full faith in India's ability to deal with terror."[61]

Even as Israeli officials worked to repair strained relations, news stories and reports continued to emerge repeating previous Israeli criticisms as well as offering new ones. For instance, the ZAKA team's claims that Indian forces may have killed Jewish and Israeli victims were re-published by Indian and international papers.[62] A December 1 *India Today* article began: "If Israel is grieving the death of its eight citizens in the November 26 attacks in Mumbai, its terror experts cannot help regard it with a sense of déjà-vu. The attacks were a near repeat of the Savoy hotel attacks of March 1975 carried out by the Palestine Liberation Organisation (PLO)."[63] The article quoted Jonathan Fighel of Israel's International Policy Centre for Counter-Terror, who emphasized that "[o]ne cannot ignore the similarities between the Savoy attack and the present Mumbai attack." Fighel also suggested the Indian response was primitive and under-resourced: "From what I have seen on TV, it looks as the [Indian] assault forces were not equipped with special typical counter terror arms, clothing, night vision, laser viewfinder, ballistic shields, [and] special helmets with communication devices."[64]

Such claims had clear corollaries and comparisons built into them, namely that India's lack of modern counterterror and intelligence credentials were in stark contrast to those of Israel. A roundup article noted the implications of Israeli critiques: "That's no way to kill terrorists, they seem to be saying; our ladder is much better than yours."[65] And as time went on, some Israeli media commentators began to more explicitly articulate implications of previous Israeli criticisms, namely that India had something to *learn* from Israel. A *Jerusalem Post* op-ed argued: "Israel's experience offers some lessons [for India]: Depend on yourself, be willing to face unfair criticism to engage in self-defense, take counterterrorism very seriously, mobilize your citizens as an active warning system and decide when and where to retaliate."[66] In other words, according to these accounts, Indian authorities should welcome 26/11 as an opportunity to become more like Israel.

In contrast to previous days, these ongoing Israeli criticisms and recommendations began to spark pushback from Indian Foreign Ministry officials. They accused ZAKA officials of "selling all kinds of stories to journalists looking for stories, and taking credit for things they didn't do."[67] Enraged by the unrestrained and highly public nature of the Israeli officials' criticisms of them, Indian officials shot back, calling Israeli indictments of Indian incompetence "an embarrassment" for the Israelis.[68] As Israeli officials realized that their various criticisms were getting out of hand, they shifted into full-scale damage control. Olmert praised the "brave response and determination" of the Indian forces, and an Israeli Foreign Ministry official suggested that ZAKA had come on its own accord, commenting, "It is not exactly clear what they [the ZAKA officials and volunteers] are doing there [in Mumbai]."[69] This messaging de-escalated a potentially serious diplomatic dispute. One journalist commented on the efficacy of having various high-level Israeli officials backpedaling and doing their best to suppress and disavow their previous criticisms, noting that after the early stages of a significant "diplomatic headache," suddenly "the controversy simply disappeared."[70]

The reasons for Israel's shift in tone were rather transparent. At the time, commentators pointed out that Israel was already one of India's main military suppliers, and many lucrative weapons deals at the national level were at risk of being lost.[71] A *Jerusalem Post* op-ed columnist worried that "all the negative chatter in Israel will only lead to a wasted opportunity for building up support and unity" between the two countries, citing an unnamed Israeli official: "Barak's comments [criticizing Indian authorities] are not helpful, and the Indians are very sensitive. [. . .] Our relations with them are *also* a matter of national security."[72] Israeli Foreign Ministry representatives expressed their displeasure with the various criticisms by Israeli security experts and ZAKA officials. One complained that "[t]hese guys are mouthing off" and that "[w]e're really upset about these people." His concern was clearly about the lucrative weapons contracts on the line, stressing that "[w]e're talking about billions of dollars."[73] As a *Daily Beast* article commenting on these developments noted: "as far as the Israeli Foreign Ministry is concerned, the most helpful thing the country's counterterror specialists can do now? Simply hold their tongues," lest they give Indian authorities a reason to cancel weapons deals already in the works.[74] These attempts to silence Israeli security experts, however, were only partially realized. The Israeli private military intelligence firm DEBKA published a report on December 3 calling out the "failure of Indian intelligence" and further insisting that Al-Qaeda was responsible for the attacks.[75]

Despite some Israeli experts' refusal to fall in line, Israeli diplomatic and military officials continued to shift away from their prior critical posture. Their focus turned to reconciliation and damage control in order to preserve existing bilateral ties and weapons deals. During this period, a range of Israeli and Indian officials began to make the case for various Israeli-inspired responses to the attacks. Olmert and Indian Prime Minister Manmohan Singh both made public statements pledging increased counterterrorism coordination, and stories emerged suggesting that forms of intelligence cooperation were already underway in tracking down those responsible for planning 26/11.[76] At this time jingoistic calls for Israeli-inspired air strikes against Pakistan also became prominent in Indian media debates.[77]

While these air strikes never materialized, representatives of Israel's homeland security industry made the case that India should adopt Israeli "solutions." Reports emerged that Israel's homeland security industry was looking to exploit 26/11 in order to further expand its reach in India with Israeli schadenfreude on full display. A December 3 article in the Israeli business newspaper *Globes* reported: "The Israel Export and International Cooperation Institute (IEICI) believes that Israel [. . .] could benefit from India's misfortune." It quoted IEICI chairman David Arzi as saying: "Presumably, because of what has happened [during the attacks], the Indians will allocate more funding for the purchase of sophisticated anti-terrorism security equipment, such as warning systems, cameras, control systems, electronic systems and more. Israelis sell them to the Indians anyway, but there's always room to sell more."[78] The article further emphasized that Israel "has an outstanding track record as an exporter in the homeland security sector," with "solutions to offer" India.[79]

Others made the case for greater bilateral dialogue and cooperation between India and Israel. This is reflected in comments from Israeli Ambassador Mark Sofer on December 5 who suggested that the attacks would make the Indian public more aware of Israel's challenges with terrorism. He emphasized that "Israel benefits anyway from a great deal of good will in India" but also that he expected the attacks "will feed into it and generate more" because "[t]he fear of international terror is [now] much stronger in India than it was before [26/11]."[80] In other words, he argued that the experience of 26/11 would bring the countries closer together as Indians were able to better appreciate what Israelis had suffered throughout their history.

Indian advocates picked up on these calls for greater collaboration on counterterrorism and implementation of Israeli homeland security solutions. For instance, Indian corporate actors began announcing new security projects involving collaboration between India and Israel. A December 22 *Hindustan Times* article with the headline "Indian and Israeli Firms to Jointly Provide Advanced Security Systems" focused on a newly announced joint venture between the Delhi-based AP Securitas (APS) Group and the Israeli security firm ARES Group. It quoted Anil Puri, executive director of APS, who claimed that the joint venture would improve safety in India through importing expertise and technologies: "We basically are looking at being able to provide for India [. . .] advanced security systems, advanced security training and experience from all over the world [. . .] to provide for a better and safer India."[81]

Other voices added credibility to such propositions. A January 9, 2009, *Jerusalem Post* op-ed by Indian foreign policy scholar Harsh V. Pant similarly claimed that Israel offered specific lessons, tactics, and forms of expertise to India, which would be central to its fight against terrorism going forward, well beyond protecting vulnerable megacities like Mumbai:

> Israel's long experience in training, equipping and operating elite undercover units [. . .] to gather intelligence, spot targets and engage gunmen is useful for the Indian security forces facing similar situations in Kashmir and the Northeast. Other areas where Israeli know-how can be incorporated by India include tactics aimed at lowering the risk of ambush, use of infantry and commando units seeking out and destroying arms caches and terrorist bomb-making capabilities, and the use of dogs, robotics and specially trained sappers to detect hidden roadside mines.[82]

Together these excerpts illustrate how the notion that Israeli counterterrorism and homeland security offered a solution for India began to gain broad traction and "resonance."[83] It did so by proposing to "solve" a particular problem, namely India's apparent *lack* of western or even specifically Israeli homeland security approaches. This proposition gained resonance in the way it was performatively practiced and enacted by a heterogeneous network of Israeli and non-Israeli actors in relation to the event of 26/11. The network that enacted this new reality included Indian state officials, journalists, media pundits, and corporate leaders as well as Indian and international security experts and scholars. By *enrolling* this network of actors, the notion that Israeli homeland security offered a solution to terrorism in India shifted from being merely a series of generic Israeli homeland security industry talking points into a *reality.* This new reality laid the groundwork for defining the state of India's policing infrastructure and the country's *lack* of homeland security as a "problem" much more concretely than before 2008. This "problem" was framed both as a lack of modern security expertise but also as a matter of a culturally-specific

Indian backwardness on matters of internal security, a theme that I return to in subsequent chapters.

As the new reality took hold, new commercial linkages emerged to facilitate the accelerated circulation of technologies, expertise, and forms of training between Israel and India. For instance, the IEICI organized the first India-Israel Homeland Security Cooperation Forum, a trade delegation featuring fifteen Israeli homeland purveyors held in New Delhi and Mumbai between March 16 and 19, 2009, as well as a subsequent official delegation visit by the government of Maharashtra to Palestine/Israel in July 2009 (chapter 3).[84] Other Indian business groups, including the Federation of Indian Chambers of Commerce (FICCI), organized similar events in the wake of 26/11 in which Israeli homeland security industry representatives and other foreign state officials were present.[85]

In order to capitalize on this momentum, the Israeli Hollywood producer, businessman, and former spy Arnon Milchan in late 2008 founded Blue Sky International, a private security company to service elite Indian clientele, including Jamsetji Nusserwanji Tata, the owner of the Taj Hotel.[86] In addition, a January 21, 2009, press release announced a new partnership between the Indian electronic security firm Zicom and the Israeli Military Industries Academy for Advanced Security Training and Management to form the Mumbai-based firm Advanced Security Training and Management to train Indian security personnel.[87] I will return to the behind-the-scenes lobbying efforts involved in bringing some of these projects to fruition in later chapters.

ENACTING A NEW REALITY

As I have detailed above, in the coverage of 26/11 and its aftermath, Israel suddenly became extremely prominent in Indian English-language media as an exemplary model of homeland security for India to learn from. I have further suggested that an Israeli homeland security solution became a *reality* because it was practiced by a heterogeneous network of Israeli and non-Israeli actors. Here it is also useful to recall the counterpoint of Indian officials and experts in the aftermath of September 11 who failed to enact a reality of an Indian solution to those attacks (see the introduction), precisely because they proved unable to enroll the analogous network of actors to do so. In this section, I bring these two claims together. I argue that by getting involved in the event of 26/11, Israeli actors relationally produced knowledge through encounters and controversies, which in turn enrolled other actors. Yet, the *reality* of an Israeli homeland security solution to 26/11 emerged through the resolution of the emerging bilateral rift between India and Israel as both parties put their grievances aside and pledged to work together to solve a new problem, namely India's *lack* of homeland security.

Trying to understand how the idea of an Israeli homeland security solution enrolled a network of actors requires attending to how "Israel" and "Israeli homeland security" became visible in the event and were performed as sources of authority in relation to 26/11. In this task, Andrew Barry's notion of "political situations" is particularly instructive. Barry offers key insights for understanding how events are performed through contestations in ways that give rise to new forms of transnational governance. Political situations "are not given objects, but contested and evolving multiplicities," which are "performed or empracticed" through policy statements, new media, and the writings of a wide range of actors including experts, journalists, politicians, scholars, and "lay-experts."[88] Through these practices, such actors are able "claim expertise in judging the situation" and in doing so "contribute to the definition of the situation of which they are part."[89] This notion of political situations attunes us to how practices of enactment by interested parties work to *define* events, for instance, as failures or disasters in need of radical policy reform, specialized expertise, and transnational collaboration.

In this vein, we can notice that the emergence of the network detailed above was driven by the statements and practices of Israeli state and quasi-state actors. Israeli officials quite literally got involved in the emerging event by commenting on the attacks—their origins, causes, (mis)handling, and geopolitical significance—from November 27 onwards. These interventions involved a diverse range of actors from heads of state and diplomatic officials to U.S.-based pro-Israel lobbyists and rabbis to security experts and trade officials. They got to work immediately and were unrelenting throughout the event and into its aftermath, appearing in a range of Israeli, Indian, and international media. They also worked in concert by repeating common themes: that Israel had experienced similar violence before; that the attacks were focused on Israel and the West; that Israel exemplified the modern homeland security India lacked; and that Indian authorities were inept and/or not telling the truth about the true origins of the attacks.

These interventions centered Israeli perspectives and performed Israel and Israeli homeland security as authorities within the event. Efforts to situate their expertise, however, involved more than just repeating well-worn tropes and geographical imaginations about global terror and the Israeli experience. Israeli actors also relentlessly offered various forms of unsolicited assistance and advice while fiercely criticizing India's handling of the attacks as primitive and incompetent. India's initial lack of interest in Israeli overtures did not stop Israel from dispatching officials to the scene in Mumbai anyway. And as their offers went unheeded, Israeli officials upped the ante, attempting to shame their Indian counterparts into capitulation, suggesting that India's refusal to accept Israel's offers recklessly imperiled the lives of Israeli, Jewish, and other victims of the attacks. In short, Israeli actors, refusing to take no for an answer, got involved in 26/11 as it unfolded in ways that challenged Indian sovereignty over the event's meaning and management.

This relentless interventionist posture and shift in tone away from the early focus on common interests toward a more combative stance proved crucial in two distinct but interrelated ways. First, it made Israeli actors centrally visible in the event by producing sites and objects of domestic and international controversy, which featured Israeli actors and perspectives. Second, in doing so, their offers and criticisms relationally generated knowledge about the event itself, producing key parallels and comparisons between Indian and Israeli actors and their respective authorities on intelligence, counterterrorism, homeland security, policing, and disaster response. Most important for my purposes here, juxtaposing "Israel" and "Israeli homeland security" against India's (mis)handling of 26/11 did crucial work by relationally performing an "Israeli approach" to homeland security in contradistinction to an "Indian" one. In other words, by daring to compare the (mis)handling of 26/11 with the Israeli experience of fighting terrorism, Israeli actors gained traction as legitimate sources of authority in the emerging event. This paved the way for the proposition of an Israeli homeland security solution to it. Israel's homeland security greatness, that is, its status as a "big" or central actor in the event of 26/11, was achieved by drawing contrasts between India/Indians and Israel/Israelis, a process by which the former were made to look "small and provisional *in comparison*,"[90] to Israel/Israelis. Through such comparisons Israeli actors developed the idea of essential differences between these approaches as proxies for both countries' respective national essences. Israel was enacted as tough, hyper-masculine, modern, and efficient, in contrast to India as weak, effeminate, backward, and incompetent.

Israeli actors' comparisons and references to their civilization, modernity, and western-ness are anything but incidental or unique to the Mumbai attacks. This form of comparison is central to how Israel has cultivated its prowess as a model of homeland security, as I explore in the next chapter. Moreover, the comparisons and parallels they made between themselves and their (allegedly) primitive Indian counterparts have long imperial genealogies bound up with what Walter Mignolo calls the "geopolitics of knowledge" and the "colonial difference."[91] I argue that we need to pay close attention to how comparative geopolitics works as "classificatory devices," which do specific kinds of work for empire and capital by ranking and classifying people and places and privileging the enunciation of some actors over those who are being classified.[92]

As we have seen, Israeli's self-serving comparisons had specific corollaries and implications embedded within them, namely that Israel had something to teach India about homeland security. Israelis' charges of failure not only suggested that India's handling was misguided, however. They also crucially implied that things could have been otherwise, if only India *had* what Israel exemplified, that is, a modern, world-class approach to domestic security management. In doing so, Israeli criticisms enacted the Israeli approach to homeland security not simply as a source of inspiration but as a *thing* that could—and should—be exported to India as an alternative to and potential replacement for the Indian approach to domestic security. Israeli interventions thereby played important roles in performing the event itself as a disaster and failure of intelligence and governmental capacity and evidence of a lack of modern, western, or even specifically Israeli homeland security. The narratives that emerged out of these mediations became the core materials out of which the new reality was built. By the time Israeli officials began explicitly making the case in early December 2008 that India should adopt Israeli homeland security solutions, they were already mobilizing this groundwork. While such narratives were championed by Israeli officials and quasi-state actors, I have argued that they became a *reality* as they were able to enroll a wider network of non-Israeli interlocutors. So how did this take place?

By performing their own authority in relation to the attacks and India, Israeli actors became sources of knowledge through which the event was read, which in turn enrolled others. As we have seen, this knowledge was picked up by other Israeli and non-Israeli commentators as early as November 27. Thereafter, these commentators read the event through an Israeli lens, making use of Israeli criticisms as core frames of reference. In doing so, key Israeli claims about the parallels and distinctions between 26/11 and the Israeli experience with terrorism were reproduced and reified. For instance, early criticisms by Shin Bet officials and Ehud Barak as well as the later incendiary statements of ZAKA officials instantly made headlines in India, Israel, and around the world despite their highly speculative and questionable basis. In this sense, the Israeli interventions enrolled other Israeli and non-Israeli actors, who picked up and repeated Israeli claims.

The Israeli offers of assistance and accompanying criticisms were highly productive in generating controversies, which heightened their visibility as sources of authority in the event. The "(ideological) mediations" of 26/11 also helped to define "the situation itself" and the respective authority of the actors within it.[93] Indeed, it was through these contestations that the essences of the various actors and relations between them were worked out and naturalized. While productive, these interventions also faced crucial limits. As the resulting controversies spilled over and threatened to disrupt preexisting weapons deals, they were reined in. While Israel gained visibility and traction by stoking controversy and conflict, it was by resolving the controversies that the new reality of an Israeli homeland security solution began to take hold. Indian and Israeli authorities came together to pledge their unity and cooperation in fighting terrorism going forward.

Even so, the *what* of an Israeli solution was never explicitly defined. As will become clear in later chapters, the elusive quality of the Israeli solution was hardly incidental.

The audacity of Israeli criticisms proved crucial in stoking controversies and conflicts in which Israeli actors produced knowledge and gained authority. In this sense, the substance of their claims mattered. In trying to understand how the reality of an Israeli homeland security solution gained traction, however, the specific claims that Israeli actors and their allies advanced were less important than their overall critical posture, volume, and persistence. Practicing Israeli homeland security as a solution to terrorism in post-26/11 India was neither a straightforward nor a trivial matter: it required extensive resources and hard work. All of this work was notably necessary in spite of Israel's apparently privileged status as the global showroom of the homeland security state.[94] The sheer amount of politicking, spin, and labor that was required to create sites of controversy, keep them in line, and then silence and disavow them is particularly noteworthy. This translocal, relational, and specifically comparative nature of this politicking and spin are central elements of *comparative geopolitics.* Comparative geopolitics simultaneously generated key knowledge about the attacks (their origins, meaning, (mis)handling, and significance) but also about the existence, plausibility, and desirability of an apparent alternative, namely Israeli homeland security. Critical comparisons cultivated and then leveraged controversy between Indian and Israeli actors that generated the materials out of which the new reality was built. In this way, comparative geopolitics produced the conditions of possibility for new relations to emerge post-26/11 between Israel's homeland security industry and Indian state and corporate actors, which will be unpacked in later chapters.

Even as the new reality took hold, not everyone abided by its terms. A number of Israeli detractors publicly expressed skepticism about the extent to which 26/11 heralded a breakthrough in Indo-Israeli collaboration on counterterrorism and homeland security. A December 12, 2008, *New York Times* op-ed by Ami Pedahzur, a University of Texas Austin professor of Middle Eastern Studies and an Israeli terrorism expert, argued that the comparisons drawn between the handling of terrorist attacks by Israelis versus that of 26/11 were unfair and misleading. He further noted that he "would be extremely cautious about advocating the Israeli approach" in India post-26/11 in part because "[p]rotecting a huge multiethnic, multireligious country like India is far more challenging than securing a rather homogeneous, tiny state like Israel."[95] Efraim Inbar, director of the Begin-Sadat Center for Strategic Studies and longtime scholar of the Indo-Israeli alliance, expressed similar concerns. He stressed that Indian forces maintain a "more patient" and "defensive" approach to fighting the threat of terrorism than Israelis and that this difference would constrain any future collaboration.[96] Inbar further noted that the political sensitivities surrounding such collaboration would likely constrain its scope going forward.[97] Others also questioned whether Indian officials would allot the necessary funds to facilitate an Israeli homeland security solution. As Amos Yaron, former director-general of Israel's Defense Ministry with long-standing experience of working in India, argued: "I don't think it will happen. It costs a lot of money and a lot of effort. It's not the first priority right now."[98] These officials thus poked holes in the new reality by asserting that the attacks had changed little, if anything, about prospects of an Israeli homeland security solution to the attacks. This skepticism, as subsequent chapters make clear, would prove prescient.

CONCLUSION

There can be no question that Israel's homeland security industry quite literally capitalized on the unfolding political crisis of 2008 as a textbook case of what Naomi Klein has aptly called "disaster capitalism" under neoliberalism.[99] By following the actors involved in the event of 26/11, however, the chronology of this intuitive disaster-response sequence becomes less straightforward than how it later would be retrospectively rationalized (chapter 3). "Israel" and "Israeli homeland security" were not responses to the "original disaster" of 26/11.[100] Rather, as I have shown, Israeli and Jewish actors (state officials, security experts, pro-Israel lobbyists, industry boosters, ZAKA and MDA personnel, Chabad rabbis, journalists, and op-ed columnists) were present in the event of 26/11 from the outset. Their presence and criticism of the Indian response introduced the idea that Israel had something to teach India about fighting terrorism before the attacks were even declared officially over. Yet the ideas they proposed were not lying around passively waiting to get picked up. Instead, they were actively interjected into the emerging event through Israel's relentless self-promotional practices of intervention (commentary, critique, and offers of assistance) and produced through these same practices.

While taking seriously that Israel's status as a global leader in counterterrorism and homeland security were established well before 2008 and that this status had held considerable political weight in the Indian context long before the Mumbai attacks, a close reading of how Israel and Israeli homeland security got involved in 26/11 reveals that such advantages were anything but absolute, freestanding, or all-powerful. Indeed, the story I have told in this chapter raises questions about the basis and scope of the power that Israel's homeland security industry commands. While Israeli actors emerged post-26/11 in a way that often seemed authoritative and even dominant, at times they also appeared small, petty, and almost desperate to have their various offers taken seriously amid the attacks. By following the actors, the power, authority, and reach of Israel's industry comes into view as questionable and highly contingent on being accepted by others.

The reality of an Israeli homeland security solution, I argue, was not a subset of something broader, whether the global war on terror or the Indo-Israeli alliance. Rather, this reality emerged as it was enacted through situated and contingent translocal encounters. Further, such encounters did not come out of nowhere but had specific precedents. Although it is impossible to make sense of the contours of Israel's interventions into 26/11 without considering the bilateral relations that preceded and shaped them, the Israeli interventions were neither derivative of nor determined by these relations. The preexisting ties between India and Israel played multiple, competing, surprising, and sometimes even contradictory roles. India rebuffed Israeli overtures to send assistance during the attacks in spite of the entrenched geographical imaginations and material ties between both countries. Ironically, it was the preexisting contracts for Israeli military equipment that constrained the breadth of Israeli criticism about India's handling of the attacks. It was concern for these material linkages that compelled Israeli actors to disavow their early criticisms and return to more conventional narratives of unity and collaboration in the fight against global Islamic terrorism. The encounters between Israeli and Indian actors during and after 26/11 were thus crucial because although they recycled old tropes and ideological narratives, they were unruly and unpredictable and served to generate new forms of knowledge about the respective essences, locations, and authorities of the involved actors in relation to one another.

TWO

HOMELAND SECURITY PIONEERS

> Israel offers a model of success in facing up to the Third World and proving it vulnerable and weak. Israel is defiantly and victoriously offering this model for export. Beyond the fraternity of professional military men, the fraternal feeling seems to be felt by all those fighting against radical movements—searching, chasing, and destroying guerrillas and terrorists wherever they are. [. . .] When "international terrorism" is discussed in the West, Israel is often cited as the best example of standing up to it by military means.
>
> The Israeli perspective [. . .] is that of the settler-colonialist, a determined fighter who knows that war is his way of life. The identification of Israelis with Europeans fighting against natives is natural: this is exactly their lot in the world. A colonialist worldview serves as the basis for whatever dealings Israel has with the Third World.
>
> —Benjamin Beit-Hallahmi, *The Israel Connection: Whom Israel Arms and Why*

> No concrete example of an abstract can claim to be an embodiment of the abstract alone. No country, thus, is a model to another country.
>
> —Dipesh Chakrabarty, *Provincializing Europe*

INTRODUCTION

I open this chapter with a striking excerpt from Benjamin Beit-Hallahmi's classic book *The Israel Connection* because it speaks to the durability of Israel's position as a global inspiration for state strategies of violence.[1] Israel's relations with the Global South have in the intervening decades changed to some extent. Yet Beit-Hallahmi's efforts to grapple with how the Zionist colonization of Palestine is connected to global pacification remain as relevant as ever. Scholars have elaborated on the enduring centrality of Israeli doctrines, technologies, and logics in global pacification, citing Israel as a model of counterinsurgency, counterterrorism, urban warfare, and homeland security.[2]

While I draw on these highly illuminating accounts, I argue that scholars often take the Israeli model for granted. In this literature, "model" typically denotes an unparalleled and *uniquely Israeli* assemblage of expertise, ideology, and technologies developed to control, kill, and maim Palestinians, which has been progressively honed and distilled down over time to become an abstract, general example for others. As Jeff Halper elaborates, Israel "offers a model of securocratic control" that has "emerged (and continues to emerge) out of field-based necessity."[3] This model, according to Halper, represents "a coherent approach that, while constantly adapting to new situations and actors [. . .] can be taught, followed and described."[4] In such accounts, Israel is often represented as unique and unparalleled, as the only country to specialize in homeland security but also as the "most militarized" country in the world, with the highest levels of per-capita military expenditure and percentages of weapons exports as proportions of GDP.[5] In doing so, this body of work reproduces Palestine/Israel's location at the vanguard of global pacification regimes in a straightforward and unhindered way,[6] corresponding closely with commonsense and evolutionary imaginaries of modernity[7] and development as *first* here *then* there.[8]

In this chapter, I disassemble models and the practice of modeling, considering them as one part of the wider processes of fabricating homeland security. I ask how Israel's status as a security paragon, something both unique and replicable, has been *made*, *made up*, and *woven together* over time, as processes accelerated during moments of crisis. In the spirit of postcolonial and decolonial critiques of historicist accounts of modernity, I extend the thinking about knowledge production in the Zionist project specifically and in settler formations at large.[9] In *The Question of Palestine*, Edward Said notes that because Palestine served as the "site of a contest between a native presence and an incoming, basically European/Western form of advanced culture [. . .] a considerable part of the contest was conducted outside of Palestine itself."[10] Within this contest, Zionist leaders recognized that the violence necessary to expel Palestinians from their land would need to be "dignified by an *idea,* the idea was everything."[11] Said was not merely concerned with Israeli propaganda campaigns, important as they were and continue to be. He centered the production and circulation of knowledge *about* Palestine/Israel, and about Palestinians and Zionists therein, through orientalist expertise and the transnational production of "reality" of the "Zionist colonization of Palestine, its successes, its feats, its remarkable institutions."[12] As Ilan Pappé has elaborated more recently, the colonial discourse of Zionism has long been animated by contestation over what he terms "the idea of Israel," making a key distinction between this idea and the State of Israel as a living, material entity.[13] A crucial corollary of the notion of the idea of Israel is that ideas can be commodified, marketed, and even branded through their packaging in narrative form, which play key roles in mediating and contesting the violent displacement and dispossession of the Palestinians through the ongoing *Nakba*.

Following these insights, I theorize the Israel pacification model as an idea of Israel, fabricated over time through transnational encounters. Situating these processes in histories of empire and its forms of governance in Palestine and beyond, I concentrate on a number of key historical moments and banal practices through which the so-called Zionist settler-colonial experience of domination has been performatively staged and pictured[14] as a form global knowledge for others to emulate elsewhere.[15] Extending the notion of *comparative geopolitics* developed in the previous chapter, I situate models and modeling within comparative and exceptionalist imperial grammars and forms of reasoning employed to both legitimate and disavow settler-colonial conquest as well as to assert claims to universal knowledge.[16] Rather than approaching the Israeli pacification model as a thing unto itself (i.e., a distilled version of Zionist ideology and its apparatuses of domination), I situate it as part and parcel of imperial modalities of staging reals, which are narrated through comparative grammars of exceptionalist reasoning and materialized through transnational encounters. I argue that models exist only to the extent that they are enrolled by others and their essences are continuously (re)defined through forms of *translation* between actors across geographic distance and forms of difference. As a core concept in ANT, translation does not refer to a shift from one vocabulary to another. It instead seeks to capture "displacement, drift, invention,

[and] mediation," in other words the creations of novel links that in turn modify the actors being connected.[17]

In what follows, I begin by examining the circulation of pacification regimes and their assemblages of violence within histories of European colonization. I then trace how Zionist pacification strategies have emerged as inspirations and models for the world to emulate, a crucial aspect of the transnational fabrication of security projects. I focus on key encounters through which Israel's military prowess has been staged and enrolled international audiences. From there I shift the focus to the ongoing fabrication of Israel as a homeland security pioneer and model for the world, through an ethnography of Israel's homeland security industry. Methodologically, I focus on comparative imperial grammars, both as a means to understand how their surrounding narratives work to fabricate particular histories of violence as exceptional but also to unstitch their claims to universal authority. By tracing this ongoing history of fabrication, I show how the "Israeli experience" has become legible as a success story, a thing and a model to be emulated by other countries facing political violence, such as India.

TRANSNATIONAL PACIFICATION INFRASTRUCTURES

The Zionist colonization of Palestine has been carried out as a project of demographic reengineering and ethnic cleansing, underpinned by large-scale Jewish immigration and land purchases from the late nineteenth century onward. Whereas the purchasing of land through accumulation of title was a relatively easy task, Rashid Khalidi notes that the resistance of the *fellahin* to their removal from the land, which they and their ancestors had worked and lived on for generations, "was not so easily overcome."[18] As this resistance sparked violence, early Zionists depended on existing forms of state power in Palestine, initially Ottoman and subsequently British Mandatory authorities to assist their efforts to control and cultivate their newly acquired lands.[19]

In the early twentieth century, the Zionist settlers also developed their own material infrastructures of violence. By the time early British support for the Zionist cause was formalized with the Balfour Declaration of 1917, early Zionist settlers had already established their first guard organization

Bar-Giora in 1907 and its extension Hashomer (Guardian) in 1909 and were fortifying their *moshavot* with protective walls.[20] Hashomer further developed into the Haganah paramilitary force in 1920.[21] European Zionist settlers also brought their own military experience and technical know-how to produce weapons and other military equipment within Palestine.[22] By the 1920s, the settlement of Jews in Palestine known as the *yishuv* was manufacturing weapons and ammunition,[23] and in 1933 it founded the firm TAAS to manufacture mortars, rifles, and grenades.[24] By the late 1930s, the Zionists founded the private security company Hashmira Security Technologies Ltd. in order to claim land and challenge the growing Palestinian protests against the presence of the Zionists and the British.[25]

These infrastructures were also nurtured by colonial ideas, materials, bureaucratic practices and law developed across the British empire. After the initial period of British military rule from 1917 to 1920, British rule shifted to a formally civilian government in anticipation of the League of Nations–sanctioned British Mandate for Palestine beginning in 1922. The Mandate incorporated the Balfour Declaration, explicitly articulating that British tutelage in Palestine aimed to create a Jewish homeland in Palestinian territory.[26] During this period, colonial British police often led the charge in efforts to quell the growing Palestinian uprisings. While the initial Palestinian Police was comprised of just 18 British and 55 Palestinian officers, by April 1922 650 former members of the Auxiliary Division of the Royal Irish Constabulary, colloquially known as the Black and Tans during their violent suppression of the Irish rebellion in 1919 and 1920, were brought to Haifa to serve in the British Palestine Gendarmerie.[27] While this unit was formally dissolved by 1926,[28] the unrelenting Palestinian uprisings against Zionist and British presence prompted British authorities to attempt to reorganize the Palestine police.[29] As part of these efforts, they summoned security experts from across the empire, including South Asia. For instance, Hebert Layard Dowbiggin, the former inspector general of police in Ceylon and an imperial policing expert, was appointed to reorganize the police presence in Palestine in wake of the major riots that took place at the end of August 1929.[30]

As these uprisings gained momentum in Palestine, British pacification efforts drew their inspiration from British small wars and counterinsurgency campaigns in other colonial theaters beyond Ireland, including Bengal and the North-West Frontier Province, particularly in their suppression of the Palestinian Revolt (1936–39).[31] Mandate authorities drew on these colonial doctrines, techniques, and tactics but also refined and consolidated them.[32] Personnel moving across different areas facilitated this trend, including Sir Charles Tegart, an imperial police expert on terrorism who had served in the Calcutta police and was summoned to Palestine in 1937 to reform the Palestine Police. Tegart replaced smaller police stations with police fortresses known as Tegart Forts, among other measures.[33] Though British-led, these pacification efforts took place in part through collaboration with Zionist settlers in Palestine. British-Zionist death squads also known as Special Night Squads were mobilized to attack Palestinian villages under the cover of darkness.[34] The products of these collaborations also traveled beyond Palestine. For instance, the British counterinsurgency approaches developed under the Mandate influenced subsequent British and U.S. counterinsurgency campaigns elsewhere.[35]

These co-produced infrastructures laid the core groundwork for Israel's bureaucratic makeup and legal architecture tasked with managing so-called "dangerous populations" and subverting Palestinian self-determination.[36] As Noura Erakat shows, the Mandatory regime was *sui generis* in that, unlike other non-self-governing territories under British control, it was not devised to lead to Palestinian independence. Instead, this exception facilitated its own particular rules, which explicitly mandated the suppression of Palestinian self-determination as an international legal obligation. This established a self-fulfilling dynamic whereby the exception authorized new rules, which in turn facilitated the continuation of the exception.[37] These infrastructures co-produced by the British and the Zionists also gave rise to the coercive foundations of the Israeli state. Ever since their creation, Tegart Forts have remained embedded in the Palestinian landscape, becoming Israeli police stations, jails, and prisons. After the 1994 Oslo Accords, and later appropriated as the headquarters of the Palestinian Authority.[38] Similarly, early Zionist militias and weapons production became the building blocks of Israel's war economy, military-industrial complex, and security industries. Haganah, for instance, was the precursor of the Israel Defence Forces (IDF) formed after 1948, hereafter the IOF.[39]

TAAS was renamed Israeli Military Industries (IMI) and remains a major presence in Israel's weapons industry.[40] And Hashmira, later becoming a subsidiary of the global private security company G4S, emerged as Israel's largest private security company.[41] The violence employed in the Zionist project also shaped subsequent repression beyond Palestine/Israel. Early on, Israel began exporting weapons to recently decolonized states, including India.[42] Even as Israel has become a significant exporter of weapons and security technologies abroad, it continues to be a leading recipient of military aid from powerful western states, including the U.S.[43]

While the ethnic cleansing of Palestine was a material process, this violence was legitimized through exceptionalist, civilizational Zionist security narratives.[44] Early Zionist ideologues like Ze'ev (Vladimir) Jabotinsky and Theodor Herzl imagined their Jewish state as one fortressed by walls, in order to build settlements and repel the natives.[45] Herzl situated his claims in racialized civilizational terms, arguing that the Zionists would "form part of a wall of defence for Europe in Asia, an outpost for civilization against barbarism."[46] Because such figures openly declared their genocidal ambitions (and, occasionally, directed their violence at the British as well), the Zionists were interpellated as "terrorists" by Palestinians and Mandate authorities alike.[47] In response, David Ben-Gurion and other leaders attempted to differentiate the violent tactics at the center of the Zionist project from those employed in Palestinian resistance by representing Zionist violence as "the opposite of terror."[48] Post-1948, Israeli leaders employed exceptionalist language to justify their violence. Rooted in Biblical claims about the Jewish people as "divinely chosen," Ben-Gurion argued that Israel's national security predicament was a "one of a kind problem, much as [Jews] are one of a kind people."[49] Underpinning such exceptionalist claims, as Said pointed out, was what he termed the Zionist "ideology of difference," which represented Jews and the Jewish State as radically unique. But as he noted, this ideology also extended to non-Jews, because "if a Jewish state is created by and for the Jewish people, then it must be the case that non-Jews are posited as radically *other*, fundamentally and constitutively different."[50] As Nadera Shalhoub-Kevorkian persuasively argues, Zionist security narratives work as a settler-colonial "theology," using quasi-biblical claims to justify the elimination of Palestinians through their criminalization and racialization.[51] As I will show, these exceptionalist narratives were key to representing Zionist violence as an exemplary form to be imitated by others elsewhere.

Zionist exceptionalist security rhetoric was affirmed by leading western states, which from the outset treated Zionist violence differentially. As Said noted, "Israel's status in European and American public life and discourse has always been special. [. . .] On behalf of Israel, anomalous norms, exceptional arguments, eccentric claims were (and still are) made, all of them forcibly conveying the notion that Israel does not entirely belong to the world of normal politics."[52] Yet, as Said also crucially stressed, "Israel—and with it Zionism—has gained this unusual status *politically*, not miraculously: it merged with a variety of currents in the West," in part through the imbrication of American and Israeli exceptionalisms.[53] In the early post-1948 period, Israel and its allies promoted the Jewish state "as a successful replica of America—an even shinier, more robust model" and Israel's attempts to emulate the United States "confirmed its exemplary qualities" as "a paragon of modernization."[54]

This has worked to idealize and fetishize Israeli statecraft and military power as exceptionally efficient, ethical, and moral[55] and has proven particularly important in justifying Israeli violence within western liberal discourses.[56] While the image of Israel as a global pacification model was not yet fully formed before 1948, this history shows the exceptionalist narrative foundations on which the fabrication of the Israeli model would develop and mature in the years thereafter.

EPIC ENCOUNTERS

Transnational encounters in the form of spectacular military assaults, rescue operations, and practices of knowledge-making played a key role in the fabrication of Israel's image as a security model for the world. After its formal founding in 1948, Israel's exceptionalist security claims got some traction, at least to the extent that Britain and France continued to view Israel as an extension of European power in the Middle East. Facing a rapid decline of their own global influence and the rise of anticolonial nationalist movements around the world, these two imperial powers provided Israel vital geopolitical support and military aid, as did other

European states, not least Germany.[57] Britain and France further collaborated with Israel in early wars with its Arab neighbors, most notably the 1956 Suez War against Egypt. In this period, Israel's engagements with France became one of the most substantial and significant linkages in material, political, and ideological terms. France, reeling from its defeat in Vietnam in 1954 and facing growing rebellions in its North African colonies, allied with Israel against the Arabs in the Maghreb. In the course of their alliance, the French provided key expertise to Israel's covert nuclear weapons program but also took inspiration from the Israeli *kibbutz* as a model for French pacification efforts in Algeria.[58]

While the French saw Israel's settler-colonial project as an inspiration for their own, Israel's prevailing global image was hardly one of exceptional security prowess to be emulated by the world's leading powers. At the time, Israel was politically isolated. In the United States, as Norm Finkelstein has shown, "Israel practically dropped from sight in American Jewish life soon after the founding of the state," with "American Jewish intellectuals [. . .] especially indifferent to Israel's fate."[59] Even though the United States materially supported the Suez War and Israel's role therein, it viewed Israel as but one of a number of regional assets at the time, and President Dwight Eisenhower forced Israel to withdraw fully from the Sinai following the end of the crisis.[60] While the seeds of Israel's close geopolitical relationship with the United States can be traced to 1956, the United States around this time was "decidedly uneasy" about its emerging relations with Israel,[61] with Eisenhower showing little sympathy for Ben-Gurion's self-professed "security dilemmas."[62] President John F. Kennedy played a significant role in warming up to Israel, breaking the embargo that had previously blocked sales by U.S. weapons manufacturers from selling major weaponry to Israel in 1962 and declaring to Israeli foreign minister Golda Meir that the United States and Israel were already in a "special relationship," comparable only to the geopolitical ties between the United States and Britain.[63] Yet the emergent U.S. "shadow over Palestine" still took some time to take shape.[64] It was not until after the Six-Day War in 1967 that Israel's image in the eyes of the West undertook its most dramatic and categorical shift.

Israel's swift and decisive military victory over Egypt, Syria, and Jordan in the Six-Day War proved crucial in cultivating Israel's status as a model of military prowess to be emulated by the West. As an Adelphi Paper on the lessons of 1967 published by the London-based Institute for Strategic Studies quipped: "Like the campaigns of the younger Napoleon, the performance of the Israel Defence Force [*sic*] provided a textbook illustration for all of the classical Principles of War: speed, surprise, concentration, security, information, the offensive and above all training and morale."[65] While dismissing Soviet and Arab accusations that Israel represented "an outpost of Western imperialism" as utterly "absurd," the monograph tellingly praised Israelis' pioneering settler ethos, stressing that "more than any indigenous Middle Eastern people" Israelis exemplified "qualities of hard work, technical expertise, self-confidence which historians once mistakenly associated with the Protestant religion and the spirit of capitalism."[66]

The U.S. response to the events of 1967 became particularly pivotal. "Impressed by Israel's overwhelming display of force", Finkelstein notes, the United States incorporated Israel as a strategic asset, a shift that was bolstered by a sudden influx of military and economic aid, thereby rendering Israel as a "proxy for U.S. power in the Middle East."[67] Much like the French before them, however, what U.S. publics and strategic thinkers saw in the 1967 victory was shaped by comparison to the disastrous U.S. war in Vietnam. After having toured key battle sites in occupied Syria and Egypt with Israeli military officials in the aftermath of the Six-Day War, American generals returned with the impression that if armed with proper equipment, tactics, and training, conventional military battles remained winnable.[68] In light of the growing contestation around the morality of the U.S. military campaigns in Vietnam, "Israel came to provide a political model for thinking about military power and a practical example of effectiveness in the use of that power."[69] A source of endless public fascination in the 1970s, Israel came to exemplify morality but also military power through which the United States sought to re-fight its war in Vietnam.[70] Indeed, the 1967 victory "transformed Israel from its depressing prewar existence into a confident mini-empire" and into an object of global admiration.[71] Yet, as I detail in the interlude that follows this chapter, around 1967 Indian strategic thinkers were hardly unequivocally enthusiastic about this emergent image of Israel as a global exemplar of martial prowess and self-sufficiency.

The Six-Day War was just the beginning of Israel's increasingly global prominence in what came to be known as the "war against terrorism" through a series of what Melani McAlister calls "epic encounters."[72] The 1972 Olympic Games held in Munich, West Germany, brought the Israeli-Palestinian conflict "home to the world" when eight Palestinian guerrillas of the Black September group stormed the Olympic compound and took nine Israeli athletes hostage, demanding the release of two hundred Palestinians held by Israel.[73] The guerrillas went on to kill all of their hostages and the German authorities were fiercely criticized for their handling of the attack, as was Israel's refusal to negotiate with Black September. Israel retaliated by bombing ten villages in Syria and Lebanon, which Israel claimed to be militant strongholds, killing untold numbers. Initially, western media reporting on these retaliatory attacks was mixed. Yet, as their fallout began to materialize through the 1973 Arab-Israeli War, the civil war in Lebanon, new rounds of militant attacks against Israel, and the hostage-taking of OPEC ministers in Vienna in 1975, western media coverage retreated from its previous fetishization of Israeli martial prowess as a model for the West.[74]

However, laudatory western media coverage of Israel returned with the 1976 hijacking of an Air France flight from Tel Aviv by a group claiming affiliation with the Popular Front for the Liberation of Palestine. The hijackers forced the flight to land in Entebbe, Uganda, and demanded that Israel and other countries release a number of Palestinian and pro-Palestinian prisoners. Once in Entebbe, the hijackers received support from Ugandan troops. After the hijackers released all the hostages (except for the Israeli citizens and some Jewish non-Israelis), Israel mounted a bold covert rescue operation, flying commandos to Entebbe. The Israeli forces rescued the hostages, killing all of the hijackers and a number of Ugandan military personnel. In the course of the raid, three hostages and one Israeli soldier were killed. The spectacular raid instantly garnered widespread international publicity and acclaim in popular culture. This coverage valorized

Israel's technical capabilities in planning and executing the operation but also situated Israel's *will* as the decisive factor in winning while demonizing Palestinians as quintessential criminal terrorist figures.[75] Together, these epic encounters were formative in fabricating the image of Israel as an exemplar of military and counterterror prowess for the world to emulate. But they also crucially worked to position Israel as the quintessential victim of "international terrorism."[76]

These epic encounters worked in tandem with Israeli officials' attempts to explain away controversies surrounding Israeli violence. Moreover, in keeping with the "exceptionalist mode" of historical narration as a dual process of producing accounts of excellence and superiority through denial, disavowal, and erasure, Israeli officials worked tirelessly to forget and rework key patterns and events in the history of Zionist colonization.[77] Israel's attempts to explain away its history of hijacking and shooting down commercial flights illustrate this dynamic. For instance, on December 12, 1954, Israel intercepted a plane flying from Syria, forcing it to land at Lydda Airport.[78] Claiming that the plane has violated Israeli sovereignty, Israel detained five crew members and four passengers, including Syrian customs and consular officials, using them as bargaining chips to negotiate the release of Israeli soldiers held by Syria.[79] Likewise, on February 23, 1973, Israel shot down a Libyan passenger jet over the Sinai Peninsula, killing 108 passengers, claiming that the plane veered off course and stopped responding to air traffic control. While aides of Israeli Prime Minister Golda Meir acknowledged this event as a "disaster," Israeli officials refused to concede that any missteps had taken place. In a 1973 *New York Times* article, an Israeli army officer defended the action, asking: "What were we to do? [. . .] Let a Libyan plane roam at will through our airspace? How could we guarantee it wasn't a kamikaze plane loaded with explosives headed for an Israeli city?"[80] The officer further asserted that a few weeks earlier, Israel had received intelligence that Palestinians were planning to hijack and crash a passenger jet into Tel Aviv. At the time, the International Civil Aviation Association rejected these justifications, but Israel faced no sanction from powerful western states or the United Nations.[81]

Similar attempts to explain away Israeli violence continued in the years after, becoming ever more inventive. The military occupation of Palestinian territories that began in 1967 was itself not a new story in the annals of western empire. As Yael Berda details, the underlying legal architecture underpinning the occupation was borrowed directly from British colonial emergency laws, which were literally copied and pasted by Israeli officials from the British Colonial Emergency Defence regulations of 1945 as a contingency plan four years before 1967.[82] Yet as the occupation endured after 1967, Israeli officials attempted to reinvent and recast the meaning of military occupation in the western press not as a continuation of British empire but instead as an example of "living together," a notion that the *New York Times* was willing to indulge. On May 2, 1976, it ran a lead editorial calling out "Arab propagandists" for various outrages and repeating Israel's official line that the military occupation of the West Bank and Gaza represented a "model for future cooperation" and peaceful coexistence between Arabs and Jews.[83] The audacity of this claim was stunning. In Said's words, "[a] military occupation was taken as representative of good relations between people."[84]

This process of disavowing Israeli violence by representing it as a model for the world continued across a range of public, diplomatic, military, and scholarly forums in the years thereafter. The 1979 Jerusalem Conference was one of the most influential. It was organized by the Jonathan Institute, named in honor of the Israeli soldier killed in Operation Entebbe, Jonathan Netanyahu, the brother of future Israeli Prime Minister Benjamin Netanyahu. The Conference brought together U.S. and Israeli officials to debate the terms of "international terrorism" and was followed by the 1984 Washington Conference on the same topic.[85] These events enjoyed extensive international media coverage and produced a range of publications, including the popular 1984 book *Terrorism: How the West Can Win,* edited by Benjamin Netanyahu. In his 1987 review of the volume, Said called it out as a "scam," predicated on "massively inflated claims, undocumented allegations and ridiculous tautologies" but also as an incitement to anti-Arab and anti-Muslim violence based on racist civilizational motifs.[86]

Despite their lack of rigor or substance, these efforts to position Israel at the vanguard of debates on international terrorism continued to gain ground. Foreign interlocutors were enrolled in Israel's *hasbara* campaigns, which were developed to explain away Israeli violence and "sell" Israel to

America.[87] In doing so, Israeli officials and experts came to play key roles in what Lisa Stampnitsky has called "disciplining terror," namely the invention of "terrorism" as a specific political problem by a cadre of experts, institutions, and an emergent "'terrorism' industry."[88] This industry's work has depicted Palestinians as the quintessential terrorist Other (rather than a people struggling for self-determination) while presenting Israeli counterterrorism as exceptionally advanced.[89]

Through these knowledge-making practices, however, *what* Israel offered to the world was continuously updated alongside geopolitical shifts. Whereas in the 1970s and 1980s Israel sought to associate Palestinian militancy with the Soviet Union and positioned itself as the vanguard of the West against communism, after the end of the Cold War it shifted gears, increasingly focusing on the specter of so-called "Islamic terrorism."[90] By the late 2000s, Israel also began to publicly legitimate its long-standing assassination policy as a counterterrorism measure in international legal and diplomatic fora. It attempted to assert the legal right to use lethal force over the occupied Palestinian population by reclassifying the occupation under the newly invented legal category of "armed conflict short of a war."[91]

After the September 11 attacks, Israeli officials moved swiftly to redouble and update their credentials as counterterrorism pioneers. As elaborated in the introduction to this book, within days after the attacks Israel began to position its experience fighting terrorism as a precursor to the global war on terror, claiming that it had been anticipating and preparing for the tactics used in the attacks long before. Israeli officials further argued that they had invented the concept of homeland security decades before the term was coined by the George W. Bush administration in 2002, aided by a cadre of practitioner scholar-experts.[92] The ever-deepening embrace of Israeli counterterrorism by U.S. authorities after 2001 compelled U.S. authorities not only to retreat from their prior opposition to Israel's assassination policy but also to adopt Israeli legal reasoning to justify their emerging targeted killing programs.[93] Indeed, prior U.S. opposition to Israeli counterterrorism approaches gave way to ever-deepening forms of collaboration and practices of counterterrorism between the two countries through their joint imbrication in a rapidly expanding counterterrorism industry, seeking to undermine Palestinian resistance.[94]

Read in this light, the Israeli interventions into 26/11 surveyed in chapter 1 were anything but new. They represented one moment in a long pattern of exceptionalist positioning through comparative geopolitics, both in relation to high-profile global events but also through mundane knowledge-making practices. Comparison worked geopolitically to position Israeli pacification approaches as an exceptional example to follow. Thus, Israel's status as a homeland security model is not the simple culmination of the Zionist conquest of Palestine or its military operations abroad. Rather, this status has been actively fabricated over time by staging Israeli military and police power as exemplary through disavowing its long history of gratuitous violence, a process that has long relied on an "enormous labor of persuasion" to enroll and maintain an audience of adherents abroad.[95] In justifying their credulity to Israeli perspectives, the Adelphi Paper referenced above tellingly conceded that the "lack of balance in [its] sources is due less to a lack of cooperation from Arab governments than to the *extraordinary helpfulness* shown by Israeli officials, soldiers, and politicians at all levels" in supplying information.[96] As I elaborate below, moreover, Israel's model status is a work in progress. It needs to be constantly adapted and reinscribed through everyday worldly encounters.

COMPARATIVE ADVANTAGES

As I noted above, scholars frequently take for granted the so-called Israeli pacification model as a thing in the world. Yet, as I have shown in the previous section, if we alternatively situate this model as an idea of Israel historically, we come to grasp that this image is anything but new. It has emerged out of sustained work to make the Zionist project and its anti-Indigenous violence legible as an example for others elsewhere to admire and follow. But attention to the historical emergence of Israel-as-model also reveals something else, namely how this image has been continuously updated and morphed over time. It shows that being a model also means being current, in other words being *in* and *of* the moment of world politics. In telling this story, we get to the aftermath of September 11, 2001, the moment when Israel began to articulate its experience repressing and dispossessing Palestinians as a precursor to the emerging war on terror.

When Israel and its supporters first began to do so in September 2001, the term *homeland security* had not even been coined. Yet, within just a few years after the formal founding of DHS in 2002, Israel's experience was widely understood as coterminous with homeland security. So how did this all happen? In other words, how did Israel repackage its associations with counterterrorism and continue to update them in relation to the global war on terror in the years since? Which kinds of work are involved? And who carries it out?

In this section, I provide some answers to these questions, drawing on ethnographic engagements with actors and texts from the Israeli state and representatives of the country's homeland security industry. I began this work in July 2012 when I began my fieldwork speaking with key actors in this industry. Some were based in and around Tel Aviv and others in other parts of Palestine/Israel. A number of my informants' careers span many decades before 2001 and after, enabling us to understand how their work has been refashioned to suit new fads in the naming of violence over time. I was concerned with the marketing and legitimation of particular Israeli homeland security products and services to foreign clientele (training, consulting, weapons, surveillance, and fortification equipment) but also the origins and nature of these solutions. In my conversations with industry insiders, I also inquired about the nature of these offerings and how they come to be narrated and legitimated as models of homeland security for the world at large. Through this work of tracing the encounters between Israeli homeland security purveyors and the world, we come to see not only *what* this model refers to but also how it is *fabricated*, i.e., *made*, *made up*, and *woven together* through relations and comparisons across time and space.

Primacy

My Israeli interlocutors made claims about Israel's primacy in developing homeland security approaches and technologies. They suggested that they did so *before* the rest of the world. For instance, Isaac Ben-Israel, an Israeli weapons scientist and defense intellectual, stressed that "usually we [Israelis] are first to experience new ideas of . . . danger."[97] As we spoke in his office at Tel Aviv University, he referenced the downing of the Libyan plane in 1973 *not* as a misstep or failure but rather as evidence of Israel's proactiveness in anticipating new kinds of danger before the rest of the world. He explained that the decision of Israeli authorities to shoot down the jet demonstrated that already then Israel recognized the potential for "terrorists" to use commercial airliners as missiles. While conceding that the incident was a "tragedy" and had "nothing [. . .] to do with terrorism" (in the sense that the plane was not in fact being used in a militant plot), he argued that the decision could be justified because Israelis had intelligence that Fatah was planning to hijack a passenger aircraft and crash it into a tower in Tel Aviv. So, whereas the United States was "surprised" when aircraft crashed into the Twin Towers in 2001, Ben-Israel maintained that the event had been "planned thirty years before." Accordingly, he argued, Israel's counterterror expertise is "not from the past" but rather applies to "the present situation."

Similar accounts of Israel's primacy in the global war on terror were echoed by Leo Gleser, an Israeli-Argentinian former Israeli IOF colonel who participated in Operation Entebbe and founded International Security and Defense Systems Ltd. (ISDS) in the 1980s.[98] When we spoke at the *moshav* where his corporate headquarters is located just outside of Tel Aviv in 2012, Gleser noted "these things, now the people understand; [what] happened to us [Israelis] thirty years ago, others are facing this just now," in reference to challenges faced by U.S. military forays into the Islamic world since 2001. Gleser argued that Israel had been engaged in similar battles to those in the contemporary war on terror for decades, a trope featured in his firm's marketing brochure claiming that ISDS has been "fighting and winning the war on crime and terror since 1982."[99]

Other industry representatives similarly positioned Israel as a homeland security leader ahead of its time. They did so by comparing security dynamics in Palestine/Israel with other places and countries framed as "behind." For instance, a marketing representative of MER, a surveillance firm specializing in Safe City projects, noted that "[in Israel] it's self-explanatory, you don't need to convince people about the need of Safe City. But in the world, it's still something that is coming up [just now]." Amos Golan, a retired IOF lieutenant colonel, described Israel's emergence as a leader in developing homeland security "innovations" for the world. Golan served as a fighter and commander in IOF units and after retirement became CEO of Silver Shadow Advanced Security Systems Ltd., a firm that develops, manufactures, and exports small arms and security technologies. Recounting how he had turned his battlefield experiences into new "innovations," Golan stated, "I am an inventor all my life, *not* because I am a genius. I am an inventor *because I am not a genius.*" Golan explained that he never took the easy route, that is, "highway route number one" but instead took the less traveled "route 678, 100, and 5," thereby arriving at "a solution from a different direction." This unconventional approach, he argued, enabled him to stay ahead of the curve, stressing that he is "always five years before the others" and "one step ahead" in foreign countries. Golan cited the development of his most famous invention, the CornerShot, a technology that when paired with a pistol enables military and police units to shoot around corners. He explained that at first foreign customers were skeptical of the CornerShot's necessity but claimed that foreign customers who had put it into use became convinced: "After a few incidents, they said, "Yes, yes. It's better."

My informants acknowledged that the September 11 attacks formally inaugurated the paradigm of homeland security and that the term itself had American origins. As Guy Zuri, former director of aerospace, defense, and homeland security at the IEICI, explained, homeland security is an American term for "civil security" or "national security" that had since become "the common buzzword" for security outside of formal military settings in global parlance.

Yet, these figures claimed that Israel had seen all of the current dangers long before anyone else and had developed effective strategies to contain them. The implication of their narratives was clear: Israelis are homeland security pioneers and clairvoyants, giving their global clients tools to manage current dangers and anticipate future developments to remain ahead of the curve and avoid the quagmires and missteps faced by states around the world in managing global terrorism. In Golan's account, the Israeli experience was a central trope in narrating Israeli pacification strategies as the frontier of homeland security "innovation."

The Israeli Experience

Most industry actors with whom I spoke stressed that their unparalleled *experiences* made them uniquely situated to understand and manage security threats more efficiently than others. This is what Neve Gordon calls the "Israeli experience," namely the ways that Israeli homeland security purveyors have been able to commodify Israel's hands-on experience in combat and expertise in high tech and weapons as a comparative advantage.[100] Israel's "experience" with settler-colonial dispossession has been fused with the country's status as "start-up nation," an idea is captured and popularized by a book with that title.[101] As Joe Getzoff elaborates, "start-up discourse" represents a "traveling narrative about Israel's supposed economic and scientific exceptionalism" that seeks "to identify Israel as a perfect model for economic success by celebrating the state's unique cultural entrepreneurialism premised on military conscription and training."[102]

My interlocutors frequently referenced their unparalleled "Israeli experience" through assertions to embodied knowledges, approximating those from standpoint epistemology in order to assert claims about Israeli homeland security exceptionality. As the CEO of one security consultancy emphasized: "I think it's obvious that every . . . [security] consultant is talking from his own experience. . . . That's why they [clients] pay us, to talk about *our own* [Israeli] experience. Otherwise, they don't need us." Similarly, when I asked a representative from Magal S^3, a specialist in fencing and perimeter control, what gave Israeli firms their advantage over non-Israeli competitors, he responded that security *in general* should be thought of as an Israeli notion "because Israel is surrounded by enemies . . . our way of life *is* security." Marc Kahlberg, former head of tourist police in Netanya, a city that experienced suicide bombings during the Al-Aqsa Intifada in 2002, explained Israel's expertise and its relevance to the world in similar terms. The South African–born Kahlberg, who after his retirement founded MK International Security Consulting Ltd. (MKISC), argued that in managing contemporary dangers, "we start in Israel." As he elaborated during our conversation in his home office, "I'm not going to go back and talk about history, but . . . Israel's got a lot, unfortunately, to offer the rest of the free world in preventative methods of homeland security." What made Israeli security truly exceptional, he argued, was "the vast experience that we've had."

I encountered similar claims in my conversation with Avi, who after working in the counterterror and special forces unit Yamam as a fighter and instructor left to open his own training and supply firm around the year 2000. I asked Avi how (if at all) his expertise and skills as a police trainer were related to the conflicts with Palestinians and other neighboring countries historically and in the present. He responded by stressing that the duration of the "Israeli experience" is unparalleled anywhere in the world and that this makes Israeli expertise exceptional: "The *only* difference between Israeli security and other security all over the world is the experience. That's all. This is the only [difference]." When I asked Avi to elaborate, he repeated the trope of Israel's primacy in homeland security: "We are having that kind of situation since before even the country was born here. Meaning that it's become part of our life." He used his own life story as an example, noting that as far back as he could remember he knew what a terrorist was. He stressed that this was unique to Israel, arguing that Europeans arguably had five to seven years of similar experience.

While Avi invoked the memory of his childhood to assert Israel as exceptionally experienced, another trainer, Eyal, presented his body as evidence. In the middle of our conversation in his office, Eyal took off his T-shirt to show me a large bullet scar on his chest, allegedly from a Palestinian who shot him when he was working as a fighter in a special IOF unit. As he showed me the scar, he claimed that his personal experience gave him unique insights and credibility for his global clientele. While somewhat off-putting to me in the moment, I got the sense that the scar was a standard prop in his pedagogy. At the time of our interview, Eyal was the CEO of a training and combat supply company established in the mid-1990s and a seasoned trainer, claiming to have worked in more than twenty-two different countries. Like Golan, he had also developed and patented his own security technologies, some of which were displayed in his corporate office waiting room. Yet, before going into business, Eyal recounted that he had served in the *Musta'ribeen*, special forces units that pose undercover as Arabs; as a trainer and fighter in *Yamam*; and as a counterterror trainer in other IOF units. Eyal's career exemplified the embodiment and commodification of the Israeli experience.

These actors explained how Israel's embodied experience produced exceptionally skilled security personnel. As Leo Gleser claimed, "No one in the total world has the same situation [that Israel faces]," which in turn produces "good sources [personnel], very well trained, well prepared in different areas and with a good common sense, a way of thinking." Or as Avi more crudely put it, "We [Israelis] are good because we are eating this shit (for) more than seventy years." Others suggested that their exceptional experience produced an exceptional Israeli "brand" of homeland security knowhow. For instance, Guy Zuri explained that "in homeland security, Israel . . . comes as a brand." Likewise, Ari, a marketing director for a security training and risk management firm, explained that Israel had decades of experience with violence, claiming that "our reality creates this brand and it's an unfortunate reality, an unfortunate brand, but this is what brings, at the end of it, the necessity to learn something from this experience."

When I pressed Ari to elaborate whether he meant that the emergence of this brand was not of Israel's own making, as he responded tersely:

> Let me ask you this: who would *choose* this reality? If it was like Switzerland here, we would work well with our neighbors and everything would be fine. This is actually a dream for most of us, despite of what the world might think. . . . But reality creates a lot of facts in life . . . in a person's life, in a society's life and in a country's life, in the world's life.

While claiming that the dangers Israelis faced were externally imposed onto them, rather than of their own making, Ari mobilized the Israeli experience to disavow Israel's responsibility for creating its "reality," framing it as natural and externally imposed. In so doing, he also presented this reality as part and parcel of "the world's life." An IEICI PowerPoint presentation echoed this sentiment, framing Israeli homeland security as "Born of Necessity. Matured by Reality."[103] Here we can see how narratives of Zionist exceptionalism have shifted over time. Whereas Ben Gurion and early Zionist ideologues mobilized the ideology of difference to justify their violence against Palestinians, the claims to "experience" here also represent an effort to situate Zionist violence as part and parcel of "the world's life."

In explaining the exceptionality of the Israeli homeland security brand, industry actors frequently referenced Israelis' heightened sense of "security awareness." They argued that this enabled Israel to manage threats more effectively than other countries. Ari explained that because of "the awareness of the citizens," ordinary Israelis played a significant role in reducing hundreds of attacks around the early 2000s "to almost zero last year." Israel, as he explained, is "a country that promotes its awareness. Awareness is a huge part of preventing a problem because everybody has common-sense and security at the end is common-sense." Kahlberg similarly stressed the need to cultivate "awareness and alertness on a higher level" to fight threats effectively. He explained that his work involved helping others to challenge "naiveté and being complacent." This, he argued, made Israel an example of proactiveness for others to follow: "Israel has something that we can certainly offer a world that doesn't want violence, and this is what I'm doing." Bearing a striking resemblance to Said's account of how the occupation was presented as a model for the world, these officials argued that Israeli experience should be shared with others not as an example of *violence* but rather its antithesis.

As Kahlberg's reference to not wanting to talk about history further evidences, industry actors narrated the Israeli experience in ways that disavowed any responsibility for Israeli violence. They used a range of euphemisms that sanitized and naturalized this violence as inevitable, evolutionary, and positive, if "unfortunate." For instance, Golan referenced the CornerShot not as a *weapon* but "a handy tripod" and above all a "life-*saving* device." Gleser stressed that Israel was akin to a security "greenhouse" from which you can readily harvest "good people" who grow up to be highly competent in a "natural way," emphasizing that "this is very special." Others used scientific and medical analogies to reaffirm the exceptionality of the Israeli experience and its significance to justify Israel's colonial practices. Avi argued that "terror is a disease. Okay!?," stressing that all diseased people "should go to a doctor." He then asked me rhetorically, "Would you go to a doctor that has three years [of] experience or seventy-two years [of] experience? Easy as that!" He continued with the medical analogy, stating, "I have tons of medicines" and suggesting that he offers his foreign clients a variety of cures, just like a pharmacy, based on the given problem at hand. As Avi uttered these words, it occurred to me that a doctor with seventy-two years of experience would be well over ninety years old and perhaps not an exemplary medical practitioner.

Through their exceptionalist references, my interlocutors thereby narrated Israel's history of settler-colonial conquest as a "special case" of protracted violence, which exemplifies homeland security and therefore can serve as an inspiration and generalizable practical knowhow. In other words, Israeli settler colonialism becomes "not only a way of life, but a *way of viewing life*" to be shared with others.[104] The invocation of "security awareness" does crucial work here in fabricating the idea of Israel as a homeland security model. It provides a frame with which to hierarchically organize the world onto a general grid, suggesting that within that grid there are different levels of awareness and crucially conveying that threats can in principle be ameliorated or potentially even transcended. In other words, the frame of awareness places levels on a universal grid. This frame invites other nations to picture themselves as part of a wider world with Israel, in ways that both reaffirm Israel's superiority and suggest that other nations could move their position in this grid through investment and education. This invites other nations to picture themselves as part of a shared reality *with* Israel, thereby reaffirming Israel's superiority but also suggesting that they could move their position on this global grid, themes I return to in chapters 3, 5, and 6.

The Israeli Approach

The Israeli experience, according to industry representatives, produces Israeli homeland security as a brand.[105] We might see the emergence of this brand as a commodification of Israel's associations with "oppression, dispossession, colonisation and ethnic cleansing."[106] Ari's references to the "unfortunate reality" that produces Israeli homeland security as a "good general brand of knowing" evidences precisely this. In their discussions of this brand, my interlocutors also referenced an "Israeli approach" to homeland security and occasionally an "Israeli model." While explaining what the Israeli approach or model was, some made references to developing a preemptive and proactive attitude to security through awareness raising while others mentioned specific practices, tactics, and ways that Israelis train their clients in close-range shooting and the virtues of the Israeli martial art *Krav Maga*. Several of my interlocutors mentioned strategies like creating "rings" or "layers" of security, sometimes misleadingly claiming them as uniquely Israeli notions or even their own personal inventions.[107] Marc Kahlberg took credit for having invented the "Secure Zone Concept," a claim still featured on his firm's website. Others talked about their offerings in cultural and linguistic expertise.

When I asked industry actors to elucidate the specificities of the "Israeli approach," however, their accounts were far from consistent about what, exactly, defined it. Eyal noted that "the Israeli concept or my concept is that there is never 100 percent security." As he continued, "because we [Israelis] know that there is not 100 percent security, we are trying to create many layers of security." In contrast, Noam, a representative of Athena Security Implementations, an Israeli firm specializing in intelligence and consultancy services, argued that absolute security *defined* the Israeli approach to homeland security: "In security, if there is a doubt, there is no doubt. That means that if you have a doubt whether a certain issue is secured or not, then it is not secured. This is, in one sentence, our [Israeli] methodology." Thus, while Israeli homeland security insiders made common references to a distinct "Israeli approach" animating their work, when pressed to elaborate on its specificities, its essence and boundaries became more questionable.

In their attempts to define the Israeli approach or concept of homeland security, all of my interlocutors resorted to comparisons to security approaches elsewhere. Some recounted anecdotes of how they faced all kinds of misconceptions about what it means to conceptualize or practice security correctly with their clients abroad, arguing that many required a (re)education about the *true* meaning of security (chapter 5). Noam contrasted the Israeli security methodology with the "American methodology of risk assessment," which was "driven from the *safety methodology*." "The problem" with the American approach, he argued, is that safety and security are "not the same." Eyal used comparisons to explain why countries in the Global South required "our [Israeli] approach" rather than that of other countries. "I'm saying *approach*" he clarified, "because the American soldier can fight, the British soldier can fight, the Russians can fight. But to be a *trainer*, it's something else." Eyal went on to say that "to transfer the knowhow properly to your students," one must become a "teacher." Being an effective teacher, he argued, was predicated on the "Israeli approach," which he defined as a particular way of relating to foreign trainees, in contradistinction to that offered by other countries:

> We [Israelis] are a little bit different than Americans, British, [and] Europeans. Our approach [to training] is more warm. When you are feeling hospitality here [in Israel], it's because of the way we've been raised. This is the same idea when you come to train.

These comparisons worked in situ with civilizational and racialized claims. When I asked Eyal to define his unique training on "Islamic culture" and "Arabic language" (as offered on his website), he refused to answer directly, instead recounting an anecdote about how he was once approached by a police commander in some unspecified European city. As he repeatedly emphasized, "This [European] country is a very, very, very modern country, even more modern than Israel. Okay? [. . . a] total West European country. The highest of [. . . civilizational] levels." He then noted that his European client told him, "I have a problem," namely that in his city of more than a million people there were around fifty mosques. The European official allegedly told Eyal: "I'm basically blind," meaning unable to differentiate between Sunnis and Shiites, let alone which specific mosques or Muslims might be dangerous. According to Eyal, the European official therefore asked him to "analyze" and "picture" the situations in these mosques. Eyal claimed he had all the necessary credentials to solve the European police official's "problem." As he explained, "to learn the language [of European Muslims], to understand their mentality and to operate and to send agents inside or to collect people that can work from inside" are methods that "Israel is specialized in." Eyal continued: "They [Muslims/Arabs] are our cousin. We know our cousin better than everybody else, sometimes even better than they [Muslims/Arabs] know each other." Eyal's orientalist account of the value of his "expertise"[108] to his European client was predicated on a foundation of white supremacy, giving him the "knowledge" to help his European client decide who is deserving of surveillance and premature death and assisting him in meting out violence "professionally" as the case required. Like Golan and Kahlberg above, Eyal insisted that what Israeli expertise offered is a way to *save* lives and *reduce* violence.

Others challenged the idea that the Israeli approach or specific solutions were simple replicas of Israeli practices or policies used in Palestine/Israel. In explaining the distinctiveness of Israeli homeland security vis-à-vis the world, Noam noted, "no security professional—Israeli professional—really believes that [what] we use here for a certain problem will be valid for another place. . . . We are aware that we have unique circumstances." Guy Zuri similarly pointed out that in some cases, "the technology or the solutions that we can use here [in Palestine/Israel], maybe in other countries you cannot use," for example, because of different national regulations or norms. After describing the characteristics of his company's bomb shelters and modular building fortification systems, another marketing director noted, "In this case I have to admit that most of those products are specifically *Israeli* . . . products," meaning that they were developed for Israeli use only and had little appeal elsewhere. These claims can be read as simply as more evidence of exceptionalist narration in action. In Amy Kaplan's account of American imperial exceptionalism, she argues that its dual assertion of radical uniqueness and universality embedded in the idea of nation-states as models represents a key paradox. While America's radical distinction from other nations appears to signify "separateness and uniqueness," within exceptionalist narratives "exemplary status" serves as "the apotheosis of the nation-form itself and as a model for the rest of the world."[109]

Yet, upon closer inspection this convention is less paradoxical or specific to U.S. empire than it first appears.[110] Exceptionalist claims are foundational to all imperial projects, working through the kinds of geopolitical comparisons explored in chapter 1. As Ann Laura Stoler and Carole McGranahan argue, "Claiming exceptionalism and investing in strategic comparison are fundamental elements of an imperial formation's commanding grammar," stressing that within imperial formations historically "searches for comparison and claims to exceptionalism were not contradictions but compatible conventions."[111] Their focus on "the politics of comparison" serves "to foreground the relational quality of imperial formations" but also provides grounds on which the universalizing pretenses of imperial models can be destabilized and unstitched.[112] When situated in this long history, that practitioner texts on homeland security take an explicitly comparative focus is neither incidental nor new; it can be seen as attempt to resuscitate exceptionalist reasoning in the pursuit of contemporary forms of empire and statecraft in the name of security.[113]

Even though less paradoxical than it first appears, the tension between exceptionality and universality embedded in references to models is not exclusively imaginative. By stressing that conditions and approaches developed for Israel were radically specialized and/or parochial, certain officials thereby problematized the straightforward equivocation between Israeli-ness and the universal. Zuri's and Noam's comments also obliquely reference what Nick Denes terms "the underlying peculiarity of the Zionist 'experience' *vis-à-vis* the Palestinians."[114] As Denes crucially points out, while "Israel's battlefield showcases resonate from Indonesia to Iraq," it is important to keep this peculiarity close at hand to ensure that we do not unduly concede the universality of the Israeli experience and instead more readily grapple with the work entailed in replicating "Zionism's genocidal matrix" elsewhere.[115]

Israeli homeland security insiders elaborated countless examples of such adaptation to me, recounting anecdotes of how they had to reinvent themselves in order to successfully work in foreign countries and use whatever materials and personnel were available to develop functional security systems. A number claimed that what gives Israelis a competitive edge was not the inherent universality of Israeli-ness but instead the ability to adapt general insights to the specific requirements of individual clients abroad. More unexpectedly, some insisted that flexibility *defined* the "Israeli approach" to homeland security. As Zuri explained: "The Israeli approach is tailor made. It's . . . coming from our knowledge and understanding that internal security problems . . . [are] sometimes different . . . in every state." In other words, *what* the "Israeli approach" *is* depends on who is asking and what they are looking for. On the face of it, this appears to be a deeply paradoxical statement, even a contradiction in terms. Yet I heard similar claims from a range of other representatives. Gleser called this the Israeli "human factor," which he argued was a particular Israeli sensibility that enabled Israelis "to understand what they [foreign clients] need, what they are looking for."

This tension is part and parcel of what Darryl Li calls universal*ism*, namely "a structure of aspirations" and an accompanying set of practices.[116] Understanding universalism as a practice (rather than merely an ideology) helps to illuminate the complex relations between the universal and particular at work in particular situations. According to Li, universalism should not be seen as an assertion of homogeneity or universal*ity* (in the sense that something is valid in all instances) but rather as "a claim to transcend difference" by attempting to regulate and redefine it.[117] Indeed, when my interlocutors' accounts of their work are positioned as aspirations and practices of universal*ism*, their recurring references to difference come into view as efforts to transcend and rework the terms of difference as the basis of their claims to universal authority.

However, I suggest that such references to flexibility as a means of overcoming difference are not just a matter of material adaptation and developing new associations but also one of rationalization through settler disavowal.[118] For instance, while Avi constantly referenced how he understood terrorism and terrorists better than Europeans, he challenged any suggestion that Israel's homeland security expertise was somehow specific to Arabs or Muslims. He argued that this *lack* of specificity was precisely what enabled him to work abroad for foreign clients with different policing circumstances and needs. As Avi repeatedly reminded me, Israel's only comparative advantage was experience, not any hyper-specialized cultural/religious expertise. In other words, the flexibility and lack of specificity of the Israeli approach (and its foundations in Zionist settler-colonial conquest and Palestinian erasure) enable Israeli homeland security actors to leverage Israeli-ness as a comparative advantage while attempting to wash their hands clean of its associations with ethnic cleansing and genocide.

My interlocutors' attempts to define the Israeli approach to homeland security were often vague, flexible, inconsistent with one another, and at times questionable. To the extent that industry actors did define an Israeli approach to homeland security, it was through comparison to and differentiation from others elsewhere. They often did so through the use of racialized and civilizational tropes, reflecting the racial and colonial precepts of Israeli security theology. Their difficulty in defining the so-called Israeli model on its own terms and tendency to resort to comparisons to do so find direct parallels to historical literature on police models under the British empire. Richard Hawkins's reassessment of the "Irish model" of counterinsurgency policing notes "the difficulty, and importance, of defining 'model'" but also stresses that the "'Irish model' is *defined often by a contrast* [to others]."[119] As I will show next, attempts to sell the Israeli approach abroad requires continuously negotiating core tensions between Israeli-ness and worldliness as well as enrolling followers.

Making Global Authority

Firms selling training and small arms for domestic use to foreign governments benefit directly from their close collaboration with SIBAT, the International Defense Cooperation Directorate of the Israeli Ministry of Defense (IMOD). Their work requires specific authorization and licenses from SIBAT, which also assists with deal-making. The close ties between the IMOD and firms specializing in small arms and training were reflected in their promotional approaches. For instance, Avi affirmed that most foreign clients came to him by word of mouth, via a directory available at any Israeli consulate or embassy and sometimes directly from SIBAT. When I sat down with Eyal in his office, one such order came through for training work in a small Caribbean country. Eyal showed me the contract on his desktop computer screen with the SIBAT letterhead. As a result, many such firms' websites were crude and arcane, sometimes only with a few images and a contact page with an email address and a WhatsApp number. This reflects the enduring existence and importance of the Israeli "security network" in promoting Israel's homeland security industry abroad.[120]

Especially for firms with no direct link to SIBAT, however, deal-making was less straightforward. While these Israeli homeland security firms benefit from the support of IEICI and promotional websites like i-hls.com and israeldefense.co.il, which organize trade shows and delegation visits and publish online directories of companies, all the firms I spoke with referred to the persistent work in trying to make their firms known within an increasingly dense and ever more competitive field of global purveyors. While the Israeli approach was not easily or consistently defined by my informants, claims to Israeli-ness clearly played a central role in their promotional strategies nevertheless. Gleser maintained that it was advantageous "to say that we are [an] Israeli company, that we have our Israeli experience," noting that "we are *totally* Israeli." Likewise, Zuri stated the "Israeli brand . . . *is* [the] advantage." As he elaborated: "You know, when you are saying Nike, everybody has some opinion about the product. Doesn't matter if the . . . product is very good or not." These statements confirm a range of scholars' accounts of how real-world experiences and "combat-proven" credentials play an important role in the marketing strategies of individual Israeli firms and the success of the industry as a whole.[121]

A number of representatives further highlighted how the Israeli brand worked in conjunction with various forms of doing and negotiation. As one marketing director put it "look . . . we . . . Israelis, are . . . very pushy. . . . I don't want to say aggressive . . . [but] we are doing fieldwork . . . looking for opportunities . . . trying to be in field . . . as much as possible." When I asked a CEO of a training and consultancy firm how his company enters new markets, he stressed: "Only [by] being there. Fly there, be there," noting that foreign clients "have to *see you there*," meaning in their countries, to know that you exist. A representative of Orad, a perimeter security firm, similarly described doing business in Africa: "You win [contracts] not all through expertise" but instead by the "offer" of your products and services on the ground. To do business abroad, these representatives stressed, they needed to travel abroad and establish local presence and visibility, with some making specific reference to this imperative in India. As Ari recounted, while his firm already had developed a presence in Mumbai with corporate clients about a year before 26/11, the event proved fortuitous because his firm's employees were able to rescue a client trapped in one of the attacked hotels. He stressed that he later leveraged this *Indian* experience in subsequent marketing efforts, thereby enabling him to make the case that "there is an Israeli body who's really located in Mumbai and has *proven itself*" in India.

But this fieldwork is more than just about deal-making; it involves negotiating Israeli-ness. As the marketing director of an electric fencing company explained of the Israeli brand, "I don't push it . . . because some people don't like it. Even though they respect Israeli technology, there's . . . unfortunately, a lot of bad press about Israel." Some of my interlocutors suggested that the salience of the Israeli brand had a geography. As the Orad representative noted: "In Africa it [the Israeli brand] doesn't matter; in India . . . it helps a lot because Israeli companies are appreciated there; . . . but in Europe . . . you have to camouflage it." In qualifying the perils of being Israeli, Europe loomed large. A marketing representative of a firm specializing in radar sensing technologies noted that "Europe is quite difficult." As he clarified, it wasn't as though Israeli firms could not sell in Europe but stressed that this took place by "not being *identified*" as Israeli. Such challenges also prompted some to avoid making any specific references to the Israeli experience on their corporate websites. Others explained to me how they used front companies, made deals through third parties, or only focused on countries in the Global South where political sensitivities around their Israeli-ness were less constraining.

These transnational negotiations about the Israeli-ness of the Israeli approach also worked to negotiate the tension between universality and specificity within exceptionalist narration. Israeli companies leveraged their contracts and work abroad as evidence of their exemplary status. Some industry actors stressed that their exceptional credentials were developed through their work beyond Palestine/Israel as much as from their Israeli experience. While representing ISDS as "*totally* Israeli," Gleser noted that ISDS "already has been proved many times" in areas outside of Palestine/Israel. As he summarized: "This is . . . our strength . . . [being] Israeli. But we are *also* a foreign company." This foreign work is extensive and of long duration. In the 1980s, Gleser and ISDS became notorious for training death squads in Honduras and Guatemala as well as members of the Nicaraguan Contras.[122] During our conversation, Gleser cited less-known work as proof of his foreign credentials. He opened a binder to show me an old photo picturing ISDS work for the U.S. Navy in recovering wreckage from the Iranian passenger airliner it shot down over the Strait of Hormuz in 1988 by the USS *Vincennes*, which killed all 290 people on board. Gleser stressed that to get a contract from the "American navy!" was the best possible reference of his firm's capabilities and credibility as a global actor. Framed pictures covering nearly every square inch of Gleser's office walls embodied this cross-referencing and enrollment of foreign clients to perform ISDS's global authority. Gleser gave me a tour of these photos, stating that here is "something for your eyes" and going on to explain the various images of him posing with prominent foreign officials, spanning the political spectrum from various right-wingers to President Lula da Silva of Brazil.

While Gleser's foreign credentials were more extensive and high-profile than some of his competitors, the strategy of enrolling such foreign references to affirm his global authority is common. Eyal's website features images and videos of his firm's work around the world, picturing dark-skinned men from special forces units engaged in shooting and martial arts training with trainers observing. At the end of our conversation, Eyal, sharing his computer screen, gave me a world tour of the foreign forces his firm had worked with, spanning Africa, Eastern Europe, Central Asia, North America, Western Europe, and the Caribbean. From his nondescript office sandwiched between generic businesses in a suburban industrial park in the suburbs of Tel Aviv, an insider's view of global pacification infrastructures opened up, with Eyal's videos and photographs documenting his personal contributions to keeping them in place. It felt like a grotesque version of show-and-tell through the eyes of a subcontractor of contemporary empire.

In the course of my fieldwork in Palestine/Israel, several of my interlocutors attempted to enroll me as a vector to spread the gospel of Israel's homeland security. When I was setting up a meeting with one Israeli police trainer over the phone in 2019, he noted that British colonial policing approaches were the basis of Israeli security approaches and thanked me for giving Israel its British expertise, noting that if I took it back to the U.K., the British would "get the fruits of the trees that you planted," falsely assuming that because I worked at a British university I was British. He further noted that he was all too happy to meet me, in part because doing so would help spread the gospel of Israeli security approaches to the world, apparently imagining a researcher and educator to be an ideal vector to facilitate this mission. He told me that he was "keen to spread it" and that if I distribute it, it "will be a bomb!" Some also proposed that I should go into business with them. Midway through an interview in his company's boardroom, one CEO proposed that I help him sell his electric fencing technology to my university. When I declined this offer, he abruptly ended the interview, stating that he had more pressing matters to attend to.

Given how embedded Israeli security infrastructures are within its universities, the CEO's assumption that I might have been willing or able to facilitate a new business opportunity in the U.K. is perhaps understandable.[123] But it also reflects a broader strategy by Israel's homeland security industry to enroll foreign admirers (clients, officials, journalists, and researchers) as participants in fabricating its exceptional credentials. The LinkedIn page of one police trainer I met featured an image of his work visa to the United States issued in late 2001 as a counterterrorism training instructor as well as a link to a news clip from an American cable channel featuring his training of U.S. police as evidence of his worldly credentials.

As the preface to one firm's webpage featuring testimonials from clients put it: "We believe that personal experience of our clients speaks louder and stronger than any marketing material regarding our services and capabilities."[124] Other materials made similar claims, additionally citing Israel's key role in protecting western civilization. For instance, an IEICI brochure proclaimed: "The prominent position gained by Israel's security industries is reflected in a growing number of security projects that have been won by Israeli contractors in recent years. [. . .] Israeli security systems protect some of the major symbols of Western civilization, including Buckingham Palace, the Vatican, and the Eiffel Tower.[125] Echoing Eyal's account of his work surveilling mosques in a "very, very, very modern" European country, Israeli security firms perform their own exceptionality *and* universality by referencing their own key roles in the West's civilizing missions.

Thus, while drawing on key signifiers like combat-proven credentials or the Israeli experience, industry actors' dual claims to exceptionality and global authority are materialized through repeated engagements beyond Palestine/Israel. That is, their global application plays a key role in performatively enacting the so-called Israeli model as simultaneously unique and universal, not in some overarching abstract sense but instead through practices that piece fragments together. Through these encounters and practices narrated in exceptionalist grammars, the so-called Israeli model becomes an object of fascination but also a thing in the world to be reproduced elsewhere.

CONCLUSION

That few scholars have scrutinized the specific nature and meaning of the Israeli pacification model reflects the sheer hegemony of this image in popular culture and scholarship. This has been sedimented through years of repeated claims about it. Its commonsense qualities also reflect the centrality of references to models, copies, and replicas in the staging of the colonial-modern historically. While referencing a common Israeli settler-colonial view on the world through the lens of unending war and settler-colonial conquest, I argue that it is a mistake to look at this process of exceptionalist narration as logical or straightforward. Avi's claim that the very Europeans who provided Zionist settlers with key materials to carry out the *Nakba* controlled large swaths of the globe and have been pacifying struggles within their own territories for centuries had but a few years of experience fighting terrorismis not just slightly misleading. It is "beyond chutzpah," to borrow from Finkelstein.[126] But it also crucially betrays Zionism's need to discursively distance itself from its foundational European origins and enduring western support, thereby representing a slightly different form of settler disavowal than those described in this chapter.[127] The idea of a freestanding Israeli homeland security model for the world only makes sense insofar as it is distinct from other policing approaches in Europe, the United States, or elsewhere. Moreover, while combat-proven credentials play important roles in the marketing strategies of individual Israeli homeland security firms and the success of the industry as a whole, my engagements with industry actors and texts also showed the dangers of fetishizing the Israeli brand or approach as stable, coherent, or all-encompassing. The salience and value of Israeli-ness is contingent and geographically variegated and needs to be continuously negotiated across different sites.[128]

In order for it to be a thing in the world, the Israeli homeland security model needs to constantly enroll and maintain an audience of followers and admirers to keep these cracks and tensions hidden. If Israeli security is a settler-colonial theology, as Shalhoub-Kevorkian suggests, we might say that it is upheld through a quasi-evangelical process of convincing foreigners about its desirability but also the idea that it is some abstract thing unto itself that can and should be emulated by others. The rationalization of the 1973 downing of the Libyan airliner is illustrative of a broader dynamic through which Zionist settler-colonial conquest has been fabricated as an inspiration for the world. Through the encounter with the *New York Times* reporter, the quoted Israeli officer takes on a pedagogical role of explaining away Israeli mass murder to the world as justified and also outlining that such an atrocity can be seen as evidence of exceptional Israeli proactiveness in anticipating and preparing for events yet to come.[129]

In other words, the Israeli experience becomes legible as a success story, a thing and a model to be emulated through its narration to outsiders. As the 1973 event aptly illustrates, these encounters occur because of Zionist violence. But for this violence to become legible as a successful and exemplary *case* of homeland security, a great deal of exceptionalist spin and disavowal is necessary. Roxanne Dunbar-Ortiz reminds us that what distinguishes particular examples of settler-colonial domination from others "is not the amount of violence, but rather the historical narratives attached to that violence."[130] Thus, documenting the oft-overlooked work in the exceptionalist mode of historical narration and the practical encounters at work in the practice of comparative geopolitics destabilizes it and renders its remit less stable and totalizing. As Steven Salaita points out, situating Palestinians as "subjects of a contested geography" within global discussions about settler colonialism enables "dimensions of Zionist messianism and exceptionalism to become more recognizable and thus quite a bit less messianistic and exceptional than it would like the world to accept."[131] Finally, as I will explore further in the upcoming chapters, the desire to spread the gospel of Zionist homeland security resonates with elements of Hindu nationalism and the globalizing ambitions of the *Sangh Parivar*. The Indian nationalist project has long endeavored to project a particular "idea of India" to the world[132] that relies on a disavowal of Indian state violence and more recently a celebration of Indian *jugaad* as a skill, tool, ethic of industriousness and entrepreneurialism, or even a particular Indian mentality, mindset, set of values, or culture onto itself.[133] A number of subsequent chapters examine this confluence of ideologies in greater depth.

INTERLUDE—A RETICENT EMBRACE

THE PREVIOUS CHAPTER FOCUSED on the ways that epic and more mundane everyday encounters have worked to fabricate the contemporary image of Israel as a global security model over time. As I have shown, 1967 was a pivotal moment in this longer ongoing history, most notably in terms of Israel's image vis-à-vis the West and U.S. empire in particular. Indian strategic thinkers have also watched these events with keen interest and sought lessons of their own. Their reflections on Israel's emerging image as a global exemplar of martial prowess offer important points of overlap with western observers, to be sure. Yet Indian accounts also point to dissonances with western perspectives. At times, they sought to offer correctives to the myths of 1967 and subsequent Israeli military operations as miraculous and unvarnished victories.

A 1967 article published in India's oldest strategic affairs publication, the *United Services Institution Journal* (*USI Journal*), attempted a detached and clear-headed appraisal of "the military aspect(s) of the Arab-Israeli conflict," which self-consciously avoided "entering into the tangled politics of the situation."[1] While lauding the Jewish soldier's "magnificent tradition as a fighting man" dating back to Biblical times and acknowledging the defeat of Arab armies is 1967 as a highly significant geopolitical moment, its author contested prevailing interpretations of 1967 as the "100-Hour War" or as the "70-Hour Miracle."[2] "Without in any way denying the superb leadership, organisation, and performance of the Israeli army," the article stressed, "we would do well to understand that Israel's devastating initial air-blows within two hours destroyed all chance of an Arab victory."[3]

The article further challenged the prevailing terms of comparison between 1967 and the U.S. war in Vietnam at the time: "To deride Arab arms by comparing their collapse to the North Vietnamese in the face of U.S. air-power is unfair. To speak of morale, offensive action and logistics as influencing factors is somewhat irrelevant under the circumstances where Arab Armour, infantry and motor columns were sitting ducks for the Israeli air force."[4] It thus concluded that 1967 was at best a victory in a narrow sense of representing a very well-orchestrated bombing campaign against a largely defenseless adversary, nothing more. The author further pointed out that Israel's quick victory had left a number of profound and unresolved problems, not least of which were the hundreds of thousands of Palestinian refugees in the West Bank and Gaza. Nor was the author convinced that 1967 represented some final victory in Israel's battles against the Arab world. "Israel," it emphasized, "has won *this* third battle but who can say she has won *the war*?"[5] Another *USI Journal* article published a year later further condemned Israeli military assaults on its Arab neighbors as "examples of the rule of the jungle which Israeli pursues," noting that Israel's "claim for sympathy on the basis of legality and international law are manifestations of extreme cynicism."[6]

According to other strategic thinkers at the time, even this qualified Indian enthusiasm was overblown. A 1969 *USI Journal* article set out to challenge Indians' interpretations of Israel's 1967 "victory" more fundamentally. The article began: "A good many officers in the Indian armed forces have a great admiration for Israel's military achievements in the fighting of June 1967."[7] Drawing on conversations with officers of the Indian Army, Air Force, and Navy, the author found these officers to be "enthusiastic about the successes won by the Israeli military machine."[8] "This enthusiasm is also understandable," the author argued, given that "the June [1967] fighting was almost certainly the most photographed, televised and written about campaign world history" and because "all this mass of material was produced either by Israelis or by Zionist Jews, or by Pro-Zionist Gentiles."[9] While arguing that "publicity merchants, looking for large, quick sales of films, photos and books, may be forgiven for being one-sided in their lucrative enthusiasm," the author insisted that matters "should be different for detached and cool-headed professionals in the war business," that is, the contributors and readership of *USI Journal*.[10]

Adopting such a "cool-headed" and "detached" approach, the author argued, would permit a more sober picture of the strategic lessons of 1967 to come into view. "To be able to admire 'The Six Day War' one has to see it only as an event [narrowly] in those six days. But when one realises that the war of which it is an episode still being fought every single day, then that 'War' becomes something near a defeat."[11] As the author further noted, the basis of Israel's "victory" was not some miraculous ingenuity but rather its extraordinary outlay on military spending. "Israel's daily expenditure on defence is ten million Israeli pounds, or rupees 30 million, which comes to rupees 11 million per day [*sic*] for every single Jewish man, woman and child in the state."[12] As the article summarized: "If the outcome of a war *waged for 'security'* is more violence, more expense, more casualties than before the war, then surely the outcome is not a 'victory' but rather a hollow, phyrrhic [*sic*] victory, and the policy objective of the war has not been obtained but rather its exact opposite."[13]

This keen interest in Israel military affairs by Indian strategists continued in the years thereafter with a range of articles and commentary in *USI Journal* as well as other Indian strategic studies publications that emerged from the late 1960s onward such as *Institute for Defence Studies and Analyses Journal*, founded in 1968, and *Indian Defence Review* (*IDR*), founded in 1986. These publications featured articles on the lessons of Entebbe and the Yom Kippur War among others, often celebrating certain aspects of them while offering correctives to prevailing (western) interpretations of their meaning as well as articulating their lessons for India.

These Indian analysts' self-conscious emphasis on providing "detached," "cool-headed," and "balanced" readings of events in Palestine/Israel from the late 1960s onward reflected India's geopolitical location within the nonaligned bloc. In the course of this writing, we can see a steadily growing Indian veneration of Israeli military prowess, in spite of a self-professed commitment to anti-Zionism and a solidaristic, pro-Arab/Palestinian posture. The 1982 edition of Indian strategic affairs journal *The Defence Review Annual* contained a full-length article devoted to the legacy of Moshe Dayan written by an Indian lieutenant colonel. "We may or may not agree with the zionist [*sic*] cause against the Arabs," it began. "[B]ut no military commander, how arch enemy he may be of the Israelis can fail to pay tributes to the military genious [*sic*] of the one-eyed Moshe Dayan who led his command with the war cry of 'follow me' rather than 'forward.'"[14] This veneration deepened throughout the 1990s as geopolitical hostilities between India and Israel began to thaw and relations were formalized and consolidated. A 1993 volume of *IDR* celebrated the "Great Leap Forward" in Indo-Israel relations, offering insights into "the Israeli world of innovative equipage and thinking" on military strategy and counterterrorism.[15]

Even as Indian strategic thinkers celebrated Israeli security expertise and retreated from their pro-Palestinian stance throughout the 1990s and into the early 2000s, their words continued to betray a reticence to fully embrace the Israeli model *for* India. This speaks to the enduring ambivalence of Indian nationalists' embrace of western modernity but also the aspiration to rework the hierarchical terms of comparative geopolitics by asserting India's exceptional democratic credentials as a counterterrorism leader in its own right.

In a 2003 *IDR* article, prominent Indian intelligence official B. Raman recounted his recent weeklong study visit to Jerusalem. He enthusiastically reported that Israel had restored control to Jerusalem, despite "passing through hell with dozens of innocent men, women and children being ruthlessly killed by the [Palestinian] suicide bombers."[16] Raman painted a questionably harmonious picture of Palestine/Israel at the time, noting that despite the presence of "many Arab Muslims living in most Israeli cities, one has rarely come across any instance of mob anger or reprisals against the Arabs."[17] To do so, however, Raman tellingly drew a favorable comparison to *India's* (supposed) state of inter-ethnic and inter-religious harmony. "Contrary to my fears of landing in a besieged city," he recounted, "I was pleasantly surprised to find that despite the repeated massacres of innocent civilians by the jihadi terrorists, Israel has remained as calm and composed as India."[18] He continued on this theme, arguing that Israelis had much to learn from India's largely successful counterterrorist experience. Yet, much to his chagrin, he seemed to find very few (if any) Israelis receptive to this suggestion. "Despite all the talk of counter-terrorism co-operation between India and Israel, one is surprised to notice a relative lack of [Israeli] interest in India's problems due to its being the fellow-victim of jihadi terrorism. Not only the man in the street but even large sections of [Israeli] intellectuals have very limited knowledge of India and its terrorism-related problems. Nor is there a lively interest in learning from India's counter-terrorism experience, which is more subtle and sophisticated."[19]

As a seasoned intelligence official, Raman should perhaps not have been so surprised. As will become clear in chapter 5, the vast majority of Israeli homeland security officials who pursued work in India after 26/11 expressed no interest whatsoever in learning from India or Indians. I want to emphasize here, however, that even as admiration for Israeli martial prowess grew steadily over the decades, archives of Indian strategic thought make it all too clear that Indian officials were less than enthusiastic about being (re)educated on the hierarchical terms of colonial difference. This reticence reflects India's "betwixt and between" relations with imperial centers within Cold War geopolitics but also key nationalist ideologies and imperatives. Echoing the sentiments expressed by Indian officials in 2001 on CNN (see the introduction), Raman's words evidence a refusal to concede that that India was a peripheral authority in the war on terror as well as a desire to disavow the "violent heart" of Indian politics through forms of comparative geopolitics on terms of its own making.[20] Raman had "(an)other story to tell" about India's location in the global war on terror, one that built on long histories of Indian exceptionalism, a matter I return to in chapters 5 and 6.[21] And Raman was not alone in this regard. Around this time, K.P.S. Gill continued to work on his efforts to position India's counterterrorism experience as an alternative model of counterinsurgency and counterterrorism for the West, traveling to the United States in 2003 to meet with think tanks and public officials there to make this case.[22]

THREE

AFTERMATHS

> The whole country suffered heavily [after 26/11], morale was low and [there were] . . . attacks from various people, municipalities, the press people, [the] public, [the] opposition party, political backlash—all that happened. So, the [Maharashtra] government was basically at the receiving end. The police were [also] having very low morale.
>
> —Dhanushkodi (D.) Sivanandan, Mumbai Commissioner of Police (retired)

> Suddenly, after 26/11 everybody's mindset changed. That was the biggest, in some sense you could say positive [repercussions] of 26/11—that much greater *awareness* for security concerns in the minds of all concerned. Not only in the police, not only in the government, but [among] people outside. Today, security is on the agenda.
>
> —Senior IPS officer (retired)

INTRODUCTION

Whereas chapter 1 examined how the event of 26/11 became a site of geopolitical controversy and moment of opportunity for the global homeland security industry, this chapter shifts the focus toward how the event's resulting political crisis was governed by state actors in Maharashtra. In the aftermath of 26/11, Indian publics, press, and opposition politicians criticized the local and national governments' handling of the three-day siege of the city. Television channels frequently aired headlines such as "Enough Is Enough" and "Mumbai Is Angry."[1] One commentator noted: "Residents of Mumbai are grieving, but also angry. The grief is over the senseless loss of life. [. . .] The anger, however, is over what was clearly a colossal failure of governance."[2] This initial anger emerged out of the widespread perception that inept Indian state forces had been outflanked by a new kind of hyper-mobile, networked global enemy.[3]

Public outrage over this perceived defectiveness manifested in immediate and unusual ways. Union Minister for Home Affairs Shivraj Patil as well as Maharashtra's chief minister, Vilasrao Deshmukh, and deputy chief minister, R. R. Patil, were all forced out of office as elite-led protests erupted at the Taj Hotel with protestors bearing placards featuring slogans like "India has woken up. When will the politicians?"[4] Even after these resignations, the Maharashtra government faced attacks from the opposition BJP, which called for the immediate dismissal of Director General of Police (Maharashtra) A. N. Roy, Mumbai Police Commissioner Hasan Gafoor, and Additional Chief Secretary (Home) Chitkala Zutshi for failing to prevent and effectively manage the attacks.[5] This mounting public anger over the perceived negligence of the political class translated into demands for security and the wholesale reform of Indian politics.[6] These demands were articulated by the bourgeois constituency of middle-class and elite "corporate activists," which Manisha Sethi aptly calls "India Inc." India Inc.'s demands for security were also thoroughly bourgeois in character, seeking "protection *for itself*—as tax payers, creators of wealth and as citizens."[7] In short, this constituency's calls for Mumbai and India to be secured represented a demand for the state to assure its own egoism as a class.

The political fallout of 26/11, however, did not end there.

The event gave rise to contestations about where the violence originated from and how it had unfolded across the city. News stories in early December 2008 reported that witnesses had heard assailants speaking fluent Marathi during the attacks, thereby raising questions about their ostensible Pakistani origins.[8] There were also reports of occurrences at Nariman House, which appeared difficult to explain, prompting speculation of geopolitical machinations by Israel and the United States to destabilize India.[9] The circumstances surrounding the killing of sitting Anti-Terrorism Squad (ATS) chief Hemant Karkare during the attacks became one of the most prominent sites of such contestation. This concerned the sequence of events whereby Karkare, together with fellow police officers Vijay Salaskar and Ashok Kamte, had allegedly been killed by two of the Pakistani assailants behind Cama Hospital, according to the Mumbai police. But the context of Karkare's death raised deeper questions about why he was murdered and by whom.

In the run-up to 26/11, Karkare had been leading an ATS investigation into the 2006 Malegaon blasts, which had implicated high-profile Hindutva activists in Maharashtra. This had ignited a firestorm of vitriol from local Hindutva groups like Maharashtra's Hindu ultranationalist party Shiv Sena, which called Karkare out as a Muslim-sympathizer and an anti-national traitor. Just days before 26/11, Karkare received death threats. Under these circumstances, a range of voices began to insinuate that 26/11 might have provided a convenient cover for his murder by Saffron forces. In mid-December 2008, Union Minister for Minority Affairs A. R. Antulay, questioning whether Karkare was in fact killed by Pakistani assailants, called for a thorough investigation.[10] In January 2009, Vinita Kamte, the widow of Ashok Kamte, one of the police officers who was killed during 26/11, added fuel to the fire when she gave a featured interview to the Indian news channel CNN-IBN asserting that the officers had not received adequate support as they called for backup and that local state officials were actively misleading her about how and why her husband, Karkare, and Salaskar were killed.[11] While some of these claims proved more resonant and durable than others, they brought into question the veracity of the official narratives in an atmosphere of anti-politician anger and hypernationalism.[12]

In short, the event of 26/11 sparked a crisis of legitimacy of the Indian state. It gave rise to multiple, overlapping conflicts and controversies, which emerged through critiques of the Indian state's alleged negligence in securing the nation but then morphed into a broad critique of Indian politics per se.[13] As I noted in the introduction to this book, critiques of Indian policing's authoritarian and communal tendencies, corruption, lack of professionalism, and politicization were themselves nothing new. The extent of Indian policing's popular legitimacy is founded on extrajudicial violence such as torture and unlawful detention as well as fake police encounters. Before his death, Vijay Salaskar was a well-known "encounter specialist" in the Mumbai police, personally credited with killing nearly eighty people during his career. Yet, in the aftermath of 26/11, as Salaskar and his fourteen fellow officers lay dead in the morgue, concerns about Indian politicians' corruption and the police's lack of professionalization suddenly became a widely discussed topic and shifted in character.

Systemic corruption and politicization of the state apparatus were commonly attributed as the root cause of India's *lack* of modern homeland security preparedness and softness in the face of "global" "Islamic" terrorism. Under the glare of a global media spotlight and the relentless criticisms of foreign officials and experts (chapter 1), the improvised and haphazard nature of India's policing infrastructure associated with the term *jugaad*—a Hindi word with multiple connotations and valences—became primarily associated with political corruption.[14] In this context, the need for modern homeland security became a new kind of commonsense approach to redressing the various gaps and limitations of Indian approaches and infrastructures of domestic security. As the above comments from a retired senior officer put it, (internal) security was suddenly "on the agenda" after 26/11. Moreover, while human rights defenders and scholars had been sounding the alarm bells over the authoritarian drift of the Indian state for decades, the timing and circumstances of Karkare's death in particular reactivated and radicalized these concerns, bringing into question the country's (purported) status as a vibrant, multiethnic, and secular democracy.[15]

This chapter examines how Maharashtra state actors governed these overlapping conflicts and controversies over authority and truth in the year that followed. Inspired by Stuart Hall et al.'s *Policing the Crisis,* I argue that the Maharashtra government's response to 26/11 should be primarily understood as a project of "policing the security crisis."[16] Reading the event of 26/11 through Hall et al.'s conjunctural analysis offers crucial insights. Of particular importance is its close attention to historical periodizations, whereby periods of relative stability are punctuated by moments of unrest and broader crises of authority, necessitating a swift state response. As Hall et al. argue: "Crises have to be remedied, their worst effects contained or mitigated. They also have to be controlled. To put it crudely, they have to be *policed*," typically through forms of authoritarian populism and racialized "get tough" policies.[17]

As will become clear below, policing the crisis of 26/11 involved overt authoritarian and anti-political strategies of suppressing information and silencing dissent. By "anti-political," I am referring to the deliberate strategies to delimit space for political discussion and contestation. As Hall et al. make abundantly clear and many others have elaborated since, crises of state legitimacy can and do emerge within the Global North. Yet, in India and other postcolonial contexts where the state's monopoly of violence cannot be taken for granted[18] and the extent of police power is much more disaggregated, tentative, and contested, state authority and legitimacy are much more frequently and fundamentally brought into question.[19] In such contexts, the perceived "'weakness' of everyday stateness" is often counteracted by efforts to make state power hyper-visible, most commonly through violence but also other means.[20]

Reflecting this broader dynamic, I argue that policing the security crisis after 26/11 involved attempts to pacify local publics and soothe bourgeois demands for security. This included projecting a "confident" image of the local Indian state through a spectacle of police "modernization" mimetically styled as a replica of "world-class" security in the Global North. As I will show, these policing strategies relied on but also exceeded spectacles of toughness. Their central focus on "awareness-raising" represents efforts to interpellate new security subjects by recruiting them to *participate* in the local state's pacification project. Taken together, I argue that policing the security crisis was, quintessentially, a matter of policing a series of interlinked controversies. In so doing, it was a matter of policing the ontological terms of the crisis itself, that is, its causes, political responsibility, and prospects for potential resolution. Policing the crisis was simultaneously a matter of restoring social order and the authority of the Indian state but also policing the terms of the *reality* of the crisis itself. In other words, I argue, it was a matter of ontological politics. In a slightly different way than chapters 1 and 2, this illustrates how the fabrication of homeland security is bound up with the enactment of realities by weaving together a diverse array of materials in situ with wider authoritarian political imperatives and strategies.

This chapter draws on a range of textual sources, including news articles and excerpts from the police magazine *The Mumbai Protector* as well as the *High-Level Enquiry Commission* (HLEC) report commissioned by the Maharashtra government in late 2008 to provide an account of the local handling of the attacks and develop recommendations for policy reforms going forward.[21] I supplement these texts with interviews conducted with

HLEC's authors and key Maharashtra government police officials and others involved in crafting the policy response to 26/11. Drawing on these sources, I follow the knowledge controversies and conflicts to which 26/11 gave rise and track how actors attempted to suppress, negotiate, or otherwise resolve them. I begin with the appointment of HLEC and how the Maharashtra government mobilized its work in disarming public criticism and suppressing information. I then turn to the government's police modernization program and how it was justified and promoted. In the final section, I reflect on how these interventions worked to police the security crisis of 26/11.

THE HIGH-LEVEL ENQUIRY COMMITTEE

The Maharashtra government acted swiftly in response to critiques of 26/11's (mis)handling and the lingering controversies surrounding the fact pattern of what took place during the event. The first major development was establishing HLEC, headed by Ram Pradhan, a former union home secretary (retired), and Vappala Balachandran, a former IPS officer and high-ranking intelligence official. HLEC was formally appointed on December 30, 2008, ostensibly to facilitate a public reckoning of the handling of 26/11 by local police and government. It was tasked with undertaking a systematic analysis of the handling of 26/11 by the Mumbai and Maharashtra police and the Maharashtra government as well as assessing the current state of local preparedness against future attacks. Based on these findings, HLEC was to develop policy recommendations to strengthen local security preparedness, under mounting public pressure as well as the looming specter of a follow-up attack on the city. As Ram Pradhan told me when he and Balachandran were appointed, "We were very conscious that another attack might also take place," and therefore they tried to conclude their investigation as quickly as possible.

The appointment of HLEC was anything but unusual. It reflected long-standing procedural responses to political crises and concerns around policing in India, representing what amounted to a rather toothless gesture. For instance, the committee lacked any legal authority to summon witnesses, and its mandate was limited to interviews with officials from within the Maharashtra government and the Mumbai and Maharashtra state police. Its scope therefore excluded analysis of the union government's handling of the attacks, including alleged intelligence lapses by Intelligence Bureau (IB) and the Research and Analysis Wing; the role of the MHA; and the NSG-led operations during 26/11, which just weeks before had sparked intense controversy.[22]

Not only was the remit of HLEC deeply circumscribed, it was widely seen as a "lame duck committee" specifically designed to absolve senior state officials of wrongdoing.[23] A former senior Maharashtra Home Ministry official explained to me that Ram Pradhan had been selected to head the Committee because of his long-standing ties to the ruling Congress Party, claiming that he was specifically "told what to write down" by high-ranking Maharashtra government ministers and instructed not to name any names. In short, while HLEC ostensibly held out the prospect of a public reckoning about what took place during 26/11, who was responsible, and how to move forward, its capacity to carry out these tasks impartially was questionable at best. HLEC's work was further mediated by transnational influences. For instance, on December 1, 2008, the New York Police Department (NYPD) dispatched a team of three officers to Mumbai to conduct their own investigation of the tactics used in the attacks, internally publishing its own report on December 4, 2008.[24] And on January 8, 2009, NYPD Commissioner Raymond Kelly gave public testimony before the U.S. Congress about the lessons to be learned from 26/11 for the United States.[25]

On April 18, 2009, Pradhan and Balachandran submitted the report to the Maharashtra government. Its contents reflected these pressures, constraints, and influences. The report identified a wide range of lapses and structural problems in the Mumbai police, such as the duplication of duties, the lack of ammunition and basic police firearm training, and the failure to follow existing standard operating procedures (SOP). It criticized a few officials by name, including sitting Mumbai Commissioner of Police Hasan Gafoor and Maharashtra Director General of Police A.N. Roy for making operational decisions during 26/11 in Mumbai where Roy lacked jurisdiction. It also attributed a delay in the local procurement of arms and ammunition before 26/11 to an order passed by Chhagan Bhujbal during his tenure as Maharashtra's deputy chief minister in 2002, though the report referenced Bhujbal by title rather than by name.[26]

The report explicitly avoided assigning political responsibility for specific operational failures or oversights, intelligence lapses, or deficiencies in policy planning in the state of Maharashtra and the city of Mumbai. It stated: "The Committee have [*sic*] not found any serious lapses in the conduct of any individual officer."[27] It also reproduced the state's account of how the operations against the assailants unfolded (including the sequence of how Karkare, Kamte, and Salaskar were killed), making no mention of the simmering controversies surrounding the contested circumstances of their deaths.

The report's findings and recommendations also contained traces of the transnational influences noted above. It cited NYPD Commissioner Kelly's testimony to the U.S. Congress, further suggesting that there were lessons to be learned from the work of DHS in developing a policy response going forward. Here the report noted:

> the [U.S.] Department of Home Land Security [*sic*] (DHS) created several intelligence Fusion centres where the intelligence producers and the executing wings like State police, Port and Transportation Security (in-charge of Aviation Security) etc take part in constant dialogue on the likely terrorist threats based on available intelligence. This has worked well in that country [the U.S.].[28]

In short, the report neither revealed any particularly explosive new information nor provided an alternative interpretation of the causes of 26/11's alleged mishandling to that which already existed in public consciousness at the time. Instead, it largely reinforced the prevailing common sense about 26/11 as a failure of intelligence and governance while inscribing boundaries about what could be officially known about how the event unfolded or who/what was responsible.

As tepid as the report was, the Maharashtra government did not handle it in good faith. Leading politicians did their best to challenge and suppress it by refusing to table it in the Maharashtra state assembly, while selectively leaking parts to the press. And just before HLEC's scheduled public release, high-ranking Maharashtra politicians publicly attacked some of its findings and then promptly classified it, arguing that if it were made public, it would compromise the trial of the lone surviving alleged 26/11 assailant, Ajmal Kasab.[29] Local politicians thereby mobilized the Report within their broader efforts to contain the controversies surrounding 26/11's (mis) handling by "patrolling the facts" about what took place during the attacks and who was to blame.[30] This gave rise to a situation where, although there was widespread agreement that the handling of 26/11 represented a failure of governance and exposed deeper gaps in local state capacity, the Indian publics' understanding of *what* exactly had failed remained nebulous.[31]

The appointment of HLEC and the handling of its report was just one part of the Maharashtra government's broader strategy to contain and police the terms of the public debate on 26/11 with clear antidemocratic objectives. Alongside efforts to suppress the report's findings, the Crime Branch joint commissioner of the Mumbai police, Rakesh Maria, who directed operations from the control room during 26/11, stonewalled Vinita Kamte's requests for access to key records like logs during 26/11.[32] Other state officials similarly did their best to dismiss attempts to seek greater transparency and accountability. For instance, when pressed by a reporter in June 2009 about Kamte's concerns, Maharashtra's newly appointed home minister, Jayant Patil, insisted that they were baseless and had already been resolved: "I am convinced that there is no foul play. I have heard both sides of the story, Mrs. Kamte's as well as Mr. Maria's. I don't think there is any kind of mishandling."[33] Moreover, the Mumbai police's case against Kasab, which was cited as the key reason that the report had to be classified, ultimately did little to assuage doubts concerning the official narratives of 26/11, in part because it was built almost exclusively on Kasab's police interrogation rather than on external evidence like witness testimony.[34] However, the Maharashtra government's efforts to police the crisis went beyond these crude silencing strategies. The government also undertook a rapid program of police modernization involving the procurement of new weapons, vehicles, surveillance equipment, foreign experts, and trainers to contain the anti-politician backlash and build public "confidence" in local state authorities. In the next section, I sketch the key elements of this modernization program and how it intervened in the overlapping controversies and conflicts outlined above.

POLICE MODERNIZATION

Procurement

Building on existing police modernization initiatives in Maharashtra funded by the union government, police modernization accelerated rapidly in the immediate wake of 26/11.[35] Less than a month after the attacks, a new budget totaling Rs 126 crore had been sanctioned by the Maharashtra legislative assembly.[36] This budget authorized a range of new purchases including imported weaponry, a fleet of new armored vehicles and personnel carriers, speedboats, all-terrain amphibious vehicles, communication devices, night vision equipment, and new uniforms. As one former senior IPS officer who was involved in the early stages of planning explained to me: "Suddenly such a big incident happened, the biggest shock for government and society. So the government response at that time was kneejerk: do whatever you want, whatever you need. For a few months, the mindset was 'Ask for anything and . . . take it.'" D. Sivanandan, who was appointed to replace Gafoor in June 2009, similarly recalled that the Maharashtra government effectively "gave . . . carte blanche" to the Mumbai police "by saying whatever is right for the city to secure, do that." When I asked him about the procurement decisions following the attacks, he recalled, "you just walked up to the home secretary, the home minister, the chief minister . . . convinced them with a presentation. . . . It was sanctioned in one minute!"

Indeed, from speaking with officials involved in and familiar with these early decisions, it became clear to me that the purchase of new police procurements was devised as a response to the backlash against the perceived softness and incompetence of the state response to 26/11. As Jayant Patil recounted from the Maharashtra government's perspective, "we wanted to take quick decisions" on issues of procurement, particularly in light of "the sensitivity of all the issues of having good arms and ammunition." A former senior Maharashtra Home Ministry official put things more bluntly. This official explained to me that Maharashtra politicians "didn't . . . want their image to be tarnished; they wanted to come out well out of this. That's why . . . they took all those very quick decisions about empowering the [police] force, strengthening the [police] force and things like that."

As these officials began to develop their police modernization program, they were lobbied by a range of domestic and international commercial interests seeking to capitalize on 26/11's political fallout. Guy Zuri of the IEICI, whom we met in the previous chapter, recounted that in the wake of 26/11 Israeli authorities accelerated their preexisting lobbying efforts in India and approached the Maharashtra government to solicit their solutions and arrange the official visit to Tel Aviv in July 2009. He explicitly noted that it was the Israelis who approached the Maharashtra government rather than the other way around. The Israelis were hardly alone. The corporate lobby group Bombay First published a white paper in February 2009, calling on local government to "[b]uild a contingent of armed policemen thoroughly trained in the use of the latest weapons of all relevant types" and purchase a stockpile of ammunition and fleet of "fast cars, speed boats and helicopters."[37] The group further arranged visits of foreign officials to Mumbai who had been involved in responding to the September 11 attacks in the United States and the July 7, 2005, attacks in the UK.[38] Maharashtra officials recalled the sudden spike in lobbying by foreign state governments and homeland security corporations, pushing their various offerings. The above Home Ministry official recalled that after 26/11 "lots of teams had started arriving . . . from Israel from Germany and from Canada and from London, people coming and saying: 'Do this, do that, buy this, buy that, take of this, take of that, we have this, we have that.'" Balachandran likewise recounted that these foreign actors attempted to lobby him and Pradhan, claiming that "'our goods are better than these goods' and all that."

Reflecting these accelerated domestic and international lobbying efforts, the specific focus on police modernization shifted somewhat in the immediate post-26/11 period. Whereas the preexisting police modernization programs had focused on acquiring basic weaponry and equipment, the post-26/11 Maharashtra budget authorized the purchase of much more expensive imported weapons and armored vehicles to assuage public concerns about state weakness. An Indian small arms dealer, Sanjeev, was brought in to advise the Maharashtra and Mumbai police after 26/11. When we spoke in his office just outside of New Delhi, he explained to me: "People wanted to hear 'You're safe,'" which required specific visual signifiers to demonstrate this. As he continued, "The requirement of that particular time was to tell the people, 'We got Colt, we got Smith and Wesson, we got MP9 and blah, blah, blah. Now we are fully prepared to tackle any kind of a 26/11.'" As a result, the Mumbai police ordered new and expensive imported weapons including Colt M4 4.46mm carbines, MP5 and MP9 tactical machine pistols, 9mm Smith & Wesson pistols, Barrett M82/M107.5 anti-materiel sniper rifles, and grenade launchers. Another example was the fleet of Marksman bulletproof jeeps painted with desert camouflage specifically designed by the Indian automotive giant Mahindra for the Mumbai police after 26/11 (see also chapter 4). The Maharashtra government also pledged to purchase helicopters to improve response times as well as thirty-six speedboats to improve coastal security.[39] The Maharashtra government further introduced new intelligence-gathering and surveillance schemes, announcing its plan to cover Mumbai with six thousand new CCTV cameras managed by a central control room.

The post-26/11 police modernization drive also created new police units in Mumbai and Maharashtra, what Indian security expert Ajai Sahni termed "the 'Rambo model' of response" to live-fire attacks.[40] For instance, the government created its own "crack" commando squad Force One tasked with responding to live terror incidents within the metropolitan area of Mumbai clothed in new uniforms and armed with the newly acquired weapons noted above. The Maharashtra government also considerably expanded, strengthened, and restructured the Mumbai police's already-existing quick response teams (QRTs) through new training regimens, uniforms, equipment, and weapons, including AK-47s and Glock pistols.[41] These units were permanently stationed across all of Mumbai's five regional police stations under the command of their local additional commissioner of police. The government also created the Maharashtra State Security Corporation (MSSC), a force of security personnel to protect private sites, including industrial facilities, shrines, and public buildings across Maharashtra as well as new coastal police stations. To supplement these locally based units, the union government also created a NSG hub located near Mumbai.[42]

As these new forces were assembled and their new equipment was procured, local state officials leveraged their associations with military power as markers of a newfound toughness and efficiency. A *Times of India* article quoted Gafoor, who noted: "We have learnt our lessons from November 26 and want to raise one of the best forces in the world. It is high time we prepare for urban warfare."[43] To do so, Gafoor argued that Force One would be staffed by Short Service Commission Officers of the Indian Army, noting that the "grit and experience of an army officer can add more teeth to our commando squad."[44] Gafoor further explained that Force One commandos would "receive special training from the National Security Guards [*sic*] and be equipped with AK-47s, MP5 sub-machine guns and latest communication gadgets," thereby enabling the unit's commandos to fight terrorists more effectively.[45] In mid-December 2008, Jayant Patil similarly told the Maharashtra legislative assembly that Force One commandos would be armed with 250 MP5 guns to prevent a repeat of 26/11, stressing that "MP5 guns are state-of-the-art sub-machine guns that can fire 700–900 rounds a minute with a maximum range of 150 metres."[46]

I read these statements as deliberate attempts to soothe bourgeois demands for security through the leveraging of these new materials as stand-ins for modern state power. In other words, they are a response to demands by certain publics to "do something," manifesting in efforts to conjure an image of a strong state through public-facing projections of its security apparatus.[47]

Going Abroad

In addition to buying new security equipment, rebuilding the credentials of the Mumbai police also involved engaging foreign trainers and emulating police and security models. As early as December 2008, Jayant Patil announced that local police officers would be dispatched to Chicago and other cities around the world to study their security systems.[48] Local officials' claims about their new forces' "world-class" credentials were made through comparisons to famous commando and counter-terror units abroad. For instance, a *Times of India* article listed SWAT (U.S.), *Yamam* (Israel), and STAR Force (Australia) as inspirations for Force One. Maharashtra Chief Minister Ashok Chavan later made such comparisons more explicit, stating that Force One commandos would be provided with all of the necessary infrastructure to put them "on par with international counter-terrorism units" and promised that local government and police officials would "study different kind of trainings imparted in foreign countries to their anti-terror forces and ensure that such training reaches our commandos."[49]

In the months and years after 26/11, some of these pledges would be realized. The Maharashtra government dispatched a number of foreign delegations and study tours abroad, the first of which was to Palestine/Israel in July 2009.[50] The delegation was led by newly appointed commissioner D. Sivanandan and accompanied by Additional Chief Secretary (Home) Chandra Iyengar and high-ranking police officials, including Deputy Inspector General of Police S. Jagannathan (Force One), Deputy Commissioner of Police Nisar Tamboli, Superintendent of Police Rajesh Pradhan, and Inspector General of Police P. K. Jain.[51] In chapter 5, I elaborate on the details of how this visit and subsequent training sessions with Israeli experts played out behind the scenes. But here I focus on how such associations with foreign actors were explained and leveraged publicly.

In justifying the visit to Palestine/Israel and the use of Israeli trainers, Maharashtra officials mobilized comparisons similar to those deployed by Israeli officials and experts in Israeli critiques of the handling of 26/11 (chapter 1). These comparisons foregrounded India's lack of preparedness on 26/11 but also situated Israel's unapologetic "killer instinct" as a model for India. Sivanandan declared that, in sharp contrast to Israel, which responds unapologetically to terrorist attacks, India suffered from its lack of a similar "killer instinct." "For thousands of years, we [Indians] have been passively witnessing terror attacks. We never want to fight with anybody. That's what our main problem is and we lack the killer instinct." As he continued: "We cannot go and wage a war against Pakistan, China or anybody else. But Israel never keeps quiet. Israelis go on their flights, bombard the fellows (enemies), come back and keep quiet. But when we [Indians] become aggressive, we face international pressure." He concluded, "The time has come to protect ourselves and we need to take utmost safety precautions in the wake of recent audacious terror attacks."

Sivanandan's words referenced a recurring trope in Hindutva ideology, namely the image of the Hindu community as an ancient peaceful civilization being overrun and emasculated by invading (Muslim) marauders.

For instance, in his 1966 book *Bunch of Thoughts,* M. S. Golwarkar called out the "Muslim desire, growing ever since they stepped on this land some twelve hundred years ago, to convert and enslave the entire country [of Hindustan]," citing bomb blasts in Delhi at the time as but the latest "proof" of "a thousand years of their [Muslims'] naked aggression," which in turn required new measures fight back to defend Hindustan against this foreign aggression.[52] Mobilizing this trope, Sivanandan suggested that Israel and its so-called killer instinct was a key source of inspiration for India in its fight against (Muslim) terror.

Sivanandan was not alone in his praise for foreign experts and governments. Jayant Patil explained to me that the gravitation to foreign experts and trainers (including Israelis) was born out of an imperative to develop a "scientific approach" to counterterrorism, disaster management, and coordination within the Mumbai police. Another high-ranking officer in the Maharashtra police similarly emphasized: "There is no point in reinventing the wheel again when there is something better already available in the market. So if they're having some capability [elsewhere] . . . why *not* know from them?" Another sitting ATS official similarly maintained that the impulse to source Israeli trainers for Force One was driven by the need to get the "best in the field." Sivanandan was even more unequivocal, maintaining that "Israelis are considered to be the best in security matters. That's it." In other words, by citing specific purchases and sources of expertise as the "best in the field," the modernization program worked as a kind of blackmail, that is, a policy measure to which one cannot be reasonably opposed.[53]

As noted in previous chapters, Indian state officials' valorizations of Israel's security prowess were of long standing. Since the 1990s, Indian politicians and police have praised Israel as a model of efficiency and ruthlessness in striking Muslim terrorists in foreign territory and policing Muslims "at home." On the heels of the 1993 Bombay blasts, which killed 257 people, an *IDR* op-ed noted: "Since India has been coping with terrorist threats in the last decade, access to Israeli know-how on counterterrorism would be invaluable," stressing that "Indian interest in absorbing expertise to fight terrorism from Israel is justifiably high."[54] Reflecting this growing Indian interest in Israeli policing expertise, BJP leaders in 1996 advocated for the introduction of identification cards in order to differentiate between non-Hindu and Hindu immigrants, maintaining that in a similar way to which Israel is the homeland for Jews worldwide, so too should India serve as the natural homeland for all Hindus. Not coincidentally, this analogy implied that non-Hindus were not entitled to full Indian citizenship.[55] Bal Thackeray, the founder of Shiv Sena, who played a central role in fomenting Bombay's communal violence in the 1990s, rhetorically advocated for the use of the Mossad to come and train the Sena's own anti-terror force in order to address a wave of bombings and murders perpetrated by the Bombay underworld during the 1990s, though none of these plans ever came to fruition.[56]

Read in the context of these long-standing Hindutva geographical imaginaries and accompanying strategies, at least part of the appeal of traveling to Palestine/Israel for Indian officials in 2009 was to fulfil the fantasy of becoming a "hard" militarist state and, in doing so, consolidating the idea of a common Muslim Other.[57] Yet whereas the endorsements of the so-called Israeli security model by figures like Thackeray were largely rhetorical gestures before 26/11, in the immediate months thereafter local state officials could plausibly advocate for its adoption as a concrete policy measure. For instance, in justifying the visit to Palestine/Israel, Force One Additional Commissioner S. Jagannathan explained that members of the delegation would "study the systems put in place by Israel to counter terrorism and how they make their country secure" emphasizing that the way in which Israel trains its police and uses advanced technology to improve security preparedness would be top of mind.[58] Another unnamed official noted that after the visit was completed, "the team will decide on what measures could be inculcated and chalk out an elaborate plan for the much-needed overhaul in the [Mumbai police] force."[59] In other words, "learning from Israel" was portrayed as a kind of catchall solution to technical deficiencies in the Mumbai police. "Post the November 26, 2008 attack," a 2009 *Mumbai Mirror* article claimed that "Israel seems to have become the answer to *most of Mumbai police's problems.*"[60]

The delegation received positive coverage in leading national English-language news outlets, featuring participants' praise of Israel's exceptional homeland security credentials.[61] Iyengar praised Ben Gurion Airport as "the world's most well-protected airport" as well as the "high level of security checks and constant surveillance measures in place there." She further recalled being impressed by the "round-the-clock surveillance in most parts of Tel Aviv, and a constant monitoring of footage from CCTV cameras."[62] It was also reported that the delegation team had drafted a report with a list of recommendations to Maharashtra's home ministry "for simulation of the Israeli experience" in Maharashtra, with participants hinting at areas where this might take place.[63] Sivanandan proclaimed: "We will strongly recommend replication of certain Israeli solutions in India," praising their SOPs for emergency management.[64] Iyengar added that her experience with CCTV systems in Tel Aviv demonstrated the need for more cameras in Mumbai but also a "common platform" to facilitate the monitoring of new surveillance cameras being installed across Mumbai.[65] Local officials thereby mobilized their associations with Israel as evidence that their police modernization program would produce teams of commandos and a surveillance infrastructure at an elite level.

Referencing their newly established associations with Israel's "combat-proven" security knowledge (chapter 2) helped to arm the Mumbai police against charges of weakness, failure, and incompetence. Local state officials sought to mobilize this association with Israel to pacify local publics, restore a sense of order, and restore the tarnished images of politicians. While the image of Israel performed an important role here, it was but one of a range of other markers of modernization. As he explained the most important features of the modernization program to me, Sivanandan recalled that "we bought about 4,500 weapons from Germany, the U.S.," stressing that these were "all the best in the world." But local politicians and police did not just stake their fortunes on procuring new technologies, soliciting foreign experts, and associating with other states abroad behind closed doors. As Sanjeev recalled, they were also "in a hurry to show the visibility" of these newly acquired markers of modernization to local publics as a self-conscious public relations campaign to build confidence in local state capacity.

Showcasing Modernization

In late 2008 and throughout the following year, the police modernization program was actively showcased to local publics as a visual spectacle through press conferences, exhibitions, and laudatory news articles. These outlets featured images of local police posing with their new vehicles and weaponry and training in "urban warfare" simulations. A few days before the first anniversary of 26/11, *The Hindu* ran such an article covering a recent event to showcase Force One to Indian publics. "Trained on the lines of the National Security Guard (NSG)," it read, "they [Force One commandos] need only three seconds to draw out a revolver, cock it and fire six bullets." It quoted Maharashtra Chief Minister Ashok Chavan, who praised the creation of Force One as a key milestone in hardening the local police posture, recalling that "[t]he commandos practised day and night till their fingers bled."[66]

To assist with these public relations efforts, the Mumbai police also launched its new English-language bimonthly police magazine *The Mumbai Protector* in 2009. This media initiative was spearheaded by Sivanandan in partnership with the leading Indian trade promotion magazine, *New Media Communication*.[67] Excerpts from its early issues illustrate how the magazine sought to create an impression of rapid change in the capacities of the Mumbai police, styled as a "Pledge to Keep Mumbai Safe and Secure."[68] The following passage written by Sivanandan captures the magazine's core public relations strategy to project a new sense of security in Mumbai:

> It has been a year since Mumbai came under the dastardly terrorist attack on 26 November 2008. Much has happened since then. The Mumbai Police has since streamlined its overall preparedness in preventing recurrence of such events in the future. Most important, we have been able to create Quick Response Teams & Force One, an anti-terrorist combat-ready contingent comprising well-trained men armed with the *most modern weaponry and bullet-proof vehicles, complete with the state-of-the art communication equipment*.[69]

The *Protector's* early issues foregrounded the martial features of these new policy initiatives as markers of police modernization. One article emphasized that since 26/11 "the Maharashtra Government and the law enforcing authorities have [. . .] initiated several security measures *on a war-footing*," and the pages of the *Protector* featured photos of police officers posing with their newly acquired technologies, uniforms and weaponry (Figures 3.1 and 3.2).[70] The articles accompanying these images also frequently asserted

FIGURE 3.1: *Image from* The Mumbai Protector: A Magazine for the Mumbai Police *(November/December 2009).*

FIGURE 3.2: *Image from* The Mumbai Protector: A Magazine for the Mumbai Police *(November/December 2009).*

FIGURE 3.3: *Image from* The Mumbai Protector: A Magazine for the Mumbai Police *(January/February 2010).*

FIGURE 3.4: *Image from* The Mumbai Protector: A Magazine for the Mumbai Police *(January/February 2010).*

the local forces' likeness to other groups elsewhere: "In terms of weaponry, the Mumbai Police have further fortified itself [*sic*] with more Smith & Weston 9mm pistols, M4 Carbines, MP9 tactical machine guns, M82 sniper rifles, all are universally acknowledged by experts as the best anti-terrorist urban warfare equipment available in the world."[71] Quoting Joint Police Commissioner (Law and Order) Himanshu Roy, another article emphasized "a paradigm shift in our thinking, our motivation and our morale and our mindset," noting that "[t]he Mumbai Police is now supported by technology, equipment and training comparable to the best in the world."[72]

These measures self-consciously set out to restore a sense of order and build public confidence in the capacities of local police. An article authored by Sivanandan emphasized that public displays of newly acquired equipment by local forces are "meant to infuse confidence among the people of Mumbai about the preparedness of the police force to meet any terrorist attack."[73] Another segment emphasized the increasing physical fitness and agility of the Mumbai police: "A slow-moving cop with a paunch doesn't inspire much confidence in the public. Which is why Police Commissioner

D Sivanadhan [*sic*] places a hefty premium on the fitness of his force. The Top Cop is putting his men through a fitness regime by making available to them the state-of-the art gymnasiums at most police stations."[74] In short, "[t]he Mumbai Police is a confident force that inspires confidence in the public."[75]

The spectacle of police modernization thus worked as a "politics of permanent performance" though which the postcolonial Indian state came "into view"—to be seen by certain publics in particular, mediated ways.[76] Following Sankaran Krishna, we might say that the local spectacles of police modernization represented "not merely *means* to achieve certain ends of the state, but *were* the state itself."[77] This was nothing new in India's post-Independence history. As Krishna points out, "one of the hallmarks of the so-called developmental state is the extraordinary importance attached to symbolic signifiers such as science, technology, and industrialization as sources of legitimacy."[78] There is an unambiguously mimetic quality to the modernization drive with officials asserting their aspiration to become "like" foreign forces such as SWAT and Yamam and replicate them in Mumbai.[79] The spectacularization of the police modernization program aimed to present a new image of the Mumbai police as a world-class force, leveraging references to the West as a synonym of the universal. This spectacle of state power was also deeply gendered, mobilizing martial, hypermasculinized images of toughness in order to rebuild the damaged authority of the state.

The modernization program and its accompanying spectacle attempted to restore social order in Mumbai and Maharashtra by inspiring public confidence through the projection of modern security credentials but also through creating new citizen-subjects to actively *participate* in the local state's pacification project.[80] Moreover, it sought to interpellate new security subjects within middle- and upper-class constituencies in Louis Althusser's sense of the "recruitment" of ideological subjects. Using the example of the police practice of hailing a person on the street by calling out to her "Hey, you there," Althusser argues that this person is rendered into a subject through the recognition that the hail is "really" addressed to her (rather than someone else).[81]

In the post-26/11 context, the local state's "hails" to would-be Indian security subjects took place through a security "awareness raising" campaign.

Throughout the pages of the *Protector*, there is an emphasis on "[r]eaching out to the people" to "encourage participation of people towards the security of the state" and building greater security awareness among citizens with key parallels to Israeli homeland security actors' references to the centrality of awareness-raising in the previous chapter.[82] The *Protector's* September/October 2009 issue had an advertisement announcing a new initiative called "Fighting Bullets & Bombs with Your Ears and Eyes," jointly sponsored by the Mumbai Police, the Mumbai Fire Brigade, and the Indian consumer goods multinational Eureka Forbes. Under the banner of "*Jagrut Mumbaikar* [awakened Mumbaikar]—Be Secure. Be Sure," the ad emphasizes that the initiative "aims at spreading awareness among the people about crime, terrorist attacks and the preventative measures," claiming that an "initiative of this kind and magnitude has never been attempted in the history of independent India."[83] This example illustrates how the Maharashtra state sought to cultivate a particular subject position (i.e., you are a security subject) but also crucially a particular identification (i.e., an affective attachment to the local state's new security project), a process similar to that described by Deniz Yonucu as *violent interpellation*.[84] In doing so, these actions sought to build "shared, and officially constituted, sanctioned, and promoted feelings" as a means of "coordinating citizens as members of a national security state."[85] As such, it shows the need to grasp the affective and pastoral elements of fabricating homeland security in India and how these work in conjunction with the repressive dimensions of police power.[86]

POLICING REALITIES

At its most obvious and basic level, the police modernization program worked to contain the political backlash of 26/11 and assuage India Inc.'s demands for modern world-class security. State actors mobilized the spectacle of police modernization as a catchall solution to several alleged deficiencies at the local level. The spectacle of police modernization mobilized visual signifiers of modernity and toughness with the declared aim of (re)building local confidence in the state's security apparatus, styled as a "pledge" that Mumbai was now "safe and secure." As the above images from the pages of the *Protector* make all too clear, these hypermasculine signifiers of toughness attempted to counteract Indian forces' emasculation during 26/11 and rebuild their authority anew on a "war footing."

These images and their aspirations to replicate western levels of technological capability and martial power in India were themselves nothing new; they have long played central roles in the Hindu nationalist project. Although Sahni's above reference to the "Rambo model" of response was intended as a critique, it reflects the long-running valorization of the figure of Rambo as a ubiquitous icon of violent justice and revenge within India since the 1980s that nurtured the unprecedented expansion and popularization of Hindutva around this time. There have been several Bollywood remakes of *Rambo,* and the Rambo character has been appropriated to build new images of Indian manliness, thereby imbricating elements of American hegemonic masculinity into Indian popular culture and politics. As Sikita Banerjee elaborates, these forms of hegemonic masculinity served as a "cultural filter" through which young *Sainiks* (male Shiv Sena activists) defined their identities during the communal riots that engulfed Bombay during the 1990s.[87]

In the post-26/11 context, the Rambo-like qualities of the Maharashtra state's response served related though slightly different roles. They were leveraged to resolve the crisis of legitimacy sparked by the global emasculation of the Indian state through the visual spectacle of 26/11 (chapter 1). Mirroring the way that the figure of American Rambo emerged as a cultural response to the trauma of the U.S. defeat in Vietnam on the American psyche and its resulting damage to the self-confidence of U.S. empire,[88] in the post-26/11 context, visual representations of Maharashtra's own Indian Rambos posing with their new weapons, uniforms, and technologies as markers to project confidence took on a parallel reparative function for the Indian state.

It is important to note that although Maharashtra officials mobilized comparisons with the West in their own pacification project, they did so strategically in order to bolster their own *Indian* credentials. This dynamic has close parallels to what Christoffe Jaffrelot calls "strategic syncretism," namely the tendency of Hindutva ideologues to assimilate external values and ideas associated with the Other's prestige and power in a mimetic fashion, yet on terms that were strategically oriented to vindicating India's own threatened cultural heritage.[89] While I will explore the notion of strategic syncretism in greater depth in chapter 5, here I simply note that by 2009 the nature and terms of the (Israeli) comparative geopolitics detailed in the previous chapters had already begun to shift in the sense that Indian officials were mobilizing comparison on terms of their own making.

The police modernization program further assisted Maharashtra politicians in steering the public conversation about 26/11's (mis)handling and circumscribing space for a public reckoning about *what* exactly failed on 26/11 and *who* was to blame. Above, we saw how local state actors attempted to suppress any dissenting voices. In conjunction with these overtly antidemocratic silencing strategies, however, the spectacle of police modernization served some less obvious depoliticizing functions.[90] The police modernization program was portrayed in the Indian media as a straightforward and technical matter. Officials like Gafoor, Patil, and Chavan were willing to publicly concede that certain failures had taken place during 26/11 and gaps had been identified, proposing the purchases of MP5s, MP9s, carbines, and armored jeeps as a way to ameliorate these. Jagannathan, Sivanandan, and Iyengar similarly argued that Mumbai suffered from a lack of modern security preparedness and that this deficiency could be resolved through the implementation of Israeli and other foreign homeland security solutions. In my conversations with some of these officials, they defaulted to this intuitive script, arguing that their decisions were straightforward, functionally driven, and beyond the realm of interrogation, yet refusing to spell out which specific deficiencies in local preparedness these supposed solutions actually resolved. The broader spectacle of police modernization played similar roles in attempting to sidestep and drown out enduring controversies about what took place on 26/11 and who was to blame, working as a kind of "politics of *anti-knowledge*" in the sense of governing a supposed problem by circumscribing the parameters around which it could be publicly known.[91]

Here it is important to return to the Maharashtra government's handling of the HLEC report. While the modernization program enjoyed intuitive appeal within the prevailing media scripting of 26/11 as a failure of local capacity, this program did not flow out of the report's findings and recommendations.[92] The authorization of the new emergency budget in late 2008 and key procurement decisions were taken well before the report was even submitted to the government on April 18, 2009. And whereas the report focused on a series of structural and organizational problems in the Mumbai police, such as the duplication of duties, ill-defined jurisdictional boundaries, a lack of ammunition and basic police firearm training, and a failure to follow the SOPs already in place before 26/11, Maharashtra politicians showed little interest in responding to such concerns, as their classification and public rebuke of the report's findings made all too clear. Rather than accepting the report's recommendations, local politicians mobilized the police modernization program to solve Mumbai's lack of security preparedness on their terms.

In my conversations with Balachandran, he stressed the dissonances between the modernization program and the substance of the report. He repeatedly pointed out that the specific procurements and policy decisions did not come from the report's conclusions or recommendations, arguing that some aspects of the modernization program were misguided. He noted, for instance, that the report did not recommend the implementation of a new CCTV scheme, arguing that in his estimation, the use of CCTV in contexts like the U.K. was far less effective in fighting crime and terrorism than Maharashtra politicians seemed to imagine. He further recounted that he and Pradhan were asked by the Maharashtra government about the value of sending the delegation to Palestine/Israel and had questioned its value on practical grounds. As he clarified, "I'm not saying that going to foreign countries and learning it is bad . . . but their [the Israeli] system you cannot transplant it here." As he explained, he and Pradhan "did not want these people [the delegation] to go and get lessons from Israel because what they're practicing is not applicable here [in Mumbai] at all. We have a different type of public [in India]."

Balachandran's skepticism about replicating the so-called Israeli model in India did not begin in his capacity on HLEC. As a former high-ranking intelligence official, he had long-standing personal relationships with a range of foreign officials (including Israelis) and published writings prior to 26/11 calling out suggestions for India to emulate Israeli approaches to security as little more than fantasies.[93] As the substance of the report indicates, moreover, from early on he and Pradhan seemed more partial to the U.S. homeland security approaches of DHS, and Balachandran became a champion of their use in India in the years after 2008.[94] That the modernization program's priorities contradicted Pradhan and Balachandran's recommendations is significant, however. It reflects an effort to steer the conversation away from questions of basic police capacity, which HLEC had identified, an issue I return to in chapter 4.

While the modernization program did not arise out of the report's recommendations, the two are not disconnected. It was shortly after the decision to withhold the report that the government sent its delegation to Palestine/Israel. The press coverage of the visit came only a month after the government had announced its partial rejection and classification of the document, prompting the Bombay High Court and Ram Pradhan to publicly call for its release and Maharashtra BJP politician Nitin Gadkari to allege that a coverup of the failures of key officials was being orchestrated.[95] In the context of these pressures, sending the delegation to Palestine/Israel seems to have offered a temporary distraction. As Balachandran emphasized to me, it was telling that "before . . . [the] Maharashtra government even digested our Report, the first action that they took was to send a delegation to Israel," thereby insinuating that the impulse to send its officials abroad was explicitly designed as a diversion to sidestep the report's findings.

We can see this tendency more broadly in the ways that police modernization was mobilized to police the ontological terms of the security crisis after 26/11. State actors' attempts to suppress key information and contain controversies are significant, particularly in illuminating the antidemocratic and authoritarian dimensions of the Maharashtra government's response to the attacks. But they were only partially realized, in some cases themselves generating new sites of discord. For instance, Rakesh Maria's handling of Kamte's requests for information prompted Kamte to question Maria's motives and file right to information (RTI) requests. In May 2009, Kamte and Kavita Karkare, widow of Hemant Karkare, further lashed out at HLEC for absolving the sitting Mumbai police officers for their husbands' deaths, accusing the ruling government of undermining democracy.[96] Retired Indian police officer S. M. Mushrif published his book *Who Killed Karkare?* in September 2009 in Marathi and English editions, which suggested that Karkare might have been killed by a right-wing Brahmanist conspiracy.[97] And in November 2009, Vinita Kamte published a memoir of her late husband *To the Last Bullet*, which contested the official account of the circumstances of his death, based on her own investigation.[98]

I am unable to detail the full range of allegations contained in these works, though a few are worth noting. Mushrif bracketed off ongoing speculation about whether 26/11 was in fact planned and carried out by Lashkar-e-Taiba (LeT) and/or Pakistan's Inter-Services Intelligence (ISI) alone, as Indian authorities claimed, or had potentially received support from the Taliban, Al-Qaeda, the CIA, Mossad, or other pro-Zionist actors.[99] He asserted unequivocally that the "Taj-Oberoi Trident part of the Mumbai attack was a reality, with the terrorists having Pakistan connections."[100] Nevertheless, Mushrif argued that attacks around Mumbai's central railway station, Chhatrapati Shivaji Terminus (CST), and Cama Hospital "had nothing to do with the main attack at the Taj-Oberoi-Nariman House" and that Karkare had been intentionally directed toward Cama hospital to be killed by "Brahmanist elements" with direct assistance from officials within India's IB, who mobilized 26/11 as cover to carry out his murder.[101] Based on his analysis of Indian newspaper articles chronicling 26/11 day by day, Mushsrif's alternative theory of 26/11 proposed not just that the IB had failed to uncover the planning of 26/11 (and thereby prevent it, as had been widely reported) but that the IB had been directly complicit in the attacks. Mushrif further questioned the authenticity of prevailing images of 26/11, most notably the infamous photograph of Ajmal Kasab standing with an AK-47 at CST, allegedly taken from CCTV footage in the station.[102] Thus, while conceding he lacked definitive proof of *who exactly* killed Karkare, Mushrif poked holes in official accounts, situating Karkare's death as further evidence of the Indian state's complicity in Saffron terror.

To the Last Bullet similarly claimed that local state actors had attempted a cover-up of the key facts of 26/11 while making no allegations of any Brahmanist conspiracy at work. In the book, Kamte charged that she had been denied access to basic information such as the copy of the postmortem report of her late husband.[103] She further argued local state officials were effectively blaming her husband and his fellow officers for their own deaths in order to shield themselves from accountability and that HLEC had assisted these efforts by glossing over these officials' "glaring acts of incompetence" in the operational handling of 26/11.[104] Kamte further recounted how she was prevented from giving testimony to HLEC, despite her repeated attempts to do so. Crucially, however, Kamte claimed that she was not the only one being deceived. Her book recounted that through her own correspondence with Balachandran she learned that he and Pradhan only ever saw certified copies of police call logs but never the originals. When I spoke with Vinita Kamte in Mumbai in 2013, she stressed that her multiple RTI requests had yielded two different versions of call records, thereby demonstrating that the original records had been illegally tampered with. Thus, while Kamte's and Mushrif's allegations had different points of emphasis and evidence for their claims, they converged in contesting the credibility of official accounts of what took place on 26/11, claiming in slightly different ways that Indian publics were being actively misled by the government's suppression of information.

Both books also had immediate political consequences in late 2009. *Who Killed Karkare?* became an instant bestseller and went through multiple editions. When I spoke with the editor of an Urdu newspaper in 2013, he recalled that Mushrif emerged as a hero in the Urdu press, widely appreciated by Muslims for challenging the dominant state narratives at the time. In addition to questioning the official narratives of 26/11, the publication of *To the Last Bullet* further ignited a new firestorm of public controversy and infighting within the Mumbai police, with Sivanandan personally attending its official launch and Rakesh Maria threatening to resign in protest over its allegation that he had personally played a central role in orchestrating a coverup.[105] It was in the midst of these simmering controversies that the local state's spectacle of police modernization culminated, with the inaugural issue of the *Protector* published in September/October 2009 and a military-style parade on Marine Drive on the first anniversary of 26/11. When situated in this context, we can see how the spectacles of police modernization attempted to drown out and displace these ongoing conflicts and controversies and interpellate new subjects to serve in the state's ongoing security project.

In all of these respects, attempts to police the security crisis after 26/11 were simultaneously about suppressing information and actively reproducing various forms of *un*knowing but also generating forms of knowledge about the origins, causes, and nature of the crisis itself.[106] The police modernization program governed the crisis performatively in a double sense, namely by performing a particular image of the state but also working as a kind of diagnostic device.[107] By this I mean that rather than simply responding to a set of obvious preexisting policy problems, the police modernization program played a key role in constituting the core problem of Mumbai's vulnerability as stemming from a lack of modern expertise and weaponry. Purchasing new weapons and technologies, sending officials abroad, and engaging with foreign trainers implied that Mumbai's vulnerability stemmed from a lack of modern technological capability, which could, in turn, be remedied by the swift procurement of modern security solutions.

CONCLUSION

In this chapter, I have examined how the Maharashtra government responded to the crisis of legitimacy sparked by 26/11. The event ignited a firestorm of anti-politician sentiment and jingoism but also gave rise to a set of controversies and conflicts. These were initially sparked by bourgeois critiques of the Indian state's domestic security apparatus but quickly mutated and multiplied, calling into question dominant media and state narratives about the meaning, origins, and significance of the attacks. As I have shown, local state actors worked swiftly to tamp down and displace these various conflicts and controversies with a spectacle of police modernization-as-pacification, representing "policing and politicking *at the same time*."[108]

Policing the security crisis, in other words, was simultaneously an expression of authoritarian populism and a politics of truth, which attempted to enact and thereby police the ontological terms of reality itself.[109] By this I mean that the security crisis of 26/11 was governed by circumscribing the terms through which this same crisis—and the basic facts of what took place on 26/11—could be known by certain interested parties like Vinita Kamte as well as wider publics. While Kamte remained adamant in her right to seek accountability and pushed ahead in pursuit of truth and accountability, she conceded that she had run into hard limits. In our conversation, she recalled that throughout her struggle, it was telling that no public official ever seriously tried to find out what she wanted to know, let alone provide any plausible answers. In her view, it was even more shocking, if unsurprising, that the Indian media showed no interest in contesting the official line, likely out of fear of police retaliation by Rakesh Maria, who, she stressed, "is such a powerful person!"

While I am in no position to adjudicate the veracity of the allegations of a Brahmanist conspiracy in relation to 26/11, this chapter has shown that policing the security crisis went hand in hand with policing the realities of the event of 26/11 itself, in part by attempting to silence dissent.[110] Moreover, regardless of Mushrif's specific charges, the central role of Indian state actors in instigating and supervising Hindu-led communal violence is well established. It also should be emphasized that the prevailing violence that saturates Indian politics in ever more visible and brazen ways since 2014, whether forms fomented directly by Indian state actors or others, is in no way antithetical to the order of things in contemporary India—quite the contrary. As Achin Vanaik emphasizes, the sheer "frequency, scale and intensity of either routinized or episodic violence" in India "raises disturbing questions about the relationship between such violence to the existing order—and its utility for that order."[111] This points to the importance of grasping the centrality of police power not exclusively in terms of regulating social *order* but rather in generating *dis*order by actively instigating violence between different communities as pretext to carry out a permanent counterinsurgency war on radical politics, a dynamic hardly unique to India.[112] Read in this wider context, what is perhaps most significant about the government's response to 26/11 is how it managed to pacify the local anti-politician backlash under the banner of police modernization while keeping firmly in place the local policing infrastructure and wider structures of state violence.

When read carefully, even some official pronouncements to project confidence raise doubts about the extent of the state's commitment to implementing a radical overhaul of the local policing apparatus in the image of northern moderns. In an interview in the September/October

2009 issue of the *Protector*, Sivanandan began to backpedal from his bold endorsements of Israel's "killer instinct" and imminent plans to replicate an Israeli solution in Mumbai. When asked about the delegation visit, he responded: "The Israeli trip is only a study group's visit. It is too early to say that we have done any thing [*sic*] with Israel [. . .] we have [only] seen how they are working and *if* there is anything to learn from them."[113] The clear contrast in his tone from previous public statements reflects an underlying trepidation to defer to foreign experts, one that was at play in the engagements with Israeli and other foreign trainers that took place. As will become clear in chapter 5, the new reality, though important, was a temporary achievement and hardly destiny.[114]

FOUR

THE CHANGING SAME

INTRODUCTION

Political violence transforms urban landscapes.[1] When I arrived in Mumbai in October 2012, visual reminders of 26/11 remained at some of its key battlegrounds. A plaque at the memorial to police officers killed during 26/11 installed in 2009 on Marine Drive pledged to "never forget those martyrs who laid down their lives so that Mumbai may live." Nariman House remained closed to the public and was uninhabited. Although some early renovations had begun, its structure was still badly damaged. I was guided through the facility by an Indian Jew with close ties to the local Chabad movement. He took me up the concrete staircase to the room of Moshe, the surviving child of rabbi Gavriel Holtzberg and his wife Rivka, both killed during 26/11. The room's walls were still adorned with hand-painted Hebrew letters as well as a sketch of a bird carved into the plaster. On the building's upper floors, there were visible bulletholes and craters from the explosives used during 26/11.

When I visited the Leopold Café, the bulletholes in the walls had been left unrepaired to add to the venue's appeal to its tourist patrons. These examples recall the violence of 26/11 itself and how this was materially inscribed into the city's fabric in ways that kept certain memories of the

FIGURE 4.1: *Blast site inside Nariman House, Mumbai, 2012. Photo by the author.*

event alive. However, these were not the only ways that 26/11 and its repercussions lived on in Mumbai.

In this chapter, I trace how the Maharashtra government's policy responses to 26/11 materialized in the everyday built environment of the city. At a distance, the police modernization program examined in the previous chapter appears as a textbook example of the *militarization* of everyday urban space. The program gave rise to the accelerated purchase of new weapons, vehicles, and surveillance equipment and the solicitation of foreign experts and police trainers. It was justified politically as an effort to professionalize the Mumbai and Maharashtra police forces and bring the local state onto a "war footing," one mimetically styled in the image of modern and western homeland security approaches. In the years immediately thereafter, scholars noted that counterterrorism projects in India "promoted by a Western-dominated security ideology" are increasingly "determining the way that security issues are framed and [. . .] responded to," privileging "militarised and technological responses."[2] Such readings of 26/11's policy repercussions as a form of militarization (or securitization) being imposed by the Global North *onto* India (and the Global South at large) are common.[3] Indeed, post-26/11 dynamics bear close resemblance to those seen across a range of cities during the war on terror[4] and well before it.[5]

References to militarization connote a deepening reliance on aggressive tactics, weapons, and military-style infrastructures, resulting in a hardening of everyday urban landscapes.[6] These dynamics are further associated with a radical blurring of the domestic/foreign and the exceptional/everyday. These critical accounts of urban militarization have importantly challenged the neoliberal security state's most visible excesses. The powerful polemical tone of Mike Davis's classic *City of Quartz* is an excellent example of this.[7] Over time, however, many have lost this critical edge. Militarization has become common sense. That the Homeland Security Newswire, an industry website for homeland security practitioners, recently published articles on the dangers of "militarized" law enforcement demonstrates the commonsense nature of "militarization."[8]

The growing ubiquity of what Christopher McMichael calls the "militarization thesis"[9] has subjected it to critical revaluation in the Indian context[10] and beyond.[11] Critiques of this thesis do not dispute contemporary policing's reliance on heavy weaponry and surveillance technologies with clear military origins or purposes. The core concern, rather, is the thesis's reliance on "an overstated and unquestioned distinction between war and police," which implies militarization to be unprecedented and reinscribes the very binaries supposedly being erased by it.[12] References to militarization can also become an easy way to explain recent phenomena based on a "surface analysis of military aesthetics in so-called civilian life,"[13] thereby problematically decentering the political emphasis on the systemic nature of organized violence.[14] Of concern are the boundaries of police/war but also the nature of politics. The analytic of militarization can reinscribe the mythology of war and police as having previously been separate and in so doing produce a sanitized picture of politics.[15]

Such a picture of politics as antithetical to violence has always been out of step with Indian politics and to an ever-growing extent in the present as well.[16] Indeed, in India *martial* and *politics* have long been deeply entwined, ideologically and materially, and remain so. Hindu nationalism has always been a mixture of ideological production, military aesthetics, and rhetoric accompanied by effort to infuse physical strength into the majority Hindu community through training and indoctrination.[17] While it took decades to develop the popularity that Hindutva today enjoys within India and its diaspora, Islamophobia has deeply shaped many currents of Indian nationalist thought.

Taking critiques of militarization as my point of departure, the key question of this chapter is not *whether* military technologies and logics are at work in Mumbai's governance pre- or post-26/11. Instead, I seek to better understand the ever-shifting but continuous imbrications of war police and which concepts we employ to theorize them.[18] As an alternative to militarization, I build on Alison Howell's notion of "martial politics" to document how new technologies were grafted onto preexisting policing infrastructures, in patchy, ad-hoc, and fleeting ways.[19] Furthermore, I show how these changes reinscribed particular spatial and political borders around policing in Bombay/Mumbai and India more broadly.[20] Situated in the long and ongoing history of transnational and trans-temporal war-police assemblages between India and imperial metropoles, I argue that the Maharashtra government's policy response to 26/11 should be seen as an effort to fabricate Mumbai's social order by preserving rather than transforming the pre-2008 status quo police infrastructure, albeit with some important changes.[21] In doing so, this chapter charts an approach for theorizing the local materializations of homeland (in)security, which makes sense of the leveraging of warlike qualities as forms of politics, employed to negotiate and paper over the "provisional"[22] and "contingent"[23] character of police power in India today. I argue that the post-26/11 police modernization programs are akin to what Ruth Wilson Gilmore, following LeRoi Jones (Amiri Baraka), calls "the changing same," namely the redoubling of ongoing histories, structures, and regimes of violent domination under the banner of reform.[24] This chapter mobilizes the notion of the changing same to make sense of how the fabrication of homeland security in the city of Mumbai leveraged military aesthetics as semiotic markers of swift and far-reaching change. I argue that this was a political strategy to preserve the preexisting status quo under a new guise.

I draw on ethnographic encounters with police infrastructure and messaging in Mumbai gathered through walking the city between 2012–13 and again in 2019. I supplement my reflections gleaned through walking and photographing the city with interviews and informal conversations with Mumbai journalists, activists, lawyers, sales agents as well as Maharashtra officials involved in crafting the state's police modernization program. By triangulating between my own firsthand encounters with Mumbai's physical landscape, media coverage of the response to 26/11, and interviews, I trace how the response to 26/11 materialized in the urban environment of Mumbai. In so doing, I situate these developments within broader patterns of urban dispossession, fragmentation, and segregation. These patterns have defined Bombay/Mumbai since the early 1990s alongside the rise and consolidation of Hindu authoritarianism,[25] which manifested in the official change of the city's name from Bombay to Mumbai in 1995.[26]

MATERIALIZING HOMELAND (IN)SECURITY

In the years after 26/11, aspects of the police modernization program outlined in chapter 3 became visible in the city's physical landscape. In the south of the city, new vehicles, weapons, and cameras were prominently displayed to inspire public confidence. For instance, the fleet of Mahindra Marksman jeeps were stationed at the Maharashtra state government headquarters Mantralaya and CST, also commonly known as Victoria Terminus or simply "VT."[27] These vehicles were sometimes manned by QRTs clothed in camouflage uniforms or small groups of police officers, some wearing protective vests and carrying pistols and submachine guns (Figure 4.2). Additional CCTV cameras had been installed across the south of the city, including at major railway stations.

The physical infrastructures at certain private and commercial sites in south Mumbai had also undergone significant change. The Taj and Oberoi hotels, both devastated during the attacks, had installed physical security perimeters, including planters, walls, and retractable anti-crash bollard systems to allow cars to pass in and out. These hotels were now equipped with baggage scanners and CCTV systems monitored by security control rooms inside. In the case of the Taj, these physical bollard systems were

FIGURE 4.2: *Police standing guard outside of CST, Mumbai, 2013. Photo by Paramita Nath.*

FIGURE 4.3: *EL-GO Team anti-crash bollards installed at Taj Hotel, Mumbai, 2012. Photo by the author.*

initially contracted out to the Israeli firm EL-GO Team, as I learned by speaking to the firm's representatives in Tel Aviv (Figure 4.3).

Likewise, the Bombay Stock Exchange (BSE) had installed a yellow metal gate and a system of anti-ramming bollards purchased from the Israeli firm BG Ilanit Gates and Urban Elements Ltd. (BGI) (Figures 4.4 and 4.5).[28] And like CST and Mantralaya, at the Taj and the BSE there were also Marksman jeeps with police personnel on site standing or sitting on plastic chairs adjacent to the vehicles.

Major train stations like CST and Churchgate had installed metal detectors at their main entrances. Although the metal detectors were ostensibly installed to reassure commuters that their security was being taken seriously, their manifestations seemed to signal a tacit admission by the local state that securing the facility was impossible. Unlike in other Indian cities like New Delhi, where public transport passengers are frisked and have their luggage scanned before entering the metro, I noticed that at CST and other Mumbai train stations passengers could pass through the scanners without being stopped, even if they had triggered the machine's

FIGURE 4.4: *BGI anti-crash bollards and security gate, Bombay Stock Exchange, Mumbai, 2013. Photo Paramita Nath.*

FIGURE 4.5: *BGI anti-crash bollards and security gate, Bombay Stock Exchange, Mumbai, 2013. Photo by the author.*

alarms. Many such stations and entrances lacked scanners altogether, and even in instances where a scanner was installed, passing through the scanners was entirely voluntary. Where scanners were present, there were often large gaps between them, which enabled commuters to walk around the machines if they chose (Figure 4.6).

Some of the most common changes to Mumbai's physical security infrastructure, however, had little to do with police *modernization* as such. One of the more noticeable changes was the increased physical fortification of strategic sites. These included the Bombay High Court and railway terminals like CST as well as police stations, like the Maharashtra police headquarters in Colaba a few blocks away from the Gateway of India

FIGURE 4.6: *Scanners at entrance of CST, Mumbai, 2013. Photo by Paramita Nath.*

and the Office of Mumbai's Commissioner of Police opposite Crawford Market. These fortifications took various forms, including improvised bunkers constructed out of sandbags and/or concrete blocks, typically manned by police constables armed with Indian Small Arms System (INSAS) rifles or vintage British Sterling submachine guns (Figure 4.7). Even with the arrival of newly purchased weapons, the antique weapons remained in commission. As a former Maharashtra Home Ministry bureaucrat explained to me, "for the time being they [antique weapons] are being used" because police personnel "need weapons and until such time as we are able to give each a newer weapon, he has at least got *something*." From speaking with such officials, I got the impression that these old weapons would not be phased out anytime soon. In other words, the arrival of new technologies supplemented, rather than replaced, preexisting police infrastructures.

During my travels across the city, I noticed other kinds of security perimeters set up at numerous sites to control movement, including the Gateway of India adjacent to the Taj (Figures 4.8 and 4.9). These barriers were constructed from low-tech steel roadblocks called *nakabandi*, which are prevalent across India. While the use of stop-and-search tactics using

FIGURE 4.7: *Sandbag Bunker, CST, Mumbai, 2013. Photo by Paramita Nath.*

nakabandi have long been a staple of the Mumbai police, after 26/11 their usage became more widespread in response to public pressure to "do something" or "appear to be proactive."[29] Thus, rather than signifying a shift from "civil" to "militarized" approaches to policing Mumbai, the introduction of "new" homeland security logics and technologies merged with the preexisting policing repertoires and physical infrastructures.

It is important to stress that well before 2008, Mumbai was one of the most heavily fortified cities in India with large swaths of its territory under the direct or indirect control of the Indian navy, army, and the Mumbai city and Maharashtra state police. Walking the city provided me with constant reminders that much of the city's infrastructural fabric is "of war."[30] The city's deep connection to colonial and imperial military violence lives on in the naming of the city itself, for instance the area of south Mumbai known as "Fort," named after Fort George, which was built by the East India Company. The city's connection to ongoing forms of military violence was further made visible to me through other semiotic markers. At Lion Gate, the entrance of the Naval Dockyard in south Mumbai, a sign warned would-be intruders in Hindi and English that the compound was

FIGURE 4.8: *Line of barriers, Taj Hotel/Gateway of India, Mumbai, 2013. Photo by the author.*

FIGURE 4.9: *Line of barriers, Taj Hotel/Gateway of India, Mumbai, 2013. Photo by Paramita Nath.*

a "HIGH SECURITY DEFENCE AREA" and that "TRESPASSERS MAY BE SHOT."

Likewise, the rollout of the police modernization program also included various forms of security messaging. Some of this was clearly intended to boost public confidence, reassuring certain publics that they had a "right" to security and that surveillance was for *their* benefit. A sign on a scanner at Churchgate Station read "Security Check is for the Benefit of the Passengers, Kindly Cooperate with the Railway Officials," further noting underneath that "Being Safe Is Your Birth Right! [*sic*]." Along my journeys through the city, I also found signs echoing the DHS campaign "If You See Something, Say Something."[31] One sign instructed commuters that "ALERTNESS BEGINS WITH YOU!," warning that "[t]he bag next to yours may not belong to an everyday commuter." Signs like these worked to boost security awareness and alertness as per programs aimed at interpellating new security subjects referenced in early issues of the Mumbai *Protector* (chapter 3). Barriers outside of the BSE had similar messages, though struck a more conciliatory even apologetic tone. One read "thank you for your co-operation" and "sorry for the inconvenience."

These forms of "banal" antiterrorism attempted to foment a sense of everyday unease but also facilitate the kinds of "dialogue with the people" that D. Sivanandan had called for in 2009 (chapter 3).[32] Much like the physical security measures above, however, these newer forms of messaging supplemented and augmented, rather than replaced, preexisting ones. One *nakabandi*, which I encountered near Mumbai's port area, warned passersby not to handle "unidentified object [*sic*]," instructing them to call the police to assist with the removal of such items (Figure 4.10).

In contrast, a sign at CST gave instructions (in Hindi) to publics about how to handle such objects and notify police about them:

> Your safety is in your hands. If you find unclaimed objects or vehicles near your area of residence, bring them to the notice of the nearest police station at once. Promptly keep sacks of sand around the unclaimed object to ensure that no one touches it—once blocked, take the residents away from it and inform the other residents of nearby areas—don't crowd and cooperate with the police once informed.

FIGURE 4.10: *Nakabandi, Near Yellow Gate Police Station, Mumbai, 2013. Photo by Paramita Nath.*

At various suburban railway stations across the city, I encountered WANTED posters published by the Maharashtra ATS featuring pictures of four young Muslim men and a reward of Rs. 10 Lacs (Figure 4.11).

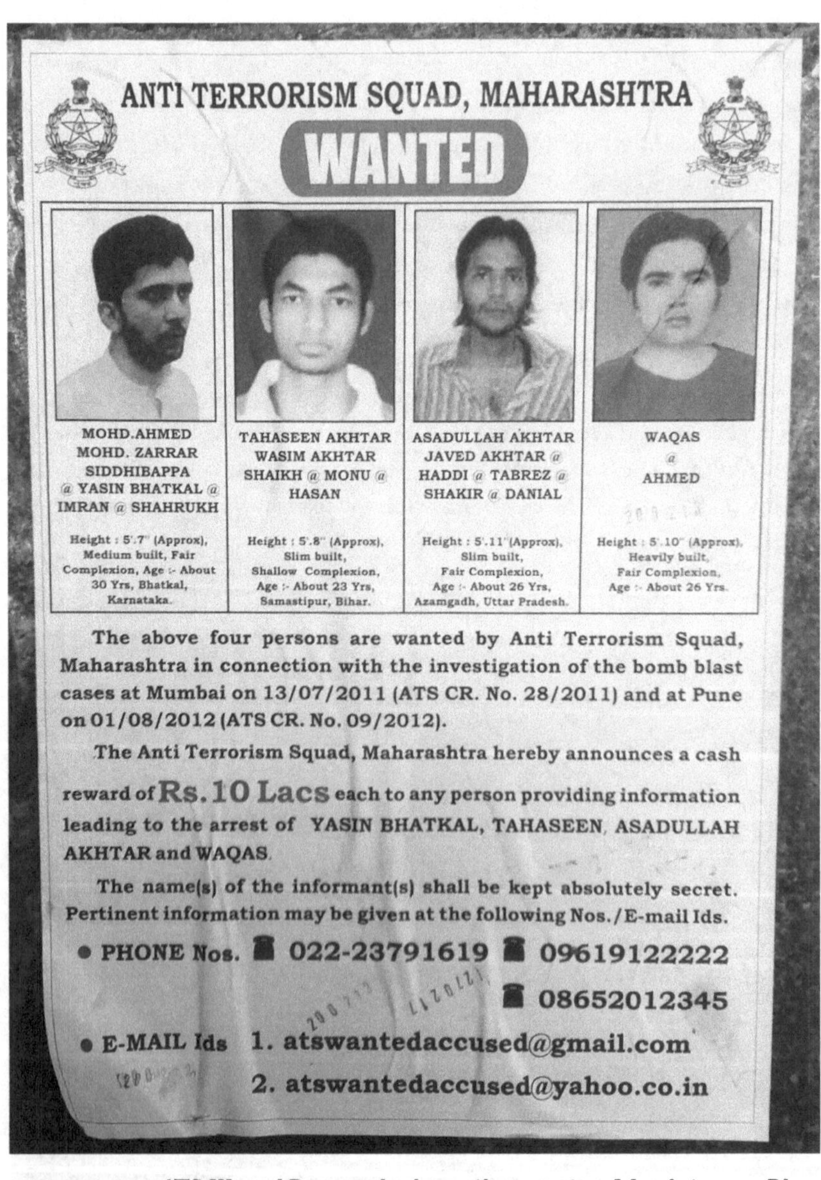

FIGURE 4.11: *ATS Wanted Poster, suburban railway station, Mumbai, 2012. Photo by the author.*

In Mumbai, police modernization thereby materialized in the form of hybrids or "mixtures" of different elements, grafting new weapons, surveillance cameras, vehicles, uniforms, and signs onto preexisting infrastructures while leaving the latter in place.[33] The uneven implementation of metal detectors at CST illustrates how new technologies were not just layered onto preexisting infrastructure; such projects also materialized in uneven, patchy, and superficial ways. The metal detectors were not the only example of this. By 2011, journalists reported that the majority of purchased speed boats were lying unused due to a lack of trained personnel[34] and because funds were never allotted to purchase fuel for the new fleets.[35]

This hybridized character of the police modernization program resonates with discussions of imperial *bricolage* characterized by a piecemeal and partial adoption of certain elements while leaving others behind.[36] In so doing, these hybrids modified certain preexisting elements of Mumbai's urban fabric and added certain new ones, yet hardly in the radically unprecedented or all-encompassing way that militarization tends to connote. It is important to mention that not all the promised measures to secure the city came to fruition. For instance, early pledges by Maharashtra politicians to purchase helicopters never moved forward and efforts to modernize police infrastructure in Mumbai were plagued by ongoing controversies, corruption, and allegations of mismanagement.

CRACKS IN THE FAÇADE

The procurement process for new security infrastructure and its materialization or, rather, the lack thereof was marked by characteristics associated with the Hindi notion of *jugaad*. The term *jugaad* cannot be translated into a single English word. Rather, it has multiple connotations in Hindi. *Jugaad* is often used in relation to corruption in India but is also associated with "actions that involve 'quick and dirty' fixes or problem solving through improvisation, especially in a context of scarce resources."[37] As Beatrice Jauregui's rendering of this idiom elaborates in the context of Indian policing, *jugaad* represents a kind of "make do" or "can do" ethos and associated practices that are characterized by "continual improvisation, recombination, and recreation in both senses of 'play' and 'remaking.'"[38] Following Jauregui, I argue that the *jugaad*-like qualities of the response to 26/11 reflect the "provisionality" of police power in contemporary India, in the sense of their impermanence and instability.

The modernization program, particularly the process of procuring new equipment, was plagued by controversies and charges of corruption. While the HLEC report cited a lack of adequate protective gear as a key reason why so many police officers died unnecessarily during 26/11, efforts to procure such items proved less than straightforward. After repeated delays, an insufficient number of protective vests arrived. Yet, many of the procured vests as well as the bomb disposal suits proved defective, sparking major corruption scandals involving key ministers in the Maharashtra government.[39] There were further bribery scandals surrounding the purchase of overpriced speedboats as well as significant delays in the tendering and rollout of Mumbai's CCTV scheme, which were reported in the press during my time in the city.[40]

In my conversation with residents of the city, they consistently alleged systemic incompetence and corruption. A Mumbai crime reporter recounted rumors that the decision to buy MP5s was made because of D. Sivanandan's close personal connections to a dealer promoting this particular weapon in India. A businessman I met in the city saw it similarly. He had lobbied unsuccessfully to sell foreign-manufactured speedboats to the Maharashtra government after 26/11. He recalled that local state officials had no idea what they were looking for and, as a result, deferred to various agents and contractors like himself in key decisions on procurement. According to this businessman, local authorities' ignorance compelled them to purchase "junk" from unscrupulous agents, rather than the vessels he was promoting, which he claimed to be of extremely high quality. As one senior Mumbai crime editor of a leading Indian national daily recalled, "It was *not* that [the police] tried all these guns and . . . [then] shortlisted [them]." Rather, he stressed, some officers simply thought that some weapons were better than others and then purchased them on a whim.

Other journalists questioned the modernization program's priorities and rationality. While media coverage of 26/11 implied that local forces lacked modern automatic rifles, subsequent reports emerged that the Mumbai police had a cache of 247 AK-47s on hand during 26/11 but that these weapons were not made available to Mumbai police officers during the attacks.[41] This raised questions about why the procurement of new (and much more costly) imported weapons took on such urgency after 26/11. Other newly procured items plainly lacked any obvious tactical purpose. One of the most striking examples of this was the M82/M107 .50-caliber anti-materiel rifles mentioned in chapter 3 featured in the *Mumbai Protector* (Figure 4.12). In 2009, *The Hindu* reported that the Mumbai police had procured and showcased these weapons to publics even though they could not be tested by local authorities because they exceeded the capacities of local police firing ranges.[42]

Other local journalists commented on how ill suited many of the newly purchased procurements were to the local environment. One Mumbai journalist explained to me that many of the flashy weapons purchased, like MP9 submachine guns, were of questionable utility in such a densely

FIGURE 4.12: *Image featuring officer holding M82/M107 .50-caliber anti-materiel rifle (center) from* The Mumbai Protector: A Magazine for the Mumbai Police *(January/February 2010).*

populated urban environment, which if ever used would inevitably cause unwarranted collateral damage. He chuckled as he noted the distinct *lack* of similarity between the visual appearance of Force One commandos donning maroon berets (chapter 3), with the balaclavas and high-tech helmets typically worn by special operations forces in the Global North. Another journalist noted that the Marksman jeeps lacked air-conditioning and became unbearably hot during the day, thereby compromising their operational utility in the event of future attacks. Walking the city, I noticed that these jeeps often had newspapers pasted in their front windows, apparently to ameliorate this.

Several high-ranking officials went even further as they questioned the very premise of police modernization (i.e., the procurement of new weapons and technologies) as a solution to 26/11. As one former senior officer emphasized, "it's *not* that we had really outdated armory or weapons, it's not that. I think the issue is more complex than that." Another retired officer further stressed that "simply saying that . . . we were . . . not modernized and so unable to deal with it [26/11]—it is not that . . . Bombay city had . . . sophisticated weapons." He further commented on the impulsive and ill-considered attempts to respond to 26/11 through the rapid police modernization program, suggesting that the political imperative to soothe demands for security generated misguided priorities. He recalled that 26/11 put the Maharashtra government "in a panic mode," causing them to respond "in a reactionary way . . . [by] pump[ing] in funds." As he summarized: "It's like trying to . . . close the gate after the horse has bolted."

While local public officials questioned the need to buy new equipment, they nevertheless insisted that the modernization program had achieved its most important political objectives. For instance, though stressing that the focus on buying flashy new weapons was essentially ill conceived, the above officer nevertheless insisted: "Whatever has been done as a result of the creation of Force One has produced tremendously good results . . . I mean for developing confidence." As he explained, "You know, if you see a QRT vehicle standing somewhere in public, it inspires confidence." Even Vappala Balachandran, who relentlessly criticized the government's response to 26/11, conceded that "when you see a [bulletproof] vehicle like this or the policemen are all over, fairly heavily armed, the public are a bit confident." In other words, state officials insisted that the response to 26/11 had worked by restoring a sense of social order in the city.

In my conversations with police officers, a number did their best to convince me that by global standards Mumbai remained a very safe city. To make this case, some drew a separation between the dangers posed by unusual security events like 26/11 and the general state of everyday safety in the city. As one senior officer explained:

> *Unlike* many, many countries around the world, Mumbai, I would say, it's still the safest city for a common citizen at any given point of time. . . . Which does not mean that crime doesn't take place, it does, sure. But it is not *unsafe*. . . . Therefore, when . . . people [are] going in for [to buy] private security [this] is more for other reasons: maybe it will give them a little more sense of status or sense . . . [of] comfort, [but it's] not to say that if they *didn't* have the [private] security they would be robbed or something; it doesn't happen like that. . . . [During 26/11] there was] a breach of security or . . . a terrorist attack. . . . [But] you can still have . . . an attack of terror . . . [without] affecting the *safety* of a lot of people.

I certainly do not take this statement as an accurate portrayal of everyday life for many Mumbaikars, particularly its minoritized communities, an issue I return to below. What concerns me about this statement here, however, is twofold. First is the officer's attempt to represent the city of Mumbai to a foreigner as a place of exceptional safety, potentially deserving greater global recognition than it is typically afforded, a theme I return to in the next chapter. Second is the officer's distinction between *security* as exceptional and *safety* as the realm of the ordinary, the everyday. In other words, it speaks to the political and ideological bordering of police work.

A number of other officials invoked this distinction by referencing the modernization program in contradistinction to "law and order" policing. When I asked a senior officer about how the new weapons were rolled out after 2008, he stressed that these were "not for the *whole* force." He and other officers saw the issue of police modernization as a matter of getting the best weaponry to Force One and QRTs, emphasizing that the police modernization program had little to do with the practice of everyday policing. Another former senior officer noted, "I have always believed that . . . terrorism [policing] is very different from normal policing," stressing that "normal" policing chiefly concerned efforts "to police the society" at large. A senior Force One officer put things more categorically, arguing that matters of law and order and counterterror policing are "*totally* different." Another top Force One official later elaborated a similar claim in an interview published on the Indian news site NDTV.com: "Every constable does not fight terrorism. We have NSG and Force One to fight terrorism. We don't expect the beat constable to fight terrorism. He does not do that anywhere in the world. He is the first line of defence, but not the ultimate line."[43]

The distinction that these officers made between modernization efforts for select forces versus everyday law and order policing led me to two conclusions. First, the vast majority of public officials whom I spoke with portrayed 26/11 as an exceptional, one-off event. A senior officer who had served in Maharashtra's ATS lamented that "too much emphasis has definitely gone into empowering . . . [on] more arming and more equipment," noting that in general terrorism will focus on the use of IEDs as a 26/11-style attack will likely prove to "be a very rare thing." Likewise, as former Maharashtra home minister Jayant Patil, under whose tenure many key post-26/11 policy decisions were made, bluntly put it: "In India we are very serious when incidents happen [but] as the time passes, we think 'No, no, no it's not going to happen again' . . . [and] forget about it. That is how we survive." This reflects the broader tendency of Indian police officials to view and portray breakdowns in (urban) social order as exceptional rather than routine events.[44]

Second and relatedly, police officials viewed counterterrorism policing as distinct from policing per se, reflecting the highly disaggregated nature of the Indian state and sovereignty. Jinee Lokaneeta's focus on what she calls the "contingency" of Indian police power is helpful here. Lokaneeta grapples with tensions between the ideological imperatives of police power and "the structural contingencies that render the police unable to operate in a unitary way."[45] In contrast to the central importance of discretion in police power,[46] contingency is structural in nature and developed as a counter to prevailing ideas of "unified, rule-based policing."[47] In other words, whereas discretion relates to selective application of police power at micro scales, contingency is a defining structural feature of the operation of police power in India.

It is precisely this lack of unity referenced in the distinction between ordinary and security policing that has been cited by mainstream Indian security commentators as the central source of India's vulnerability to future attacks. In his critiques of the Indian state's modernization programs after 26/11, Ajai Sahni has argued that "the strategic success of India's counterterrorism responses will depend overwhelmingly on the capacities, mandate and effectiveness of its 'general forces,'" referencing the alleged success of "broken windows" policing strategies in New York City.[48] Much to his dismay, however, the capacities of these "general forces" never received much attention in the years after 2008 in Mumbai or across India.

Officers' insistence on a fundamental separation between security and everyday order-making or safety is important in another sense as well. What is striking and notable about their insistence on a categorical separation between the exceptional and the ordinary is the contrast it draws vis-à-vis prevailing understandings of homeland security as an "all-encompassing" approach to domestic surveillance and territorial control,[49] which explicitly sets out to erase boundaries between different elements of the domestic police apparatus under a highly centralized and streamlined system of information-sharing known as intelligence "fusion."[50] As my Israeli informants from chapter 2 repeatedly stressed, the Israeli conception of (homeland) security takes as its starting point that no distinctions between different spheres can exist.[51] And as will become clear in the next chapter, Israelis who sought work on homeland security projects in India often encountered sharp contradictions in how they conceptualized domestic security from those of their Indian counterparts.

To be clear, the point here is not to imply that the borders of policing in Mumbai (or anywhere) are somehow immutable. Rather, it shows the need to apprehend policing's borders as "conceptual" rather than "absolute"[52] and as the subject of continuous remaking and negotiation.[53] This does not mean that the policing of terrorism as such is somehow tangential to Indian policing[54] or that the Indian state is soft—indeed, quite the opposite.[55] The Indian state has some of the most draconian antiterrorism laws in the world, which enable the surveillance and persecution of India's Muslim communities in particular.

POLICING SUSPECT COMMUNITIES

The Mumbai police has long been deeply implicated in the city's communal tensions, particularly during the 1992–93 riots sparked by Hindutva activists' demolition of the Babri Masjid in Ayodhya, Uttar Pradesh. During these riots, the long-standing anti-Muslim bias within the Hindu majority police force became increasingly apparent. The police issued "shoot to kill" orders that targeted Muslim demonstrators while showing lenience toward those from the Hindu community.[56] This occurred even though the minority Muslim population was the primary victim of the violence perpetrated by the police and Hindu activists.[57] As Thomas Blom Hansen details, the communal riots in the 1990s represented a particular formative moment in a much longer-standing program of political marginalization of Muslims in the city, fueled by the Mumbai police's portrayal of Muslim areas and Muslims as "security problems" and quintessential outsiders.[58] As Arjun Appadurai elaborates, the 1992–93 riots "translated the problem of scarce space into the imaginary of cleansed space, a space without Muslim bodies."[59]

In my interviews with police officers, I often noticed that they seemed less fixated on what the prospects of a modern homeland security infrastructure offered them than I had anticipated. Rather, they were more eager to share their thoughts on policing dangerous classes and various Others. Many of my interviews with police officers contained numerous references to these xenophobic imaginative geographies of threat. Unprompted and irrespective of the question posed, many of my interlocutors expounded on what they thought was the most important or pressing danger facing the city. These responses covered a number of common tropes, such as the issue of anonymous "floating" migrant populations from rural India, the specter of Muslim-instigated communal riots, "anti-national" efforts to "indoctrinate" and "radicalize" local Muslim youth, the threats posed by so-called "urban Naxals," and the alleged connections between local criminal groups and global criminal-terrorist syndicates stretching from

Mumbai to Dubai and Pakistan. Here, references to the notorious gangster Dawood Ibrahim frequently came up.[60]

At the time, this recurring pattern frustrated me. I had spent months tracking down these often elusive individuals, intending to solicit their reflections on Mumbai's infrastructure of security preparedness in a technological sense, only to be treated to a rambling account of their own personal views on which dangerous Other they deemed to be most menacing.[61] A few even suggested some background reading for me to come to terms with the real threats facing the city and the nation like that of SIMI. Some distance from these encounters, however, allowed me to understand that officers' recurring references to dangerous Others were in no way a distraction from my central concern about efforts to secure the city after 2008.

Their accounts of danger in the city were foundational to how these officials approached their work and what motivated their actions. Most obviously, their accounts reaffirmed the well-elaborated communal nature of the Mumbai police and the racialized, casteist, and classed imaginaries and agendas that animate its work. Particularly since the 1990s, the imaginative geographies of Hindutva representing Muslims as a dangerous and foreign presence have materialized in the physical landscape of the city through its ghettoization and fragmentation. Muslim-majority districts have been labeled as "Pakistan" and their residents as "Pakistanis" and "anti-nationals," resulting in fewer governmental resources being directed to these areas.[62] This has in turn produced systemic levels of poverty, poor health, lack of education, high crime rates, and consolidation of criminal networks, which legitimize more intensive policing of these same areas. For instance, Muslim-majority districts have higher density of police *chowkis* (police stations or outposts) than in Hindu areas and Muslim slums are often categorized and policed as "notorious areas."[63] In addition, the policing of Muslim-majority ghettoes like Nagpada, Byculla, Dongri, Kurla, Mira Road, Bhiwandi, and Mumbra is underpinned by dense networks of *khabris* (spies), working as informal arms of the local state.[64] The imaginative and material fragmentation and ghettoization of the city has not merely fallen along communal but also class and caste lines. Abdul Shaban has detailed the spatialization of Mumbai into three metaphorical spaces, namely "Hindustan," "Dalitsthan," and "Pakistan," with Dalits often forming "buffer zones" between higher-caste Hindus and Muslims.[65]

My conversations with police officers pointed to the fact that the bulk of their work centered on the biopolitical quotidian regulation of everyday life in the metropolis,[66] a task for which existing Indian policing infrastructures would do just fine. The above-cited WANTED posters illustrate this. The posters make it all too clear that the local state was and continues to be fixated on policing Muslim bodies and livelihoods as the quintessential "suspect community" threatening the city and the nation.[67] Indeed, the "marking of the Muslim population as suspect" has long been and remains the *sine qua non* of the Indian police.[68]

The growth of surveillance infrastructures in conjunction with networks of *khabris* has no doubt assisted in this xenophobic mission in Mumbai and across India.[69] But as the Yahoo and Gmail accounts listed on the wanted posters allude to, this persecution is not entirely contingent on new high-tech instruments of control and violence from the global homeland security industry. It unfolds with near-total impunity but also relative ease.[70] As Shaban notes, in light of the profound economic and social vulnerabilities that all minorities (but Muslims in particular) face in Mumbai, it has long been "easy to jail them and apply tough and draconian laws," whether TADA, POTA, or the Maharashtra Control of Organised Crime Act (MCOCA).[71] Mumbai schoolteacher Wahid Shaikh's harrowing personal account of his and others' wrongful conviction in the 2006 Mumbai blasts case[72] makes this all too clear. Seen in this light, the patchy, superficial, and broadly conservative nature of the response to 26/11 does not evidence a lack of capacity for state violence and is certainly no cause for celebration. Nor should we conclude that the symbolic and spectacular elements of the Maharashtra response to 26/11 are inconsequential.

The spectacle of police modernization programs and the engagement with Israel's homeland security industry have a rather different set of meanings in relation to Mumbai's Muslim community than they do to those who called for a "hard" response to the attacks, like "Israeli-style" airstrikes on Pakistan (chapter 1). Through the local state's engagements with Israel's homeland security industry after 2008, the imaginative geography of "cleansed space" was again reinscribed in the locality. These associations reinforced the already existing patterns of political subjugation and the Mumbai police's prejudicial attitudes and violence toward the city's minorities. And some of my interlocutors emphasized that the transnational influences on local police post-26/11 went beyond mere symbolism. When I asked the editor of a Mumbai Urdu newspaper about how the Israeli training of local police was received by Muslims in the city, he was unequivocal that "Mossad is involved" and he and other Muslim residents reacted negatively to this. "If an Israeli officer comes to give training or the Indian government goes to Israel for the training," he explained, "that is a negative thing" because the State of Israel is not merely a threat to Palestinians but to all Muslims. According to him, local police officials' engagements with Israelis could only but redouble their very well-elaborated anti-Muslim prejudices, impunity, and violence.

The Mumbai-based activists and human rights defenders whom I spoke with further elaborated these concerns. As Teesta Setalvad, a prominent Mumbai-based journalist and human rights activist told me, "We are being affected . . . by the *global* perception of the terror issue," which she suggested had a detrimental effect on local police agencies by reinforcing prejudicial and racist attitudes, particularly toward Muslims. She noted that Indian police authorities "don't necessarily look at the evidence on the ground after a terror attack" but instead tend to "operate with a preconceived belief that only a Muslim minority can do that." This tendency, she argued, is at least partly the result of India's deepening geostrategic partnerships with the United States, Israel, and the U.K. and the "cross-state nexus" between the antiterror wings of the police agencies from these foreign countries. As she explained, these prejudices in turn create biases within prosecutions of terror cases against Muslim youth while allowing Hindu terror groups to avoid prosecution.

While local police and government officials did their best to explain their engagements with Israel's homeland security industry as a dispassionate apolitical matter driven by the imperative to get "the best in the field" (chapter 3), I clearly touched a nerve when I asked D. Sivanandan how Mumbai's minorities received news of these initiatives. His tone quickly went from cagey to confrontational. "You can wonder yourself, because it is nothing connected with your research or anything like that. It's going ahead at that point of time and it was the right thing to do. Nobody, no Muslim, no Hindu ever asked questions!" He then declared the interview over, making it all too clear that my question was beyond the pale.

Of course, Muslims and others in the city of Mumbai and across India did ask questions about such matters and continue to (see the epilogue).[73] During my time in Mumbai, I spoke with a few local activists who have worked to unearth and mobilize against the connections between the Mumbai police and Israel, convinced like the Urdu editor that local authorities had a close and ongoing working relationship with Mossad. And there was certainly some reason to suspect as much. The ex-Mossad chief Danny Yatom, who criticized India's handling of 26/11 during the attacks (chapter 1), visited Mumbai in late 2009 to lobby on behalf of his own security advisory firm, which was reported in the Indian press.[74] I also found some evidence of local actors' enduring connections with elements of Israel's security industry. In 2013, I spoke with a Mumbai-based Indian private businessman. He claimed to have been involved in facilitating small arms deals between Israeli manufacturers and central Indian paramilitary forces, operating under the jurisdiction of India's MHA. The businessman had nothing but praise for Sivanandan, stressing that the former commissioner instantly grasped the value of Israeli homeland security solutions for Mumbai and "*never* said no to a meeting!" Likewise, Samuel Marshall, a well-established Jewish food commodity trader whose family immigrated to India from the U.K. in 1920, reportedly made some inroads into the homeland security business in India after 2008.[75]

As will become clear in the next chapter, the engagements between the state of Maharashtra and Israel's homeland security industry were less than seamless. As Sivanadan's terse response to my question further alludes to, those challenging state agendas face retribution in the form of threats, imprisonment, and other forms of state and vigilante violence. Shahid Azmi, a Mumbai lawyer who had been falsely convicted and incarcerated for terror-related offenses and then exonerated, became one of the most successful lawyers defending other wrongfully accused suspects in Indian terrorism cases. In 2010, Azmi was gunned down in his office. At the time, he was defending a suspect falsely accused in the plotting of

26/11. Setalvad, who led the charge in building a legal case against Narendra Modi for his central role in the 2002 Gujarat pogroms as the state's chief minister, has faced repeated charges, intimidation, and imprisonment since Modi's subsequent political rise in national politics. These types of overt violent silencing are also manifested in the broader patterns of segregation and political representation across Mumbai and Maharashtra. Around the time I conducted the first phase of my fieldwork in Mumbai, there was not a single sitting Muslim MP in Maharashtra, although Muslims represented 42.4% of Maharashtra's urban population.[76] In this sense, we might read anti-politics in a slightly different way to that explored in chapter 3, namely as the denial of the right *to* politics or right to the city.[77]

When situated in this broader context, it becomes clear the state's claims about police modernization were never *for* everyone and were likely treated by many with indifference from the outset. When I spoke with the editor of a local Marathi newspaper, he stressed that while middle classes and elites of Mumbai took to the streets after 26/11 to protest politicians' perceived negligence in protecting them, the city's poor instead "began to internalize what happened," viewing the attacks as yet another example of the fact that "this is the kind of life we have to live." As he pointed out, that approximately four thousand Mumbaikars die annually from rail accidents alone likely gave poor residents ample reason to be skeptical about the state's apparent newfound interest in homeland security. In other words, state officials' bold pledges that Mumbai would be secured were not a response to the general public but rather to certain sections of India's urban "civil society."[78]

During my travels on the suburban rail lines across the city, I found visual references to the endurance of the prosaic life-truncating dangers that the Marathi editor had mentioned as well as state efforts to police travelers' behavior in relation to these dangers. A series of posters affixed to suburban trains warned commuters to be vigilant against getting run over. One set of images portrayed individuals and families with small children attempting to cross the train tracks (Figure 4.13). Below a listed emergency help line it read: "Your life is invaluable not only for you but your family too. Please don't cross the railway line. This is dangerous and a legal offence." Another poster had a closeup picture of a man's face in a state of shock in

FIGURE 4.13: *Posters on suburban trains, Mumbai, 2012. Photo by the author.*

FIGURE 4.14: *Poster on suburban train, Mumbai, 2012. Photo by the author.*

three frames as he is run over by a train, with a call to act responsibly as well as warnings about dangers and potential punishment: "Be a responsible citizen. Don't cross the railway line and stop others from doing so. This is dangerous and a punishable offence" (Figure 4.14). Other messages seemed to defy any kind of "dialogue" with ordinary residents of the city. One sandbag bunker at CST had a message scribbled in English that read "PLEASE NO ENQUIRY." While the structure was ostensibly installed in order to project confidence, the message on it struck a notable contrast to the welcoming and apologetic tone of the signs at BSE. At the site where the vast majority of 26/11's less-than-glamorous victims lost their lives, commuters were told to carry on and specifically not to ask any questions.

CONCLUSION

This chapter traced how the police modernization program outlined in chapter 3 materialized in the city of Mumbai. Newly procured security equipment was integrated into the city's preexisting urban landscape, creating new visual representations of security and continuing to interpellate Mumbaikars as actors, active or passive, into the security state. Moreover, the police modernization program was woven together as a *fabric* of homeland security comprised of various constituent threads. This fabric, however, did not replace a preexisting fabric of policing. Rather, it came into being as an improvised and hybridized bricolage of old and new, high- and low-tech components. Through the specifically local practices of *jugaad,* these internationally inspired and sourced components were woven together into a patchy and sometimes questionable fabric of homeland security.

Importantly, I have highlighted how the police modernization program was woven into the city's existing infrastructure, an infrastructure that reminds us that Bombay/Mumbai is a colonial and postcolonial city that has long been imbricated with war. In doing so, I have challenged the implied temporarily of militarization (i.e., the movement from a nonmilitarized state to a militarized one).[79] My analysis goes beyond a critique of military aesthetics. I have endeavored to grapple with the martial in a political register, which addresses the particular ways in which military aesthetics are mobilized in police power to pacify publics and govern dangerous classes, yet without treating these dynamics as exceptional—geographically or temporally.

In this chapter, I have further contested the implicit teleology embedded in the notion of militarization by qualifying the extent to which the initial political impulse to modernize local police infrastructure in the image of homeland security has been sustained over time. I have drawn attention to the fickle and fleeting political commitment to projecting an image of radical reform under the banner of modernization. This is what Jayant Patil's above references to "survival" alludes to: namely, the political imperative to do just enough to subvert calls for structural change, including potentially the programs of police professionalization historically undertaken by forces in the Global North.[80] Thus, we might read the *jugaad*-like qualities of the police modernization program as physical manifestations of Vanaik's paradox (see the introduction), namely the limited interest in developing a professional police force by Indian politicians and key sections of the capitalist class, despite their enduring reliance on structures of violent repression.

This returns us to questions about the corruption, politicization, and coloniality of Indian policing as barriers to transformation through reform. References to a combination of the corruption, politicization, and coloniality of the Indian state are the principal way in which mainstream Indian policy commentators and journalists explain the key dynamics discussed in this chapter as well as the broader durability of the colonial policing structures since Independence. This resonates with my findings to some extent. As I have shown, the purchase of overpriced and defective equipment seems readily explicable by the corruption of senior police officers and leading ministers in the Maharashtra government. Likewise, the political imperative to act swiftly led to the procurement of weapons and equipment without careful strategic planning. The coloniality of Indian policing is undeniable, with key continuities of the Raj's "colonial terror" enduring after Independence in 1947.[81] It is precisely the endurance of this structure that has produced the tentative, provisional, and contingent nature of Indian policing, manifesting in the patchy and uneven nature of Mumbai's policing infrastructure. Yet this state of affairs cannot be understood as a lack or an absence but instead represents a key element of what Zoha Waseem calls the "post-colonial condition of policing."[82] Here the notion of *jugaad* helpfully brings together questions about political corruption with the profoundly violent and authoritarian but also questionable nature of police power in India today through its dual connotations as productive and constraining.[83]

We should not conclude that nothing at all happened after 26/11 or that the prevailing durability of the already-existing police infrastructures and logics is somehow insignificant. Rather, I argue it is evidence of what Gilmore calls "the changing same" in the sense that the reformist project of police modernization in Maharashtra post-26/11 has politically mobilized military aesthetics as visual signifiers of radical transformation as a deliberate political strategy to preserve the preexisting status quo and redouble its violent foundations. Perhaps most important is how the project of fabricating homeland security in Mumbai—though styled as transformational change through a language of modernization—has served to entrench the long-standing policing of Muslim bodies and livelihoods as the quintessential suspect community in both material and ideological registers.

CODA

I returned to Mumbai in late 2019. Some aspects of the early physical response to 26/11 were still in place. The long line of *nakabandi* remained at the Gateway of India, as did the scanners at CST and Churchgate. Likewise, luxury hotels like the Oberoi and Taj remained heavily fortified. In some cases, the visible markers of modern homeland security had since multiplied. For instance, the number of visible surveillance cameras had grown considerably at CST since I left the city in 2013. As I walked around Colaba, I noticed a contingent of NSG vehicles passing by the Taj, with a personnel carrier and jeeps and long ladders strapped to the roof of one of the jeeps. Likewise, at the BSE, there were still a number of permanently stationed police personnel on site and a large truck hand-painted with camouflage and MUMBAI POLICE emblazoned in large white lettering on its side adjacent to a now-faded sign bearing the words "sorry for the inconvenience." Nariman House had been completely renovated as a memorial to 26/11's victims, which opened to the public in November 2019. The building had also been heavily fortified with surveillance cameras looking over the narrow alleyway below.

During this visit, I followed up with a local journalist. He confirmed that the CCTV scheme had been completed in two phases of five thousand cameras each. He also noted that other less visible surveillance projects had been put into place, for instance a plan requiring local shopkeepers to install cameras in their buildings, the footage from which could be monitored in a centralized police control room. The Mumbai police has also embedded new antiterror cells at all ninety-three local police stations with dedicated personnel in ways that seemed to directly challenge officers' insistence of some categorical distinction between security and law and order policing.[84] As large-scale protests unfolded in Mumbai and across India over the Citizenship Amendment Act (CAA) in late December 2019, new surveillance capabilities like facial recognition software were also being put to work, resulting in mass arrests and the deportation of some foreigners across India.[85]

Other dimensions of the physical security infrastructure that were once prominently displayed between 2012 and 2013, however, had receded from public view. The Marksman jeeps that had been prominently displayed in front of CST and behind the Taj with armed officers standing by were no longer present at these sites. Likewise, virtually all the sandbag outposts around CST with their armed police personnel had since been removed. Other elements had shifted in purpose and/or location. At the anti-CAA protests in Mumbai, Marksman jeeps were used for crowd control with armed officers standing on the back bumpers of the vehicles to get a better view of the crowd passing by.

Other physical structures previously installed around the city had undergone modification in a highly improvised *jugaad*-like fashion. At the BSE and Bombay High Court some of the sandbag structures had been replaced with more permanent bunkers built with brick or stone; some were covered with marble with surveillance cameras installed overhead. At the BSE, meanwhile, although certain parts of the BGI perimeter security system like the yellow gates and retractable bollards remained intact as before, the BGI logos stamped on the bollards had been erased. On one of my visits to the site, I observed contractors taking apart the structures and modifying them with handheld metal grinders (Figures 4.15a and b). Although the system had been purchased to project an image of modern homeland security at the center of India's financial capital, in the intervening decade its respective Israeli-ness vs. Indian-ness had become an open question.

FIGURES 4.15A AND B: *BGI bollards being modified, Bombay Stock Exchange, Mumbai, 2019. Photos by the author.*

FIVE

ENCOUNTERING DIFFERENCE

> Israel's long experience in training, equipping, and operating elite undercover units deployed in Palestinian towns and villages to gather intelligence, spot targets, and engage Palestinian gunmen, is useful for the Indian security forces facing similar situations in Kashmir and the Northeast. Other areas where Israeli know-how can be incorporated by India include tactics aimed at lowering the risk of ambush, use of infantry and commando units seeking out and destroying arms caches and terrorist bomb-making capabilities, and the use of dogs, robotics, and specially trained sappers to detect hidden roadside mines. [. . .]
>
> [But] There are differences of perception between India and Israel on the issue of terrorism. [. . .] Another issue has to do with the way in which terrorism is handled. While India can learn much from Israel's tackling of terrorism within its borders and sponsored by regional adversaries, there are limits to how far India sees Israel's strategy as a viable one. It views Israel's tough policy toward contentious neighbors and the Palestinians as an approach which has not brought peace and security, but has rather served to entrench hatred in the Arab world. As such, many Indians believe the strategy is not a model for their own situation.
>
> —Harsh V. Pant, "India-Israel Partnership: Convergence and Constraints"

INTRODUCTION

The Indian foreign policy scholar Harsh V. Pant wrote the passage quoted in the epigraph above in a 2004 article published in the journal *MERIA: The Middle East Review of International Affairs*.[1] We briefly met Pant in chapter 1, where he argued for increased Indo-Israeli counterterrorism cooperation in a January 2009 *Jerusalem Post* op-ed. To make this claim, he used the first paragraph of the above 2004 excerpt word for word. Yet, in the original article, Pant voiced considerable skepticism about whether

Israeli counterterrorism offered a model *for* India. Among other things, Pant cited the intractable differences in perceptions and practices of counterterrorism between the two countries as a core impasse. Pant was not the first to draw attention to the role of difference as an impediment to export of the Israeli security model to India and certainly will not be the last.[2] As we saw in chapter 3, Vappala Balachandran explained that Israeli security approaches could not be "transplanted" to India because of core differences in the character of the two countries' respective publics.

On the face of it, these references to differences as impediments to counterterrorism collaboration seem intuitive enough. After all, India and Palestine/Israel are in many indisputable ways *different,* in terms of size and scale and religious, ethnic, and linguistic makeup as well as material conditions such as levels of wealth and industrialization. Yet, upon closer inspection, the problem becomes less straightforward. Israel's and India's common and connected histories of British colonization have profoundly shaped structures of policing, warfare, governance, and legal regimes in both contexts. These histories have also produced significant homologies between Palestine/Israel and India, in the sense of correspondence of certain type or structure—though not always function—between things.[3] These include common legal structures and logics in India and Palestine/Israel. For instance, India's UAPA and Israel's Counter-Terror Law both employ similar instruments (including administrative detention and movement restrictions) as well as definitions, which have their origins in colonial-era emergency legislation.[4] Such laws also fit within corresponding architectures of racism in both contexts, owing in large measure to shared legacies of partition, which define citizens in contradistinction to various racialized Others.[5]

These regimes have produced the historical and enduring presence of large disenfranchised and displaced Muslim and Indigenous populations in both contexts, which are routinely targeted by state violence. Despite India's and Israel's misleading exceptionalist democratic claims (Israel as the supposed "only democracy in the Middle East" and India as the "biggest democracy in the world"), in practice both operate as effective ethnostates or, in Azad Essa's terminology, as "hostile homelands."[6] Thus, while taking seriously the many and significant differences between Palestine/

Israel and India, Pant's references to difference cannot be taken at face value. Rather, we need to approach them within the contours of nationalist projects and the frame of comparative geopolitics. As previous chapters have argued, comparative references to difference are (geo)political acts that do various forms of political work for empire, capital, and nationalist projects alike.

This chapter focuses on the roles that difference played in efforts to fabricate (Israeli) homeland security in India after 26/11. In critical scholarship on security regimes and the global war on terror, attention to difference in terms of civilizational reasoning and racial Othering has long and rightly been a core concern. Attention to other roles and forms of difference, however, have received limited attention, albeit with important exceptions.[7] For instance, drawing on Edward Said's frames of geographical imagination and contrapuntal analysis,[8] Rupal Oza elaborates on how fighting the common specter of "Islamic" terrorism has brought India into a triad with the United States and Israel.[9] Such accounts also crucially explain the reversal of India's pro-Palestinian stance and Israel's emergence as India's leading weapons supplier.[10] While making some space for thinking about difference across space and time, these accounts concentrate on how India has been folded into the dominating discourse of U.S. empire. As such, they do not tell us much about how forms of historical differences and local specificities are at play in the transnational fabrication of security projects.

Responding to this gap, I seek to write difference back into the stories that we tell about hegemonic projects like capital, empire, development, security, and the like. More specifically, I explore what happened to difference when Israeli homeland security officials encountered India as an actual place rather than just as an object of analysis and ridicule. Drawing on interviews with Israeli trade and marketing representatives, experts, advisors, weapons dealers, and police trainers as well as Maharashtra police officers and government officials, I focus on three sets of encounters between these actors: the 2009 official delegation visit by the Maharashtra government to Palestine/Israel; post-2008 Israeli trainings of police in Maharashtra; and business dealings between Israeli security firms and Indian state and nonstate actors. Through my analysis of these worldly encounters, I pay particular attention to their contingencies, including their indeterminate and unpredictable nature and the kinds of conflict and struggle at work therein. I show how my informants routinely explained the contingencies and contestations through references to difference. Thus, this chapter is an attempt to think through the work that difference performs in transnational pacification projects and on whose terms.

Extending Dipesh Chakrabarty's notion of "the politics of difference," I argue that we need to pay attention to difference in order to recover the ways that incommensurable social orders endure alongside hegemonic projects.[11] Doing so enables us to grapple with how references to difference are at work in hegemonic projects of western modernity, yet in a way that refuses to fully abide by these forms of reasoning. References to difference have long been central to upholding western modernity as a universalist project by explaining difference away and Othering it. Partha Chatterjee captures this tendency through what he calls the "rule of colonial difference."[12] More specifically, the rule of colonial difference enshrined the universality principle of modern government through the objectification of the colonized as the exceptional Other, often through racial signification.[13] While the rule of colonial difference emerged out of colonization, importantly it is not merely at work in rigidly defined colonial situations. Rather, the rule of colonial difference endures in multiple situations and forms. As I show in this chapter, Israeli security peddlers all treated India as a backward place with impoverished and feminized inhabitants deemed by them to be lacking in modern rationality. Furthermore, their own racialized, gendered, and classed "ideologies of difference" profoundly shaped their encounters with Indians.[14] This reflects Israeli officials' historic contempt for the impoverished peoples of the Global South and echoes longstanding colonial discourses about the applicability of modern regimes of power vis-à-vis the colonized.[15] Thus, the rule of colonial difference remains at play in the contemporary politics of security.

However, the rule of colonial difference also shapes struggles over identity in the contemporary world as the basis of what Chatterjee calls "postcolonial difference."[16] As I illustrate below, the engagements between Israelis and Indians did not merely play out within the parameters and conventions of the rule of colonial difference (i.e., on the Israelis' terms).

They were also profoundly shaped by currents in Indian nationalist thought and practice, namely the dual desire to selectively assimilate certain aspects of western culture seen as efficient and desirable such as technological prowess and combine them with the spiritual greatness of the East.[17] Here it is useful to recall Christophe Jaffrelot's crucial observation that the emergence of Indian nationalist thought broadly and Hindutva doctrine in particular "resulted from an ambivalent reaction to the West and Islam." He points out that although Hindu nationalists "imitated features of the Other—to whom they attributed superiority," they did so "in order to resist the Other more effectively rather than become like the Other."[18]

This is Jaffrelot's "strategic syncretism," a term employed to denote that the content of Hindutva ideology derives in large measure from material appropriated from the cultural values of groups seen as adversaries of the Hindu community, situating the production of Hindu nationalist ideology as a process principally devised to "vindicate a threatened culture."[19] The encounters that this chapter surveys are structured by this underlying ambivalence about the terms of mimesis between India and the West and the simultaneous imperative to vindicate "Indian-ness" through forms of relationality.

Thus, the *politics of* (post)colonial difference refers to the multiple, elastic, and sometimes contradictory ways in which difference is deployed in asserting claims to identity, nationhood, sovereignty, and authority. As Homi Bhabha notes, "the representation of difference is [. . .] always also a problem of authority."[20] It must also be emphasized that the terms and boundaries of the politics of (post)colonial difference are never settled one way or the other. While informed by particular histories and ideologies (colonial, anticolonial, and postcolonial), their terms and boundaries remain uncertain and subject to ongoing renegotiation. This is what the parentheses around the (post) in (post)colonial are intended to signify. Moreover, references to difference reflect how (post)colonial differences are at play in the negotiations of multiple *reals* in the sense of different forms of the social but also to incommensurable orders or worlds. As I elaborate below, there are not just multiple reals but also multiple *kinds* of difference at work in the politics of (post)colonial difference, although they do merge and overlap. Some of the most obvious relate to forms of culture and/or (national) identity, whereas others relate to human and physical geographies such as demographics, landscapes, and climatic conditions. Others are more squarely ideological, both colonial/imperial as well as nationalist.

By tracing the encounters between representatives of Israel's homeland security industry and Indian officials after 2008, this chapter opens space for a consideration of more disruptive forms of difference to enter into discussions of global pacification regimes. The point of this chapter is to reflect on what grappling with difference enables, both conceptually and politically. Writing difference (back) into the stories that we tell about capital, empire, and globalization means engaging with how these projects seek to hierarchically organize and govern places and populations. But it also requires grappling with the forms of incommensurability that structure and sometimes interfere with these same projects. This in turn bears on how we think about global power. In the case of this particular story, writing difference (back) in changes the terms through which we think about the basis of the power that Israel's homeland security industry commands. Rather than appearing coherent and all-powerful, analytic attention to the multiple roles difference played in this industry's encounters with India and Indians reveals the contingency of the authority it commands. Thinking difference more carefully further raises questions about the natures and presumed universality of human subjectivity, a theme I return to in chapter 6.

SHOWCASING ISRAELI HOMELAND SECURITY

As elaborated in previous chapters, the IEICI organized an official Maharashtra government delegation to visit Palestine/Israel in July 2009.[21] The delegation was led by newly appointed Mumbai police commissioner D. Sivanandan and accompanied by the Additional Chief Secretary (Home) Chandra Iyengar and a number of police officials: Deputy Inspector General of Police (Force One) S. Jagannathan, Deputy Commissioner of Police Nisar Tamboli, Superintendent of Police Rajesh Pradhan, and Inspector General of Police P. K. Jain.[22] Over the course of five days in early July 2009, the team toured Palestine/Israel, visiting Jerusalem to meet the city's police chief and visit a local police training center. Members also attended several events such as a seminar on "Secure Cities" in Tel Aviv, visited the port of Ashdod, and undertook "field visits" to Ben Gurion Airport and to the headquarters of Israeli companies that manufacture security technologies.[23] After the visit, it was reported that the delegation team drafted a report with a list of recommendations to Maharashtra's home ministry "for simulation of the Israeli experience" in Maharashtra (chapter 3).[24]

In keeping with Israel's status as the world's homeland security showroom, both organizers and participants suggested that the primary objective of the delegation was to "showcase" Israeli homeland security approaches. Guy Zuri, the former director of the Aerospace, Defense, and Homeland Security Technology Industries Division at IEICI, played a central role in organizing the delegation visit. When we spoke at IEICI headquarters in a shiny office tower in Tel Aviv in 2012, Zuri situated the delegation as part of the IEICI's broader efforts to "penetrate" the Indian internal security market, efforts that began in 2007. He recalled that the tour involved a mix of different activities from official meetings with Israeli police and government agencies, multiple days of business meetings, "industry days," and a "live demonstration of Israeli technology." All these activities, he claimed, are typical for such official visits by foreign governments. As he understood it, the Maharashtra team "came to Israel to learn" and thereby get "a set of knowledge" for "fighting terror" and "establishing the right homeland security solutions."

Yet, as he stressed, the Israeli hosts as well as their Indian counterparts also understood the delegation visit as a "business opportunity" to showcase Israeli companies and their products to a wider array of potential Indian customers. Zuri suggested that the visit proved "very interesting" and fruitful, in part because there was a general understanding of at least some common (domestic) security challenges facing India and Israel, respectively. As he explained, like Israel, India is "facing a big terror problem" at its borders but also within its territory, thereby giving Indians the impression that they "can learn from us [Israelis]." Yet, echoing Pant's trepidations about competing "perceptions," he qualified that Indians "also feel that they are facing some different [threats]" than those experienced by Israelis. Zuri, moreover, was quick to point out that what happened after the delegation left was out of the IEICI's hands. Once the initial "matchmaking" phase (i.e., the delegation visit itself) was over, he noted, the Israeli security companies would be more or less on their own as they "took it to the next step" and worked out their projects with Indian clients.

The highly suggestive metaphors that Zuri used to describe the delegation visit are neither new nor incidental. Efforts to promote conventional weapons sales from Israel to India have also long relied on similar terms of reference. A 2009 promotional video from the Israeli weapons firm Rafael depicts an Israeli man donning sunglasses and a leather jacket dancing with multiple Indian women and singing in highly sexualized and gendered language in front of phallic objects adorned with jasmine flowers, pledging to build a durable geopolitical partnership. While gazing into the Israeli man's eyes, one woman sings, "I need to feel safe and sheltered, secure and protected." The Israeli man in turn promises "to defend you, fulfil your expectations, shield you and support you, [and] meet my obligations."[25]

Members of the Maharashtra delegation recalled the experience in broadly similar terms to those of Zuri and evidenced a partial willingness to consider entering into the kinds of "matches" that the IEICI sought to make. Like Zuri, they framed the visit's significance in terms of "showcasing" Israel's homeland security industry as well as specific kinds of technologies, weapons, and systems. As Rahul, a senior IPS officer, summarized: "Basically it was a showcasing of Israel: they [the Israelis] wanted to showcase their equipment, their Safe City concept." Rahul explained that he and the other delegation participants "just wanted to see firsthand. . . what kinds of things they [Israelis] have to offer," because Israel is "one of the largest sellers of equipment across the world" and was "one place where *everything* could be showcased."

The encounters, which took place through this showcasing, nurtured a sense of commonality between the urban security "problems" of India and Israel, respectively. When I asked Rahul what struck him as particularly relevant for Mumbai, he recalled seeing videos and photos of Jerusalem that depicted "skirmishes between Muslims and Jews" and the kinds of tactics and equipment used to manage them. As he remarked, "This is all relevant to our cities also; we have similar kinds of problems here [in Mumbai/India]." In this sense, Rahul agreed with Zuri that both parties had a shared understanding of certain domestic threats facing Israel and India, respectively, thereby opening some possibilities for collaboration to manage such problems and reinscribing the racialized specter of a (common) Muslim Other threating both countries (see also chapters 3 and 4).

Maharashtra delegation participants were impressed by what they found in Palestine/Israel. They portrayed their experiences in an overwhelmingly positive light, stressing that traveling there offered the opportunity to experience successful security systems in action. One participant remarked: "Israel is very impressive. Their training . . . is very systematic. I found the whole thing very impressive." The Indian officials were not merely impressed by Israeli homeland security, however. Experiencing it firsthand reified both its exceptional status and its specificity in contradistinction to India's *lack* of homeland security. As Rahul explained: "You see, Israel is one of the safest countries surrounded by enemies all around so they have to survive and they [do] survive. Their security system is one of the most foolproof I've found and I experienced it there." Rahul went on to emphasize that the Israelis "had these systems in place . . . which we don't have . . . [in India] at all. . . . So you could see them *in action.*" Rahul further explained that seeing this firsthand was critical in transforming Israeli security systems from mere abstractions into tangible entities, stressing that "seeing was believing." In other words, for the Maharashtra delegation participants, experiencing Palestine/Israel through firsthand encounters consolidated Israel's status as an exemplary model of and convenient one-stop shop for all things homeland security.

The delegation also shaped participants' visions for police procurement and policymaking. Rahul stressed that it was through the knowledge gained from such foreign excursions that "you are able to analyze and assess their [Israel's] equipment" and clarify "what you exactly . . . have in mind." This, he argued, "gives you more perspective" for updating Indian counterterror strategies, the kinds of technologies to be procured, and the general desirability of a more modernized police infrastructure. He claimed that experiencing Israeli systems firsthand gave him the impression that India might be able to import some Israeli technologies and that if they did so, India would "certainly be much more efficient and much more capable" in its fight against terrorism and other ongoing threats. Rahul even suggested that the experience sparked discussions about potential security infrastructure projects, including the CCTV scheme that was rolled out in Mumbai in the years after 2009 (chapter 4).

Despite their unequivocally positive impressions of Israel as having exceptionally "foolproof" security systems, Maharashtra participants generally framed the "lessons and borrowings" they derived from the visit in broad platitudes.[26] When I asked Sivanandan if there was something that particularly impressed him during the visit, he responded: "No, they [the Israelis] were very good. That's it. They were very good." Indeed, the delegation participants' accounts were most striking for their circularity. Through my conversations with these officials, it became apparent that the most important lesson that they all came away with was the underlying premise of their visit, namely that Israel is the undisputed global leader in homeland security. Some Maharashtra officials went further, stressing that the delegation's purpose and significance were not about finding a *solution* to anything but rather something less tangible. When I asked one participant whether there was something particularly impressive about the Israeli homeland security "solutions" observed during the tour, they responded: "There are no *solutions*. . . . It's a question of how . . . in a situation like this in these issues [of terrorism], what is your preparedness, how are you prepared?" This response troubled the publicly declared purpose of the visit in 2009 as a first step toward replicating an "Israeli approach" to or "model" of homeland security in Mumbai as a practical strategy for preventing future attacks in the city.

Some Maharashtra officials concluded that Israel's security prowess rested on certain cultural or structural attributes specific to the Israeli state and society. According to them, this meant that Israeli approaches could not be literally transferred to Maharashtra/India. As Rahul explained of Israel, "Their [security] systems are slightly better [than India's] because their policy is different [and] their people are different. Their people are more security conscious [than Indians] because they have been fighting a war ever since they're born." Sivanandan, who had publicly lauded the Israeli model and advocated for the adoption of Israeli solutions (chapter 3), expressed deep skepticism about its underlying relevance to Mumbai. As he bluntly put it: "Israel is only 7 million [in] population; [in India] we are talking about 1.2 billion people! The Israeli model will [therefore] not be applicable to India." Thus, rather than reading the Israeli homeland security model as a universal standard and "thing" to be exported or emulated, as the Israeli architects of the delegation had presumably hoped, Maharashtra officials seemed to deduce that Israel's homeland security exceptionality was culturally and historically specific and tied to place, making it both *im*mobile and radically out of place in Maharashtra/India. In these senses, at least, Rahul and Sivanandan seemed to take Israel's claims to exceptionality quite literally. Difference was viewed as an impediment to, rather than the basis of, Israel's universality. Such portrayals echo longstanding currents in Indian strategic thought, which explicitly reference material differences between Israel and India and the "special character" of Israel as impediments to collaboration on counterterrorism with India.[27]

Maharashtra officers further challenged the commensurability of conditions of life in Palestine/Israel vis-à-vis India and the accordant relevance of Israeli homeland security solutions. Both Rahul and Sivanandan were quick to point out that despite *some* common security problems (like unruly urban Muslims), the sheer scale of India made its challenges fundamentally different from those faced by Israel. This raised questions about the utility of some of the Israeli systems in relation to India. Rahul noted that "some of the things we have seen" in Palestine/Israel "would be a problem" to implement in India because of radical differences in population size. He emphasized that "the numbers in our country are humongous and the crowds that we have we didn't see anywhere in Israel, or anywhere in the world." Thus, while their visit to Palestine/Israel clearly confirmed to Maharashtra officials that Israel is an exemplar of homeland security, they seemed to be rather less convinced that replicating Israeli approaches in India was necessary or practically possible.

Maharashtra officials' encounters with the showcasing of Israeli homeland security reinforced core terms of colonial difference upon which the delegation was predicated. To some extent, it also abided by imperial conventions of modeling and exceptionalist narratives. Israeli difference was reified and re-produced as technological exceptionalism, which included hierarchies of knowledge and authority as well as the idea of potential common urban security problems between Israel and India. Yet Maharashtra officials' impressions of Palestine/Israel also called into question the notion of Israeli exceptionality as the basis of universality by representing Israeli difference-as-parochiality. The officials suggested that the relevance of anything they saw in Palestine/Israel to Mumbai/Maharashtra was at best an open question; it would need to be determined after the visit had come to an end.

As Rahul recalled, after the delegation concluded, he and his colleagues drafted and submitted their final report to the Maharashtra government. He noted that the broad strokes of the report suggested that the security systems "are working very fine in Israel and there is no harm in trying some of them" in Mumbai. "But then," he continued, "whenever the trials are given, we tell the vendors to come and demonstrate the abilities in India." Rahul explained that he and other Indian officials were "not concerned with how your system performs [. . .] *there*." Rather, they wanted to see how they work on the ground in a tropical climate and conditions radically unlike those found in such foreign countries like Israel, the U.K. or the United States. This, he suggested, required that foreign vendors like the Israelis "have to come and showcase their capability in *my* country." While these references to difference point to material distinctions between India and Palestine/Israel, they are also much more than this. They also reflect the historical and enduring Indian ambivalence to the western Other, echoing the partial credulity to foreign counterterrorism models expressed by K.P.S. Gill (introduction) and B. Raman (interlude). In the next section, I explore how these demonstrations and trainings played out. The reservations of some Maharashtra officials about the utility of Israeli homeland security approaches would prove to be more than hypothetical. Other sites of friction also emerged.

ON THE GROUND

Beginning in 2009, Indian media reported that Israelis were training special units in the Mumbai and Maharashtra police. By speaking with Israeli actors and Indian senior officers who were directly involved in or familiar with these activities, I got a sense of the texture of these encounters and what, if anything, they produced. Certain Maharashtra officials mentioned specific contributions from the Israeli trainers who worked with local forces. One former officer spoke of Israeli trainers' expertise in "built-up area intervention" for hostage rescue and disaster management as well as some "good practices" in shooting and training in the Israeli martial art *Krav Maga*. Likewise, Rahul noted that Israeli and other foreign trainers taught the Maharashtra police how to prepare themselves for "urban warfare." When I spoke with a high-ranking officer in Maharashtra's ATS, he maintained that the single most important post-2008 development was the rise of "mental preparedness" among police officers, which he saw as a matter of developing a new sense of "confidence." Such confidence, he argued, was a direct outcome of the expertise, SOPs, equipment, and training imparted by the Israelis and other foreign experts. Another senior officer similarly emphasized that foreign trainers helped units in the Maharashtra and Mumbai police to develop mock drills, simulations, and other "actually-faced scenarios" from real-life experiences in the field. Echoing themes from chapters 3 and 4, he argued this helped to "build confidence" in the newly created local anti-terror units and improve overall levels of security preparedness against future terrorist attacks.

Israeli officials who engaged with the Maharashtra police agreed with key aspects of these accounts. They suggested that their encounters had been generally productive and to some extent improved security preparedness in Mumbai. Leo Gleser was all too happy to take credit for building up Force One, noting that "we developed there [in Mumbai] one of the first units of counterterrorism." He further emphasized that Force One was able to cultivate some "very good people" and that overall, India's approach to managing the threat of terrorism had improved over the decade since 26/11: "I think that India today is different" than in 2008 and unmistakably for the better. Gleser further qualified that modern homeland security preparedness was not something that could simply be brought to India on a moment's notice: "I think *that* takes time."

However, Indian actors' accounts of foreign training troubled the idea that Israeli expertise, models, and/or solutions could be smoothly transferred from one location to another. As we have seen above, some delegation participants questioned whether or in what sense the Israeli model was even relevant to Mumbai/India, suggesting that radical differences in scale, societal makeup, and culture placed constraints around the importation of certain Israeli approaches and technologies. Some Maharashtra officers claimed that these barriers could be overcome by adapting the insights of Israelis and other foreign experts to the Indian context. As Aditya, a retired high-ranking officer in the Maharashtra police, pointed out, "Whatever expertise you acquire abroad, unless you can assimilate and adapt it to Indian conditions, your unit will never be successful." Aditya further emphasized that "it is *not* that we adopted the whole [Israeli] training." In other words, he suggested that Israeli and other foreign forms of knowledge had to be indigenized in order to make them compatible with India's radically different scale and conditions like population, climate, and cultural makeup, making reference to the challenge of "translating"[28] and "indigenizing"[29] security projects across space.

But as these officers explained this adaptation, it became increasingly clear that they meant highly partial and selective application or even *non*-application of their newly acquired knowledges. A senior Maharashtra officer tellingly emphasized that, even after foreign trainers were gone, "you can [still] decide which to follow and which *not* to follow." Sivanandan, who had retired from the police and become chairman of the private security consultancy firm Sucurus First, explained that foreign experts and sales agents "come on their own as a private people [. . .] trying to sell their wares so you can select what you like" and that "it's not that we [Indians] *have to* get influenced by them and go buy from them."

While maintaining that the Israelis and other foreign experts and trainers were welcomed and proved useful, all of the Maharashtra officers with whom I spoke underscored their own credentials, authority, and sovereignty. They were adamant that the foreign training that local officers received did not displace or replace *Indian* approaches or models. According to them, Israeli and other foreign trainers merely supplemented the roles of Indian trainers from the Indian Army and national paramilitary bodies like the NSG. All categorically rejected any suggestion that a foreign model—Israeli or otherwise—had been taken up by the Maharashtra state and the Mumbai city police. When I asked a senior IPS officer in the Maharashtra police about the previously reported use of an Israeli model in building up Force One, he replied: "We don't have any such model.

Our models are Indian!" These Maharashtra officials consistently stressed that getting foreign expertise did not mean giving foreign actors free rein to define how things should be done; Indian officials were in control and determined the terms of engagement.

Even officers who suggested that adaptation was key to making foreign expertise useful acknowledged that this outcome was not always possible. Aditya explained that when Israeli experts arrived in Mumbai to train local forces, they showed him and other officers a training video. The video, he said, depicted a scenario in which a terrorist suspect with an Arab appearance was intercepted by security personnel just before carrying out a grenade attack in Tel Aviv. Aditya recalled that he had serious doubts about the utility of this approach in Indian conditions, because "the scale, the magnitude, [and] the numbers [in India] are *very* daunting." He then asked the Israeli trainer to accompany him to CST at rush hour. Aditya laughed as he recalled that immediately upon observing the scene at CST, the Israeli trainer told him: "I withdraw my remarks. These things won't work here." In this narrative, difference was thus cited as a fundamental, irreconcilable impediment to the utility of Israeli homeland security approaches in the Indian context.

Some Israeli security officials made similar references to difference as impediments to collaboration. Gleser qualified the limitations of what ISDS was ultimately able to impart to his Indian police counterparts by citing core differences between India and Israel in population and society. He emphasized that "India is big. [. . .] It is a very big country and [has] a lot of people." Echoing Aditya's above impressions of Israeli society and security systems as irreducibly different, Gleser further noted the importance of societal and ideational barriers, stressing that "our [Israeli] society and the Indian society are very different, *very* different." He referenced the lack of a general familiarity of handling modern firearms in India as compared to Israel, suggesting that this placed limits on what he could achieve in working with special forces there. Invoking colonial stereotypes of Indians as quintessentially weak and effeminate, Gleser explained that few officers in India had experience carrying weapons and that even the officers who *were* armed "are so old" and therefore "not efficient" at providing armed responses to specific emergencies. Gleser, however, was not simply content to agree with his Maharashtra counterparts that contextual differences placed boundaries around what they could achieve through working together and leave it at that. Nor did he frame such difficulties as a threat to his carefully crafted public persona as a macho, globe-trotting "Jewish cowboy."[30] Rather, he attempted to Other these frictions as evidence of Indian difference in the sense of ignorance or backwardness. He complained that Maharashtra authorities proved unwilling to purchase all the "good equipment" that ISDS had recommended, resulting in considerable limitations of their levels of preparedness.

Some Maharashtra officials, however, poked holes in the basis of Israeli claims to authority and its implicit hierarchy. Rahul maintained that the various foreign trainers (including the Israelis) who arrived after 2008 to assist local forces were all roughly similar and interchangeable. He recalled that "after 26/11 a lot of people across the world came to help us: the Americans came, the U.K. fellows came, the Israelis were willing to train" the local forces. While the foreign trainers were supposed to embody and exemplify their respective national essences and exceptional qualities, Rahul and his colleagues' experiences of their training suggested otherwise. As Rahul recalled, after having gone through a training course, he and other fellow officers concluded that the various forms of foreign training were interchangeable. "The training" as he put it, "is the same, basically. [. . .] You know, almost 90 percent they're the same: 5–10 percent there could be a difference in various organizations across the world." Thus, foreign trainers proved unable to demonstrate their uniqueness from one another. This prompted Rahul to suggest that foreign trainers (including the Israelis) were less than forthcoming about their *real* secrets, noting that "no government or [. . .] agency shares 100 percent with any other [foreign] agency."

In addition to being all roughly similar to each other, Rahul further suggested that Israelis and other foreign trainers were not radically different from Indian experts and trainers who also provided training to the Maharashtra police after 2008. "Whatever they shared," he noted of these foreign trainers, "we found that there was hardly any difference with what we're doing [in India]." The only things that really made the foreign forces truly exceptional, according to him, was that "they had better *systems* and better *equipment.*" Rahul concluded that although these powerful foreign countries and their special forces were indeed more efficient than their Indian counterparts, this stemmed from how these foreign forces were organized and equipped rather than from specialized tactics, expertise, or skills unavailable in India. The Israelis and other foreign experts proved unable, in Rahul's terminology, to convincingly "demonstrate the[ir] abilities in India," both in the sense of their relevance but also in terms of their uniqueness, value added, or necessity. Thus, whereas Aditya had stressed that some of the Israeli advice and tactics were inapplicable to material conditions in Maharashtra, Rahul highlighted foreign experts' lack of uniqueness and stressed the different resources between rich and poor countries. Rahul thereby refused to be Othered on the terms of colonial difference.

In my conversations with some of the Israelis involved in these interactions, I found striking traces of these Maharashtra officers' unwillingness to treat Israeli actors deferentially and commit to them as well as the rifts that this lack of deference produced. Gleser stressed that Indian authorities did not always accept his advice as readily as he might have expected. Based on this experience, he concluded that "the Indian mentality is not a simple one," stressing that India "is not an easy country to work [with]." Avi, the Israeli trainer we met in chapter 2, had worked with Force One as well as a number of other police training projects in India until around 2013. Avi was less restrained in his criticisms. He called out Indians' strange "attitude" and suggested that they were not exactly straightforward to deal with. When I asked him about this experience working in India, he remarked: "Indians are very complicated persons. Very. . . . Their attitude to life is different than us [Israelis]. First of all, they don't like to pay. Then they think that they can copy you. After five minutes they . . . take someone [else, i.e., another consultant/trainer . . .] and start work. Crazy stuff!" He went on: "That's why Israeli people don't like to go" to India to do work on domestic security. Some minutes later in our conversation after we had moved on to another topic, he added, referring to India, "I hate that country!"

Maharashtra police and Israeli trainers disagreed about why they did not develop a durable partnership on homeland security, and some of their accounts are diametrically opposed. Both groups of actors projected the sources of difficulty onto the other in ways that preserved their own authority as the norm. Whereas Maharashtra officials suggested that Israelis were either out of place and/or less than impressive in their offerings, Israeli trainers reverted to classic imperial tropes of the ignorant and slippery native, suggesting that the Indians proved unwilling to do what they recommended or were not interested in paying for their expertise because of their strange "mentality" or "attitude." While their accounts were inconsistent in terms of who or what was to blame, they broadly agreed that the encounters were characterized by considerable disagreement about how to approach domestic security. These differences proved intractable. In other words, the necessary conditions for any ongoing relationships were not met.

What is of greatest interest to me here, however, is how interactions on the ground in Maharashtra unsettled Israeli claims to exceptional expertise and their pretense of privileged, universal authority. In a narrow technical sense, the Maharashtra officials' accounts show a core skepticism about the relevance of Israeli approaches and the Israeli model vis-à-vis India/Mumbai, reflecting themes from Pant's remarks that opened this chapter. Like Pant, the Maharashtra officials saw Israel as an inspiration but not necessarily as a model *for* Mumbai/India. They were also unwilling to treat Israelis deferentially as all-knowing experts who could secure Mumbai/Maharashtra. Some Maharashtra officials took a certain pleasure in explaining to me how they had exposed certain Israeli recommendations and the Israeli model as provincial or even questionable. As I explore next, there are echoes of this lack of deference in the broader efforts of Israel's homeland security industry to "penetrate" India.

PENETRATING INDIA

In this section, I elaborate upon Israeli security officials' reflections on their work in India. As earlier chapters have noted, some Israeli homeland security firms entered India before 2008, but many more came thereafter, offering various solutions. These offerings covered a wide range of technologies like small arms, access control systems, anti-ramming bollards, gates, fences, and surveillance equipment as well as consulting services in risk management, intelligence, and police training. Some of these Israeli firms benefited immediately from 26/11's political fallout, selling new weapons and technologies to units in the Indian military and to central and state police forces. For example, Force One and other Indian commando units procured a number of CornerShot pistol modifications as well as "sense-through-the-wall" imaging systems from the Israeli firm Camero-Tech.[31] When I spoke with a Camero representative at the company's corporate headquarters in Kfar Netter, he enthusiastically recalled that 26/11 "did *great* job for us" by demonstrating "the need . . . for internal security" in India and providing the necessary budgets to the Mumbai and New Delhi police to purchase Camero's systems. Other Israeli homeland security ventures in India also matured. After 2008, BG Ilnalit Gates and Urban Elements Ltd. (BGI), which manufactures anti-ramming bollards and roadblocks, moved all of its production to India to take advantage of cheaper labor costs, as I found out from speaking to the firm's representatives at the trade show IFSEC and Homeland Security India in 2012. BGI later formed its Indian subsidiary, BGI Egintech Private Ltd., based in Ahmedabad, ultimately winning a number of major contracts in the luxury hospitality sector.

Yet large-scale and long-term contracts in the public sector in Maharashtra and beyond did not materialize, as many Israeli homeland security firms and trade officials had hoped.[32] There was broad consensus among Israeli homeland security insiders that expectations of a sudden and sustained spike in demand were wildly overblown, particularly in relation to the Indian state. As one Israeli CEO lamented, despite all the talk of rapid change after 2008, the public sector demand for his services "didn't change at all." As will become clear below, the capacity to acquire contracts with Indian state agencies and corporations varied considerably among the various Israeli companies I spoke with. I survey these varied experiences of Israeli firms working in India, paying particular attention to how forms of *Indian difference* were cited by these actors as impediments to their work. These references spanned the pace and timescales of business dealings, "business cultures" and "mentalities," but also "attitudes" and ways of conceptualizing and practicing domestic security.

Representatives who worked to position Israeli firms in India referenced a range of frictions and difficulties related to the timescales of business development. Guy Zuri explained that in Palestine/Israel most security firms think on timescales of a few months or years and that for them such horizons are "very long term." But he emphasized that in "India it's not like that." In India, winning public tenders, arranging partnerships, and developing these into tangible projects takes many years of sustained activity at high cost with uncertain returns. A number of other representatives raised similar concerns. One marketing director described an Indian public corporation to which he sold his fencing systems to as "very, very slow, like a dinosaur . . . slow to take decisions and change." Another noted, "In India . . . everything is urgent until they [Indians] have to respond or take action. We are waiting patiently. . . ." Some Israeli representatives lacked the patience or resources to sustain this ill-defined wait. Eyal, the CEO of an Israeli police and counterterrorism training firm we met in chapter 2, recalled that he had attempted to get work in India after 2008 "but, like divers, you need a huge tank of oxygen to succeed in diving in the Indian Ocean, like we [Israelis] say. You need a lot of patience. You need a huge budget for marketing and penetration into the country and I couldn't. I didn't succeed."

Echoing Zuri's claims about different timescales of business dealings in India, other representatives suggested that Indian "slowness" reflected the country's peculiar "business culture," which Israeli firms were ill accustomed to working with. As Ari, a marketing director of an Israeli firm specializing in various forms of security and police training as well as risk consultancy services, explained, "A lot of Israeli companies did not take into consideration a very big matter that we felt on our own flesh: the cultural differences. Not just the locals but the business culture." Indeed, almost all the Israeli homeland security representatives with experience in India with whom I spoke with made some reference to this "business culture" and the challenges it posed to their work, suggesting that Indian clients were slippery, cheap, and hard to deal with (see also chapter 6). When I asked Uriel Bin, founder and CEO of the Israeli fencing company D-Fence, about his experiences there, he responded: "I'll tell you a joke. India is saying all the time 'Mr. Bin, Mr. Bin, money no problem, money no problem!' I said: 'Big problem!' They say 'Why?' I say: 'Because I am the Jew . . . and you are the Indian and I need the money in *this* generation!'"

Thus, utilizing key elements of a classic antisemitic joke, Bin emphasized that as a Jew, he was not willing to entertain business deals without clear profits. As he summarized about doing business in India, "I don't like [it], if you ask me."

Gleser explained his experience of business dealings with Indians in strikingly similar racist terms. When I asked him to clarify his references to Indians' difficult "mentality" (above), he said that he meant this both in relation to the practice of training and advising Indian forces but also in relation to business dealings, implying that the two were inextricable. He maintained that every imaginable matter with his Indian counterparts was subject to "bargaining and dealing," comparing the challenges posed by Indians' strange "mentality" to haggling over the price of something you want to buy. In general, he claimed that the process is straightforward: "You ask how much. He looks at you and he says 20. You say 10. He says 12. You say 8. Then you buy for 10." Such haggling, he suggested, normally "takes one minute" but that "the same in India will take one hour!" Likewise, a representative from perimeter security firm Orad similarly emphasized that although Orad was "very active" in India for a time, successfully bidding on Smart City tenders, "we decided to go out of the Indian market," citing "the mentality of the Indians" as well as the lower-than-expected profit margins. He began to laugh as he recalled that he had come to the conclusion that "profits . . . do not exist actually in India for companies like us."

I got my own firsthand experience of Israelis' struggles with the so-called Indian "mentality" and "business culture" in a meeting in Mumbai with an Israeli sales agent working for an Israeli security firm that specialized in access control systems and anti-ramming bollards. During our meeting, Moshe, the agent, was interrupted by a phone call from a representative of an Indian subsidiary of a European technology company, after which a tense exchange between the two men ensued. At numerous points in the conversation, Moshe screamed at his Indian client, reminding him of Moshe's strict policy of not performing services or supplying products until after receiving full payment. During the call, Moshe repeatedly stated that he did not *need* the client's business and that the client should feel free to seek another supplier if the client did not like his policies. After some minutes of arguing back and forth, the two men seemed to have worked out an arrangement amenable to both. Yet after Moshe hung up the phone—sweating and still visibly exasperated—he noted how much he hated living in Mumbai and that he could not wait to return to Israel as soon as he got the chance.

As we have seen, Israeli representatives complained about various difficulties they experienced related to Indians' "slow," peculiar, and "difficult" style of doing business, which they attributed to India's strange and backward "business culture," "attitude," and "mentality." Their experiences working in India also prompted some Israelis to question whether Indians truly wanted an Israeli security *solution* or if they even understood what getting one would require. Moshe expressed frustration with his Indian clients in the luxury hotel sector in Mumbai, who he claimed were always trying to cut corners. He said that they did this by procuring their security products through multiple suppliers or opting not to pay to have their systems properly serviced. Others went even further, suggesting that Indians did not truly grasp the meaning of security and were unwilling to do what was necessary to get a real solution to the various risks and threats they faced. As Noam, of Athena Security Implementations, explained:

> Indians are not looking for a *solution,* they are looking for a *technology* to solve their problem. To get a good security solution, you need to have a good combination of technology, manpower and procedures and protocols. They don't invest anything in the other two, just in technology. They call it "gadget." Not to diminish them but this is how they think about it. For them, it is nice to have stuff. You cannot convince an Indian company or the Indian government to buy *consulting*, to buy *knowhow*; they will buy only *equipment.*

Noam maintained that Indians either did not understand security or otherwise had a rather different conception of it from the (Israeli) vision that he was selling. In doing so, he also referenced the fixation on the purchase of new security "gadgets" and limited appetite for structural reform within Indian state's responses to 26/11 discussed at length in chapters 3 and 4. According to Noam, these challenges, among others, prompted Athena to give up on India as a potential new growth market.

Israelis' frustrations with India's alleged lack of "security awareness" (chapters 2 and 3) were not unique to the post-2008 period. Israeli homeland security officials cited this issue as a long-standing barrier to "market penetration." A December 3, 2008, article from the Israeli business newspaper *Globes* cites Uriel Bin, who notes: "A spiritual country like India finds it difficult to think about security. So we had a tough job to penetrate the market [before 2008]. But they [Indians] now realize that something is changing and are becoming receptive."[33] In the article, Bin suggested that this alleged "cultural" or "conceptual" barrier would recede after 26/11 as Indians woke up to the reality of global terrorism. When I spoke with Bin in 2019, he had changed his mind. While noting that the Indian military was all too eager to buy weapons from the major players like Rafael and Elbit Systems, he claimed that selling to Indian law enforcement agencies was an entirely different story. He stressed that these domestic Indian agencies were less than "serious" about security and lacked the necessary "dedication" to achieve it. After struggling to find the right words to capture what he meant, he settled on a comparison: "China it's *so* serious, Hong Kong *so* serious, India not so [serious]." He went on to explain that India's "mentality" was not one which you could really work with on domestic security projects.

One of the things that initially surprised me was the sheer crudeness of what Israeli officials said about India and Indians behind closed doors, despite the two countries' ever-deepening bilateral linkages. They often resorted to crude hierarchies of colonial difference and unfavorable comparisons. When I asked an Israeli consular official stationed in Mumbai what he thought of the city, he told me that it was an endlessly fascinating place. However, he went on to note that after a recent trip to Hong Kong, he was struck how utterly "perfect" Hong Kong was in contradistinction to Mumbai. Hong Kong, as he eloquently put it, is "like New York but with Chinese people in it." He went on to suggest that if all the world's major cities were stacked on top of each other with the best at the top, Hong Kong would take the position of the penthouse. Mumbai, in contrast, would be "the place where they keep the garbage." Such remarks, of course, reflect more about their authors than the places they describe. As such, they crucially gesture to the hierarchies that they imagine structure the world.

Some Israeli security companies I spoke with found ways to do business in India and some claimed to have done well, in spite of their self-described challenges of scale, the Indian security "mentality," the "business culture," and Indians' alleged lack of understanding of or even lack of interest in achieving real security. A few congratulated themselves for their advances in cultural competency vis-à-vis India, perhaps the next frontier of "innovation" of the Israeli "start-up nation."[34] As Ari explained, "It's about adaptation to cultural differences. I won't say it was easy for us at the beginning, but we were willing to adapt [to India] . . . it's a Darwinian thing." Another noted, "Sometimes you have to adapt to the market and not try to change or educate it." Yet the vast majority of firms I spoke with were forced to shift entirely to the private sector, focusing mostly on the luxury residential and hospitality industries and relying on Indian sales agents and consultants to carry out deal-making.

Others had withdrawn from India entirely, based on a combination of economic calculation and the sheer frustration of interacting with their Indian counterparts. As Zuri explained, although some Israeli firms had success right after 2008, by 2010 the majority of these firms had returned to Israel, largely empty-handed. With regard to IEICI's progress in "penetrating" India to date, Zuri summarized that "we are not there *yet*." Likewise, in an email correspondence, one Israeli homeland security marketing official responded to my inquiry about his firm's activities in India with the following: "As for homeland security in India I do not think that I have much to offer [in relation to your research] as I understood long back that I do not know how to play the 'selling to government game' in India so we are focusing on selling to private companies and approach quote[s] to government only through [a] third party."

My Israeli interlocutors did their best to rationalize their struggles and limited success in India as evidence of Indian backwardness. As the marketing director of an electric fence company told me, Indians are "just reactive, which is one of their problems." Gleser similarly noted that life for most Indians is an unrelenting struggle for basic existence, noting that "people need to fight for every day, [just] to live" and stressing that many go hungry. While driving me to catch a bus back to Tel Aviv after our meeting just north of Herzliya, Avi remarked that India is a "fucking crazy country." He noted that Indian children have their kidneys stolen and sold on the black market as a way to drive home the county's unparalleled depravity. According to Gleser and Avi, India's general poverty and backwardness helped explain why fully committing to the totalizing project of homeland security was not necessarily a top priority. Or as Guy Zuri put it, the Indian domestic security market "is kind of immature." Noam went a step further, explaining Indians' apparent lack of interest in the full range of his firm's services as evidence of their ignorance and lack of modernity and leadership. "Indians," he told me, "are servants in nature . . . they were born to serve and they don't feel comfortable at all being leaders . . . of *anything*!"

Amid these racist efforts to explain away their encounters in India, a few officials reflected upon what their experiences said about them and their claims to universal, expert authority. Noam told me a story that bore a striking resemblance to Aditya's account of taking an Israeli trainer to CST. Noam recalled that after arriving in New Delhi in 2009 to pursue potential business opportunities with local authorities (including a proposal for a security system for the city's public transit system), he visited New Delhi's main train station at rush hour. He recounted that just after entering the premises he found himself overtaken "by something I can only suppose was about a million people at the same time in the building," claiming that "you had to move or you were killed!" He described the chaotic scene as analogous to "a stream of ants going in various directions," noting that he lost control and struggled to even decipher "what is the real current, where it will take me?" He told me that after having managed to walk to the other side of the station, he concluded: "Due to the size and the amount of people [in India], some of the [security] problems they have are not really solvable. There is nothing I can offer them. There is no way, from a security point of view, that you can do a *real* management of threat for a million people in one hour." Thus, even as he railed against Indians as natural-born "servants," Noam conceded that his encounter with India humbled him and fundamentally called into question whether he, as an Israeli, was in any position to educate Indians on how to manage their domestic security planning. As someone from a country of roughly seven million people "with very distinct enemies," he asked rhetorically: "From *where* do we [Israelis] take the courage, the vanity, to try to tell a nation of 1.25 billion people how to manage [their internal security]?"

Thus, in spite of their global expert credentials, India proved to be an especially difficult country for Israel's homeland security industry to "penetrate," owing to a range of specifically Indian differences and peculiarities.[35] The Israeli actors with whom I spoke all explained their respective fates in India through references to *Indian difference*, with a particular focus on so-called "business culture." Ari explained that Indian business culture "broke a lot of attempts of other companies from Israel over there [in India]," emphasizing that "regardless of the reputation of Israelis, we have found it very hard" to work in India. As we have seen, some officials like Ari claimed that they were able to manage to mediate so-called Indian differences better than others. Yet, the vast majority of Israelis I spoke to presented Indian difference as unsurmountable and conceded defeat. I found out some years after speaking with Moshe that he had since moved on from the security business to manage operations in India for a large Israeli firm working in the diamond trade, a vibrant and long-standing sector of trade between India and Israel. This seemed to suggest that it was not Indian "business culture" per se but rather something more particular about selling homeland security to Indians and educating them about its value and necessity, issues I return to in chapter 6.

Even some Israelis who had success in India suggested that in a world full of danger and other more straightforward and "serious" customers, India was just not worth the extra effort and costs. After elaborating on Indians' impossible "mentality" through his experiences of haggling with Indian counterparts above, Gleser explained: "If you have time [for that], do it. I don't have time. Do you understand?" So while maintaining that he still had many possibilities to work in India, Gleser stressed that he did not need the business badly enough to stay. He clarified that it was not because he did not like India, which he claimed he did, making mention of its "very impressive cultural things" but rather that he simply lacked the patience to work there. Bin similarly explained that he had gotten some contracts in India just after 2008 working with luxury real estate developments in Mumbai catering to Bollywood clientele and that similar prospects were still available to him. However, having just returned from a business trip to China, Bin claimed that India was no longer of significant interest and that East Asia, North America, and Europe would be the primary regions of focus in his marketing strategy going forward. Avi similarly remarked: "I will go to train them [Indians] if they need, but you know, I prefer not [to]." In light of his self-described failure to "penetrate" the Indian market above, Eyal similarly recounted: "So I said: 'Thank you. Call me when you need us,'" though he had little expectation that any calls from India would be coming anytime soon.

Even though India proved difficult, frustrating, even impenetrable for some Israeli officials, this does not mean that nothing of consequence happened. In my meeting with one Israeli informant on the outskirts of Tel Aviv, he showed me a photo of a police trainer who had once worked for his firm as a subcontractor in India. The photo depicted the trainer and his wife posing together with a Maharashtra police official and his wife, all dressed in *saris* and *kurtas* and smiling for the camera. When I later spoke with this pictured trainer, he confirmed that he had developed a close personal relationship with this Maharashtra police official and remained in contact even today. Moreover, the Israeli firms that did manage to get work in India mobilized these contracts to further reinforce their authority as global experts. Until 2021, ISDS's website featured the Mumbai police among its many global clients. In this sense, Indian clients became just the latest reference that proved Israel's credentials as the global pioneer of homeland security (chapter 2).

CONCLUSION

In this chapter, I have argued that we need to pay attention to difference to recover the ways in which incommensurable social orders endure alongside hegemonic projects. Doing so enables us to grapple with how references to difference are at work in projects of universalism and their attempts to transcend difference (chapter 2), yet without assuming their capacity to achieve these ends in practice.[36] Despite significant tensions and limitations of postcolonial theory,[37] its engagements with questions about difference and universality are instructive, if incomplete.[38] In particular, postcolonial theory's engagements with difference demonstrate the impossibility of modernity's and capitalism's claims to universality and coherency but also spell out how difference matters in conceptual terms. As Gurminder Bhambra argues, it is crucial but insufficient to simply recognize difference: "'Difference' also has to *make a difference* to the assumptions that informed the initial enquiry."[39] In this case, a focus on difference helps to destabilize the self-implied universality of (Israeli) homeland security and the hierarchies of knowledge and authority underpinning its claims to universality.

Indian and Israeli actors' accounts of their encounters do not provide a singular or definitive narrative of how difference mattered. Even though their accounts have striking overlaps, they also represent difference differently and to different ends, sometimes in contradictory ways. These accounts cannot, therefore, be taken at face value; instead they should be understood within the frame of comparative geopolitics broadly and more specifically the grammars of imperial exceptionalism and hierarchies of colonial difference. As illustrated in the quotation from Uriel Bin in *Globes*, the idea was that through the experience of 26/11 India (finally) woke up to the new reality of global terrorism and that this recognition would prompt a radical modernization of India's domestic security infrastructure in the image of (Israeli) homeland security. More specifically, by making reference to essential differences between Israeli and Indian approaches to policing and domestic security, Israeli homeland security solutions were framed as quintessentially modern and inherently superior to the "backward" Indian repertoires (chapter 1). The ostensible aim of Israeli actors was to bring Indian domestic security governance in line with (or at least closer to) Israeli approaches by transcending, overwriting, or otherwise mitigating the (supposed) essential differences between them through technology, training, and education. These terms thus implied a particular hierarchy of knowledge and authority upon which new forms of relationality would unfold after 26/11.

The encounters between Israeli homeland security officials and their Indian counterparts were shaped by these underlying terms of engagement. Israelis' recurring reliance on the sexualized and gendered terminology of "matchmaking" with and "penetrating" India is highly suggestive of the terms through which they approached their work in India, seeing themselves in commanding positions of authority and control and India/

Indians as the submissive recipients of their experience, technology, and expertise. Maharashtra officials' accounts upheld key elements of this script; they all affirmed that Israeli homeland security exemplified a modern approach to domestic counterterrorism that was lacking in India. And yet, these encounters were hardly determined by these terms.

Maharashtra officials were largely unconvinced about the replicability (or even desirability) of the Israeli model in Maharashtra/India, even challenging the notion that there were any quick-fix Israeli homeland security solutions to be had. Despite referencing shared urban security problems, Maharashtra officials portrayed India and Indians as, for the most part, *un*like Israel and Israelis. Further, they suggested that engagements with Israel's homeland security industry were never envisaged to displace or replace their own Indian models of policing, emphasizing that the terms of mimesis would be of their making in the vein of strategic syncretism, that is, selectively borrowing certain ideas and elements of (Israeli) homeland security while leaving others behind to service the Indian nation. This exemplifies what I call *the politics of (post)colonial difference* but also speaks to its intersection with forms of Indian exceptionalism[40] and Hindu exceptionalism.[41] That a popular book by a Hindutva writer took as its title *Being Different* speaks to the broader nationalist underpinnings of and the enduring resonance of this reasoning. The book, which bears an endorsement from Narendra Modi, mobilizes a focus on "how India differs from the West" as an explicit challenge to "Western universalism" and "Western civilization."[42]

While Maharashtra officials' reservations about the replicability of the Israeli model were often couched in technical concerns about applicability of specific technologies, tactics, practices, or systems, their skepticism exceeded these narrow terms. It reflected a broader unwillingness to treat Israelis deferentially and a refusal to abide entirely by the terms of imperial exceptionalism through which the Israeli homeland security model is typically narrated. Indian officials instead sought to shift onto the terrain of Indian exceptionalism, a dynamic I return to in the next chapter. Indeed, through the encounters between Israeli and Indian officials, the imperial conventions of modeling broke down as did the presumed authority of Israeli security experts to speak from a position of unquestioned privilege. My Israeli officials' self-described "penetration failures" suggest that their masculinized security credentials "went soft,"[43] with some conceding that in India they lost their "vanity" and "courage" to speak as macho, all-knowing experts. While analytically challenging, the messiness of these accounts is also politically instructive as it illuminates the political nature and contingencies of the encounters between Israeli and Indian actors.[44] They also make visible uncertain boundaries between the colonial, postcolonial, and even the anticolonial in ideological and practical terms.[45]

Furthermore, these accounts capture instances of what John Law and Wen-Yuan Lin call "moments of disconcertment."[46] Through these encounters the underlying imperial terms of engagement largely broke down, as did the presumed authority of Israeli officials to speak from a position of unquestioned, universal privilege. As Law and Lin point out, moments of disconcertment in (post)colonial encounters "are mostly Othered," and as we have already seen, this is precisely what happened.[47] Israeli officials resorted to classic imperial and colonial tropes to explain away their fraught encounters with Indians and India, attempting to Other Indian difference as deficiency. The representations of India as backward and Indians as ignorant, slippery, and hard to deal with by those who see themselves as exemplars of civilization and modernity reflect the language and strategies of historical empire as well as contemporary corporate efforts to engage with India as an emerging market—projects that never had any qualms about resorting to the naked orientalism of "India is different, India is different, India is different."[48] However, as Law and Lin point out, critical attention to the representations of cultural difference in worldly encounters can be productive. They suggest that if we "trace the stories that narrate and enact differences," we can find opportunities to uncover how multiple reals intersect and are negotiated in practical engagements. Following Helen Verran, they argue that when different worlds and metaphysics intersect, "their disjunction is experienced as *bodily disconcertment.*"[49]

Building on these insights, I suggest that Israelis' narrations of their experiences in India, even in the crude, racist, and dehumanizing terms with which they are enunciated, illuminate how Israeli claims of expertise were destabilized through encounters with a different world. Israelis' characterizations of India as unruly ("a fucking crazy country") and vast and slow-moving ("like the Indian Ocean," "like a dinosaur") as well as their disdain for the place ("I hate that country!") evidence their feelings of exasperation with India and Indians for not regarding them with the seriousness they anticipated. A focus on the accounts of these moments of disconcertment also crucially reflect the negotiation of multiple, different worlds, or reals in Annemarie Mol's sense of ontological politics.[50] Their references to *bodily* disconcertment through accounts of Indian "cultural differences" being "felt on our flesh" as well as to experiences of being overtaken by "a stream of ants" in a Delhi train station capture embodied feelings of disorientation under different conditions. Accounts of needing "a huge tank of oxygen to succeed in diving the Indian Ocean" similarly evoke Israelis' feelings of being out of their depth in India. They are testaments, in other words, to embodied feelings of being out of place.

As I elaborated in chapter 2, negotiating various differences (geographic, cultural, economic, linguistic, political, and so on) between Palestine/Israel and various elsewheres was nothing unusual, according to my Israeli interlocutors. Many saw flexibility as a definitive aspect of their work across diverse contexts, even the very essence of the Israeli approach to homeland security. Yet, as the above narratives illustrate, these very same actors suggested that in India, their typical strategies for mitigating, repressing, papering over, or otherwise overcoming such differences proved less effective than usual. They explained that India proved unusually challenging, not merely in terms of practically adapting their knowhow to different material conditions. What made India unusually frustrating was the prevailing ambiguity about what, if anything, any potential job prospect might yield. And representatives who remained, like Ari, argued that their success required that they adapt to India instead of trying to get Indians to work on their (Israeli) terms.

But as many of the disparaging Israeli narratives of India and Indians make clear, the vast majority of my Israeli interlocutors were unwilling to do this. If working in India required that they take on a subservient role without large, predictable profits, most just could not be bothered. This point seems critical to understanding why India proved especially difficult for Israeli firms to navigate. That India is different from Palestine/Israel—though undeniable—does not in and of itself tell us much about why so many Israeli security officials found themselves out of their depth in India. What proved crucial, rather, was Indians' unwillingness to fully capitulate to working under the terms of colonial difference and its corresponding conventions and hierarchies upon which Israeli security authority relies and seeks to enshrine as a form of global pacification.

Thus, while models and modeling are notions developed by colonizers and capital on their terms to suit their needs, I have shown that attention to actually-existing practices at work in fabricating (Israeli) homeland security in India opens up new possibilities. It can help us find ways to "unstitch"[51] modeling in different ways than abstract critique makes possible. Following the actors at work in actually-existing pacification projects and the politics of (post)colonial difference at play therein can demonstrate how projects of universalism and their supporting ideological architectures might unravel or even fail, showing the importance of thinking about expertise as a historically constituted phenomenon and outcomes of relational networks or "alliances" (rather than merely as specialized forms of knowledge).[52]

As the next chapter explores, in the years after 2008 Indian capital self-consciously sought to rehabilitate security's standing in India and foster greater appreciation for it through educational strategies aimed at raising greater "security awareness" or "consciousness" across India.

SIX

EDUCATING A MARKET

> While the Indian market for security technologies is huge, the challenge is to effectively match industry and end users to produce projects *tailored for "the Indian situation."*
>
> —U.S. diplomatic cable, October 16, 2009[1]

INTRODUCTION

On the morning of June 25, 2012, I arrived at the Elizabeth II Conference Centre in Westminster, London, where registration opened for delegates at Securing Asia 2012. While billed as "The Asian Homeland Security and Counter Terror Summit," Securing Asia 2012 focused primarily on India and its linkages with the U.K. It was co-organized by a collection of Indian and U.K. state agencies and corporate partners including Security Watch India (SWI); Global Energy Private Ltd. (India); the UKTI Defence and Security Organization; the Aerospace, Defence Security, and Space Group; and the International Professional Security Association (IPSA). Upon arrival, I was ushered through an airport-style metal detector, after which I was given my "delegate package," including an event guide, a badge, and a customized nylon Securing Asia 2012 conference briefcase. I proceeded to the third floor, where the event would soon begin. On the right side was the Fleming Room, with exhibitor booths representing organizations including Security Watch U.K. (SWUK), the Asian Business Club, and Saab Security as well as a range of other firms manufacturing single products like anti-crash bollards and cyber security technologies. On the left side was the Whittle Room, where the programming for the event would take place over the next three days.

After getting some coffee from a refreshment table, I found my way to the Whittle Room to await the "welcome note" at 8:40 a.m. to be delivered by Harry Dhaul, director general of the Independent Power Producers Association of India and founding member of SWI, one of Securing Asia's main sponsors. Behind the stage was a large screen with the SWUK and Securing Asia 2012 logos in bold orange lettering emblazoned on it. The seating plan was arranged by importance, with speakers and visiting trade delegations at the front and the general delegates, like myself, sitting in rows of chairs at the back. As I awaited the welcome address, the Whittle Room began to fill up with other delegates, including scholars, diplomats, think tank representatives, exhibitors, and ex-military officials. Among them I caught my first glimpse of Dhaul, wearing a wide-brimmed black hat and trailed by a bodyguard as he made his way to the stage, warmly greeting members of the audience along the way.

After taking the stage and welcoming delegates, corporate sponsors, and exhibitors, Dhaul got down to business. "Why Securing *Asia*?" he asked. "Why *Asia* and not *the world*?" The reason, he maintained, is that Asia suffers from a unique set of challenges including large population growth, rising threats, and a sense of discontent that stems from not yet being able to fully participate in a rapidly globalizing world. "Why *London*?" Dhaul then asked. As he clarified, "London for us [Asians] is *still* the center of the world." He then reflected on Securing Asia's defining features and key goals, emphasizing that there were official delegations from twenty-three Asian countries. While this was impressive, he stressed that there could have been many more delegates if it were not for the fact that several delegates had not dropped out at the last minute because of visa problems. Dhaul used this as an opportunity to explain that the "problem is bureaucracy" and that the private sector is where the real solutions to contemporary governance challenges are to be found.

Despite his staunchly neoliberal, pro-business tone, Dhaul repeatedly claimed that the event was *not* fundamentally about making money and was instead about "raising awareness." Dhaul drew a contrast between Securing Asia and leading global industry trade shows like Eurosatory and Counter Terror, stressing that these other events merely focused on showcasing the latest in weapons and security technology and facilitating trade in the security field. In contrast, Dhaul emphasized that Securing Asia was additionally focused on "raising the cerebral quotient" about debates on homeland security challenges across Asia. He further stressed that different "perceptions" and "worldviews" were important to better understanding and managing contemporary security problems, presenting Securing Asia as a "neutral platform" for dialogue and collaboration where "West meets East."

Securing Asia 2012 was, as captured by Dhaul's remarks, many things at once. It was a self-styled "exhibition" and a "summit" to position "Asia" as the next big homeland security market. The Event Guide proclaimed: "Bringing Asia closer to you, Securing Asia 2012 is not just an event but 'the' event you can't afford to miss. A first of its kind, this event offers a curtain raiser for select companies, with an exposure to a market estimated at $1 trillion over the next 7 years."[2] Yet, the event was also presented as a "cerebral platform" for overcoming a range of "cultural barriers" impeding cooperation on homeland security between "Asia" and "the West." Intriguingly, Securing Asia's programming and materials suggested that its hard-nosed imperatives of opening markets, facilitating business transactions, and maximizing profits were to be realized through self-described "cerebral" activities, which on the face of it appear tangential to greasing the gears of neoliberal disaster capitalism.

While marketed as a "first of its kind" event, Securing Asia 2012 was merely the latest iteration of events organized by Indian and global capital to build a new Indian homeland security market in the years after 26/11. In this chapter, I draw on ethnographic accounts of these corporate-led efforts to *stage* and *educate* an Indian homeland security market, including Securing Asia 2012 (London), IFSEC and Homeland Security India (Noida), Challenges for India's Homeland Security (New Delhi), New Age Risks (New Delhi) as well as a closed-door conference in Mumbai. While many purveyors at the Indian homeland security events that I attended were from the Global North, these events also made space for others, including significant numbers of Chinese and Indian firms. I situate these efforts as a universalist project of world-making and subject-formation, which I group under the banner of *fabricating Indian homeland security*. Like historical world exhibitions that played crucial roles in building the representative machinery of the colonial-modern,[3] events like Securing Asia sought to simultaneously bring India *to* the West and western modernity *to* India in the form of homeland security in order to remake India in this western image.[4] As such, it is a performative process of world-making through market-making.[5] This takes us back to Tim Mitchell's account of the *making* of the economy, out of which this book's theorization of homeland security's fabrication draws its inspiration.[6]

However, to speak of the *fabrication of Indian homeland security* as I do in this chapter requires defining the performativity of economics more precisely. By "economics" I refer to a range of knowledges, actors, and technologies related to market-building but which are by no means limited to the formal academic discipline of economics. Drawing on key insights from ANT, a focus on the performativity of economics and market-related activities concerns not merely how economic worlds are known and represented but also the ability to *produce* and *transform* said worlds through the "interweaving of "words" and "actions."[7] Michel Callon calls this dynamic "performation," capturing the ways in which statements and their worlds become entangled and coevolve through confrontations and struggles between competing actors and agendas.[8] As will become clear in this chapter, a focus on the performative dimensions of fabricating Indian homeland security helps to recuperate the oft-overlooked struggles and failures therein.

Under the banner of *fabricating Indian homeland security*, I draw attention to the involved actors' efforts to enact a new field of investment and trade on homeland security in India. I show how new networks of actors were enrolled as a means to "educate" an Indian homeland security market, in the parlance of industry boosters. Here homeland security—presented as a simultaneously western/modern *and* universal conception of security—works as an arbiter of and proxy for (Indian) rationality. As I will show, the various actors involved in fabricating an Indian homeland security market relied on and reproduced grammars and forms of reasoning predicated on the racialized hierarchies of colonial difference (chapters 1, 2, and 5). They also sought to transcend these differences by finding ways to regulate and process them, using strategies related to but distinct from those explored in chapters 2 and 5.[9]

As Dhaul's remarks suggest, educating an Indian homeland security market involved more than just exporting security solutions from the Global North to India/Asia. Rather, central to this project was the goal of interpellating a new Indian security subject by raising Indians' levels of security "awareness" or "consciousness." This subject resembles *homo securitas*, the quintessentially neoliberal entrepreneurial citizen-subject of Man with a soul committed to security.[10] Like the general figure of *homo securitas*, security boosters sought to create an Indian citizen-subject who appreciates and espouses certain (homeland) security affects and is fully committed to police powers.

While most of these educational activities have been targeted at potential Indian homeland security clientele (government and police officials, corporate actors, policymakers, and so on), the project of raising security consciousness also had broader Indian publics in its crosshairs. I argue that this figure of *homo securitas* is not a freestanding and totalizing subject; rather it is a relation of Othering employed to regulate difference as forms of irrationality and backwardness. In other words, working within the structure of racial capitalism, this project of market-making has been and remains entwined with contemporary forms of empire and race-making.[11]

Inspired by Sylvia Wynter's critique of Man-as-human, I am concerned with the fabrication of *homo securitas* in the Indian context and the ways in which modern security, in tandem with its desired subject, becomes an arbiter of humanity and rationality. Tracing the secular genealogy of Man from its Christian roots in Medieval Europe, Wynter shows how the Christian/Other dichotomy morphed into the Man/Other binary alongside the rise of a secular rationality.[12] Not incidentally, the emergence of Man-as-human took place alongside the expropriation of Indigenous territories and the enslavement of Black peoples of Africa. According to Wynter, the question of Man is always already a colonial question inextricably tied with material dispossession. Interestingly, Wynter argues that the key struggle of the contemporary world will be over "the ongoing imperative of *securing* the well-being of our present ethnoclass (i.e. Western bourgeois) conception of the human" as though it were representative of the human species per se.[13] Thus, educating Indians in the image of *homo securitas* needs to be understood as an attempt to bring homeland security *to* India and secure the western bourgeois conception of Man-as-human. When read closely, security boosters' fraught attempts to create Indian *homo securitas* challenge the self-implied universality of (homeland) security but also the western episteme of Man-as-human.

I begin by outlining the efforts by Indian capital and their global partners to stage 26/11 as a paradigm shift in the governance of India's internal security. Through five vignettes, I proceed to unpack the strategies employed by these actors to overcome a set of self-described challenges of Indian homeland security by identifying and processing so-called "Indian difference." In the final section, I connect these strategies and their consequences to the rule of colonial difference explored in previous chapters. I argue that when we read these strategies closely, including how they are received and challenged by their intended audiences, the universal pretenses of (homeland) security are destabilized.

STAGING A PARADIGM SHIFT

In the wake of 26/11, a range of stakeholder meetings, policy conferences, and trade shows took place across India in attempts to radically refashion India's approach to internal security. These events were organized through collaborations between Indian subsidiaries of global management consultancies, Indian chambers of commerce, and global security promoters, including KPMG, Pinkerton, PricewaterhouseCoopers, McKinsey and Co., the Federation of Indian Chambers of Commerce and Industry (FICCI), the Associated Chambers of Commerce and Industry of India (ASSOCHAM), and the U.K.-based International Fire and Security Exhibition and Conference (IFSEC). These events were often accompanied by publications such as market reports, white papers, surveys, and other promotional materials, some of which have been referenced in previous chapters.[14] Many of these reports and events engaged with Indian state agencies including the MHA, often featuring state officials from these institutions as speakers and delegates.

Within these industry discourses, 26/11 was staged as a paradigm shift in India's threat perception and its appetite for homeland security. Industry reports proclaimed that 26/11 made visible new domestic security threats, which in turn fostered a greater appreciation of homeland security by the Indian state, Indian capital, and civil society. A 2009 FICCI report notes: "The 26/11 Mumbai attacks and the rising tide of Maoist violence have definitively changed the ways in which both the public and private sectors deal with extreme events," claiming that there has been a "paradigm shift in threat perception by Corporate [*sic*] in India."[15] Based on this premise, these texts and events suggested that new opportunities to buy and sell homeland security in India abound. As a KPMG-ASSOCHAM report noted: "A significant market opportunity exists in several domains comprising the [Indian] Homeland Security sector such as police modernization, critical infrastructure protection and counter-terrorism activities."[16] "Given the Government's focus on securing the country from all threats arising from a weak Homeland Security scenario," it continued, "the outlook for this sector in India is bright."[17] A few years later, an industry website put things more exuberantly, featuring a MHA official who claimed that the "Indian Homeland Security Market would literally [*sic*] be exploding in terms of the opportunities for the private industry in the next 5 years" (Figure 6.1).

FIGURE 6.1: *Screenshot from SWI website. Source: securitywatchindia.org.in, 2014.*

In their efforts to bring an Indian homeland security market into being, industry texts, events, and actors employed familiar neoliberal economic reasoning. They made the case for viewing terrorist attacks as a major threat to India's overall economic stability, arguing that after 26/11 India could no longer afford *not* to invest more in homeland security if it wished to maintain its status as a vibrant emerging economy on the world stage. The FICCI report noted:

> As India rises from a colonial past and shakes away socialist lethargy to reclaim its rightful place among the world's biggest and most influential economies, it is constantly being challenged repeatedly by unexpected and unprecedented means of terrorism.[18]

It continued, "a secure India is critical for our sustained economic progress [. . .] the time for platitudes and rhetoric is long gone," stressing that "[u]nless drastic measures are taken, there can be no assurance that India will be able to prevent the next major attack, and to reassure the global investor about the 'India rising story.'"[19] Another report expressed similar concern that large-scale terror attacks can have negative economic impact in the form of reduced credit ratings and a downturn in tourism.[20] "Given such potential damages," it argued, "Homeland Security is increasingly becoming critical to the *overall security* of the country," suggesting that the Indian government is already allocating increased budgets and attempts to "create a structured approach to Homeland Security of India [*sic*]."[21] These texts sought to document, consolidate, and capitalize on the growing profile of homeland security in India. Market reports also identified the economic gains that Indian homeland security held as a growth sector. They called on the Indian state to devote much larger budgets for things like police modernization as well as transform the governance structures for procurement procedures surrounding domestic security in order to make them more transparent, dynamic, and efficient. Such documents further suggested that modernizing India's domestic security infrastructure would require greater engagement with private industry.[22]

Representing interested parties (Indian and global capital, management consultancies, and the global homeland security industry), these texts sought to seize on the post-26/11 sense of collective insecurity as a moment of opportunity for a new shared vision of capitalist growth under the banner of "Indian homeland security." They had a triumphalist, self-congratulatory, and anti-political tone, calling on politicians to get out of the way and enable the market to redress India's domestic security challenges once and for all (chapters 1 and 3). However, they also cited a number of concrete challenges that needed to be overcome in order for this paradigm shift to materialize. The KPMG-ASSOCHAM report cited key challenges of Indian homeland security such as the "disorganized nature of Homeland Security apparatus [*sic*] in India" and "High entry costs and other associated risks" such as "bureaucratic delays" and a highly opaque procurement process.[23] Other industry documents further mentioned issues of awareness about rising threats, cultural and geographic difference, and questions about the universality of homeland security as a concept and set of practices. Thus, the project of fabricating Indian homeland security was self-consciously defined by its protagonists as a struggle rather than a fait accompli. I explore these issues in greater detail below as I examine how they were addressed in the course of industry events and publications.

EDUCATING AND INFORMING THE MARKET

The industry events that I attended focused on boosting demand by flooding India with new products and services and showcasing them to potential buyers and sales agents. For instance, IFSEC and Homeland Security India was held in a 1,500-square-meter venue in Noida just outside of New Delhi in early November 2012 (Figure 6.2).

The conference hosted 250 vendors and 8,627 participants, showcasing a wide range of Indian and foreign purveyors (including two Israeli firms) that offered everything from surveillance cameras to fencing, drones and vehicles for domestic use (Figures 6.3a, 6.3b, and 6.4).[24]

The brochure from IFSEC and Homeland Security India stated that the event would help in "educating and informing the market, keeping Indian security professionals at the cutting edge of industry developments."[25] In industry parlance this was often referred to as "educating the market," the process whereby potential customers are exposed to new security solutions and, as a result, become aware of their self-implied necessity and desirability.

FIGURE 6.2: *Entrance to IFSEC and Homeland Security India, Noida 2012. Photo by the author.*

While the scale of IFSEC and Homeland Security India was significantly larger than most industry events in India, the imperative of market education was apparent across all. At the 2013 Challenges for India's Homeland Security held in New Delhi, a representative from the security division of an Indian tech startup argued in his presentation that the need for security was based on a "universal truth," stressing that "security is as old as human evolution." Throughout history, he argued, we have always been trying to adopt the "best solutions" and that recent trends are just a continuation of this long evolutionary progression toward security for all.

Other industry groups framed this mission in terms of raising "awareness" about homeland security in India. For instance, SWI, a New Delhi–based corporate lobby group founded in October 2009 to spearhead India's homeland security revolution with Dhaul at its helm, explained its raison d'être as follows:

> Our mission is to assist in the transformation of the India homeland security apparatus [*sic*] to meet [. . .] challenges by bringing in new technologies, training methods and *awareness*, through the involvement of the

FIGURE 6.3: *BGI Engitech Pvt. Ltd. booth at IFSEC and Homeland Security India, Noida 2012. Photo by the author.*

FIGURE 6.4: *BGI Engitech Pvt. Ltd. booth at IFSEC and Homeland Security India, Noida 2012. Photo by the author.*

FIGURE 6.5: *Ashok Leyland police vehicle on display at IFSEC and Homeland Security India, Noida 2012. Photo by the author.*

> international homeland security industry. SWI is one of the few international platforms which provide cutting-edge information for technology providers and investors about the emerging opportunities in the Indian homeland security market.[26]

To do so, SWI organized a circuit of conferences and trade shows like its flagship Securing Asia abroad to exhibit the Indian homeland market as ready for greater engagement with western purveyors. Securing Asia's event guide stated that a core goal of the event was to "open doors, quite literally" for "Western suppliers" of homeland security, thereby facilitating access to "a trillion dollar market [. . .] waiting to be tapped."[27] In line with this goal, it had thirty-nine vendor booths where a range of Indian and international security purveyors could mingle with conference delegates. Among them I spotted a representative of the Israeli "digital intelligence" firm Cellebrite, notorious for its software that enables state agencies to unlock the mobile phones of activists and alleged dissidents. The three-day event featured presentations by a range of speakers including some of the attending vendors, giving them platforms to extol the virtues of their products and services and the kinds of problems they could resolve.

These kinds of staged opportunities for market education were standard fare at such events. At Challenges for India's Homeland Security, representatives made similar pitches about what their products and services offered to the homeland security of a modernizing India. In a presentation entitled "Cost-Effective Day and Night Surveillance," a representative of the French firm Photonis outlined his firm's products. His presentation focused on the virtues of Photonis's "Nocturn camera core" stressing that it is an all-in-one product where "everything is in one camera" and has the additional virtue of being able to be mounted onto weapons. He claimed that Photonis was "number one in the world" in night vision and was quick to point out that "security is *lacking* some night vision in India." "That is why I'm here," he later stated, "so maybe we should talk!?" He finished by reminding delegates: "You can wait for years, but *you* have to decide!" The Photonis representative's claims were recurring at such events. His claims illustrate how homeland security purveyors attempted to package their products and services as exceptional and world-leading but also develop more particular sales pitches geared to Indian needs and desires.

While the Photonis representative received no questions from the audience, other presentations seemed to spark genuine enthusiasm, sometimes even revelation. At the same event, a representative of India's National Disaster Response Force and Civil Defence gave a presentation on the challenges and opportunities of employing RFID and GPS technologies to track down missing weapons but complained that existing solutions remained "primordial." In the Q&A session afterwards, a sales manager from the audience told the director that he was "very intrigued by what you are saying" and that the technology for tracking down missing weapons already exists, recommending that they connect later to discuss the matter further. Indeed, some industry actors with whom I spoke referenced the key importance of industry events in making them aware of new products on the global market. The Indian small arms dealer Sanjeev, whom we met in chapter 3, noted that trade shows provided him with key opportunities to discover new products and solutions of which he might have otherwise been unaware. As he explained, "When I am working the [trade] show, I walk up to a guy and say: 'Do you have a solution like *that*?'" Educating and informing the market, however, went beyond simply showcasing modern homeland security solutions *to* India and enrolling Indians as clients. It also involved efforts to network and collaborate more effectively.

BUILDING ENDURING NETWORKS

Fabricating Indian homeland security was a matter of enabling western homeland security purveyors to make new connections with potential Indian clients. The programming at Securing Asia 2012 constantly reminded attendees of the benefits of collaborating between Asia and the West, presenting these connections as a continuation of long-standing mutually beneficial ties. At the event, James Brokenshire, the U.K. minister for crime and security, spoke of the "historic bond" between the U.K. and Asia (India in particular) and how this relationship could be further consolidated through collaboration on homeland security, thereby framing the British empire as an inspiration for contemporary transnational business ventures. Similar claims were echoed at a closed-door policy conference hosted by a local lobbying group in partnership with a visiting U.K. trade delegation in Mumbai in early 2013. Flanked by a poster reading "BUSINESS IS GREAT Britain," the chairperson of the local host organization welcomed the speakers and guests of the delegation and its accompanying corporate representatives from major weapons and surveillance firms. Emphasizing that 26/11 caused such significant "trauma" that it was still "echoing with gunfire," the chairperson presented the event as the latest in a pattern of international solidarity and collaboration that the attacks gave rise to, which would give India the tools it needed to finally modernize its domestic security architecture. Quoting Helen Keller, he proclaimed: "*Alone* we can do so little; *together* we can do so much!"

To realize these possibilities, speakers constantly reminded the audience that for sustainable and mutually beneficial solutions to materialize over the long term, it was incumbent on conference attendees to make the connections last. The head of the U.K. delegation urged delegates to "make sure you know how to keep in contact" to ensure that the day's focus on building connections between visiting firms and the Maharashtra government did not go "up the chimney and into the atmosphere" once the event came to a close. Likewise, at Securing Asia 2012, event organizers and speakers constantly stressed to participants that it was incumbent on them to build the connections for the Asian homeland security market to come to fruition. After a presentation by a visiting foreign state official, Dhaul intervened, calling on delegates to actively think about how to build enduring networks that "go *beyond* the event."

Yet industry events did not merely press their attendees to network more; they also provided advice, competencies, and expertise on how networking should be approached and carried out.[28] In the Securing Asia Event Guide, a diagram suggested that networking was a key part of realizing its core mandate of linking "Asian Security Buyers" and "Global Security Suppliers" (Figure 6.6).

In this same diagram, successful "networking" is presented as contingent upon preexisting knowledge of the "Asian legal framework" and "how to do business in Asia." Echoing similar concerns to those voiced by the Israeli homeland security purveyors in chapter 5, numerous vendors complained to me about the difficulties they were facing in accessing Indian

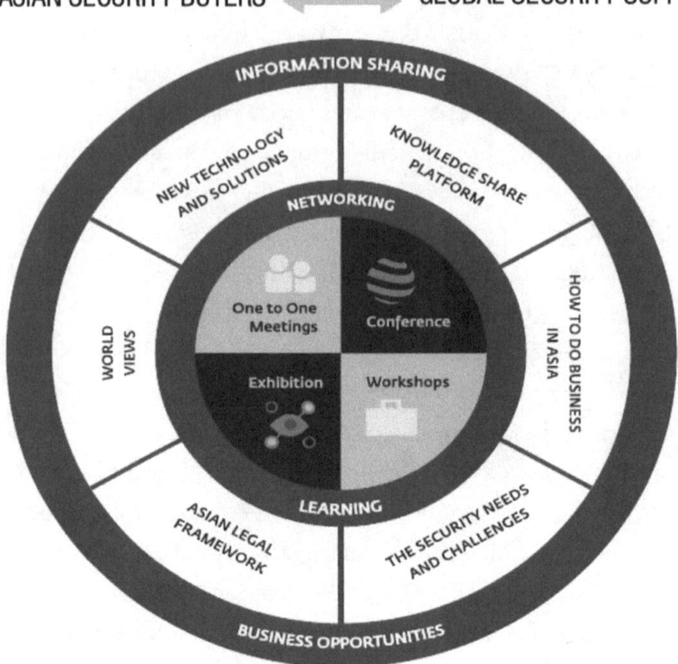

FIGURE 6.6: *Diagram from Securing Asia 2012. Source: Securing Asia 2012 Event Guide.*

clients, particularly in the public sector. Anticipating these challenges, industry events attempted to educate foreign homeland security purveyors about the overall landscape of the Indian homeland security market and the specific dangers and pitfalls it posed. In his address at Securing Asia 2012, an executive from an Indian brand management consultancy, spoke about the current state of the Indian business environment. He stressed that in India "nothing is how you see it." The executive claimed that although the country holds immense commercial opportunities as an export market for homeland security, it is a deceptive environment with slippery and unscrupulous Indian agents and partners waiting to "screw you" along the way. As a partial solution, these events provided advice on *how* to network and collaborate more profitably and offered concrete suggestions and forms of expertise. At Securing Asia 2012, specialist consultants and agents provided solutions to the challenges of doing business in Asia.

Some ex-officials further claimed that they had the ability to open doors to certain Indian government agencies, whereas others offered services for how to approach business dealings with Indian partners.

As the brand management executive's remarks allude to, however, rather than simply being represented as a matter of gaining access to the right official, industry forums represented these networking challenges as irreducibly cultural in nature. Accordingly, a number of area specialists made presentations to conference delegates, attempting to explain the culture of various Asian countries and offered their consultancy services about how to network properly through their knowledge of local customs, etiquette, and the ability to read social cues. Thankfully, according to such representatives, cultural competencies could be purchased from them to avoid falling into traps or otherwise getting "screwed," inviting participants to get in touch if they wanted more information. These references to cultural competency as a means of overcoming cultural difference were thus represented as utilitarian strategies to overcome the key challenges of networking successfully in India and Asia more broadly. Such strategies attempted to picture and process Indian difference by giving western homeland security purveyors the knowledge and skills to understand its sources and find ways to mitigate the various (cultural) barriers standing in their way. These forms of cultural knowledge and skills were represented in industry discourses as a necessary but insufficient condition for securing India. Securing Asia 2012's programming, for instance, suggested that bringing homeland security to India could not be reduced to transactions between buyers and sellers of homeland security solutions. Fabricating Indian homeland security was also about transforming Indians' "awareness" *about* and appreciation *for* homeland security as a new paradigm of governance.

RAISING AWARENESS

Echoing claims made by Israeli homeland security purveyors in chapter 2 as well as themes in the pages of the Mumbai *Protector* (chapters 3 and 4), industry discourses framed awareness raising as key to cultivativating different dispositions and subjectivities of Indians vis-à-vis homeland security. A 2009 Bombay First white paper suggested that Indians "need to urgently take steps to change our attitude towards security." It continued: "Every

Government Authority, and more particularly the police should give the utmost importance both in words and action to security," insisting that "Nobody should belittle security."[29] It further stated: "Our objective should be two-fold, i.e. public attitude should change, and the [state] authorities should be better prepared. One depends upon the other."[30] The inaugural issue of the FICCI-Pinkerton India Risk Survey similarly positioned itself as "an attempt to sensitise Government about emerging risks and dangers they pose, so that well planned strategic policy decisions can be made and implemented."[31] This imperative of raising the profile of certain dangers also involved educating India about the meaning and value of homeland security as a new paradigm of governance in need of urgent state and corporate intervention. A 2010 KPMG-ASSOCHAM report pledged its commitment to "creating more awareness *about* Homeland Security in the country," presenting homeland security as an alternative, modern perspective on domestic security planning to the current status quo in India.[32]

This project of cultivating awareness about homeland security in India was also central to SWI's work. It cited boosting "security awareness" within India as central to its broader mission of Indian homeland security: "SWI works towards a secure tomorrow by enhancing security awareness and consciousness in Indian industry and civil society."[33] Its website further noted that "SWI has been organizing conferences globally to create security consciousness among [Indian] citizens, industry and the [Indian] government," arguing that such events are "[c]reating the groundwork for improved homeland security."[34] To lay this "groundwork," SWI sought to educate domestic "stakeholders" (domestic state officials, security purveyors, investors) through a range of seminars and workshops across Indian cities, including Secure City 2012, held first in New Delhi in September 2012 and followed by a three-city tour of Ahmedabad, Mumbai, and Kolkata. SWI also published white papers and promotional materials on security issues facing India and Asia as well as generating a news feed featuring a compilation of related news articles and reports.

As these texts allude to, a focus on cultivating greater homeland security awareness or consciousness cannot be decoupled from the strategies of educating the Indian market or networking detailed above. One SWI publication entitled "Guiding India to a Secure Future" featured an image depicting SWI's work as having four core inter-related aspects: "create," "promote," "provide," and "educate" (Figure 6.7). These activities were framed as mutually constitutive and complementary, working to redress "the threats *of* Homeland Security" in the sense of the dangers facing the nation.[35] But they were also framed as resolving "threats" *to* the project of Indian homeland security, like that of Indian bureaucracy and a lack of demand for new products and services among relevant stakeholders.[36]

While the themes of different industry reports, events, websites, and pamphlets overlap and converge, it is also useful to point out some of their points of dissonance. For example, events like Securing Asia 2012 were primarily focused on exhibiting the Indian/Asian homeland security market as ready to be tapped, requiring that western purveyors be educated to deal

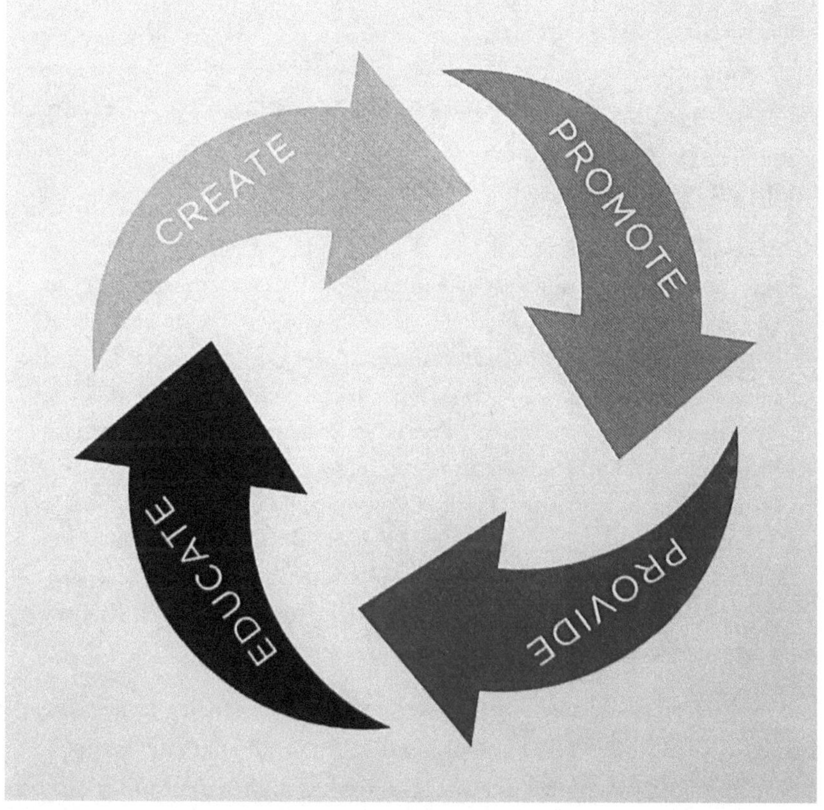

FIGURE 6.7: *Image from "Guiding India to a Secure Future." Source: Security Watch India.*

with the peculiarities of Indian business culture. In partial contrast, events like IFSEC and Homeland Security India as well as consultancy reports coauthored by bodies like FICCI and ASSOCHAM were more focused on educating would-be Indian buyers and boosters to appreciate the necessity of homeland security as a new paradigm of governance. Thus, within the project of fabricating Indian homeland security, the imperative of raising awareness was situated as a strategy through which India's *in*security could be overcome by enabling Indians to finally wake up to the necessity of a homeland security approach and taking steps to shift into this new (modern) paradigm. Indeed, industry boosters framed efforts to educate Indian homeland security subjects as a way to overcome Indian tradition, backwardness, and culture by reeducating the "Indian mind."

THE INDIAN MIND

These efforts to raise security awareness represent a continuation of longer-standing campaigns in India and elsewhere.[37] A 1971 *USI Journal* article expressed its desire to raise India's "security consciousness" and outlined a campaign to realize this goal:

> There is no doubt that security consciousness can be created by taking suitable measures. It is, however, a continuing process, something which can be created only during a period of time. In countries where the majority of people are educated, and where a large portion of the population has had some service in the armed forces or other defence activities, there would be a great amount of security consciousness in existence. [. . .] Due to various historical and other factors, an awareness [of security] does not now exist [in India], but has to be created. In this, the news media and leaders of all walks of society have to bear responsibility. There is a definite need for initiating a campaign to create security consciousness in the nation. The need is, perhaps, as urgent as that of population control for the future of the [Indian] nation, and a comparable campaign is called for.[38]

In the aftermath of 26/11, this desire to increase security awareness returned with a sudden vigor and urgency in India. Industry actors began to argue that reeducating the Indian mind should be the first order of business in modernizing India's domestic security infrastructure. The 2009 FICCI report claimed that "[u]ltimately, all the great battles are fought in the mind," suggesting the "battle" over Indian homeland security should be no different.[39] This focus on the Indian mind was also a central theme of subsequent industry publications and trade events. "Guiding India to a Secure Future" presented SWI as a "Catalyst for Thought Leadership," with an image of a range of such leaders, including K. P. S. Gill superimposed on a map of India (Figures 6.8 and 6.9). The same document also

FIGURE 6.8: *"Catalyst for Thought Leadership." Source: Security Watch India.*

Past Events

The Challenge of terrorism to India's Infrastructure and Economy

SOME OF THE PARTICIPATING COMPANIES INCLUDED

Thales India Pvt. Ltd.; Eldyne Electro Systems Pvt. Ltd.; Oil and Natural Gas Corporation Ltd.; Delhi International Airport (P) Ltd.; Maharashtra State Power Generation Co. Ltd.; Hindustan Petroleum Corporation Limited; Dell International Services India Pvt. Ltd.; Indian Oil Corporation Limited; Infosys Technologies Limited; Delhi Development Authority; Jaiprakash Associates Limited; National Security Guard; Mahanagar Gas Limited; L 3 Communications; L&T Infra; Gas Authority of India; Tata Advanced Systems; Cairn India; HCL Technologies, etc.

The Honorable Michael Chertoff

Mr. Gopal K Pillai

Mr. Shekhar Dutt

H.E. Mr. Tejendra Khanna

Ms. Elaine Dezenski

Mr. H.S. Brahma

Dr. Tobias Feakin

Mr. Shyam Mehra, IPS (Rtd.)

Mr. Leo Gleser

Guiding India to a Secure Future 23

FIGURE 6.9: *List of participating companies at previous SWI events. Source: Security Watch India.*

has an image of foreign homeland security officials, including former U.S. DHS secretary Michael Chertoff as well as Leo Gleser of ISDS, the latter of whom we met in chapters 2 and 5.

As I have noted above, Securing Asia 2012 was styled as a key battlefield for this epic struggle over "thought" and "mindsets," taking place through dialogue and debate among interested parties. Alongside its imperatives of networking and opening doors, it was presented as a "cerebral platform" for overcoming a range of cultural barriers and "world views," which were standing in the way of Indian homeland security, through strategies of "information sharing" and "learning" (Figure 6.6). As Dhaul's opening remarks illustrate, Securing Asia 2012's programming was characterized by liberal tropes about coming together to work across difference through dialogue. Yet the event's cerebral focus was also notably manifested in its organizational structure with substantial programming time and physical venue space devoted to inter-civilizational debates in the form of roundtables and keynotes featuring a mix of well-known scholars from elite British and international universities, like King's College, London and American University as well as prominent think tanks, including the Royal United Services Institute and the Brookings Institution. Some of these discussions also featured high-profile current and former public officials including former Labour politician and leading Iraq War proponent Jack Straw, international security experts, and industry representatives, all debating the key challenges facing the future of Asia and how they could be resolved.

At Securing Asia 2012, the first such panel discussion was entitled "Understanding the Asian Mindset, Attitudes, and Perceptions." It had three panelists: the chief belief officer at an Indian corporate conglomerate; a professor from King's College, London; and a former Pakistani ambassador. As spelled out in the event guide, the premise of this session was debunking various "myths" inherent in western views on security by giving space for authentic Asian perspectives to emerge. It promised to bring a "historical and cultural perspective" on "values and beliefs" and to reveal the difference between "the western view vs. the reality" by "busting myths" about perceptions of security in India today.[40]

In keeping with this focus, the panelists ruminated on the importance of security "worldviews," implying that there are differences between the western and the Asian/Indian versions. Couched in platitudes about human desires and needs, the crux of the belief officer's message was that western perspectives on security fail to adequately appreciate the specificities of India, reflecting a long-standing tendency to undervalue the key contributions of Indian civilization. As an example, he noted that because there is no harmony in Indian music, westerners historically wrote it off as primitive, thereby neglecting its true complexity and value. He finished by asking the audience to consider whether we should "allow" or "correct" different security worldviews, leaving this question unanswered. The next address, by the King's College professor, was entitled "Understanding the Indian Mindset and the Sociopolitical Challenges," and it continued with similar themes. Like the belief officer, the professor reified contrasts between Indian and western perspectives on security and the importance of reconciling them, though he was similarly thin with the specifics.

While such presentations often lacked any clear conclusions or even discernible arguments as such, they mobilized cartoonishly crude caricatures of Indian and western culture. Their general takeaway was that although changing mindsets and beliefs was crucial to securing Asia, this could not be realized by simply imposing western security perspectives *onto* Indians. They intimated Indians could no longer be seen as passive recipients of western knowledge and civilization; the western view had to (finally) contend with the reality of India and adapt accordingly. This reflects the strategic dimensions of strategic syncretism elaborated in previous chapters. That is, although the Indian actors involved in fabricating Indian homeland security were ostensibly seeking to emulate western approaches and remake India in their image, these same actors also mobilized this project to vindicate India as a historically threatened culture and recuperate Hinduism's overlooked civilizational contributions to the world. This is evidenced in the belief officer's insistence that despite the well-known deficiencies of India's approaches to *security*, India has made its own substantial contributions to art and culture that cannot be overlooked. Such reasoning represents a cornerstone of Indian exceptionalism. As Kate Sullivan's account of Indian exceptionalism in the context of Indian diplomacy elaborates, its key tenets include the notion that India has a unique capacity to offer moral leadership in world affairs and that the inherent moral and spiritual "genius" of Indian civilization needs to be combined with certain elements of European enlightenment for the former to realize its full potential in the contemporary world.[41]

While most industry events and texts did not spell out cerebral concerns or challenges of difference in Indian homeland security as schematically as Securing Asia, strikingly similar themes and strategies were present across all of them. These events and their accompanying texts focused on transforming ideas and norms surrounding how India and Indians see, understand, and imagine domestic security by translating and tailoring (western) homeland security ideas and solutions to Indian conditions. In his remarks at the Mumbai policy conference, a U.K. official stressed that "our countries couldn't be more different." To elaborate, he noted that Britain is a small, cold island and India is a vast country with climatic diversity and a huge population. Yet the official remained hopeful about the prospects of collaboration across these differences, because both countries face the same threats. During a panel discussion that followed, a representative from a major U.S. weapons manufacturer further sought to assuage any concerns that the delegation was trying to impose its technological solutions onto India. He patronizingly praised Indian security consumers as some of the "most intelligent I have ever had the privilege of working with," pledging his unwavering commitment to working to suit their needs on their terms.

Other event programming focused on the need to transform existing norms around how Indians imagined homeland security and went about developing solutions. At IFSEC and Homeland Security India, Rajiv, a consultant from a leading Indian corporate management consultancy, criticized what he called a "commoditized approach to solution architecture," using the example of equating e-governance with the buying of new computers. He contrasted these with his recommendation for a "holistic security agenda" based on citizen engagement. When we spoke a few days later in his corporate office in New Delhi, Rajiv explained that the key challenge of Indian homeland security was not, in fact, really a "security problem" at all, at least not in the narrow technical sense of managing threats and risks. Instead, he argued, India's homeland security challenge stemmed from a deeper "problem of governance," invoking the endurance of a "colonial mindset" as the key impediment to his and other experts' ongoing efforts to secure the Indian nation. As he emphasized, "we [Indians] want to control, not to govern." He claimed that some people in the Indian government are in the "twenty-second century," enlightened to the real value of investing in homeland security as an economic and political necessity. As Rajiv explained, however, the vast majority of Indians remained in the "twelfth century" clinging to a backward "colonial" mentality of punishing individual crimes and failing to resolve systemic governance issues around a more effective and comprehensive approach to the management of the nation's domestic security. Rajiv stressed that Indian homeland security was not at all like homeland security in the West and that "internal security" was a more useful descriptor, which had more resonance among Indian officials and publics.

Rajiv's reflections suggested that in spite of industry boosters' efforts to educate Indians about the necessity of adopting modern/western homeland security approaches, the concept was not yet hegemonic in the Indian context. Rajiv's comments echo a long-standing concern among Indian security analysts and practitioners about Indian leaders' lack of security consciousness,[42] reflecting a broader postcolonial anxiety among Indian elites and educated classes about not being there *yet.*[43] This supposed deficiency has also long been of concern to strategic thinkers in the Global North, who have ruminated on India's (supposed) absence of "strategic thinking" and the historical factors and peculiar cultural attributes, which impede such thinking from taking shape in India.[44]

Such discussions raise questions not merely about the universality of *homeland* security but security per se. Indeed, the above-cited 1971 *USI Journal* article with which I opened this section obliquely questions security's self-implied universality. On one hand, it takes as its foundational premise the notion that "security consciousness is inherent in *all living beings*," that is, a universal. Yet as the article elaborates, "[s]ecurity has different shades of meaning" and further emphasizes that creating security *consciousness* represents "a continuing process, something which can be created *only during a period of time*."[45] In other words, although its reflections on how to "remedy" India's lack of security consciousness are based on the premise that security is an inherent and universal characteristic of all living beings, it suggests that cultivating consciousness is a contingent and uncertain historical process, one that might never materialize in the Indian context.

My own ethnographic engagements with the project of fabricating Indian homeland security suggest that this process remains not merely elusive but also illusory. Part of the reason for this is that many of the boosters of Indian homeland security were operating on the flimsy "once was blind but now can see" narrative.[46] In other words, they seemed to assume that the project of educating this market was principally an epistemological matter. Yet the success of fabricating Indian homeland security necessarily extended beyond the realms of the mind and of belief. Here one of the most crucial insights of ANT's engagements with performativity is that performativity includes but also goes beyond the realms of language, discourse, and human minds and into the materialities of sociotechnical worlds. Their accounts of the performativity of economics explicitly leave open "the possibility of events that might refute, or even happen independently of, what humans believe or think."[47] Moreover, Rajiv's comments speak to an unwillingness of Indians to fully capitulate to the terms of corporate-led efforts to fabricate Indian homeland security in the image of the West, as I explore next.

'UNRULY' SUBJECTS

At industry events there was an excitement about the prospect of replicating western homeland security prowess in India. At the closed-door conference in Mumbai, a high-ranking minister in Maharashtra's government pledged his commitment to large-scale CCTV projects across Maharashtra, projects that were inspired by London's nominally exemplary approach to surveillance. He reflected that London's unparalleled success in surveillance had shaped his own thinking about security and police modernization, after experiencing it firsthand years before as a student in London. Yet, echoing themes explored in chapter 5, not all Indian state officials sounded like pacified subjects of *homo securitas* lining up to be reeducated, at least not on the terms dictated to them by the global homeland security industry and their Indian elite collaborators.

During industry events, some Indian state officials shared their skepticism and hesitations about the idea of replicating homeland security in India. At the Mumbai conference, a high-ranking Indian police officer dampened expectations about what might be achieved through collaboration with the visiting western firms. He emphasized the importance of addressing security challenges gradually in stages rather than all at once, beginning with the "low-hanging fruits" and then, perhaps, moving onto more ambitious goals. He was also less sanguine than other figures at industry events about the prospect of fully transcending differences between the U.K. and India through dialogue. He stressed that Mumbai is a city of "alarming proportions" and that domestic security challenges are extremely difficult to manage, even with the aid of new technology from "advanced" countries like the U.K. In light of these concerns, he stressed that it was crucial to draw attention to the specificities of security "in our context," noting that any foreign tactics or technologies would need to be "dovetailed" into local conditions of Mumbai if they were to prove workable at all.

At other events, Indian state officials more explicitly challenged key industry tropes. Some questioned whether an influx of new perspectives, ideas, or modern technologies offered fixes to structural deficiencies of India's domestic security infrastructure. At IFSEC and Homeland Security India, a former police official from the Indian state of Uttar Pradesh gave a presentation on whether modern homeland security solutions would have prevented 26/11 or could prevent future ones. He asked the audience rhetorically, "Can technology really secure the nation?," answering definitively in the negative. He stressed that even the most modern CCTV system would never have stopped the assailants who carried out 26/11, noting that surveillance is only helpful in prosecuting terrorist attacks after they have already occurred. What really ailed India, he argued, was not a lack of modern technology but rather the absence of a "structural system" of policing and threat management.

Other police officials challenged the very idea that terrorism should be the top priority for Indian homeland security going forward. At New Age Risks in New Delhi, held to launch the 2013 edition of the FICCI-Pinkerton India Risk Survey, the keynote speaker, a retired IPS officer and member of India's National Disaster Management Authority, acknowledged that 26/11 "shook all of us." But he then challenged the prevailing industry trope that the attacks signified the emergence of a new kind of threat, noting that the only thing that made the event of 26/11 novel was that a few rich people got killed. While arguing that an "attitudinal change needs to take place" in Indian security thinking, he explicitly challenged the industry trope that 26/11 did or should signify some "paradigm shift" in threat perceptions. The change, he suggested, should instead address the everyday dangers and risks facing people in poor rural states like Orissa.

Others went even further in troubling the idea of homeland security as quick techno-fixes to gaps in India's domestic security infrastructure. At Challenges for India's Homeland Security, a police official from Bhopal gave a presentation entitled "Modernising Police Forces to Stay Ahead," which criticized the slow-moving and bureaucratic nature of police procurement processes across India. He further called for greater integration of IT-based systems into Indian policing moving forward. The presentation, however, seemed to offer few, if any, new opportunities for engagement by the attending representatives of foreign firms to cash in on. The official explicitly pushed back against the suggestion that Indian police needed some reeducation or even that the West represented the standard of modernity to be striven for. Here he praised India's Unique Identification (UID) number system[48] as an unparalleled global achievement in "civilian biometrics," stressing that *India*, rather than the West, is "*really* the leader in IT!" The police official's attempt to reclaim the UID system as an exceptional and overlooked success story for the world reflects the long-standing ambitions of Indian exceptionalism and the attempts by the *Sangh Parivar* to weigh in on and shape world affairs.[49] It also evidences the closely related attempts by Indian state and corporate actors to celebrate *jugaad* as an ability, a skill, a particular tool or formula, an industrious and entrepreneurial ethos, a mentality, a tradition, a set of values, and even a specific Indian "culture" unto itself.[50] Thus, we see echoes of Hindutva writers' celebration of India's claims to "being different," which are mobilized to validate the inherent genius of Indian civilization as an alternative to western universalism (chapter 5).

Indian state officials' objections to or qualifications of industry tropes show how industry boosters' attempts to educate the subject of Indian *homo securitas*—that is, to interpellate Indians into the world-making project of homeland security—came up short. These tensions certainly reflect a different understanding of security and threat perception in India vis-à-vis the West, which a range of others have elaborated at length in other contexts.[51] But these tensions are more than this. They point to the existence of a different subjectivity, one that refuses to fully capitulate to western actors and Indian corporate elites' (expected) terms of engagement. This suggestion must be carefully qualified in order to avoid falling into the trap of replicating the racist terms of colonial difference at work in efforts to fabricate Indian homeland security. Sanjay Seth's account of histories of western educational practices in colonial India is particularly instructive. Seth reveals the only partial extent to which the British achieved their goals of remaking India and Indians in the image of the modern West. He unearths evidence of a broad failure to produce modern Indian subjects, suggesting that this testifies to the existence (and endurance) of a *different*, that is, non-Occidental, subjectivity. Rather than signifying that Indians were premodern (as colonial discourses would have it), Seth reads this as evidence of the limits of western knowledge. As he notes, to the extent that western knowledge failed to remake Indians in its image, "it never became fully adequate to knowing India."[52]

Following Seth, I argue that when read carefully, Indian state officials' skepticism about and refusal to fully indulge the project of replicating western homeland security unsettles the self-implied universality of western (homeland) security knowledge but also the subject-oriented epistemology of modernity undergirding efforts to export this knowledge to India. This in turn prompts a rethinking of the terms of subjectivity and modernity. As Seth writes, we need to look for ways to

> "think" this difference without substantializing it into another "subjectivity" [. . .]. We need to search for forms of thought which allow us to recognize that there have been and are ways of thinking the world other than modern, occidental ones; but also ways of thinking difference without invoking the Subject and without setting into motion an anthropology which ceaselessly transforms human beings into Man.[53]

In other words, while demonstrating the existence of multiple subjectivities in relation to security projects is crucial, we should not stop there. We also need to challenge the presumed universality implicit in the very notion of subjectivity, which suggests that "there is only ever one norm, and all difference is a deviation from it, or a journey toward it."[54] Situating the unruliness of the Indian subject vis-à-vis the world-making project of homeland security requires grappling with difference on different terms than those of the colonial-modern, namely on ontology rather than merely epistemology.

CONCLUSION

This chapter has argued that fabricating Indian homeland security represents a universalist project in the sense of inscribing homeland security both as an arbiter of modernity and rationality and as a structure of aspirations to transcend differences. As we have seen, this project has been undertaken as an attempt to bring homeland security to India and thereby remake the country and its people in the image of the (modern) West. To be sure, its recurring references to 26/11 as an awakening or paradigm shift further reflect its ambitions to bring India deeper into the orbit of U.S. empire and the global war on terror.[55] Yet the project of fabricating Indian homeland security is not simply about securing an already-existing neoliberal economic order of things in India. Rather, it has been self-styled as a civilizing mission that reinscribes global racial hierarchies and the long-discredited subject-oriented rationality associated with post-Enlightenment modernity on which these same hierarchies are founded. This arrogant reason asserts a singular universality by laying its "epistemological privilege" over other forms of knowledge, in effect proclaiming its own coherence and rationality by writing off "all other subjectivities as inadequate, fragmentary, and subordinate."[56]

The underpinning coloniality and racism of this universalist vision is significant. Industry boosters' attempts to further entrench imperial and colonial economic continuities into postcolonial India were hardly well hidden. Brokenshire openly declared that the U.K. government's desire to mobilize the project of Indian homeland security was a means to consolidate and deepen the "historic bond" between Asia and the West. The tagline of the 2013 iteration of Securing Asia was "Bringing Asia to Your Doorstep."[57] Furthermore, the very premise that India's domestic security needed to be modernized in the image of homeland security only makes sense insofar as the West was seen as ultramodern and India as primitive and therefore in need of western knowledge.

Following directly from these colonial precepts, the project of fabricating Indian homeland security has been a project of (re)education. Its core framing of the Indian mind as a key impasse to the realization of Indian homeland security might well have been plucked directly out of the educational programs of the British Raj. British colonial educational practices in India took as their key target the Indian mind and consciousness, based on their modernist presumption that "all actions, social practices, and institutions" represent "expressions and manifestations of ideas and belief."[58] It should be noted that belief itself is a quintessentially modern category.[59] Just as crucially, corporate efforts to position appreciation *for* and proficiency *in* homeland security worked as arbiters of Indians' rationality and humanity. In Rajiv's telling, Indians' enduring attachment to a premodern logic of punishment and limited commitment *to* or understanding *of* homeland security reflects Indians' unwillingness or inability to govern like the modern rational subject of Man. In other words, being (or not being) *homo securitas* becomes a proxy for humanity-as-whiteness in Wynter's sense. Thus, fabricating Indian homeland security is a project that operates, in Lisa Tilley and Robbie Shilliam's terms, as a "raced market"; it is predicated on and works to reinscribe racial categories, stereotypes, and hierarchies of knowledge between the Global North and the Global South.[60]

While fabricating Indian homeland security is a racial project founded on a hierarchy of humanity, its concern with difference goes beyond simply reinscribing this western ideology of domination. It is also crucially concerned with performatively enacting reals and processing differences. After 26/11, boosters of India's homeland security revolution attempted to systematically identify and categorize India's supposedly peculiar security beliefs and mentalities and transcend these through an epistemological process of reeducating the Indian mind. The underlying logic underpinning these efforts was that although India's lack of modernity stems from historical, cultural differences (as well as its historical subjugation by western empire), these could, in principle at least, be overcome through training and education. While industry actors have employed trivializing ideas, concepts, and strategies to identify and overcome forms of Indian difference, this does not mean that questions of difference, subjectivity, ontology, or culture are themselves trivial matters or represent mere glosses for these projects' true objectives. "Neoliberalism," as Mitchell reminds us, "does not lie behind a screen."[61] Rather, references to debate, mutual understanding, and transcending difference should instead be situated as central to the painstaking *groundwork* of trying to process and mediate difference, which did not always go as planned. Indian actors broadly and state actors in particular have proven to be rather unruly homeland security subjects.

This can in turn prompt a reconsideration of the universal pretentions of security per se. As others have already stressed, conceptions of security are contextually bounded and therefore must be translated and adapted to in order to circulate geographically.[62] As rich and insightful as these accounts have been, they and parallel attempts to challenge the prevailing Eurocentrism of security studies fall short.[63] Despite their ostensible efforts to challenge the implied universality of (western) ideas and practices of security, their commitment to the framework of securitization nevertheless reifies security as a universal. That is, even while exploring differences in how security is imagined and practiced across contexts, such accounts replicate liberal conceptions of security as a transcendental value and social good that all people can and should aspire to. In doing so, they contribute to a broader problematic tendency in international relations and social theory to reify "ontological security" as a normative political horizon by disciplining and marginalizing nondominant forms of subjectivity that challenge the ontological security/insecurity episteme.[64]

When security is instead approached as a colonizing, historical project of pacification, as I have done in this book, a different and more fruitful account of security's universalist pretenses and (ostensible) ontological primacy opens up. This chapter shows the imperative of grasping security's colonial, world-making ambitions while refusing to concede their pretenses to universality and rationality, thereby pushing pacification theory further. Although the efforts to educate the subject of *homo securitas* elaborated in this chapter have some specificity, they are less novel than they might appear. They emerge out of long histories of the police power that accompany and the emergence and consolidation of a system of bourgeois rule broadly understood to be synonymous with modernity.[65] When we pay close attention to the particular strategies employed to realize Indian modernity via homeland security, however, what we see is not a struggle to consolidate bourgeois rule alone; it is also crucially a struggle to stitch together the "one-world world" as a single, coherent totality governed by Man.[66]

CODA

As I write this book, the project of fabricating Indian homeland security remains ongoing, and its boosters continue to proclaim its boundless growth as a global market opportunity. Some of these cite the rise of Prime Minister Narendra Modi as a boon to this project. A recent market report notes: "The intrinsic need to protect its people has catapulted India's Homeland Security sector into unprecedented growth," noting that Modi's "push for domestic manufacturing of defence equipment including homeland security equipment under his 'Make in India' campaign has tremendously aided this growth."[67] While the "Make in India" slogan is highly misleading and itself bound up with Hindu exceptionalism,[68] it references some important developments. Between 2021–22 India's weapons exports have reportedly reached an unprecedented new height of Rs 13,000 crore, a significant increase of which 70 percent comes from manufacturing in the private sector.[69] As before, such efforts continue to have significant backing from sections of India's corporate elite, including FICCI, which still has a desk dedicated to homeland security.

This suggests that a field called "Indian homeland security" has indeed been fabricated as a sector of economic and political activity within which various governmental and corporate projects are ongoing. In this sense, at least, the performative dimensions of efforts to fabricate Indian homeland security have succeeded. While these breathless claims about boundless future growth are recurring, the early grand vision of remaking the Indian state in the image of homeland security as articulated by groups like SWI and FICCI have grown less confident and ambitious. Securing Asia was held twice between 2012 and 2013 and then rebranded itself as Securing Asia and Africa in 2014, apparently finding the remit of Asia unduly constraining. Since then, it stopped running altogether, and SWI's website is no longer in operation. The organization has all but disappeared.

This does not seem to be because its sponsors and architects deemed India or Asia to be secure or because India is now sufficiently homeland security "conscious" or "aware" to no longer need any further education. When I followed up with a close associate of Harry Dhaul in 2022 who was involved in Securing Asia, he blamed Dhaul personally for SWI's collapse. He complained that Dhaul was unable to stay focused on Asia/India and "kept on changing the focus" unnecessarily. He further explained that Dhaul ultimately lost interest in "securing Asia" after realizing that this project was not going to be as straightforward or profitable as he had initially anticipated. He noted that Dhaul, not being from the security field, was naïve and overly optimistic about the newfound optimism for homeland security. Dhaul's associate noted that enthusiasm for homeland security in India after 26/11 never really coalesced into a well-defined agenda on police modernization, prompting him to shift his own focus to promoting events more focused around traditional military and defense issues. In the end, then, it seems that Dhaul's claim that Securing Asia was *not* primarily about making money proved prescient, if in an unintended way.

Even if such projects did not meet their own targets, they have nevertheless done important work in legitimating and expanding police power in contemporary India and certainly enabled some of their boosters to extract profits. Yet Indian internal security never became modern. Just like during the British empire itself, "India was not (is not) proto-Europe."[70] But Europe has never been modern either.[71] And modern thought is not itself terribly apt in making sense of what modernity is or how it comes into being, in India or anywhere else.

CONCLUSION

IN THIS BOOK, I have explored how homeland security is fabricated across space and time. To tell this story, I have focused on the event of 26/11 and how media pundits, state officials, and homeland security boosters framed it as the moment when India woke up to the new reality of "global," "Islamic" terrorism. Hence the idea that 26/11 was India's 9/11. Though hegemonic, this representation did not go unchallenged. As Arundhati Roy argued in an essay entitled "9 is not 11," published in the Indian magazine *Outlook* on December 22, 2008, "November isn't September, 2008 isn't 2001, Pakistan isn't Afghanistan and India isn't America."[1] The documentary filmmaker Anand Patwardhan further called out the emerging impulse to seek American and Israeli homeland security solutions to 26/11, arguing that this would "lead us [Indians] further into the abyss." Patwardhan did not merely critique such impulses as misguided but also notably emphasized their underlying futility. As he pointed out:

> India is for many reasons a quintessentially soft target. Our huge population, vast landmass and coastline are impossible to protect. The rich may build new barricades. The Taj and the Oberoi can be made safer. So can our airports and planes.

Yet, protecting Mumbai's railway stations, trains, bus stops, buses, and markets, Patwardhan argued, was another matter altogether, stressing that "no amount of homeland security can save us."[2] At the time, Roy's and Patwardhan's critiques represented rare attempts to destabilize the emerging bourgeois desire to bring homeland security to India. Yet, in the following decade, Roy's and Patwardhan's words have proven remarkably prescient.

Less than three years after 26/11, another attack rocked Mumbai. On the evening of July 13, 2011, twenty-six people were killed and another 130 wounded in coordinated bombings at Dadar West, Zaveri Bazaar, and the Opera House. Repeating a familiar pattern, the Maharashtra government took the attacks as an opportunity to learn from abroad. Maharashtra's home minister, R. R. Patil, was dispatched to Scotland Yard to study London's video surveillance approach. In an op-ed published in the *Sunday Guardian*, Vappala Balachandran challenged the premise of this move, repeating his skepticism concerning the Indian delegation sent to Israel in 2009 (chapter 3). Balachandran argued that "[f]oreign jaunts, purchase of equipment or recruitment of more policemen will not improve our counter-terrorist methodology," insinuating that the renewed impulse to send its officials abroad in 2011 was a deliberate attempt to avoid serious restructuring of the city's security infrastructure, which he and Ram Pradhan had recommended in the HLEC report two years earlier.[3] Reporting on the 2011 blasts, Naresh Fernandes, a Mumbai journalist, echoed Patwardhan's skepticism about homeland security solutions. Fernandes argued that "[n]o matter how many security cameras are installed and how many check posts are established at traffic junctions, it won't be long before another determined terrorist hides an explosive device under an umbrella."[4] However, in contrast to the political consequences of 26/11 (chapter 3), the 2011 blasts received no significant backlash from the media or publics. If anything, this muted response seemed to signal an admission that little could have been done to prevent these most recent attacks or mitigate their lethal consequences.

As I began my fieldwork in 2012, I frequently reflected on the similarities and differences between the respective responses to 26/11 and the 2011 blasts. How was the event of 26/11 constituted as an exceptional moment in India's post-Independence history? How did homeland security materialize in India in the years thereafter? What roles did homeland security play in India politically and otherwise? How did the impulse to modernize India's police infrastructures square with its persistent coloniality? Would I be able to find evidence of Israel's homeland security industry's mark on India's politics or physical landscapes of Mumbai or elsewhere across the country? Throughout this book, I have provided answers to some of these questions. In the concluding pages of *Fabricating Homeland Security*, I reflect on what the fate of homeland security in India might tell us about homeland security more broadly, including its imperial and colonial origins and world-making ambitions. I find Roy's and Patwardhan's refusals to equate 26/11 with 9/11 analytically and politically instructive in challenging the myth of homeland security and attempting to think beyond it, within India and in the world at large.

As I have illustrated in this book, efforts to remake India and Indians in the image of homeland security partially came to fruition and did particular kinds of work in constituting the event of 26/11 itself. Indeed, as I have shown, "Israel" and "Israeli homeland security" as well as some Israeli and Jewish actors (state officials, security experts, pro-Israel lobbyists, industry boosters, ZAKA and MDA personnel, Chabad rabbis, journalists, and op-ed columnists) were present in the event of 26/11 from the outset. Their presence and criticism of Indian authorities paved the way for various solutions to the attacks before they were even declared officially over (chapter 1). This was itself nothing new. It was but the latest iteration of longer-standing efforts by Israeli actors to locate and position Zionist pacification efforts in Palestine as a model for the world through exceptionalist narration (chapter 2). As I have argued, we need to understand the fabrication of homeland security within these ongoing histories of empire and their strategies of obfuscation and disavowal.

In the years after 26/11, homeland security's global mission served some global and Indian constituencies well enough. Local state actors were able to police the crisis of authority that 26/11 gave rise to under the banner of police modernization rather effectively (chapter 3). Evidence of this can be seen in the return of some of the very politicians who became objects of the wave of anti-politician anger. R. R. Patil, who was initially forced to resign from office in 2008, returned less than a year later with objections from the BJP but limited broader political fallout. Around this time, Chhagan Bhujbal, referenced in the HLEC report for his failures to adequately equip the Mumbai police properly prior to 26/11, became Maharashtra's deputy chief minister.

Furthermore, certain state actors who had overseen the initial handling and responses to 26/11 later became security experts in the private sector. For instance, during my time in Mumbai I met a former high-ranking NSG official who had played a central operational role in the widely criticized operations during 26/11 at the Taj and Oberoi hotels and Nariman House (chapter 1). After his retirement he became a security expert at a leading Indian management consultancy, advising major corporations and Indian government agencies. Several other prominent Indian officials, irrespective of their parts in the (mis)handling of previous crises, rode the wave of homeland security in India after 26/11.

Yet the mission to remake India and Indians in the image of homeland security did not materialize in ways that many, including Israelis, initially imagined or desired it would. Despite all of their best efforts to exploit 26/11 as a moment of opportunity (chapter 1), the Israeli homeland security industry's attempts to "penetrate" India mostly came up short (chapter 5), as did Indian capital's broader strategies to educate an Indian homeland security market (chapter 6). And to the extent that homeland security materialized in the city of Mumbai, it did so in highly patchy, ad-hoc, and often questionable ways. Newly procured weapons, equipment, and technologies were woven into the city's preexisting police infrastructure in a *jugaad*-like fashion (chapter 4).

India, in all kinds of ways, was not (and still is not) America (or Israel), to borrow Roy's phrase. During my time in India, I found evidence that the initial enthusiasm for replicating homeland security in India had waned (chapters 4, 5, and 6). Even D. Sivanandan, who had previously declared that his top three priorities as Mumbai's police commissioner would be "terrorism, terrorism and terrorism," was singing a rather different tune by late 2012. At a public roundtable, Sivanandan argued that "[c]orruption [. . .] is a bigger threat than terrorism," further pointing out that "[s]ecurity [. . .] is considered a waste of investment by both the government and the private sector." He concluded, "In some ways we are prepared while in others we are not," conceding that regardless of the local state's best efforts, the terrorists would invariably remain "four steps ahead of us."[5] Likewise, the 2019 FICCI-Pinkerton Risk Survey (the last published issue to date) conceded that the category of Terrorism and Insurgency "has slipped into the fifth position" of perceived importance in India after Corruption Bribery and Corporate Frauds; Natural Hazards, Crime, and Political and Governance Instability.[6] Thus, the political and elite commitments to homeland security as a strategy to fight terrorism seemed to have dissipated. Part of the reason for this is that the political pressure exerted by India Inc. proved less than formidable in the longer term, precisely because it was never rooted in any meaningful mass constituency. When I spoke with the Marathi editor we met in chapter 4, he stressed that the elite-led demands for security never had any grassroots basis or appeal, noting that the event of 26/11 represented little more than "a glamorized melodrama of the rich." As a result, the pressure that India Inc. initially exerted on the political class in the aftermath of 26/11 proved less than formidable.

In trying to make sense of this state of affairs, critics often frame the country's policing infrastructure as exceptionally backward and therefore incapable of delivering policing's ostensible goal of security for all. Policy commentators frequently argue that Indian politicians are incapable of even understanding what security is, let alone practicing it in an efficient way because their political imperatives to resort to theatrical but ineffective strategies. When I spoke with Ajai Sahni in his office at the Institute for Conflict Management in New Delhi in 2013, he explained that "the *illusion* of security is infinitely more important to the [Indian] political establishment than the creation of *actual* security or *actual* capability of response." According to Sahni, moreover, Indian politicians' lack of understanding of *real* security was precisely what led them and others to embrace the idea that emulating foreign models of homeland security after 26/11 would secure Mumbai and the nation. The fixation on such foreign models, Sahni noted, reflected "an *idiotic* view, it's not myopic. Myopic is too flattering. This is stupidity. . . . It is at the level of extreme ignorance that these things are being discussed and obviously the consequences are never going to be achieved."

As I have elaborated earlier chapters, such critiques of the Indian state predate 26/11 by many decades. They have been central concerns throughout India's post-Independence history, often articulated by former Indian state officials, who have become some of the most persistent critics of Indian policing and advocates for its reform. In *Police and Politics in India*, former IPS officer Kirpal Dhillon writes that "Indian police continues to be a prisoner of mid-nineteenth-century enactments, colonial concepts, antiquated legal systems and mindsets." He continues: "Indian political and bureaucratic classes are woefully deficient in security consciousness. Even when a new organization is set up specifically to look after national security in all of its various aspects, it often fails to approach its task with precision and concentration."[7] Such accounts further suggest that Indian policing's focus on protecting politicians and maintaining *order* is anomalous and out of step with what modern professional policing can and should achieve.

Such accounts overlap with more radical critiques of the Indian state. As prominent Mumbai human rights lawyer Colin Gonzalves observed on December 20, 2008, "What the people of India expected was that the governments would give careful thought to making the police a professional fighting force oriented to the security of ordinary citizens of India rather than operating, as it does now, as the protectors of politicians."[8] Yet, as Gonzalves noted, nothing of the sort was likely to take place. Gonzalves's objections to the authoritarian character of Indian policing are entirely different from those of Sahni. Sahni, the son-in-law of the late K. P. S. Gill, has long worked to rationalize and legitimate Indian state violence. The two founded the Institute for Conflict Management in the late 1990s and worked closely together to, among other things, improve India's strategic thinking but also to push back against international human rights groups documenting the recurring atrocities carried out by Indian forces. Despite the very different politics of figures like Gonzalves versus those of Sahni and Gill, they share a common conception of Indian policing and hence the definition of Indian security as an absence or a lack.

These critiques offer insights into understanding the state of internal security in contemporary India. The enduring coloniality of Indian policing is undeniable, with key continuities in its structure and the tyrannical violence it instantiates enduring post-Independence. Furthermore, a focus on the theatrical dimensions of Indian state power resonates with some of my own findings. In chapter 3, I documented how the political imperative to act swiftly compelled the Maharashtra government to procure weapons and equipment that lack any obvious tactical purpose. As we saw in chapter 4, moreover, such decisions seem to have been made in the absence of systematic planning and marked by recurring corruption.

Reading these dynamics as evidence of lack of *real* security, however, is a mistake. Although the illusory, theatrical, incompetent, and politicized nature of security in India are often read as exceptional, such claims, when situated within critical theorizations of police power, become difficult to sustain. Indian policing, like all forms of policing, has its own particular genealogy and hence a degree of specificity, which this book and others have elaborated in detail. These specificities have both structural and cultural elements.[9] Yet Indian policing's mythic, illusionary, colonial, and antidemocratic features; "political" nature; and predominant focus on order-making rather than prosecuting "crime" are anything but anomalous. What is often framed as "security theater" (in contradistinction to the real thing), in other words, is better understood as just *security*. Police have never set out to "serve" or "protect" ordinary people from anything, nor should anyone hope that they might; they are there to serve and protect themselves.[10]

As Manisha Sethi crucially points out, the prevailing idea that Indian police violence stems primarily from a lack of resources or general incompetence represents a dangerous and self-serving mythology in its own right. This mythology enables Indian state officials to wash their hands of their systematically prejudicial treatment of minorities (especially Muslims) under the banner of counterterrorism, thereby obfuscating the core objectives that this prejudicial violence serves.[11] Sahni's suggestion above that the imperative of replicating western homeland security models in India stems from a combination of stupidity and ignorance importantly obscures the ways in which the fabrication of homeland security in India has worked to advance mass surveillance and the Indian state's permanent counterinsurgency war against its political enemies. Thus, while this book has argued that homeland security never materialized in India in the "modern" form its architects desired, some of the resulting institutions that did materialize, like the NIA, have been weaponized with considerable efficiency.[12] The NIA gives the central Indian state jurisdiction to investigate alleged offenses in any police station across the country and has dramatically increased the success rate in the conviction of terror-related charges.[13]

Thus, homeland security's fate in India should not be understood as evidence of India or Indians being premodern. Rather, I argue that it reflects the existence of different reals or worlds as well as the endurance of non-Occidental subjectivities into contemporary India (chapters 5 and 6). Moreover, the fragile, fraught, and tentative attempts to remake India in the image of homeland security points to a broader story about homeland security itself, its paradigm, and its global mission. Approaching homeland security as fabricated (*made, made up*, and *woven together*), as I have done in this book, provides us with an opportunity to unsettle the prevailing image of homeland security as an all-encompassing, universal paradigm of contemporary governing.

UNSETTLING HOMELAND SECURITY

As I have argued throughout this book, critically engaging with the emergence of homeland security and its globalizing ambitions requires taking it seriously, yet actively refusing to abide by its own conventions and the forms of active forgetting on which it is predicated. In particular, I have suggested that we question the term's misleading claim to radical novelty. As Amy Kaplan observed as early as 2003, the rising salience of "homeland" at the time was not altogether new. It was a return that mobilized "comforting images of a deeply rooted past to legitimate modern forms of imperial power."[14] When properly situated in this long and ongoing history of imperial and (settler)colonial pacification projects and the exceptionalist narratives through which they are waged (chapter 2), the project of homeland security comes into view as rather less exceptional and unprecedented than it might otherwise appear.

This book argues that when read carefully, efforts to fabricate homeland security in India offer new ways to unsettle the notion of homeland security and the models thereof, which go beyond abstract critique. As we have seen, homeland security is a self-consciously global mission that has attempted to remake the world in its image. Yet, this does not mean that what Brendan McQuade calls the "prose of pacification" organized under the banner of homeland security is all-powerful.[15] While India has long been thoroughly imbricated in imperial pacification projects, it has never served as some passive backdrop onto which they could be projected. Their encounters have always been negotiations, some of which are surprisingly contingent and uncertain and reflective of the multiple social orders that endure in the world. Thus, rather than treating these challenges as tangential to the story of fabricating homeland security, I have embraced the fragment and fragmentary analysis to tell a different story of homeland security's global mission.

Donna Haraway suggests that "staying with the trouble" of contemporary planetary crisis means considering which stories to tell about this crisis and how to tell them.[16] Anna Tsing similarly argues that as we think about possibilities for life in the ruins of capitalism and empire, we need to better differentiate between the stories we know from stories we need to know by cultivating "arts of noticing."[17] Inspired by this impulse to tell different stories, I suggest that when read carefully, homeland security's encounters with India reveals how truly "alien" homeland security is to much of the world, even places and societies deeply imbricated in empire and capitalist social relations.[18] As Roland Barthes points out, myths have histories but also geographies.[19] This means that myths have boundaries and limits as well; they are not everywhere the same.

The difficulties and impasses in fabricating homeland security in India can enable us to return to an often overlooked if not entirely forgotten matter, namely the term's underlying meaning or substance. In the early years of the global war on terror, Jodi Dean incisively noted that the term homeland security "*does not mean anything* but anticipates the possibility of meaning."[20] "We should not forget," Dean continued, "that even as the Department of Homeland Security seems to *secure* the term by repeating and inscribing it another space, 'homeland security,' for those of us who refuse to be interpellated by it, means nothing at all."[21] Following Dean, the frictions and difficulties encountered in bringing homeland security to India illustrate Indians' partial refusal to become fully interpellated by this world-making project. If we follow Dean's claim through and pay attention to how homeland security's encounters with India and Indians played out, we see how meaningless the term remains there.

Indeed, even Indian security practitioners with whom I spoke openly expressed their reticence to commit to the project of homeland security, which they were ostensibly working for and materially benefiting from. In January 2012, I met up with the NSG official I noted above who had become a security consultant at the café in the Taj Hotel in Mumbai. He was visiting the city on a business trip. As we discussed his work and his experience of 26/11, the consultant explained that the majority of new security measures that were instituted after 26/11 were futile. He noted that the only thing that hotels could do to protect themselves would be to install bollards to protect them from a vehicle bomb attack, as the Taj Hotel had done with the assistance of Israeli companies (chapter 4). Yet he argued that all other measures such as checking under incoming cars with mirrors and scanning guests' luggage was a complete waste of time and money. The vast majority of security systems, the consultant maintained, were simply to give the *impression* that something was being done. He was not convinced by any of it, arguing that the response to 26/11 was wildly out of proportion to the threats that India faced. When we met up again some weeks later in New Delhi outside another luxury hotel where the guards were tasked with looking under incoming cars with mirrors, he wryly noted that the demand for new so-called homeland security solutions serves the needs of "the mirror industry" rather than those of everyday people in India. His ambivalence about homeland security reflects Indians' refusals to become fully interpellated into the figure of Indian *homo securitas*.

Dean's reflections also gesture to something else, namely that homeland security gets "secured" by the vast material infrastructure and spatiality that institutions like DHS and the IOF provide. Moreover, it is such infrastructures that secure the term in place, to use Dean's phrase. Her reflections help to make sense of homeland security's *in*security in India, a country where the vast infrastructure of DHS did not exist either before or after 2008 and likely never will. Even industry reports, which set out to raise awareness about the value of homeland security in India, sometimes make reference to the sheer disparity between the size of its political economy in the United States versus India. Citing a market report from hsrc.biz, an infographic from the 2010 KPMG-ASSOCHAM report mentioned in chapter 6 noted that India represents 3.6 percent of global spending on homeland security, in contrast to the United States at 33 percent.[22] While the report represented this difference as a crucial opportunity for future growth in India, it nevertheless points to the profound gulfs in the material investment in the necessary infrastructures to sustain the myth of homeland security. What makes the practice of Indian security meaningfully distinct is that it more readily exposes the fabricated nature of police power per se, precisely because the material, political, and ideological groundwork necessary to sustain the myth of security are less plentiful.

Another revelation about homeland security that becomes visible through its encounters with India are the varied and sometimes competing roles that forms of difference play within global pacification projects (chapter 5). These cover the well-elaborated roles of these projects in policing what W. E. B. Du Bois called the global "color line" and its underpinning hierarchy of colonial difference.[23] But fabricating homeland security also involves the negotiation of multiple reals in the sense of ontological politics. Despite the global homeland security industry's attempts to overcome the self-described problems of "Indian difference" with epistemological strategies like (re)educating the "Indian mind" (chapter 6), the challenges that these actors were up against were primarily ontological rather than epistemological. When we pay attention to the strategies to fold India into the "one-world world" of the global war on terror, we repeatedly encounter enactments of multiple, sometimes rather incompatible worlds or reals, reflecting global incommensurabilities. In other words, homeland security's encounters with Indians and India repeatedly enacted a fractiverse[24] or pluriverse[25] rather than a universe. As I have argued here, understanding the world-making project of fabricating homeland security requires attention to how differences are enacted and negotiated in practice relationally, rather than approaching them as natural, stable, or preordained.

Finally, homeland security's encounters with India provide new grounds to challenge the universalist pretentions not merely of *homeland* security but of security per se. The most common translation of *security* in Hindi is *suraksha*, a Sanskrit-derived construct and hybrid of two words *su* (well, good) and *raksha* (protection, guard). *Suraksha* is also frequently translated as "safety."[26] While *su* and *raksha* are both very old words, *suraksha* appears to be a more recent coinage. The first translation I have found is in the 1968 Indian government document *Glossary of Administrative Terms*.[27] There, security is translated both as *suraksha* and as *pratibhuti*, a Sanskrit-derived word that in contemporary Hindi-English dictionaries is translated as "security, deposit," "bond," or "bail."[28] Yet, in earlier Hindustani dictionaries of the late nineteenth century, such as the 1866 edition of Forbes's *A Dictionary, Hindustani and English*, *suraksha* does not appear. There, *security* is translated using words with Arabic and Persian etymologies.

A genealogy of *suraksha* exceeds the scope of this book. However, that *suraksha* appears to be a post-Independence coinage is potentially significant. The resort to Sanskrit (rather than the available preexisting vocabularies in Persian or Arabic) could indicate an attempt to distance the lexicon from India's neighbor, Pakistan. Furthermore, the apparent recentness of *suraksha*'s coinage in Hindi seems related to the enduring tentativeness of security and its surrounding ideologies, affects, and practices in the Indian context. Thus, I suggest that security does not enjoy broad resonance in contemporary India. As of yet, it is not common sense. This is not to suggest that forms of territorial control and property relations associated with concepts and practices of security are in any way alien to India or South Asia. The historical translation of security to words like *pratibhuti* denote the well-established property relations in South Asia that precede European colonization and how these continue to relate to ideas about security in India today. It is, however, to raise new questions about the actually existing extent of security's universality.

As I noted in chapter 6, existing scholarship on the translation and indigenization of security regimes and discourses across contexts often fall short by effectively reproducing liberal conceptions of security as a universal value or need. As I have emphasized throughout the previous chapters, Marxian theorizations of security-as-pacification have long challenged security's false universalism by situating its central ideological roles in legitimating processes of accumulation and their surrounding structures of violence. Although pacification projects are universal in the sense that they unfold in the name of capital,[29] Indian state officials and significant sections of Indian capital remain surprisingly less than enthusiastic about being "deceived in the name of security."[30] I read this reticence not as some definitive contradiction but as a crack, an opening, and even a riddle that might serve as the basis for extending existing challenges to security's self-implied universality[31] and forever-ness.[32]

EPILOGUE

AS I NOTED IN the introduction to this book, the story of fabricating homeland security in India overlaps with but is not equivalent to the wider and longer-running story about the relations between Palestine/Israel and India. The rise of Narendra Modi within Indian national politics and the broader entrenchment of Hindu authoritarianism have been profound developments in their own right and ones deeply connected to both of these stories. Under Modi's BJP-led governments, Indo-Israeli bilateral relations at the national level have multiplied and deepened significantly. This is perhaps best evidenced by the rapid growth of conventional weapons sales from Israel to India, which rose by 175 percent between 2015 and 2019.[1] Not coincidentally, during this India became Israel's single largest weapons market by a significant margin.[2]

In this climate, concerns about the "Israelization" of India resulting from collaboration on policing have grown ever more widespread and urgent. Critics suggest that under Modi's emboldened BJP government, the "Hindutva fantasy" is now finally "realising itself," particularly in Kashmir.[3] There have also been collaborations on India's "smart border" along the Line of Control between the Indian- and Pakistani-controlled areas of disputed territory of Jammu and Kashmir.[4] Reports further suggest that a range of police forces, including the Punjab Police, routinely train in Israel.[5] In 2015, the Indian Police Service announced a program to collaborate on counterterrorism, counterinsurgency, and low-intensity warfare with Israel's National Police Academy by sending Indian officers to Palestine/Israel on field trips.[6] In 2018, *The Times of India* reported on ongoing efforts to build a police training center in Modi's home state of Gujarat in collaboration with Israeli partners.[7] On a domestic level, the Indian state under Modi's tenure has extensively weaponized the surveillance software Pegasus developed by Israeli firm NSO Group against up to two thousand of its political opponents, with at least three hundred targeted devices verifiably infected.[8] And although the practice of housing demolition is of long standing in India, it is now shifting in nature and meaning, being explicitly weaponized as retribution for the (alleged) subversive political activity of Indian Muslims in a way that is said to be inspired directly by Israeli practices against Palestinians.[9]

These developments are all profoundly concerning in any number of ways. They seem to suggest that under current BJP rule, India's historical reluctance to fully embrace Israeli homeland security may soon come to an end, if it has not vanished already. Without ruling anything out, however, I am somewhat skeptical of this suggestion for a few reasons. First, I want to recall that almost identical reporting emerged in the aftermath of 26/11. It was in part by reading this reporting that I began this project on the questionable premise that 26/11 was a game-changing historical moment in the story of India's internal security vis-à-vis Israel. As a rule, mainstream press reports of engagements between Israeli actors and Indian police agencies need to be treated as public relations, albeit sometimes evidencing significant forms of engagement. Second, my conversations with Israeli homeland security insiders, small weapons dealers, and police trainers up until 2019 strongly suggest that bilateral relations at the national level (including the sale of large-scale conventional weapons systems) is a different *world* than that of dealing with the governments and police forces of Indian states. I have reason to suspect that boundaries between these different worlds will remain, even though there may be political and economic circumstances that could destabilize them. Third, in conducting research for this book, I have come to the conclusion that there are significant differences between selling objects like weapons, scanners, through-the-wall radars ("gadgets") vs. selling consulting or training. From the numerous Israelis I spoke with, those who sold such gadgets seemed to have had a far more positive impression of engaging with India and Indians. In contrast, those contractors seeking to train local forces and develop large-scale surveillance projects fared less well. Thus, without insisting on some categorical distinction between these two types of homeland security solutions, there is reason to anticipate that Israel's efforts to export gadgets will continue to be more successful than some other activities that occur under the banner of fabricating homeland security in India. In any case, however, doing justice to how the rise of Modi, the BJP, and Hindutva bears on the project of fabricating homeland security exceeds the scope of this book.

NOTES

Introduction

1. "America's New War: Terrorist Attacks Cause Gridlock; President Encourages CIA," *The Point with Greta van Susteren,* CNN, 26 September 2001.

2. For instance, I spoke to a retired member of the Indian Army who recalled that some U.S. military officials visited training academies in Pune, Maharashtra, in the early 2000s in relation to planning for the U.S.-led counterinsurgency campaigns of the war on terror, though he suggested that these engagements ultimately proved very limited and short-lived. In archives of *Pratividrohi,* the flagship journal of the Indian Counterinsurgency and Jungle Warfare School (CIJWS), I also found a number of photos from the early 2000s depicting visits by U.S. forces to the CIJWS training grounds at Vairengte in India's northeastern state of Mizoram.

3. Lee Hockstader, "Israelis Say U.S. Could Learn from Their Tactics," *Washington Post,* 13 September 2001.

4. See for instance Martin Peretz, "Counting," *The New Republic,* 24 September 2001.

5. Lisa Hajjar, "International Humanitarian Law and 'Wars on Terror': A Comparative Analysis of Israeli and American Doctrines and Policies," *Journal of Palestine Studies* 36, no. 1 (2006): 21–42; Stephen Graham, *Cities Under Siege: The New Military Urbanism* (New York: Verso, 2010); Derek Gregory, *The Colonial Present: Afghanistan, Palestine, Iraq* (Malden, Mass.: Blackwell, 2004).

6. Amy Kaplan, *Our American Israel: The Story of an Entangled Alliance* (Cambridge, Mass.: Harvard University Press, 2018), 257.

7. Neve Gordon, "The Political Economy of Israel's Homeland Security/Surveillance Industry," Working Paper III, *The New Transparency: Surveillance and Social Sorting,* 2009; Neve Gordon, "Israel's Emergence as a Homeland Security Capital," in *Surveillance and Control in Israel/Palestine: Population, Territory, and Power,* ed. David Lyon, Elia Zureik, and Yasmeen Abu-Laban (New York: Routledge, 2011), 134–53.

8. Ahmad H. Sa'di, "Israel"s Settler-Colonialism as a Global Security Paradigm," *Race and Class* 63, no. 2 (April 2021): 21–37; Naomi Klein, "Laboratory for a Fortressed World," *The Nation,* 14 June 2007, www.thenation.com/article/laboratory-fortressed-world; Antony Lowenstein, *The Palestine Laboratory: How Israel Exports the Technology of Occupation around the World* (London: Verso, 2023).

9. Sanjay Seth, *Subject Lessons: The Western Education of Colonial India* (Durham, N.C.: Duke University Press, 2007), 9.

10. "National Strategy For Homeland Security," Office of Homeland Security, July 2002, 1–2, emphasis added.

11. Nadav Morag, *Comparative Homeland Security: Global Lessons* (Hoboken, N.J.: John Wiley & Sons, 2011), 1, 362, emphasis added.

12. Morag, *Comparative Homeland Security*, 9, emphasis added.

13. Morag, *Comparative Homeland Security*, 9.

14. Alex Lubin, "From Home Rule to Homeland: Counterterrorism as a Way of Life," *American Quarterly* 74, no. 3 (2022): 556–62; Rhys Machold, "Reconsidering the Laboratory Thesis: Palestine/Israel and the Geopolitics of Representation," *Political Geography* 65 (2018): 88–97.

15. Azad Essa, *Hostile Homelands: The New Alliance between India and Israel* (London: Pluto Press, 2023), 10–13.

16. For instance, in the early 1980s, reports emerged that Indian Army officers traveled to Israel for an anti-hijacking course and that former Indian Prime Minister Rajiv Gandhi's personal security planning was being assisted by Israeli experts. See Bidanda M. Chengappa, "Indo-Israeli Relations: The Great Leap Forward," *Indian Defence Review* 8, no. 3 (July 1993): 108.

17. Efraim Inbar, "The Indian-Israeli Entente," *Orbis* 48, no. 1 (2004): 97.

18. Nicolas Blarel, *The Evolution of India's Israel Policy: Continuity, Change, and Compromise since 1922* (New Delhi: Oxford University Press, 2014); P. R. Kumaraswamy, *India's Israel Policy* (New York: Columbia University Press, 2010); Rupal Oza, "India's relations with Israel and Palestine: Tracing a tectonic shift," *Society and Space Open Site*, September 18, 2014.

19. Reece Jones, *Border Walls: Security and the War on Terror in the United States, India, and Israel* (London: Zed Books, 2012); Rupal Oza, "Contrapuntal Geographies of Threat and Security: The United States, India, and Israel," *Environment and Planning D: Society and Space* 25, no. 1 (2007): 9–32; Vijay Prashad, *Namaste Sharon: Hindutva and Sharonism under U.S. Hegemony* (New Delhi: LeftWord Books, 2003).

20. P. R. Kumaraswamy, "India and Israel: Emerging Partnership," *Journal of Strategic Studies* 25 (2002): 202.

21. K. P. S. Gill, "Terrorism, Institutional Collapse, and Emergency Response Protocols," in *Terror and Containment: Perspectives on India's Internal Security*, ed. K. P. S. Gill and Ajai Sahni (New Delhi: Gyan Publishing House, 2000), 275–76.

22. Gill, "Terrorism, Institutional Collapse," 280.

23. Cited in Reece Jones, "Geopolitical Boundary Narratives, the Global War on Terror, and Border Fencing in India," *Transactions of the Institute of British Geographers* 34, no. 3 (July 2009): 292.

24. POTA replaced the Terrorist and the 1985 Disruptive Activities Prevention Act (TADA), which lapsed in 1995.

25. Oza, "Contrapuntal Geographies," 20.

26. Jones, "Geopolitical Boundary Narratives," 293.

27. "Indian Intelligence Agencies Lack Coordination: Experts," Indo-Asian News Service, 20 October 2004.

28. Ajit Doval, "Terror Tactics Change, but Do We?," *Hindustan Times*, 10 September 2007.

29. Doval, "Terror Tactics Change."

30. Doval, "Terror Tactics Change."

31. 'Israel for Sharing Technology with India', *Assam Tribune*, 14 October 2006.

32. Arjun Sen, "Raytheon Eyes $1-Bn Indian Civilian Business by 2018." Indo-Asian News Service, 21 November 2008.

33. Neelesh Misra, "Advantage Militants as Law Lacks Teeth," *Hindustan Times*, 1 January 2008.

34. Ramesh Bhan, "Indian, US Officials Discuss Security, Prevention of Terrorism," *United News of India*, 28 September 2008.

35. Varghese K. George, "'Can't Give up War on Terror,'" *Hindustan Times*, 28 September 2008.

36. For instance, a 1993 *Pratividrohi* article argued that India suffered from a key structural problem, namely that the country's armed forces were primarily structured to meet foreign (rather than domestic) aggression and that India's "plethora of para-military forces and the police" lacked the "adequate capability to meet the threat posed by insurgents, secessionists and the like." In response it asked whether "we [Indians], like the USA and Israel, [should] raise a separate force to deal with internal security threats? Or should our Armed forces be structured and trained to meet all kinds of threats," including *internal* ones? S. S. Grewal and B. K. Khanna, 'Low Intensity Conflict in the Indian Context', *Pratividrohi* (September 1993): 15.

37. "A Nation That Cannot Afford to Sleep," *Hindustan Times*, 28 November 2008.

38. Pramit Pal Chaudhuri and Aloke Tikku, "Homeland Security: Who Is in Charge Here?," 3 December 2008.

39. Manisha Sethi, *Kafkaland: Prejudice, Law, and Counterterrorism in India* (Gurgaon, India: Three Essays Collective, 2014), 7–8.

40. Arvind Narrain, *India's Undeclared Emergency,* chapter 3. NADGRID was formed in 2009, but the NCTC never came to fruition, facing intense political opposition from certain leaders of Indian states, who objected to its far-reaching powers.

41. Rahul Bedi and Damien McElroy, "India Asks for Foreign Help to Hit Terrorists," *The Daily Telegraph* (London), 3 December 2008.

42. Prem Prakash, "Anger against Politicians Is Justified: We Need Accountability," *Hindustan Times*, 19 December 2008.

43. Veena Das, *Critical Events: An Anthropological Perspective on Contemporary India* (Oxford: Oxford University Press, 1996).

44. Myriam Anna Dunn Cavelty and Kristian Søby Kristensen, eds., *Securing "the Homeland": Critical Infrastructure, Risk, and (In)Security* (Abingdon, England: Routledge, 2008); Donald E. Pease, "The Global Homeland State: Bush's Biopolitical Settlement," *Boundary 2* 30, no. 3 (2003): 1–18; Michael Sorkin, ed., *Indefensible Space: The Architecture of the National Insecurity State* (New York: Routledge, 2008).

45. Jodi Dean, "Anticipating Homeland Security," *Communication and Critical/Cultural Studies* 4, no. 2 (June 2007): 209.

46. Jon Coaffee and Peter Rogers, 'Rebordering the City for New Security Challenges: From Counter-Terrorism to Community Resilience," *Space and Polity* 12, no. 1 (2008): 101–18; Stephen Graham, "'Homeland' Insecurities? Katrina and the Politics of 'Security' in Metropolitan America," *Space and Culture* 9, no. 1 (2006): 63–67; Stephen Graham, "Cities and the 'War on Terror,'" *International Journal of Urban and Regional Research* 30, no. 2 (2006): 255–76.

47. Jon Coaffee and David Murakami Wood, "Security Is Coming Home: Rethinking Scale and Constructing Resilience in the Global Urban Response to Terrorist Risk," *International Relations* 20, no. 4 (2006): 503–17.

48. Shailza Singh, "The 'Homeland Security Moment' in International Politics: Implications for the Third World," *International Studies* 58, no. 3 (July 2021): 387–88.

49. "Homeland Security Budget," The Costs of War, June 2021, https://watson.brown.edu/costsofwar/costs/economic/budget/dhs.

50. Singh, "The 'Homeland Security Moment,'" 388.

51. Matthew Dallek, *Defenseless Under the Night: The Roosevelt Years and the Origins of Homeland Security* (New York: Oxford University Press, 2016); Eli Jelly-Schapiro, *Security and Terror: American Culture and the Long History of Colonial Modernity* (Oakland: University of California Press, 2018); Amy Kaplan, "Homeland Insecurities: Some Reflections on Language and Space," *Radical History Review* 85, no. 1 (2003): 82–93.

52. Aziz Rana, "Settler Wars and the National Security State," *Settler Colonial Studies* 4, no. 2 (April 2014): 171–75.

53. Patricia Owens, *Economy of Force: Counterinsurgency and the Historical Rise of the Social* (Cambridge: Cambridge University Press, 2015); Laleh Khalili, *Time in the Shadows: Confinement in Counterinsurgencies* (Stanford: Stanford University Press, 2013); Kim A. Wagner, "Savage Warfare: Violence and the Rule of Colonial Difference in Early British Counterinsurgency," *History Workshop Journal* 85 (April 2018): 217–37.

54. Deepa Kumar, "Terrorcraft: Empire and the Making of the Racialised Terrorist Threat," *Race and Class* 62, no. 2 (October 2020): 34–60; Alex Lubin, "'We Are All Israelis': The Politics of Colonial Comparisons," *South Atlantic Quarterly* 107, no. 4 (October 2008): 671–90; Joseph A. Massad, *The Persistence of the Palestinian Question: Essays on Zionism and the Palestinians* (Abingdon, England: Routledge, 2006).

55. Kaplan, "Homeland Insecurities," 85–88, emphasis added.

56. Alex Lubin, *Never-Ending War on Terror, Never-Ending War on Terror* (Berkeley: University of California Press, 2020); Somdeep Sen and John Collins, eds., *Globalizing Collateral Language: From 9/11 to Endless War* (Athens: University of Georgia Press, 2021); Nikhil Pal Singh, *Race and America's Long War* (Oakland: University of California Press, 2017); David Vine, *The United States of War: A Global History of America's Endless Conflicts, from Columbus to the Islamic State* (Oakland: University of California Press, 2020).

57. Foucault, *Security, Territory, Population: Lectures at the College De France 1977–1978,* ed. Michel Senellart, trans. Graham Burchell (New York: Picador, 2007); Markus Dirk Dubber and Mariana Valverde, eds. *The New Police Science: The Police Power in Domestic and International Governance* (Stanford: Stanford University Press, 2006).

58. Mark Neocleous, *The Fabrication of Social Order: A Critical Theory of Police Power* (London: Pluto Press, 2000); Jelly-Schapiro, *Security and Terror.*

59. Laleh Khalili, "The New (and Old) Classics of Counterinsurgency," *Middle East Report*, no. 255 (2010); Joseph MacKay, *The Counterinsurgent Imagination: A New Intellectual History* (Cambridge: Cambridge University Press, 2023); Alfred W. McCoy, *Policing America's Empire: The United States, the Philippines, and the Rise of the Surveillance State* (Madison: University of Wisconsin Press, 2009); Stuart Schrader, *Badges Without Borders: How Global Counterinsurgency Transformed American Policing* (Oakland: University of California Press, 2019)

60. Karl Marx, "6: On the Jewish Question," in *Karl Marx: Selected Writings*, ed. David McLellan, 2nd ed. (Oxford: Oxford University Press, 2000), 61.

61. Neocleous, *Fabrication of Social Order*, 44.

62. Markus Dirk Dubber, *The Police Power: Patriarchy and the Foundations of American Government* (New York: Columbia University Press, 2005).

63. Mark Neocleous, *Critique of Security* (Edinburgh: Edinburgh University Press, 2008).

64. Aníbal Quijano, "Coloniality of Power and Eurocentrism in Latin America," *International Sociology* 15, no. 2 (2000): 215–32; Aníbal Quijano, "Coloniality and Modernity/Rationality," *Cultural Studies* 21, no. 2–3 (2007): 168–78; Cedric J. Robinson, *Black Marxism: The Making of the Black Radical Tradition* (Chapel Hill: University of North Carolina Press, 2000).

65. Ben Brucato, "Policing Race and Racing Police: The Origin of U.S. Police in Slave Patrols," *Social Justice* 47, no. 3/4 (161/162) (2020): 115–36.

66. Ben Brucato, "Fabricating the Color Line in a White Democracy: From Slave Catchers to Petty Sovereigns," *Theoria* 61, no. 141 (December 2014): 30–54; Rhys Machold and Catherine Chiniara Charrett, "Beyond Ambivalence: Locating the Whiteness of Security," *Security Dialogue* 52, no. 1 Suppl (November 2021): 38–48.

67. Mark Neocleous, "'A Brighter and Nicer New Life': Security as Pacification," *Social and Legal Studies* 20, no. 2 (2011): 191–208.

68. Mark Neocleous, George Rigakos, and Tyler Wall, "On Pacification: Introduction to the Special Issue," *Socialist Studies/Études Socialistes* 9, no. 2 (2013).

69. Didier Bigo, "Liaison Officers in Europe: New Officers in the European Security Field," in *Issues in Transnational Policing*, ed. James Sheptycki (London: Routledge, 2000), 67–99; Didier Bigo, "The Möbius Ribbon of Internal and External Security(ies)," in *Identities, Borders, Orders: Rethinking International Relations Theory*, ed. Mathias Albert, David Jacobson, and Yosef Lapid (Minneapolis: University of Minnesota Press, 2001), 91–116.

70. Mark Neocleous, *War Power, Police Power* (Edinburgh: Edinburgh University Press, 2014); Micol Seigel, *Violence Work: State Power and the Limits of Police* (Durham, N.C.: Duke University Press, 2018).

71. Schrader, *Badges Without Borders*, 15.

72. Ranajit Guha, "The Prose of Counter-Insurgency," in *The Small Voice of History*, ed. Partha Chatterjee (Ranikhet, India: Orient BlackSwan, 2009), 194–238.

73. Richard Hawkins, "The 'Irish Model' and the Empire: A Case for Reassessment," in *Policing the Empire: Government, Authority, and Control, 1830–1940*, ed. David M. Anderson and David Killingray (Manchester: Manchester University Press, 1991), 18–32; Peter Robb, "The Ordering of Rural India: The Policing of Nineteenth-Century Bengal and Bihar," in *Policing the Empire: Government, Authority, and Control, 1830–1940*, ed. David M. Anderson and David Killingray (Manchester: Manchester University Press, 1991), 126–50.

74. David Arnold, *Police Power and Colonial Rule: Madras, 1859–1947* (New Delhi: Oxford University Press, 1986); David H. Bayley, *The Police and Political Development in India* (Princeton: Princeton University Press, 1969).

75. Radha Kumar, *Police Matters: The Everyday State and Caste Politics in South India, 1900–1975* (Ithaca, N.Y.: Cornell University Press, 2021); Radhika Singha, "Settle,

Mobilize, Verify: Identification Practices in Colonial India," *Studies in History* 16, no. 2 (August 2000): 151–98.

76. Radhika Singha, "'Providential' Circumstances: The Thuggee Campaign of the 1830s and Legal Innovation," *Modern Asian Studies* 27, no. 1 (February 1993): 86.

77. Beatrice Jauregui, *Provisional Authority: Police, Order, and Security in India* (Chicago: University of Chicago Press, 2016).

78. Deana Heath, *Colonial Terror: Torture and State Violence in Colonial India* (Oxford: Oxford University Press, 2021).

79. Singha, "'Providential' Circumstances," 85.

80. Arnold, *Police Power and Colonial Rule*, 230.

81. Kumar, *Police Matters*.

82. Gagan Preet Singh, "Property's Guardians, People's Terror: Police Avoidance in Colonial North India," *Radical History Review* 2020, no. 137 (May 2020): 54–74.

83. Arnold, *Police Power and Colonial Rule*; Priyamvada Gopal, *Insurgent Empire: Anticolonial Resistance and British Dissent* (London: Verso, 2019).

84. Jyoti Belur, "Police Use of Deadly Force: Police Perceptions of a Culture of Approval," *Journal of Contemporary Criminal Justice* 25, no. 2 (May 2009): 237–52; Beatrice Jauregui, "Just War: The Metaphysics of Police Vigilantism in India," *Conflict and Society* 1, no. 1 (2015): 41–59; Santana Khanikar, *State, Violence, and Legitimacy in India* (Oxford: Oxford University Press, 2018); Rachel Wahl, *Just Violence: Torture and Human Rights in the Eyes of the Police* (Stanford: Stanford University Press, 2017).

85. Achin Vanaik, *The Painful Transition: Bourgeois Democracy in India* (London: Verso, 1990), 92.

86. Thomas Blom Hansen and Finn Stepputat, "Introduction: States of Imagination," in *States of Imagination: Ethnographic Explorations of the Postcolonial State*, ed. Thomas Blom Hansen and Finn Stepputat (Durham, N.C.: Duke University Press, 2001), 14.

87. Gurminder K. Bhambra, *Rethinking Modernity: Postcolonialism and the Sociological Imagination* (Houndmills, England: Palgrave Macmillan, 2007).

88. Donna J. Haraway, *Simians, Cyborgs, and Women: The Reinvention of Nature* (London: Free Association Books, 1991); John Law, "After ANT: Complexity, Naming, Topology," in *Actor Network Theory and After*, ed. John Law and John Hassard (Oxford: Blackwell, 1999), 1–14.

89. Donald A. MacKenzie, *Inventing Accuracy: A Historical Sociology of Nuclear Missile Guidance* (Boston: MIT Press, 1990).

90. Annemarie Mol, "Ontological Politics: A Word and Some Questions," in *Actor Network Theory and After*, ed. John Law and John Hassard (Oxford: Blackwell, 1999), 74.

91. Craig Gilmore, "Foreword (Foreword) to the Second Edition," in *Police: A Field Guide*, ed. David Correia and Tyler Wall (London: Verso, 2022).

92. Timothy Mitchell, *Colonising Egypt* (Berkeley: University of California Press, 1991); Timothy Mitchell, "The Stage of Modernity," in *Questions of Modernity* (Minneapolis: University of Minnesota Press, 2000), 1–34.

93. John Law, "What's Wrong with a One-World World?," *Distinktion: Journal of Social Theory* 16, no. 1 (2015): 126–39.

94. Ann Laura Stoler, *Duress: Imperial Durabilities in Our Times* (Durham, N.C., and London: Duke University Press, 2016).

95. Mikhail M. Bakhtin, *The Dialogic Imagination: Four Essays*, trans. Caryl Emerson and Michael Holquist (Austin: University of Texas Press, 1981); Mariana Valverde, *Chronotopes of Law: Jurisdiction, Scale, and Governance* (Oxford: Routledge, 2015).

96. Timothy Mitchell, *Rule of Experts: Egypt, Techno-Politics, Modernity* (Berkeley: University of California Press, 2002), 82–83.

97. Mitchell, *Rule of Experts*, 83.

98. Bruno Latour, *Pandora's Hope: Essays on the Reality of Science Studies* (Cambridge, Mass.: Harvard University Press, 1999), 127.

99. William Walters, "Rezonong the Global: Technological Zones, Technological Work and the (Un-)Making of Biometric Borders," in *The Contested Politics of Mobility: Borderzones and Irregularity*, ed. Vicki Squire (Abingdon, England: Routledge, 2011), 51–73.

100. Bruno Latour, *Science in Action: How to Follow Scientists and Engineers through Society* (Boston: Harvard University Press, 1987).

101. I attended Securing Asia 2012 (June 25–27, 2012, London), International Fire and Security Exhibition and Conference (IFSEC) and Homeland Security India (November 1–3, 2012, New Delhi, Challenges for India's Homeland Security (March 15, 2013, New Delhi), and New Age Risks 2013 (March 22, 2013, New Delhi) as well as a closed-door policy conference in Mumbai. These were hosted through collaborations between groups representing Indian capital and a range of foreign governments, focusing on building a new Indian homeland secuity market for foreign and Indian purveyors.

102. Headley is an American citizen currently serving a prison sentence on terrorism charges. Headley is alleged to have carried out various activities for the Pakistani militant group Lashkar-e-Taiba, including scouting and mapping the targets for 26/11. Prior to his incarceration, Headley had also worked as an informant for the U.S. Drug Enforcement Agency.

103. Brian Balmer and Brian Rappert, eds., *Absence in Science, Security, and Policy: From Research Agendas to Global Strategy* (Basingstoke: Palgrave Macmillan, 2016); Mat Coleman, "State Power in Blue," *Political Geography* 51 (2016): 76–86; Marieke de Goede, "The Chain of Security," *Review of International Studies* 44, no. 1 (January 2018): 24–42; William Walters, "Secrecy, Publicity, and the Milieu of Security," *Dialogues in Human Geography* 5, no. 3 (November 2015): 287–90.

104. Skunk water is a putrid-smelling liquid developed in Palestine/Israel and used by the IOF in their pacification efforts against Palestinians. It is routinely sprayed on demonstrators but also into Palestinian homes to terrorize and intimidate them and fragment communities. See Mikko Joronen, "Atmospheric Negations: Weaponising Breathing, Attuning Irreducible Bodies," *Environment and Planning D: Society and Space* 41, no. 5 (2023): 765–83.

105. Anna Lowenhaupt Tsing, *Friction: An Ethnography of Global Connection* (Princeton: Princeton University Press, 2005), 271.

106. Donna J. Haraway, *Staying with the Trouble: Making Kin in the Chthulucene* (Durham, N.C.: Duke University Press, 2016).

107. Darryl Li, "Lies, Damned Lies, and Plagiarizing 'Experts,'" *Middle East Report*, no. 260 (2011): 5.

108. John Law, *After Method: Mess in Social Science Research* (Abingdon, England: Routledge, 2004).

109. Talal Asad, "Thinking about Terrorism and Just War," *Cambridge Review of International Affairs* 23, no. 1 (2010): 3–24; Verena Erlenbusch, "How (Not) to Study Terrorism," *Critical Review of International Social and Political Philosophy* 17, no. 4 (2014): 470–91; Charles Tilly, "Terror, Terrorism, Terrorists," *Sociological Theory* 22, no. 1 (2004): 5–13.

110. Joseph McQuade, *A Genealogy of Terrorism: Colonial Law and the Origins of an Idea* (Cambridge: Cambridge University Press, 2020).

111. Jasbir K. Puar, *Terrorist Assemblages: Homonationalism in Queer Times* (Durham, N.C., and London: Duke University Press, 2007); Kumar, "Terrorcraft."

112. Edward Herman and Gerry O'Sullivan, *The "Terrorism" Industry: The Experts and Institutions That Shape Our View of Terror* (New York: Pantheon Books, 1989); Lisa Stampnitzky, *Disciplining Terror: How Experts Invented "Terrorism"* (Cambridge: Cambridge University Press, 2013).

113. Christos Boukalas, *Homeland Security, Its Law, and Its State* (Abingdon, England: Routledge, 2014), 1–2.

114. Stuart Hall et al., *Policing the Crisis: Mugging, the State and Law and Order*, 2nd ed. (Houndmills, England: Palgrave Macmillan, 2014), 1.

115. Hall et al., *Policing the Crisis*, 1.

116. Darryl Li, *The Universal Enemy: Jihad, Empire, and the Challenge of Solidarity* (Stanford: Stanford University Press, 2019), 26.

117. Lisa Stampnitzky, "Can Terrorism Be Defined?," in *Constructions of Terrorism: An Interdisciplinary Approach to Research and Policy*, ed. Michael Stohl, Richard Burchill, and Scott Howard Englund (Berkeley: University of California Press, 2017), 11–20.

Chapter One

1. Various official and non-official sources have competing figures on the total numbers of deaths and their respective breakdowns by nationality. I take the above-cited figures from a dossier compiled by the New York Police Department (NYPD). See "Mumbai Attack Analysis," New York Police Department (NYPD) Intelligence Division, 4 December 2008. The Mumbai Police charge sheet for 26/11 has slightly lower count of overall deaths as well as slightly different breakdowns of victims by nationality.

2. "A Nation That Cannot Afford to Sleep," *Hindustan Times*, 28 November 2008.

3. Neve Gordon, "The Political Economy of Israel's Homeland Security/Surveillance Industry," Working Paper III, *The New Transparency: Surveillance and Social Sorting*, 2009.

4. Claudia Aradau and Rens van Munster, *Politics of Catastrophe: Genealogies of the Unknown* (Abingdon, England: Routledge, 2011); Stuart Elden, *Terror and Territory: The Spatial Extent of Sovereignty* (Minneapolis: University of Minnesota Press, 2009); Andrew W. Neal, "'Events Dear Boy, Events': Terrorism and Security from the Perspective of Politics," *Critical Studies on Terrorism* 5, no. 1 (April 2012): 107–20; A. Closs Stephens and N. Vaughan-Williams, eds., *Terrorism and the Politics of Response* (Abingdon, England: Routledge, 2009).

5. Stephen Graham, *Cities Under Siege: The New Military Urbanism* (New York: Verso, 2010); Naomi Klein, *The Shock Doctrine: The Rise of Disaster Capitalism* (Toronto: Vintage Canada, 2007).

6. Veena Das, *Critical Events: An Anthropological Perspective on Contemporary India* (Oxford: Oxford University Press, 1996).

7. Michel Callon, "Some Elements of a Sociology of Translation: Domestication of the Scallops and the Fishermen of St. Brieuc Bay," *Sociological Review* 32, no. 1 Suppl (1984): 211.

8. Cf. Closs Stephens and Vaughan-Williams, *Terrorism and the Politics of Response*; Elden, *Terror and Territory*.

9. Andrew Barry, "Political Situations: Knowledge Controversies in Transnational Governance," *Critical Policy Studies* 6, no. 3 (October 2012): 324–36; Andrew Barry, "The Politics of Contingency: Events, Travelling Models, and Situations," Gefördert von der DFG, 2016.

10. Walter D. Mignolo, "The Geopolitics of Knowledge and the Colonial Difference," *South Atlantic Quarterly* 101, no. 1 (January 2002): 57–96.

11. The notion of political situations offers an extension and partial corrective of ANT that I build on further. While ANT's impulse to question hierarchies of knowledge, power, and location is highly productive, it also poses certain dangers of its own, particularly in its potential to flatten differences between actors entirely as well as sideline questions about the racialized and colonial dimensions of power in relation to techno-science. These are serious dangers. See Sandra Harding, ed., *The Postcolonial Science and Technology Studies Reader* (Durham, N.C.: Duke University Press, 2011). Moreover, while ANT grapples with the politics of comparison to some extent, the concept of comparative geopolitics takes more seriously the historical and contemporary roles that comparison plays within imperial and colonial projects and their surrounding discourses.

12. Micol Seigel, "Beyond Compare: Comparative Method after the Transnational Turn," *Radical History Review* 2005, no. 91 (2005): 62–90.

13. Ann Laura Stoler and Carole McGranahan, "Refiguring Imperial Terrains," *Ab Imperio* 2006, no. 2 (2006): 32.

14. "World Rallies Behind India in Anti-Terror Fight," Indo-Asian News Service, 27 November 2008.

15. Herb Keinon and Judy Siegel-Itzkovich, "MDA, ZAKA Dispatch Teams to Mumbai," *Jerusalem Post*, 27 November 2008.

16. Keinon and Siegel-Itzkovich, "MDA, ZAKA Dispatch."

17. Tim McGirk, "Israel Reacts to the Mumbai Massacre," *Time*, 28 November 2008. See also Yaakov Katz, "Israeli Officials Say India Mishandled Hostage Situation. Israel Offers Aid, but Not Sending Commando Units to Mumbai," *Jerusalem Post*, 27 November 2008.

18. Keinon and Siegel-Itzkovich, "MDA, ZAKA Dispatch."

19. Katz, "Israeli Officials Say."

20. "India's Rescue Efforts 'Premature and Badly Planned,' Says Israel," *Hindustan Times*, 27 November 2008.

21. Harel, "India Declines Israeli Offer of Aid Delegation to Mumbai," *Haaretz*, 28 November 2008. An armed Israeli security officer from Mumbai was also arrested by Indian police on the evening of November 26 en route to Nariman House. See "Israeli Consulate's Mumbai Security Chief Arrested En Route to Chabad House Rescue," *Haaretz*, 30 November 2008.

22. MDA is Israel's national emergency medical, disaster response, blood bank, and ambulance service. The organization predates the formal founding of Israel in 1948 and collaborates with other arms of the Israeli state.

23. Keinon and Siegel-Itzkovich, "MDA, ZAKA Dispatch." ZAKA is a nongovernmental religious Haredi organization, which specializes in the collection of dead bodies and body parts from sites of "unnatural" deaths and transporting them to morgues according to strict Jewish religious laws. Founded in the late 1990s by Yehuda Meshi-Zahav, previously leader of the ultra-Orthodox Jewish militia *Keshet*, ZAKA has been and remains a highly controversial organization for a variety of reasons. While ZAKA claims itself as a nongovernmental organization, its credibility has often been questioned in light of the organization's deep and enduring ties to the Israeli state and its *hasbara* campaigns. Before his death in 2022, Meshi-Zahav was implicated in recurring patterns of rape and sexual assault, including against minors. See "ZAKA Is Not a Trustworthy Source for Allegations of Sexual Violence on October 7," *Mondoweiss*, 30 December 2023.

24. Keinon and Siegel-Itzkovich, "MDA, ZAKA Dispatch."

25. McGirk, "Israel Reacts to the Mumbai Massacre," emphasis added.

26. McGirk, "Israel Reacts to the Mumbai Massacre."

27. Ritu Sharma, "Eight, Including Jewish Centre Rabbi, Stuck in Nariman House," Indo-Asian News Service, 28 November 2008.

28. McGirk, "Israel Reacts to the Mumbai Massacre."

29. "Israel Calls Indian Troops Handling of Mumbai Terror Siege 'Risky and Premature,'" *Hindustan Times*, 28 November 2008.

30. Tobias Buck, "Israel Offers Assistance to End Mumbai Siege," *Financial Times*, 28 November 2008.

31. Anshel Pfeffer, "9 Dead in Mumbai Chabad House Attack; Israel to Help Identify Bodies," *Haaretz*, 28 November 2008.

32. Buck, "Israel Offers Assistance to End Mumbai Siege."

33. "Israeli Media Calls India's Reaction 'Slow, Confused,'" *News18*, 28 November 2008.

34. Damian McElroy, "Mumbai Attacks: Foreign Governments Criticise India's Response," *The Telegraph*, 28 November 2008.

35. Harel, "India Declines Israeli Offer of Aid Delegation to Mumbai."

36. Pfeffer, "9 Dead in Mumbai Chabad House Attack; Israel to Help Identify Bodies."

37. Subhash K. Jha, "Israel Concerned about Rabbi Held Hostage, to Send Rescue Team," Indo-Asian News Service, 28 November 2008.

38. Daniel Pepper, "Breaking of Mumbai Siege Turns into Street Theatre," *The Guardian*, 28 November 2008.

39. Pfeffer, "9 Dead."

40. Pfeffer, "9 Dead."

41. Pfeffer, "9 Dead." Indian authorities have always maintained ever since that 26/11 was planned exclusively by the Pakistani-based militant group Lashkar-e-Taiba (LeT) and Pakistan's Inter-Services Intelligence (ISI).

42. "Israel Says Mumbai Terrorists Targeted Its Citizens," *Bharat Chronicle*, 29 November 2008.

43. James Blitz, "Israelis Critical of India's Response to Attacks," *Financial Times*, 29 November 2008.

44. Jason Koutsoukis, "Israeli Military Will Not Intervene; Mumbai Massacre," *Sydney Morning Herald* (Australia), 29 November 2008.

45. Ronen Medzini, "Mumbai Horror: Rescue Workers Shocked by Chabad Massacre Site," Ynetnews, 29 November 2008.

46. Muhammad Najeeb, "Hatred of Jews Spurred Nariman House Attack: Israel," Indo-Asian News Service, 30 November 2008.

47. Amos Harel, "Israeli Experts: Slow Operation Meant 'No Chance' for Hostages at Mumbai Chabad House," *Haaretz*, 30 November 2008.

48. Harel, "Israeli Experts."

49. Harel, "Israeli Experts."

50. Harel, "Israeli Experts."

51. Yaakov Lappin, "Zaka Head: Indian Forces May Have Killed Some Hostages," *Jerusalem Post*, 30 November 2008.

52. Najeeb, "Hatred of Jews."

53. Najeeb, "Hatred of Jews."

54. Najeeb, "Hatred of Jews."

55. Najeeb, "Hatred of Jews."

56. Moin Ansari, "Mumbai: Israel Calls Indian Forces Lackadaisical, Unprofessional, Incompetent, Untrained, Slow, Confused and Inefficient," *Rupee News*, 30 November 2008.

57. A. Vinod Kumar, "The Fidayeens Are Back, But We Aren't Ready," Indo-Asian News Service, 30 November 2008.

58. "Olmert: No Doubt Mumbai Attack Targeted Jewish Institutions," *Haaretz*, 30 November 2008.

59. R. R. Patil came under fire after underplaying 26/11's significance, stating, "Only a few people died, it could have been worse." See "After 26/11, R. R. Patil Returns as Home Minister," NDTV, 9 November 2009.

60. Yaakov Katz, "Israel Closely Watching India's Investigation of Mumbai Attacks. Defense Industries Concerned That Israeli Criticism of India May Jeopardize Contracts," *Jerusalem Post*, 1 December 2008.

61. Roy Dipanjan Chaudhary, "Israel Ambassador Hails India for Job Well Done," *India Today*, 1 December 2008.

62. Richard Boudreaux, "How Mumbai Attack on Jews Unfolded," *Los Angeles Times*, 3 December 2008; "Indian Forces May Have Killed Some Hostages: Report," *Hindustan Times*, 2 December 2008.

63. Sandeep Unnithan, "Mumbai Terror Attacks Similar to Savoy Hotel Attack: Israeli Terror Expert," *India Today*, 1 December 2008.

64. Unnithan, "Mumbai Terror Attacks."

65. "After Mumbai," *Mideast Mirror*, 1 December 2008.

66. Barry Rubin, "India and Israel: The Parallels," *Jerusalem Post*, 1 December 2008.

67. Herb Keinon, "State Angry at Zaka's Mumbai 'Meddling,'" *Jerusalem Post*, 2 December 2008.

68. Keinon, "State Angry."

69. Keinon, "State Angry."

70. Kevin Peraino, "Why Israel Isn't Angry," *The Daily Beast*, 3 December 2008.

71. Katz, "Israel Closely Watching"; Peraino, "Why Israel Isn't Angry."

72. Kevin Kolben, "Blowing an Opportunity with India," *Jerusalem Post*, 3 December 2008.

73. Peraino, "Why Israel Isn't Angry."

74. Peraino, "Why Israel Isn't Angry."

75. B. Raman, "The Anti-Israeli Angle," *Outlook India*, 4 December 2008.

76. Rahul Bedi and Damien McElroy, "India Asks for Foreign Help to Hit Terrorists," *The Daily Telegraph* (London), 3 December 2008.

77. Anand Patwardhan, "Free of All Zealots," *Hindustan Times*, 10 December 2008.

78. Sapir Peretz, "A Partner in Need; Officials in Israel Believe India Is Likely to Step up Demand for Israeli Products, Services, and Know-How Related to Homeland Security," *Globes*, 3 December 2008.

79. Peretz, "A Partner in Need."

80. Herb Keinon, "Looking Past Mumbai," *Jerusalem Post*, 5 December 2008.

81. "Indian and Israeli Firms to Jointly Provide Advanced Security Systems," *Hindustan Times*, 22 December 2008.

82. Harsh V. Pant, "India and Israel: A Bond Is Forged," *Jerusalem Post*, 9 January 2009.

83. William E. Connolly, "The Evangelical-Capitalist Resonance Machine," *Political Theory* 33, no. 6 (2005): 105–28.

84. "First India-Israel Homeland Security Forum Next Month," *India Today*, 24 February 2009.

85. FICCI organized the Conference on National Security and Terror held in New Delhi on December 12, 2008, which was followed up by the FICCI Task Force on National Security and Terrorism convened on February 11, 2009. These events featured top current and former national security, MHA and intelligence officials, leading Indian corporate players as well as foreign officials. A U.S. diplomatic cable dated October 16, 2009, documents the happenings of another FICCI-hosted conference that same year on the subject of Science and Technology for Homeland Security. The cable noted the presence of high-profile Indian speakers like MHA Secretary G. K. Pillai as well as various foreign state and industry actors, including Steve Swain, a representative of the Security Innovation Technology Consortia, U.K., and Avi Shavit, the Head of Homeland Security, Israeli Ministry of Industry, Trade and Labour: "India Pursues Homeland Security Technologies," Wikileaks Public Library of U.S. Diplomacy (16 October 2009).

86. Keren Blankfield, "Hollywood Heavyweight," *Forbes*, 29 March 2010.

87. "Zicom & IMI, Israel Ties up with Security Training & Education Academy," 9 January 2009, www.derivatives.capitaline.com.

88. Barry, "Politics of Contingency," 6–8; Barry, "Political Situations," 331.

89. Barry, "Politics of Contingency," 8.

90. Michel Callon and Bruno Latour, "Unscrewing the Big Leviathan: How Actors Macro-Structure Reality and How Sociologists Help Them to Do So," in *Advances in Social Theory and Methodology: Toward an Integration of Micro-and Macro-Sociologies*, ed. Karin Knorr-Cetina and Aaron V. Cicourel (London: Routledge, 1981), 277–303.

91. Mignolo, "Geopolitics of Knowledge."

92. Walter D. Mignolo and Catherine E. Walsh, *On Decoloniality: Concepts, Analytics, Praxis* (Durham, N.C.: Duke University Press, 2018), 180.

93. Barry, "Politics of Contingency," 8.

94. Naomi Klein, "Laboratory for a Fortressed World," *The Nation*, 14 June 2007; Leila Stockmarr, "Seeing Is Striking: Selling Israeli Warfare," *Jadaliyya*, 18 January 2014.

95. Ami Pedahzur, "From Munich to Mumbai," *New York Times*, 20 December 2008.

96. Peraino, "Why Israel Isn't Angry."

97. "Israel Says Mumbai Terrorists Targeted Its Citizens."

98. Peraino, "Why Israel Isn't Angry."

99. Klein, *Shock Doctrine*.

100. Klein, *Shock Doctrine*, 19.

Chapter Two

1. Benjamin Beit-Hallahmi, *The Israeli Connection: Who Israel Arms and Why*, 1st ed. (New York: Pantheon Books, 1987).

2. Stephen Graham, "Laboratories of War: United States-Israeli Collaboration in Urban War and Securitization the Urbanizing Middle East," *Brown Journal of World Affairs*, no. 1 (2010): 35–52; Stephen Graham and Alexander Baker, "Laboratories of Pacification and Permanent War: Israeli-U.S. Collaboration in the Global Making of Policing," in *The Global Making of Policing*, ed. Jana Hönke and Michael-Marcus Müller (Abingdon, England: Routledge, 2016), 40–58; Lisa Hajjar, "International Humanitarian Law and 'Wars on Terror': A Comparative Analysis of Israeli and American Doctrines and Policies," *Journal of Palestine Studies* 36, no. 1 (2006): 21–42; Lisa Hajjar, "Israel as Innovator in the Mainstreaming of Extreme Violence," *Middle East Report*, Summer 2016; Ahmad H. Sa'di, "Israel"s Settler-Colonialism as a Global Security Paradigm," *Race and Class* 63, no. 2 (30 April 2021): 21–37; Eyal Weizman, *Hollow Land: Israel's Architecture of Occupation* (London: Verso, 2007).

3. Jeff Halper, *War Against the People: Israel, the Palestinians, and Global Pacification* (London: Pluto Press, 2015), 44, 144.

4. Halper, *War Against the People*, 144.

5. Tariq Dana, "Israel's Big Business of War," The Political Economy Project, 9 January 2017; Shir Hever, *The Privitization of Israeli Security* (London: Pluto Press, 2018).

6. Rhys Machold, "Reconsidering the Laboratory Thesis: Palestine/Israel and the Geopolitics of Representation," *Political Geography* 65 (2018): 88–97.

7. Bruno Latour, *We Have Never Been Modern*, trans. Catherine Porter (Cambridge, Mass.: Harvard University Press, 1993).

8. Dipesh Chakrabarty, *Provincializing Europe: Postcolonial Thought and Historical Difference* (Princeton, N.J.: Princeton University Press, 2000).

9. Mark Rifkin, "Settler Common Sense," *Settler Colonial Studies* 3, no. 3–04 (November 2013): 322–40.

10. Edward W. Said, *The Question of Palestine* (London: Vintage, 1992), 19.

11. Said, *Question of Palestine,* 28.

12. Said, *Question of Palestine,* 21.

13. Ilan Pappé, *The Idea of Israel: A History of Power and Knowledge*, Ebook (London: Verso, 2014).

14. Timothy Mitchell, *Colonising Egypt* (Berkeley: University of California Press, 1991).

15. Ahmad H. Sa'di, "Israel's Settler-Colonialism as a Global Security Paradigm," *Race and Class* 63, no. 2 (April 2021): 21–37.

16. M. Shahid Alam, *Israeli Exceptionalism: The Destabilizing Logic of Zionism* (New York: Palgrave Macmillan, 2009); Ann Laura Stoler and Carole McGranahan, "Refiguring Imperial Terrains," *Ab Imperio* 2006, no. 2 (2006): 17–58; Alex Lubin, "'We Are All Israelis': The Politics of Colonial Comparisons," *South Atlantic Quarterly* 107, no. 4 (October 2008): 671–90.

17. Bruno Latour, *Pandora's Hope: Essays on the Reality of Science Studies* (Cambridge, Mass.: Harvard University Press, 1999), 179.

18. Rashid Khalidi, *Palestinian Identity: The Construction of Modern National Consciousness*. New York: Columbia University Press, 1997, 102.

19. Rashid Khalidi, *Palestinian Identity*, 102.

20. Bar-Giora was named after the last leader of the Jewish Revolt against the Roman Empire by Israel Shochat. Gershon Shafir, *Land, Labor, and the Origins of the Israeli-Palestinian Conflict, 1882–1914* (Cambridge: Cambridge University Press, 1989), 123–36.

21. Haim Bresheeth-Zabner, *An Army Like No Other: How the Israel Defense Forces Made a Nation* (London: Verso, 2020), 44.

22. Patrick Wolfe, "Purchase by Other Means: The Palestine Nakba and Zionism's Conquest of Economics," *Settler Colonial Studies* 2, no. 1 (2012): 133–71.

23. Bresheeth-Zabner, *Army Like No Other.*

24. Neve Gordon, "Israel's Emergence as a Homeland Security Capital," in *Surveillance and Control in Israel/Palestine: Population, Territory, and Power*, ed. David Lyon, Elia Zureik, and Yasmeen Abu-Laban (New York: Routledge, 2011), 153.

25. Juliana Ochs, *Security and Suspicion: An Ethnography of Everyday Life in Israel* (Philadelphia: University of Pennsylvania Press, 2010), 19.

26. Noura Erakat, *Justice for Some: Law and the Question of Palestine* (Stanford: Stanford University Press, 2019), 16.

27. Richard Andrew Cahill, "'Going Beserk': 'Black and Tans' in Palestine," *Jerusalem Quarterly* 38 (January 2009): 60.

28. Cahill, "'Going Beserk.'"

29. Martin Kolinsky, "Reorganization of the Palestine Police after the Riots of 1929," *Journal of Israeli History* 10, no. 2 (1989): 155–73.

30. Gad Kroizer, "From Dowbiggin to Tegart: Revolutionary Change in the Colonial Police in Palestine during the 1930s," *Journal of Imperial and Commonwealth History* 32, no. 2 (2004): 115–33.

31. Laleh Khalili, "The Location of Palestine in Global Counterinsurgencies," *International Journal of Middle East Studies* 42, no. 3 (2010): 415.

32. Matthew Hughes, *Britain's Pacification of Palestine: The British Army, the Colonial State, and the Arab Revolt, 1936–1939* (Cambridge: Cambridge University Press, 2019); Charles Townshend, "The Defence of Palestine: Insurrection and Public Security, 1936–1939," *English Historical Review* 103, no. 409 (1988): 917–49.

33. Kroizer, "From Dowbiggin to Tegart"; Yasid El Rifai, Dima Yaser, and Adele Jarrar, "Tegart's Modern Legacy: The Reproduction of Power, a Timeless Paradox," *Jerusalem Quarterly*, no. 69 (2017): 78.

34. Khalili, "Location of Palestine"; Laleh Khalili, *Time in the Shadows: Confinement in Counterinsurgencies* (Stanford: Stanford University Press, 2013).

35. Khalili, "Location of Palestine"; Georgina Sinclair, "'Get into a Crack Force and Earn £20 a Month and All Found . . .': The Influence of the Palestine Police upon Colonial Policing 1922–1948," *European Review of History: Revue Européenne d'histoire* 13, no. 1 (March 2006): 49–65.

36. Yael Berda, *Living Emergency: Israel's Permit Regime in the Occupied West Bank* (Stanford: Stanford University Press, 2017); Yael Berda, *Colonial Bureaucracy and Contemporary Citizenship* (Cambridge: Cambridge University Press, 2022).

37. Erakat, *Justice for Some*, 16.

38. El Rifai, Yaser, and Jarrar, "Tegart's Modern Legacy," 82.

39. I refer to the IDF in this way as I understand the IDF to be a euphemism for Zionist violence. As Rashid Khalidi notes, the origins of the military institutions so essential to the success of the Zionist project only meaningfully constitute "defense" in the sense of defending the "newly acquired lands against those who still claimed rights over them," namely the *fellahin*. Rashid Khalidi, *Palestinian Identity: The Construction of Modern National Consciousness* (New York: Columbia University Press, 1997), 106.

40. IMI was acquired by the Israeli weapons firm Elbit Systems in 2018.

41. Ochs, *Security and Suspicion*.

42. See Beit-Hallahmi, *Israeli Connection*; Haim Yacobi, *Israel and Africa: A Genealogy of Moral Geography* (New York: Routledge, 2016); Azad Essa, *Hostile Homelands: The New Alliance Between India and Israel* (London: Pluto Press, 2023).

43. Elias Yousif, "Factsheet: U.S. Arms Sales and Security Assistance to Israel," securityassistance.org, April 2021.

44. Eric Cheyfitz, "The Force of Exceptionalist Narratives in the Israeli-Palestinian Conflict," *Journal of the Native American and Indigenous Studies Association* 1, no. 2 (2014): 107–24.

45. Theodore Herzl, *The Complete Diaries of Theodor Herzl*, ed. Raphael Patai, trans. Harry Zohn, vol. 1 (New York: Thomas Yoselof, 1960); Ze'ev (Vladimir) Jabotinsky, "The Iron Wall—We and the Arabs," 1923.

46. Cited in Ahmad H. Sa'di, "The Borders of Colonial Encounter: The Case of Israel's Wall," *Asian Journal of Social Science* 38, no. 1 (2010): 47.

47. Joseph A. Massad, *The Persistence of the Palestinian Question: Essays on Zionism and the Palestinians* (Abingdon, England: Routledge, 2006), 1.

48. Massad, *Persistence*, 2.

49. Gil Merom, "Israel's National Security and the Myth of Exceptionalism," *Political Science Quarterly* 114, no. 3 (1999): 410–14.

50. Edward W. Said, "An Ideology of Difference," *Critical Inquiry* 12, no. 1 (1985): 42.

51. Nadera Shalhoub-Kevorkian, *Security Theology, Surveillance, and the Politics of Fear* (Cambridge: Cambridge University Press, 2015).

52. Said, "Ideology of Difference," 38.

53. Said, "Ideology of Difference," 38. Keith P. Feldman, *A Shadow over Palestine: The Imperial Life of Race in America* (Minneapolis: University of Minnesota Press, 2015); Steven Salaita, *Inter/Nationalism: Decolonizing Native America and Palestine* (Minneapolis: University of Minnesota Press, 2016).

54. Amy Kaplan, *Our American Israel: The Story of an Entangled Alliance* (Cambridge, Mass.: Harvard University Press, 2018), 6.

55. James Eastwood, *Ethics as a Weapon of War: Militarism and Morality in Israel* (Cambridge: Cambridge University Press, 2017).

56. Steven Salaita, *Israel's Dead Soul* (Philadelphia: Temple University Press, 2011).

57. Daniel Marwecki, *Germany and Israel: Whitewashing and Statebuilding*. Oxford: Oxford University Press, 2020.

58. Beit-Hallahmi, *Israeli Connection*, 8.

59. Norman G. Finkelstein, *The Holocaust Industry: Reflections on the Exploitation of Jewish Suffering*, Ebook (London: Verso, 2003), 34–35.

60. Finkelstein, *Holocaust Industry*.

61. Noam Chomsky, *Fateful Triangle: The United States, Israel, and the Palestinians* (London: Pluto Press, 1999), 66.

62. Warren Bass, *Support Any Friend: Kennedy's Middle East and the Making of the U.S.-Israel Alliance* (New York: Oxford University Press, 2003), 2.

63. Bass, *Support Any Friend*, 183.

64. Feldman, *Shadow over Palestine*.

65. Michael Howard and Robert Hunter, "Israel and the Arab World: The Crisis of 1967," *Adelphi Papers* 7, no. 41 (1 October 1967): 39.

66. Howard and Hunter, "Israel and the Arab World," 41.

67. Finkelstein, *Holocaust Industry*, 30.

68. Timothy Mitchell, *Carbon Democracy: Political Power in the Age of Oil* (New York: Verso, 2011), 187.

69. Melani McAlister, *Epic Encounters: Culture, Media, and U.S. Interests in the Middle East since 1945* (Berkeley: University of California Press, 2001), 157, emphasis added.

70. McAlister, *Epic Encounters*, 159.

71. Bresheeth-Zabner, *Army Like No Other*, 171.

72. McAlister, *Epic Encounters*, 178.

73. McAlister, *Epic Encounters*, 178.

74. McAlister, *Epic Encounters*, 181.

75. McAlister, *Epic Encounters*, 184.

76. Kaplan, *Our American Israel*, 8.

77. Cheyfitz, "Force of Exceptionalist Narratives."

78. "Syrian Airliner Seized by Israel: Plane, 10 Aboard, Is Forced Down—Damascus Sees Tie to Soldiers' Capture," *New York Times*, 13 December 1954.

79. Massad, *Persistence*, 5.

80. Terence Smith, Israelis Down a Libyan Airliner in the Sinai, Killing at Least 74; Say It Ignored Warnings to Land," *New York Times*, 22 February 1973.

81. Brian E. Foont, "Shooting Down Civilian Aircraft: Is There an International Law," *Journal of Air Law and Commerce* 72, no. 3 (2007): 695–725.

82. Berda, *Living Emergency*, 18.

83. Said, *Question of Palestine*, 39.

84. Said, *Question of Palestine*, 38–39.

85. Remi Brulin, "Compartmentalization, Contexts of Speech, and the Israeli Origins of the American Discourse on 'Terrorism,'" *Dialectical Anthropology* 39, no. 1 (March 2015): 69–119; Deepa Kumar, "Terrorcraft: Empire and the Making of the Racialised Terrorist Threat," *Race and Class* 62, no. 2 (October 2020): 34–60; Lisa Stampnitzky, *Disciplining Terror: How Experts Invented "Terrorism"* (Cambridge: Cambridge University Press, 2013).

86. Edward W. Said, "The Essential Terrorist," *Arab Studies Quarterly* 9, no. 2 (1987): 195–203.

87. Robert I. Friedman, "Selling Israel to America," *Journal of Palestine Studies* 16, no. 4 (1987): 169–79.

88. Edward Herman and Gerry O"Sullivan, *The "Terrorism" Industry: The Experts and Institutions That Shape Our View of Terror* (New York: Pantheon Books, 1989).

89. Gargi Bhattacharyya, "Globalizing Racism and Myths of the Other in the 'War on Terror,'" in *Thinking Palestine*, ed. Ronit Lentin (New York: Zed Books, 2008), 46–62.

90. Stampnitzky, *Disciplining Terror*; Kaplan, *Our American Israel*, 243.

91. Erakat, *Justice for Some*, 181.

92. See, for example, David Weisburd, Tal Jonathan, and Simon Perry, "The Israeli Model for Policing Terrorism: Goals, Strategies, and Open Questions," *Criminal Justice and Behavior* 36 (2009): 1259–78; David Weisburd et al., eds., *To Protect and Serve: Policing in an Age of Terrorism* (London: Springer, 2009).

93. Hajjar, "International Humanitarian Law and 'Wars on Terror'"; Craig A. Jones, "Lawfare and the Juridification of Late Modern War," *Progress in Human Geography* 40, no. 2 (April 2016): 221–39; Craig Jones, *The War Lawyers: The United States, Israel, and Juridical Warfare* (Oxford: Oxford University Press, 2020).

94. Erakat, *Justice for Some*, 191.

95. Latour, *Pandora's Hope*, 104.

96. Howard and Hunter, "Israel and the Arab World," preface, emphasis added.

97. Ben-Israel is best known for developing a mathematical equation for destroying Hamas and other Palestinian militant organizations by arresting or killing its members. Ben-Israel was featured in Yotam Feldman's 2013 documentary on Israel's weapons industry *The Lab* in relation to this work. Also see Eyal Weizman, *The Worst of All Possible Evils: Humanitarian Violence from Arendt to Gaza* (London: Verso, 2012).

98. Edward Herman and Gerry O'Sullivan, *The "Terrorism" Industry: The Experts and Institutions That Shape Our View of Terror* (New York: Pantheon Books, 1989), 134.

99. International Security and Defense Systems Ltd. Corporate Brochure, International Security and Defense Systems Ltd. (ISDS), accessed 7 June 2014, www.isds.co.il.

100. Neve Gordon, "The Political Economy of Israel's Homeland Security/Surveillance Industry," Working Paper III, *The New Transparency: Surveillance and Social Sorting*, 2009, 42.

101. Dan Senor and Saul Singer, *Start-Up Nation: The Story of Israel's Economic Miracle* (Toronto: McClelland & Stewart, 2009).

102. Joseph F. Getzoff, "Start-up Nationalism: The Rationalities of Neoliberal Zionism," *Environment and Planning D: Society and Space* 38, no. 5 (October 2020): 813.

103. "HomeLand Security Industry: Born of Necessity. Matured by Reality," Israel Export and International Cooperation Institute (IEICI), n.d.

104. Beit-Hallahmi, *Israeli Connection*, 240, emphasis added.

105. Erella Grassiani, "Commercialised Occupation Skills: Israeli Security Experience as an International Brand," in *Security/Mobility: Politics of Movement*, ed. Matthias Leese and Stef Wittendorp (Manchester: Manchester University Press, 2017), 37–56.

106. Pappé, *Idea of Israel*, 10.

107. The concept of "rings" or "layers" of security is in no meaningful way uniquely Israeli. See, for instance, Jon Coaffee, "Rings of Steel, Rings of Concrete, and Rings of Confidence: Designing out Terrorism in Central London Pre and Post September 11th," *International Journal of Urban and Regional Research* 28, no. 1 (2004): 201–11.

108. Gil Eyal, *The Disenchantment of the Orient: Expertise in Arab Affairs and the Israeli State* (Stanford: Stanford University Press, 2006).

109. Amy Kaplan, *The Anarchy of Empire in the Making of U.S. Culture* (Cambridge, Mass.: Harvard University Press, 2002), 16.

110. Jasbir K. Puar, *Terrorist Assemblages: Homonationalism in Queer Times* (Durham, N.C.: Duke University Press, 2007), 8.

111. Stoler and McGranahan, "Refiguring Imperial Terrains," 29.

112. Stoler and McGranahan, "Refiguring Imperial Terrains," 56.

113. See, for instance, Nadav Morag, *Comparative Homeland Security: Global Lessons* (Hoboken, N.J.: John Wiley & Sons, 2011).

114. Nick Denes, "From Tanks to Wheelchairs: Unmanned Aerial Vehicles, Zionist Battlefield Experiments, and the Transparence of the Civilian," in *Surveillance and Control in Israel/Palestine: Population, Territory, and Power*, ed. Elia Zureik, David Lyon, and Yasmeen Abu-Laban (London: Routledge, 2011), 188.

115. Denes, "From Tanks to Wheelchairs," 189.

116. Darryl Li, *The Universal Enemy: Jihad, Empire, and the Challenge of Solidarity* (Stanford: Stanford University Press, 2019), 12.

117. Li, *Universal Enemy*, 12.

118. Sara Salazar Hughes, "Unbounded Territoriality: Territorial Control, Settler Colonialism, and Israel/Palestine," *Settler Colonial Studies* 10, no. 2 (April 2020): 216–33; Areej Sabbagh-Khoury, "Memory for Forgetfulness: Conceptualizing a Memory Practice of Settler Colonial Disavowal," *Theory and Society*, 7 July 2022; Nikhil Pal Singh,

"Racial Formation in an Age of Permanent War," in *Racial Formation in the Twenty-First Century*, ed. Daniel HoSang, Oneka LaBennett, and Laura Pulido (Berkeley: University of California Press, 2012), 276–301.

119. Richard Hawkins, "The 'Irish Model' and the Empire: A Case for Reassessment," in *Policing the Empire: Government, Authority, and Control, 1830–1940*, ed. David M. Anderson and David Killingray (Manchester: Manchester University Press, 1991), 22–23, emphasis added.

120. Oren Barak and Gabriel Sheffer, "Israel's 'Security Network' and Its Impact: An Exploration of a New Approach," *International Journal of Middle East Studies* 38, no. 2 (2006): 235–61.

121. Graham, "Laboratories of War"; Erella Grassiani, "Performing Politics at the Israeli Security Fair," *Policing and Society* (June 2022): 1–17; Halper, *War Against the People*.

122. Herman and O'Sullivan, *"Terrorism" Industry*, 135. Noam Chomsky elaborates on the veneration of Israel as a security "model" for a number of other Latin American dictators during this period at length. Chomsky, *Fateful Triangle*.

123. Somdeep Sen, "Antagonistic Landscapes," *Environment and Planning C: Politics and Space* 39, no. 4 (June 2021): 705–21; Maya Wind, *Towers of Ivory and Steel: How Israeli Universities Deny Palestinian Freedom* (New York: Verso Books, 2024).

124. "Max Security testimonials page," accessed 1 February 2014, https://www.max-security.com/testimonials/.

125. "Israel HomeLand Security Industry," Israel Export and International Cooperation Institute, 2010.

126. Norman G. Finkelstein, *Beyond Chutzpah: On the Misuse of Anti-Semitism and the Abuse of History* (Berkeley: University of California Press, 2005).

127. Patrick Wolfe, "Settler Colonialism and the Elimination of the Native," *Journal of Genocide Research* 8, no. 4 (2006): 389.

128. See also Nivi Manchanda and Sharri Plonski, "Between Mobile Corridors and Immobilizing Borders: Race, Fixity and Friction in Palestine/Israel," *International Affairs* 98, no. 1 (January 2022): 183–207.

129. Just before the September 11 attacks, Israelis also shot down a Cessna aircraft that had entered Israeli airspace from Lebanon using similar reasoning to that in 1973 to justify it. See Foont, "Shooting Down Civilian Aircraft."

130. Roxanne Dunbar-Ortiz, *Loaded: A Disarming History of the Second Amendment* (San Francisco: City Lights Books, 2018), 42.

131. Salaita, *Inter/Nationalism*, 156.

132. Perry Anderson, *The Indian Ideology*, 2nd ed. (London: Verso, 2021); Sunil Khilnani, *The Idea of India* (London: Penguin Books, 2004).

133. Beatrice Jauregui, *Provisional Authority: Police, Order, and Security in India* (Chicago: University of Chicago Press, 2016), 83.

Interlude—A Reticent Embrace

1. Fanga La, "The Arab Israeli War," *United Services Institution Journal* LXXXXVII, no. 408 (July 1967): 214.

2. La, "Arab Israeli War," 228.

3. La, "Arab Israeli War," 228.

4. La, "Arab Israeli War," 228.

5. La, "Arab Israeli War," 230.

6. Arjun Thapan, "The Arab-Israeli Conflict June 1967 and Its Origins," *United Services Institution Journal* LXXXXVIII, no. 412 (July 1968): 295.

7. GH Jansen, "A Study of Indian Reactions to Israel's Military 'Victory,'" *United Services Institution Journal* LXXXXIX, no. 417 (October 1969): 387.

8. Jansen, "Study of Indian Reactions," 387.

9. Jansen, "Study of Indian Reactions," 387.

10. Jansen, "Study of Indian Reactions," 387.

11. Jansen, "Study of Indian Reactions," 388.

12. Jansen, "Study of Indian Reactions," 389.

13. Jansen, "Study of Indian Reactions," 389.

14. C. B. Khanduri, "Moshe Dayan: The Military Commander," *The Defence Review Annual*, 1982, 59.

15. Bidanda M. Chengappa, "Indo-Israeli Relations: The Great Leap Forward," *Indian Defence Review* 8, no. 3 (July 1993): 107–8.

16. B. Raman, "My Jerusalem Diary," *Indian Defence Review* 18, no. 3 (September 2003): 9.

17. Raman, "My Jerusalem Diary," 9.

18. Raman, "My Jerusalem Diary," 8.

19. Raman, "My Jerusalem Diary," 10.

20. Thomas Blom Hansen, *The Law of Force: The Violent Heart of Indian Politics*. New Delhi: Aleph Book Company, 2021.

21. Dipesh Chakrabarty, "The Difference-Deferral of (a) Colonial Modernity: Public Debates on Domesticity in British Bengal," *History Workshop Journal* 36 (1993): 30.

22. Rhys Machold, 'India's Counterinsurgency Knowledge: Theorizing Global Position in Wars on Terror', *Small Wars and Insurgencies* 33, no. 4–5 (July 2022): 796–818.

Chapter Three

1. Sevanti Ninan, "Do We Deserve This?," *The Hindu*, 7 December 2008.

2. Kalpana Sharma, "Governance Failures and the Anti-Political Fallout," *Economic and Political Weekly* 43, no. 49 (June 2008): 13.

3. Caren Kaplan, "The Biopolitics of Technoculture in the Mumbai Attacks," *Theory, Culture, and Society* 26, no. 7–8 (2009): 301–13.

4. Rama Lakshmi, "Official Quits amid Public Anger at India"s Leadership," *Washington Post*, 1 December 2008.

5. "Force One, State-of-Art Guns to Guard Mumbai," *Telegraph India*, 18 December 2008, https://www.telegraphindia.com/india/force-one-state-of-art-guns-to-guard-mumbai/cid/516164.

6. Suhas Palshikar, "In the Shadow of Terror: Anti-Politician or Anti-Politics?," *Economic and Political Weekly* 43, no. 50 (2008): 10–11; Tania Roy, "'India's 9/11': Accidents of a Moveable Metaphor," *Theory, Culture, and Society* 26, no. 7–8 (2009): 314–28.

7. Manisha Sethi, *Kafkaland: Prejudice, Law, and Counterterrorism in India* (Gurgaon, India: Three Essays Collective, 2014), 165.

8. Abdul Hameed, "Mumbai Attack: Terrorists Spoke Marathi?," *TwoCircles.Net*, 29 November 2008.

9. Yoginder Sikand, "Mossad-CIA Connection to Mumbai Terror Attacks?," *Countercurrents*, 29 November 2008.

10. "Antulay Raises Doubts over Karkare's Killing," *Economic Times*, 17 December 2008.

11. "'Why Did No Backup Arrive for My Husband?,'" *Hindustan Times*, 15 January 2009.

12. Raveena Hansa, "The Mumbai Terror Attacks: Need for a Thorough Investigation," in *Mumbai Post 26/11: An Alternative Perspective*, ed. Ram Puniyani and Shabnam Hashmi (New Delhi: SAGE Publications India, 2010).

13. Roy, "'India's 9/11': Accidents of a Moveable Metaphor"; Sharma, "Governance Failures and the Anti-Political Fallout."

14. Beatrice Jauregui, "Provisional Agency in India: Jugaad and Legitimation of Corruption," *American Ethnologist* 41, no. 1 (2014): 76–91.

15. Biju Mathew, "As the Fires Die: The Terror of the Aftermath," *Samar: South Asian Magazine for Action and Reflection*, 1 December 2008, http://www.samarmagazine.org/archive/articles/275.

16. Stuart Hall et al., *Policing the Crisis: Mugging, the State, and Law and Order*, 2nd ed. (Houndmills, England: Palgrave Macmillan, 2014), 397.

17. Hall et al., *Policing the Crisis*, 332.

18. Veena Das and Deborah Poole, eds., *Anthropology in the Margins of the State* (Oxford: Oxford University Press, 2004).

19. Paul Amar, *The Security Archipelago: Human-Security States, Sexuality Politics, and the End of Neoliberalism* (Durham, N.C.: Duke University Press, 2013); Graham Denyer Willis, *The Killing Consensus: Police, Organized Crime, and the Regulation of Life and Death in Urban Brazil* (Berkeley: University of California Press, 2015); Teresa P. R. Caldeira, *City of Walls: Crime, Segregation, and Citizenship in São Paulo* (Berkeley: University of California Press, 2000); Guillermina Seri, *Seguridad: Crime, Police Power, and Democracy in Argentina* (New York: Continuum, 2012).

20. Thomas Blom Hansen and Finn Stepputat, "Introduction," in *Sovereign Bodies: Citizens, Migrants, and States in the Postcolonial World*, ed. Thomas Blom Hansen and Finn Stepputat (Princeton, N.J.: Princeton University Press, 2005), 29.

21. Ram Pradhan and Vappala Balachandran, "Report of the High Level Enquiry Committee (HLEC) on 26/11 (Appointed by the Maharashtra Government Vide GAD GR No: Raasua.2008/C.R.34/29-A, 30th Dec 2008)," 2009.

22. While most of the initial criticisms of the NSG operation focused on its delayed deployment from Delhi, some Indian commentators also contested the efficacy of the tactics employed by NSG forces on the ground in Mumbai during 26/11 as well as its operational structure. See Praveen Swami, "Mumbai Siege Turns Spotlight on Crisis within NSG," *The Hindu*, 12 December 2008.

23. Aditi Pai and Swati Mathur, "Lame Duck Committee to Investigate 26/11," *India Today*, 31 December 2008.

24. The dossier was later made public but was initially classified. It contains evidence from a range of sources, including photos from inside Nariman House taken by the ZAKA team (see chapter 1).

25. Director of the U.S. Federal Bureau of Investigation (FBI) Robert S. Mueller also later gave testimony to the Council on Foreign Relations on February 23, 2009, noting the "unprecedented access to evidence and intelligence" provided by Indian authorities to U.S. officials. Cited in Vappala Balachandran, "Dealing with Aftermath of Attacks: Lessons from Mumbai and Elsewhere on What to Do and What Not to Do," The Future of International Cooperation in Countering Violent Extremism, St. Antony's College, Oxford University, 2010.

26. Harinder Baweja, "Why Can't You See The 26/11 Report?," *Tehelka*, 22 August 2009.

27. Pradhan and Balachandran, "Report," General, Section 4.

28. Pradhan and Balachandran, "Report," Section D, 3.73.

29. Harinder Baweja, "Why Can't You See The 26/11 Report?," *Tehelka*, 22 August 2009. The HLEC report was not officially made public until 2019, after more than a decade of lobbying for its release.

30. Richard V. Ericson, "Patrolling the Facts: Secrecy and Publicity in Police Work," *British Journal of Sociology* 40, no. 2 (1989): 205–26.

31. An article published in the investigative magazine *Tehelka* in June 2009 pointed out that "the events of that night [November 26, 2008] are only too well known, but the truth is not," stressing that "there are critical questions that the Mumbai Police need to answer." Harinder Baweja, "Slaughter House Files," *Tehelka*, 13 June 2009.

32. Rana Ayyub, "In the Eye of the Storm," *Tehelka*, 12 December 2009; Krishna Kumar, "Did Police Tweak 26/11 Sequence?," *Mail Today*, 6 June 2009.

33. Rana Ayyub, "'Gafoor Was Promoted, Not Transferred,'" *Tehelka*, 27 June 2009.

34. In building their case against Kasab, the Mumbai police put together a charge sheet (dossier of evidence) that later led to his conviction and execution in 2012. However, the dossier presented little evidence gathered through investigations. The charge sheet also entirely left out the sequence of events at Cama Hospital, an omission that only raised further doubts and speculations about what took place there and why. See Raveena Hansa, "India's Terror Dossier: Further Evidence of a Conspiracy," *Countercurrents*, 9 February 2009.

35. Prior to 2008, various government initiatives at the union level, such as the Modernisation of Police Force (MFG) Scheme and the Mega City Policing (introduced from 2005 onwards) were in place, specifically geared toward equipping Mumbai's police with new weapons and other security technologies. Although the latest installment of the MFG Scheme was in place by 2000 (and scheduled to run until 2009), Maharashtra's procurement process was moving slowly, stalled by the highly bureaucratic and poorly defined procurement process and a lack of approved testing laboratories.

36. Sapna Agarwal, "No Consensus on Security Plan Even a Month after Mumbai Attacks," *Business Standard*, 27 December 2008.

37. "Citizens' Action Group (in Association with Bombay First) (Formed under G.R. No. Mumbai Vikas 2004/C.R. No 12/2004/Special Projects 'White Paper on Crisis Management in Mumbai,'" Bombay First, February 2009.

38. "Citizens' Action Group."

39. Agarwal, "No Consensus on Security Plan Even a Month after Mumbai Attacks."

40. Ajai Sahni, "A Triumph of Form over Content," *Seminar*, 2009.

41. "Force One, State-of-Art Guns to Guard Mumbai," *Telegraph India*, 18 December 2008.

42. Other local hubs were also set up in Chennai, Kolkata, and Hyderabad and later Ahmedabad.

43. Somit Sen, "Once in the Army, Now in Force One," *Times of India*, 19 December 2008.

44. Sen, "Once in the Army."

45. Sen, "Once in the Army."

46. "Force One, State-of-Art Guns to Guard Mumbai."

47. Marisol LeBrón, *Policing Life and Death: Race, Violence, and Resistence in Puerto Rico* (Oakland: University of California Press, 2019), 229.

48. "Force One, State-of-Art Guns to Guard Mumbai."

49. "Maha's Elite Counter Terror Unit Force One Becomes Operational," *Business Standard*, 25 November 2009.

50. This was not the first time an official delegation from the Maharashtra government had been dispatched to Palestine/Israel, though it does appear to have been the first Maharashtra government visit there in relation to security reform. For instance, in the 1990s Maharashtra Chief Minister Sharad Pawar led an agricultural delegation to Palestine/Israel. See Bidanda M. Chengappa, "Indo-Israeli Relations: The Great Leap Forward," *Indian Defence Review* 8, no. 3 (July 1993): 108.

51. Sagnik Chowdhury, "Security Tips from Tel Aviv and High-End Training," *Indian Express*, 26 July 2009.

52. Cited in Christophe Jaffrelot, ed., *Hindu Nationalism: A Reader* (Princeton, N.J.: Princeton University Press, 2009), 119–20.

53. William Walters, "Editor's Introduction: Anti-Policy and Anti-Politics: Critical Reflections on Certain Schemes to Govern Bad Things," *European Journal of Cultural Studies* 11, no. 3 (2008): 281.

54. Bidanda M. Chengappa, "Indo-Israeli Relations: The Great Leap Forward," *Indian Defence Review* 8, no. 3 (July 1993): 108.

55. Thomas Blom Hansen, *The Saffron Wave: Democracy and Hindu Nationalism in Modern India* (Princeton, N.J.: Princeton University Press, 1999), 220.

56. Thomas Blom Hansen, *Wages of Violence: Naming and Identity in Postcolonial Bombay* (Princeton, N.J.: Princeton University Press, 2001), 99.

57. Rupal Oza, "The Geography of Hindu Right-Wing Violence in India," in *Violent Geographies: Fear, Terror, and Political Violence*, ed. Derek Gregory and Allan Pred (Routledge: New York and London, 2007), 153–74.

58. Deeptiman Tiwary, "Cops Get Israeli Answers for Terror," *Mumbai Mirror*, 12 July 2009.

59. Deeptiman Tiwary, "Mumbai Cops to Take Lessons from Israel," *Mumbai Mirror*, 11 July 2009.

60. Tiwary, "Cops Get Israeli Answers," emphasis added.

61. See for example, Ritu Sarin, "No 26/11 Repeat: Maharashtra Shops for Israeli Solutions," *Indian Express*, 13 July 2009.

62. Sagnik Chowdhury, "Security Tips from Tel Aviv."

63. Ritu Sarin, "From Israel, Lessons on Fighting Terror," *Indian Express*, 21 July 2009.

64. Sarin, "From Israel."

65. Chowdhury, "Security Tips from Tel Aviv."

66. Meena Menon, "A Smart Anti-Terror Force for Mumbai Now," *The Hindu*, 25 November 2009.

67. The Mumbai *Protector's* archives can be found at: https://www.theprotector.in/mumbai/. New Media Communication also subsequently partnered with the Consulate General of Israel in Mumbai to launch its business magazine "Indo-Israeli Business" in 2009, publishing a special issue on Israeli homeland security solutions in 2010: "Israel's Innovative Homeland Security Solutions," *Indo-Israeli Business*, September–November 2010.

68. "We Pledge to Keep Mumbai Safe and Secure," *The Mumbai Protector: A Magazine for the Mumbai Police* I, no. 2 (Nov-Dec) (2009): 9-16.

69. D. Sivanandhan, "View from the Top," *The Mumbai Protector: A Magazine for the Mumbai Police* 1, no. 2 (Nov-Dec) (2009): 6, emphasis added.

70. "We Pledge," emphasis added.

71. "We Pledge," 9.

72. "We Pledge," 10.

73. Sivanandhan, "View from the Top," 6.

74. "Stay Fit, Eat Healthy Diet," *The Mumbai Protector: A Magazine for the Mumbai Police* 1, no. 2 (Nov-Dec) (2009): 84–86.

75. "We Pledge," 10.

76. Blom Hansen, *Wages of Violence,* chapter 8.

77. Sankaran Krishna, *Postcolonial Insecurities: India, Sri Lanka, and the Question of Nationhood* (Minneapolis: University of Minnesota Press, 1999), 131.

78. Krishna, *Postcolonial Insecurities,* 131.

79. Homi K. Bhabha, *The Location of Culture* (London: Routledge, 1994).

80. Ben Brucato, "Fabricating the Color Line in a White Democracy: From Slave Catchers to Petty Sovereigns," *Theoria* 61, no. 141 (December 2014): 30–54; Stuart Schrader, "To Secure the Global Great Society: Participation in Pacification," *Humanity: An International Journal of Human Rights, Humanitarianism, and Development* 7, no. 2 (2016): 225–53.

81. Louis Althusser, *On Ideology* (London and New York: Verso, 2008), 48.

82. "We Pledge," 16.

83. "Jagrut Mumbaikar—Joint Initiative on Citizens' Safety and Security: Fighting Bullets & Bombs with Your Ears and Eyes," *The Mumbai Protector: A Magazine for the Mumbai Police* 1, no. 1 (September/October 2009): 26.

84. Deniz Yonucu, *Police, Provocation, Politics: Counterinsurgency in Istanbul* (Ithaca, N.Y.: Cornell University Press, 2022), 77.

85. Joseph Masco, *The Theater of Operations: National Security Affect from the Cold War to the War on Terror* (Durham, N.C.: Duke University Press, 2014), 18.

86. Jinee Lokaneeta, *The Truth Machines: Policing, Violence, and Scientific Interrogations in India* (Ann Arbor: University of Michigan Press, 2020).

87. Sikata Banerjee, "Warriors in Politics: Religious Nationalism, Masculine Hinduism, and the Shiv Sena in Bombay," *Women and Politics* 20, no. 3 (September 1999):

1–26; Sikata Banerjee, *Gender, Nation, and Popular Film in India: Globalizing Muscular Nationalism* (London: Routledge, 2016).

88. Lynda Boose, "Techno-Muscularity and the 'Boy Eternal': From the Quagmire to the Gulf," in *Cultures of United States Imperialism*, ed. Susan Jeffords and Donald E. Pease (Durham, N.C.: Duke University Press, 1993), 581–615.

89. Christophe Jaffrelot, "Hindu Nationalism: Strategic Syncretism in Ideology Building," *Economic and Political Weekly* 28, no. 12/13 (1993): 517–24.

90. Cf. Andreas Schedler, "Introduction: Antipolitics—Closing and Colonizing the Public Sphere," in *The End of Politics? Explorations into Modern Antipolitics*, ed. Andreas Schedler (London: Macmillan Press, 1997), 1–20; Jonas Hagmann, "Security in the Society of Control: The Politics and Practices of Securing Urban Spaces," *International Political Sociology* 11, no. 4 (December 2017): 418–38; Jonas Hagmann, Hendrik Hegemann, and Andrew Neal, "The Politicisation of Security: Controversy, Mobilisation, Arena Shifting," *European Review of International Studies* 5, no. 3 (2018): 3–29.

91. Lisa Stampnitzky, *Disciplining Terror: How Experts Invented "Terrorism"* (Cambridge: Cambridge University Press, 2013), 187; see also Claudia Aradau, "Assembling (Non)Knowledge: Security, Law, and Surveillance in a Digital World," *International Political Sociology* 11, no. 4 (2017): 327–42.

92. Åshild Kolås, "The 2008 Mumbai Terror Attacks: (Re-)Constructing Indian (Counter-)Terrorism," *Critical Studies on Terrorism* 3, no. 1 (2010): 83–98.

93. Vappala Balachandran, "An Essay on Mossad," *The Pioneer*, 18 March 2007.

94. My point here is not to imply that Balachandran or Pradhan had some hidden agenda. Yet it is notable that Balachandran was invited to speak at a number of international conferences on homeland security and counterterrorism in the years after 2008 including the Asia-Pacific Homeland Security Summit (Honolulu, November 2009) and went on to write a number of articles in homeland security trade publications.

95. Harinder Baweja, "Why Can't You See The 26/11 Report?," *Tehelka*, 22 August 2009.

96. "Wives of Kamte, Karkare Question Clean Chit," *Indian Express*, 28 May 2009.

97. S. M. Mushrif, *Who Killed Karkare? The Real Face of Terrorism in India*, 1st ed. (Delhi: Pharos Media and Publishing, 2009). Mushrif also later submitted a detailed thirty-five-page "note" with the information he had compiled about the (alledgedly) true perpetrators of 26/11 to the U.S. Department of State's Reward for Justice Program, a copy of which he shared with me. According to Mushrif, he never received any reply about his application to the program.

98. Vinita Kamte and Vinita Deshmukh, *To the Last Bullet: The Inspiring Story of Braveheart Ashok Kamte*, 1st ed. (Pune, India: Ameya Prakashan, 2009).

99. Mushrif, *Who Killed Karkare?*, 185.

100. Mushrif, *Who Killed Karkare?*, 185.

101. Mushrif, *Who Killed Karkare?*, 227–28.

102. Mushrif, *Who Killed Karkare?*, 205–6.

103. Kamte and Deshmukh, *To the Last Bullet*, xiii.

104. Kamte and Deshmukh, *To the Last Bullet*, 61.

105. Rana Ayyub, "In the Eye of the Storm," *Tehelka*, 12 December 2009.

106. Linsey McGoey, "The Logic of Strategic Ignorance," *British Journal of Sociology* 63, no. 3 (2012): 533–76; Linsey McGoey, "Strategic Unknowns: Towards a Sociology of Ignorance," *Economy and Society* 41, no. 1 (2012): 1–16.

107. William Walters, "Editor's Introduction: Anti-Policy and Anti-Politics: Critical Reflections on Certain Schemes to Govern Bad Things," *European Journal of Cultural Studies* 11, no. 3 (2008): 275.

108. Yonucu, *Police, Provocation, Politics*, 15, emphasis added.

109. Rhys Machold, "Policing Reality: Urban Disorder, Failure, and Expert Undoings," *International Political Sociology* 14, no. 1 (2020): 22–39.

110. It is important to note, however, that some of the concerns Mushrif raised live on to some extent in India today, though do not get comparable media coverage to that which *Who Killed Karkare?* garnered in 2009. See "Anand Patwardhan on 'Reason' in the Time of the RSS," *The Caravan*, 6 April 2019. Indeed, Mushrif published a follow-up book to *Who Killed Karkare?* in 2014 entitled *26/11 Probe: Why Judiciary Also Failed?* [*sic*]. But this time around there was virtually no media coverage, nor any resulting political pressures or controversies resulting from his incendiary charges that India's IB interfered in judicial processes related to 26/11.

111. Achin Vanaik, *The Rise of Hindu Authoritarianism: Secular Claims, Communal Realities* (New York: Verso, 2017).

112. Kia Meng Boon, "'The Only Thing Is You Have to Know Them First': Protest Policing and Malaysia's BERSIH Protests (2011–2016)," *Small Wars and Insurgencies* 33, no. 4–5 (July 2022): 868–901; Deborah Cowen and Neil Smith, "'Martial Law in the Streets of Toronto':G20 Security and State Violence," *Human Geography* 3, no. 3 (2010): 29–49; Bernard E. Harcourt, *The Counterrevolution: How Our Government Went to War Against Its Own Citizens* (New York: Basic Books, 2018); Desirée Poets, "The Securitization of Citizenship in a 'Segregated City': A Reflection on Rio's Pacifying Police Units," *Urbe. Revista Brasileira de Gestão Urbana* 7 (May 2015): 182–94; Deniz Yonucu, "Urban Vigilantism: A Study of Anti-Terror Law, Politics, and Policing in Istanbul," *International Journal of Urban and Regional Research* 42, no. 3 (2018): 408–22.

113. D. Sivanandhan, "Tackling Terrorism: My First Priority," *The Mumbai Protector: A Magazine for the Mumbai Police*, 2009, emphasis added.

114. John Law, "What's Wrong with a One-World World?," *Distinktion: Journal of Social Theory* 16, no. 1 (2015): 126–39.

Chapter Four

1. Arjun Appadurai, *Fear of Small Numbers: An Essay on the Geography of Anger* (Durham, N.C.: Duke University Press, 2006); Martin Coward, *Urbicide: The Politics of Urban Destruction* (London: Routledge, 2009); Ward Berenschot, *Riot Politics: India's Hindu-Muslim Violence and the Everyday Mediation of the State* (London: Hurst & Co., 2011); Sara Fregonese, *War and the City: Urban Geopolitics in Lebanon* (London: I. B. Tauris, 2019); Stephen Graham, ed., *Cities, War, and Terrorism: Towards an Urban Geopolitics* (Oxford: Blackwell, 2004); Adam Ramadan, "Destroying Nahr El-Bared: Sovereignty and Urbicide in the Space of Exception," *Political Geography* 28, no. 3 (2009): 153–63.

2. David Barnard-Wills and Cerwyn Moore, "The Terrorism of the Other: Towards a Contrapuntal Reading of Terrorism in India," *Critical Studies on Terrorism* 3, no. 3 (2010): 385–89.

3. Paul Amar, *The Security Archipelago: Human-Security States, Sexuality Politics, and the End of Neoliberalism* (Durham, N.C.: Duke University Press, 2013), 20.

4. Jon Coaffee, *Terrorism, Risk, and the City: The Making of a Contemporary Urban Landscape* (Aldershot, England: Ashgate, 2003); Martin Coward, "Network-Centric Violence, Critical Infrastructure and the Urbanization of Security," *Security Dialogue* 40, no. 4–5 (2009): 399–418; Stephen Graham, *Cities Under Siege: The New Military Urbanism* (New York: Verso, 2010); Zoltán Glück, "Security Urbanism and the Counterterror State in Kenya," *Anthropological Theory* 17, no. 3 (2017): 297–321.

5. Peter. B. Kraska and Victor E. Kappeler, "Militarizing American Police: The Rise and Normalization of Paramilitary Units," *Social Problems* 44, no. 1 (1997): 1–18.

6. Allen Feldman, "Securocratic Wars of Public Safety," *Interventions* 6, no. 3 (2004): 330–50; Henry A. Giroux, "War on Terror: The Militarising of Public Space and Culture in the United States," *Third Text* 18, no. 4 (2004): 211–21.

7. Mike Davis, *City of Quartz: Excavating the Future in Los Angeles* (London: Verso, 1990).

8. Casey Delehanty, "Police with Lots of Military Gear Kill Civilians More Often than Less-Militarized Officers," *Homeland Security Newswire*, 2 July 2020; Tom Nolan, "Militarization Has Fostered a Policing Culture That Sets Up Protesters as 'The Enemy,'" *Homeland Security Newswire*, 3 June 2020.

9. Christopher McMichael, "Pacification and Police: A Critique of the Police Militarization Thesis," *Capital and Class* 41, no. 1 (2017): 115–32.

10. Beatrice Jauregui, *Provisional Authority: Police, Order, and Security in India* (Chicago: University of Chicago Press, 2016), 145.

11. Deborah Cowen, "Militarism? A Mini Forum," *Environment and Planning D: Society and Space*, 5 September 2012; Mark Neocleous, *War Power, Police Power* (Edinburgh: Edinburgh University Press, 2014); Stuart Schrader, "Cops at War: How World War II Transformed U.S. Policing," *Modern American History* 4, no. 2 (July 2021): 159–79; Micol Seigel, "Always Already Military: Police, Public Safety, and State Violence," *American Quarterly* 71, no. 2 (July 2019): 519–39.

12. McMichael, "Pacification and Police," 129.

13. Alison Howell, "Forget 'Militarization': Race, Disability and the 'Martial Politics' of the Police and of the University," *International Feminist Journal of Politics* 20, no. 2 (2018): 131.

14. Ruth Wilson Gilmore and Craig Gilmore, "Beyond Bratton," in *Policing the Planet: Why the Policing Crisis Led to Black Lives Matter*, ed. Jordan T. Camp and Christina Heatherton (London: Verso, 2016), 173–200.

15. Howell, "Forget 'Militarization.'"

16. Angana P. Chatterji, Thomas Blom Hansen, and Christophe Jaffrelot, eds., *Majoritarian State: How Hindu Nationalism Is Changing India* (Oxford: Oxford University Press, 2019); Thomas Blom Hansen, *The Law of Force: The Violent Heart of Indian Politics* (New Delhi: Aleph Book Company, 2021); Christophe Jaffrelot, *Modi's India: Hindu*

Nationalism and the Rise of Ethnic Democracy, trans. Cynthia Schoch (Princeton, N.J.: Princeton University Press, 2021).

17. Christophe Jaffrelot, ed., *Hindu Nationalism: A Reader* (Princeton, N.J.: Princeton University Press, 2009).

18. Neocleous, *War Power, Police Power.*

19. "Martial" draws attention to the imperative of attending to "war-like relations or technologies and knowledges that are "of war."" Rather than setting out to understand how "normal politics" are contaminated by "militarization," however, martial politics begins from the premise that martial relations are inherent to (liberal) politics and 'enacted on those who are racialized, Indigenous, disabled or otherwise constituted as a threat to civil order'. Howell, "Forget 'Militarization,'" 118.

20. Steve Herbert, "The Normative Ordering of Police Territoriality: Making and Marking Space with the Los Angeles Police Department," *Annals of the Association of American Geographers* 86, no. 3 (1996): 567–82; Steve Herbert, *Policing Space: Territoriality and the Los Angeles Police Department* (Minneapolis: University of Minnesota Press, 1997).

21. Jan Bachmann, Coleen Bell, and Caroline Holmqvist, eds., *War, Police, and Assemblages of Intervention* (London: Routledge, 2015).

22. Jauregui, *Provisional Authority.*

23. Jinee Lokaneeta, *The Truth Machines: Policing, Violence, and Scientific Interrogations in India* (Ann Arbor: University of Michigan Press, 2020).

24. Ruth Wilson Gilmore, *Golden Gulag: Prisons, Surplus, Crisis, and Opposition in Globalizing California* (Berkeley: University of California Press, 2007), 189; Ruth Wilson Gilmore, "Race, Prisons, and War: Scenes from the Gilmore History of U.S. Violence," *Socialist Register* 45 (March 2009): 84.

25. Paul R. Brass, *Theft of an Idol: Text and Context in the Representation of Collective Violence* (Princeton, N.J.: Princeton University Press, 1997); Julia M. Eckert, *The Charisma of Direct Action: Power, Politics, and the Shiv Sena* (New Delhi: Oxford University Press, 2003).

26. Thomas Blom Hansen, *Wages of Violence: Naming and Identity in Postcolonial Bombay* (Princeton, N.J.: Princeton University Press, 2001).

27. CST was subsequently officially renamed Chhatrapati Shivaji Maharaj Terminus (CSMT).

28. After 26/11, BGI formed an Indian subsidiary, BGI Egintech Private Limited based in Ahmedabad, India.

29. Jyoti Belur, "Police Stop and Search in India: Mumbai Nakabandi," *Policing and Society* 21, no. 4 (2011): 240–41.

30. Howell, "Forget 'Militarization.'"

31. Joshua Reeves, "If You See Something, Say Something: Lateral Surveillance and the Uses of Responsibility," *Surveillance and Society* 10, no. 3/4 (December 2012): 235–48.

32. Cindi Katz, "Banal Terrorism," in *Violent Geographies: Fear, Terror, and Political Violence*, ed. Derek Gregory and Allan Pred (New York: Routledge, 2007), 349–62.

33. Sarah Franklin, *Dolly Mixtures: The Remaking of Genealogy* (Durham, N.C.: Duke University Press, 2007).

34. J. Dey, "Taking the Wind out of Mumbai's Sails," *Mid Day*, 18 March 2011.

35. Surendra Gangan, "Speedboats Guzzle Fuel Worth Rs60 Crore, Maharashtra Grapples for Funds," *Daily News and Analysis*, 11 October 2011.

36. Ann Laura Stoler and Carole McGranahan, "Refiguring Imperial Terrains," *Ab Imperio* 2006, no. 2 (2006): 17–58.

37. Beatrice Jauregui, "Provisional Agency in India: Jugaad and Legitimation of Corruption," *American Ethnologist* 41, no. 1 (2014): 77.

38. Jauregui, *Provisional Authority*, 47–52.

39. "Probe Points at Violation in Bomb Suits Purchase in Mumbai," *Daily News and Analysis*, 6 February 2012; Sandeep Unnithan and Bhavna Vij-Aurora, "India Doesn't Learn: Four Years after 26/11, Intelligence Wars within and Ill-Equipped Security Paint a Frightening Picture of Unpreparedness," *India Today*, 16 November 2012.

40. C. Unnikrishnan and Sanjeev Shivadekar, "Anti-Corruption Bureau Starts Inquiry into Speed Boat Row," *Times of India*, 27 August 2012.

41. Nikhil S. Dixit, "On 26/11, Cops Had 247 AK-47s, but They Stayed under Lock and Key," *Daily News and Analysis*, 24 December 2009.

42. Praveen Swami, "Mumbai Police Modernisation Generates Controversy," *The Hindu*, 8 April 2009.

43. Tejas Mehta, "Mumbai Ko Haath Lagana Mushkil Hi Nahin Namumkin Hain: Anti-Terror Chief Quotes 'Don,'" NDTV, 27 November 2014.

44. Hansen, *Law of Force*, 36.

45. Lokaneeta, *Truth Machines*, 163.

46. Dubber, Markus Dirk, and Mariana Valverde, eds., *The New Police Science: The Police Power in Domestic and International Governance* (Stanford: Stanford University Press, 2006); Mark Neocleous, *The Fabrication of Social Order: A Critical Theory of Police Power* (London: Pluto Press, 2000); Tyler Wall and Travis Linnemann, "No Chance: The Secret of Police, or the Violence of Discretion," *Social Justice* 47, no. 4–5 (2020): 19.

47. Lokaneeta, *Truth Machines*, 163.

48. Ajai Sahni, "Counter-Terrorism: The Architecture of Failure," *Eurasia Review*, 28 February 2012. For critical accounts of the origins and nature of broken windows see: Alex S. Vitale, *City of Disorder: How the Quality of Life Campaign Transformed New York Politics* (New York: NYU Press, 2008); Jordan T. Camp and Christina Heatherton, eds., *Policing the Planet: Why the Policing Crisis Led to Black Lives Matter* (London: Verso, 2016).

49. Amy Kaplan, *Our American Israel: The Story of an Entangled Alliance* (Cambridge, Mass.: Harvard University Press, 2018), 257.

50. Brendan McQuade, *Pacifying the Homeland: Intelligence Fusion and Mass Supervision* (Berkeley: University of California Press, 2019).

51. Also see Juliana Ochs, *Security and Suspicion: An Ethnography of Everyday Life in Israel* (Philadelphia: University of Pennsylvania Press, 2010).

52. Micol Seigel, *Violence Work: State Power and the Limits of Police* (Durham, N.C.: Duke University Press, 2018), 14.

53. Stuart Schrader, *Badges Without Borders: How Global Counterinsurgency Transformed American Policing* (Oakland: University of California Press, 2019).

54. K. S. Subramanian, *Political Violence and the Police in India* (New Delhi: SAGE Publications India, 2007); Jinee Lokaneeta, *Transnational Torture: Law, Violence, and State Power in the United States and India* (New York: New York University Press, 2011).

55. Santana Khanikar, *State, Violence, and Legitimacy in India* (Oxford: Oxford University Press, 2018).

56. Thomas Blom Hansen, "Governance and State Mythologies in Mumbai," in *States of Imagination: Ethnographic Explorations of the Postcolonial State*, ed. Thomas Blom Hansen and Finn Stepputat (Durham, N.C.: Duke University Press, 2001), 222.

57. Brass, *Theft of an Idol.*

58. Blom Hansen, *Wages of Violence*, 149.

59. Arjun Appadurai, "Spectral Housing and Urban Cleansing: Notes on Millennial Mumbai," *Public Culture* 12, no. 3 (2000): 644–49.

60. Vyjayanthi Rao, "How to Read a Bomb: Scenes from Bombay's Black Friday," *Public Culture* 19, no. 3 (2007): 567.

61. Stephen J. Collier and Andrew Lakoff, "Distributed Preparedness: The Spatial Logic of Domestic Security in the United States," *Environment and Planning D: Society and Space* 26, no. 1 (2008): 7–28.

62. Abdul Shaban, "Ethnic Politics, Muslims, and Space in Contemporary Mumbai," in *Lives of Muslims in India*, ed. Abdul Shaban (London: Routledge, 2018), 209–23.

63. Hansen, *Law of Force*, 85.

64. Shaban, "Ethnic Politics," 215.

65. Shaban, "Ethnic Politics," 222.

66. Blom Hansen, *Wages of Violence.*

67. Sharib Ali, "Politics of Terror: The Mecca Masjid Blast Case," *Economic and Political Weekly* 48, no. 34 (2013): 36–46; Nicole Nguyen, *Suspect Communities: Anti-Muslim Racism and the Domestic War on Terror* (Minneapolis and London: University of Minnesota Press, 2019).

68. Manisha Sethi, *Kafkaland: Prejudice, Law, and Counterterrorism in India* (Gurgaon, India: Three Essays Collective, 2014), 56–57.

69. Arvind Narrain, *India's Undeclared Emergency: Constitutionalism and the Politics of Resistance* (Chennai: Context, 2021).

70. Sethi, *Kafkaland*, 58.

71. Abdul Shaban, "Ghettoisation, Crime, and Punishment in Mumbai," *Economic and Political Weekly* 43, no. 33 (2008): 70.

72. Abdul Wahid Shaikh, *Innocent Prisoners* (New Delhi: Pharos, 2017).

73. Rehnan Ansari, "Mumbai NGOs Urge India to Snap Ties with Israel," TwoCircles.net, 15 May 2012; Sayeed Hameed, "What Are We Learning from Israeli Security Experts?," *The Milli Gazette*, 2 August 2010.

74. Vaihayasi P. Daniel, "Mossad's Ex-Chief on the Lessons of 26/11," *Rediff*, 25 November 2009.

75. A 2018 Indian news story suggested that after the 26/11 attacks, Marshall became involved in facilitating some homeland security deals in India, noting that he represents players including the Israeli firm Tamar Group, which produces explosives, detection technologies, bomb control expertise, and x-ray scanning equipment. Rahul Nayar, "India and Israel: A People to People Link," *Free Press Journal* (India), 18 January 2018.

Guy Zuri went to work for the Tamar Group just after he left his position at the IEICI in 2012. Even after some email exchanges and a few short telephone conversations, Marshall refused to speak with me.

76. Laurent Gayer and Christophe Jaffrelot, "Introduction: Muslims of the Indian City: From Centrality to Marginality," in *Muslims in Indian Cities: Trajectories of Marginalisation*, ed. Laurent Gayer and Christophe Jaffrelot (New Delhi: HaperCollins India, 2012), 1–22.

77. Don Mitchell, *The Right to the City: Social Justice and the Fight for Public Space* (New York: Guilford Press, 2003).

78. Partha Chatterjee, *The Politics of the Governed: Reflections on Popular Politics in Most of the World* (New York: Columbia University Press, 2004); Partha Chatterjee, *Lineages of Political Society: Studies in Postcolonial Democracy* (New York: Columbia University Press, 2011).

79. Howell, "Forget 'Militarization,'" 118.

80. Schrader, "Cops at War."

81. Deana Heath, *Colonial Terror: Torture and State Violence in Colonial India* (Oxford: Oxford University Press, 2021).

82. Zoha Waseem, *Insecure Guardians: Enforcement, Encounters, and Everyday Policing in Postcolonial Karachi* (London: Hurst Publishers, 2022).

83. Jauregui, *Provisional Authority.*

84. Vijay Kumar Yadhav, "Anti-Terrorism Cell Is Mumbai Police's Best Kept Secret," *Hindustan Times*, 15 November 2018.

85. The Citizenship Amendment Act (CAA) of 2019 was passed into law by the Indian Parliament on 11 December 2019. It amended the Citizenship Act of 1955, providing pathways to citizenship to certain persecuted minorities from countries neighboring India but notably excluding Muslims from such countries, many of which are Muslim majority. CAA's explicit focus on excluding Muslims from citizenship ignited major uprisings across India and widespread international criticism in December 2019. These uprisings in turn faced intense repression from the Indian forces and armed vigilantes.

Chapter Five

1. Harsh V. Pant, "India-Israel Partnership: Convergence and Constraints," *MERIA: The Middle East Review of International Affairs* 8, no. 4 (2004). The journal was previously hosted by the Israeli think tank IDC Herzliya, recently renamed Reichmann University.

2. P. R. Kumaraswamy, "Indo-Israeli Military Relations: Prospects and Limitations," *Indian Defence Review* 8, no. 3 (July 1993): 45–52.

3. Patricia Owens, *Economy of Force: Counterinsurgency and the Historical Rise of the Social* (Cambridge: Cambridge University Press, 2015), 7.

4. Yael Berda, "Managing 'Dangerous Populations': How Colonial Emergency Laws Shape Citizenship," *Security Dialogue* 51, no. 6 (2020): 557–78.

5. Yael Berda, *Colonial Bureaucracy and Contemporary Citizenship* (Cambridge: Cambridge University Press, 2022).

6. Azad Essa, *Hostile Homelands: The New Alliance Between India and Israel* (London: Pluto Press, 2023); also see Christophe Jaffrelot, *Modi's India: Hindu Nationalism and the*

Rise of Ethnic Democracy, trans. Cynthia Schoch (Princeton, N.J.: Princeton University Press, 2021).

7. Ayla Göl, "Editor's Introduction: Views from the 'Others' of the War on Terror," *Critical Studies on Terrorism* 3, no. 1 (2010): 1–5; Pinar Bilgin, "Security in the Arab World and Turkey: Differently Different," in *Thinking International Relations Differently*, ed. Arlene B. Tickner and David L. Blaney (Abingdon, England: Routledge, 2012), 27–47.

8. Edward W. Said, *Culture and Imperialism* (New York: Vintage, 1994).

9. As Oza argues, the United States, Israel, and India have become united through a "'contrapuntal geography' based on a macabre camaraderie anchored in a discourse of strategic alliance and common enemy." Oza notes that "the emergence of this triad rests on a shared discourse of Muslim terror based on a collapsed understanding of time and history that is then used to justify and deploy violent measures of repression." Rupal Oza, "Contrapuntal Geographies of Threat and Security: The United States, India, and Israel," *Environment and Planning D: Society and Space* 25, no. 1 (2007): 29.

10. Rupal Oza, "India's Relations with Israel and Palestine: Tracing a Tectonic Shift," *Society and Space Open Site*, September 18, 2014.

11. Through his engagement with Marx, Chakrabarty poses this question in terms of how capital is able to produce a standardized measure of labor out of diverse human beings in order to facilitate a generalized form of commodity production. Rather than approaching difference in terms of "natural" characteristics of individuals and reifying these qualities as eternal and ahistorical, Chakrabarty is motivated by a concern with "writing 'difference' back into" the stories we tell about capital. Doing so, he argues, enables us to explore the "real" in the sense of different forms of the "social," as well as incommensurable orders within the temporality of capital, which challenges the latter's coherence. Dipesh Chakrabarty, *Provincializing Europe: Postcolonial Thought and Historical Difference* (Princeton, N.J.: Princeton University Press, 2000), 92.

12. Even as they facilitated the export of certain institutions and forms of governance to India historically, British officials consistently questioned the universality of modern forms of power. As Chatterjee argues, although such colonial officials in India all shared a "belief in the self-evident legitimacy of the principles that are supposed universally to govern the modern regime of power," within colonial discourse up until the early twentieth century there was a "steadfast refusal to admit the universality of those principles." As Chatterjee elaborates, although British proposals to develop "responsible government" for Indians were premised on the assumption that policies deemed to be successful in western communities could, in principle, be applied to India and should be because of their inherent superiority, key British officials and thinkers concluded that such premises were false. They cited the endurance of a deep-seated "Indian tradition," which allegedly precluded Indians from being able to understand and practice impersonal forms of government. Partha Chatterjee, *The Nation and Its Fragments* (Princeton, N.J.: Princeton University Press, 1993), 16.

13. Chatterjee, *Nation and Its Fragments,* 20.

14. Edward W. Said, "An Ideology of Difference," *Critical Inquiry* 12, no. 1 (1985): 38–58.

15. Benjamin Beit-Hallahmi, *The Israeli Connection: Who Israel Arms and Why*, 1st ed. (New York: Pantheon Books, 1987).

16. Chatterjee, *Nation and Its Fragments*, 33.

17. Partha Chatterjee, *Nationalist Thought and the Colonial World: A Derivative Discourse* (London: Zed Books, 1993), 50–51.

18. Christophe Jaffrelot, ed., *Hindu Nationalism: A Reader* (Princeton, N.J.: Princeton University Press, 2009), 24.

19. Christophe Jaffrelot, "Hindu Nationalism: Strategic Syncretism in Ideology Building," *Economic and Political Weekly* 28, no. 12/13 (1993): 523.

20. Homi K. Bhabha, *The Location of Culture* (London and New York: Routledge, 1994), 128.

21. There were also a number of nongovernmental delegations from India, including one from the Tata Group, which traveled to Palestine/Israel following 26/11 in order to undergo security training for a number of different divisions of the company's operations in India. Other failed Tata ventures in Israel later also surfaced in relation to ongoing corruption investigations of Israeli Prime Minister Benjamin Netanyahu.

22. Sagnik Chowdhury, "Security Tips from Tel Aviv and High-End Training," *Indian Express*, 26 July 2009.

23. Ritu Sarin, "No 26/11 Repeat: Maharashtra Shops for Israeli Solutions," *Indian Express*, 13 July 2009.

24. Ritu Sarin, "From Israel, Lessons on Fighting Terror," *Indian Express*, 21 July 2009.

25. This video was first aired at the exhibition Aero India Bangalore in 2009: https://www.youtube.com/watch?v=ktQOLO4U5iQ.

26. Laleh Khalili, *Time in the Shadows: Confinement in Counterinsurgencies* (Stanford: Stanford University Press, 2013).

27. Kumaraswamy, "Indo-Israeli Military Relations," 51.

28. Holger Stritzel, "Security as Translation: Threats, Discourse, and the Politics of Localisation," *Review of International Studies* 37, no. 5 (2011): 2491–2517; Holger Stritzel, "Security, the Translation," *Security Dialogue* 42, no. 4–5 (2011): 343–55.

29. Itty Abraham, "Segurança/Security in Brazil and the United States," in *Words in Motion: Toward a Global Lexicon*, ed. Carol Gluck and Anna Lowenhaupt Tsing (Durham, N.C.: Duke University Press, 2009), 21–39.

30. Yossi Melman, "Jewish Cowboy," *Haaretz*, 29 March 2009, https://www.haaretz.com/1.4898997.

31. Shishir Gupta, "Post 26/11, NSG Aims for Corner Shot Weapons, 'Through-the-Wall' Radars," *Indian Express*, 6 November 2009.

32. It was reported by NDTV in 2010 that Israeli trainers provided three sessions of fifteen days each to Force One in the two years prior but also that there were insufficient funds for additional sessions. See "26/11: No Force in Force One," NDTV, 26 November 2010, http://www.ndtv.com/article/india/26-11-no-force-in-force-one-68649.

33. Sapir Peretz, "A Partner in Need; Officials in Israel Believe India Is Likely to Step up Demand for Israeli Products, Services, and Know-How Related to Homeland Security," *Globes*, 3 December 2008.

34. Joseph F. Getzoff, "Zionist Frontiers: David Ben-Gurion, Labor Zionism, and Transnational Circulations of Settler Development," *Settler Colonial Studies* 10, no. 1 (2 January 2020): 74–93; Rhys Machold, "Staying with the Failures: Iron Dome and Zionist

Security 'Innovation,'" in *Encounters with Colonial Power: Emergent Spaces of Violence and Struggle in Palestine*, ed. Mikko Joronen and Mark Griffiths (Lincoln: University of Nebraska Press, 2023), 122–48; Antti Tarvainen, "The Modern/Colonial Hell of Innovation Economy: Future as a Return to Colonial Mythologies," *Globalizations*, 21 March 2022, 1–23.

35. The self-described challenges of "market penetration" faced by Israeli security firms in India also have historical precursors closely connected to India's historic relationship with the Soviet Union which authorized India to manufacture Soviet military hardware during the Cold War. See Beit-Hallahmi, *Israeli Connection*, 24.

36. Tariq Jazeel, "Singularity: A Manifesto for Incomparable Geographies," *Singapore Journal of Tropical Geography* 40, no. 1 (2019): 5–21.

37. As Gurminder Bhambra spells out, there is a core tension between postcolonial theory's imperatives to privilege difference and valorize multiple identities while also accounting for systemic relations of domination. Gurminder K. Bhambra, *Rethinking Modernity: Postcolonialism and the Sociological Imagination* (Houndmills, England: Palgrave Macmillan, 2007), 30. Relatedly, Vivek Chibber's critique of postcolonial theory, though it has significant problems in its own right, does importantly raise questions about whether Indian elites' historical embrace of modernization was primarily driven by ideas and/or ideology (as some postcolonial theorists suggest) rather than material circumstances. Vivek Chibber, *Postcolonial Theory and the Specter of Capital* (London: Verso Books, 2013). Some other problems relate to the ways in which prominent postcolonial scholars engage with the Indian state in ways that obfuscate India's own colonial projects in locations like Kashmir. See Goldie Osuri, "Imperialism, Colonialism, and Sovereignty in the (Post)Colony: India and Kashmir," *Third World Quarterly* 38, no. 11 (November 2017): 2428–43.

38. Alexander Anievas and Kerem Nişancıoğlu, "Limits of the Universal: The Promises and Pitfalls of Postcolonial Theory and Its Critique," *Historical Materialism* 25, no. 3 (December 2017): 36–75; David L. Blaney and Arlene B. Tickner, "Worlding, Ontological Politics, and the Possibility of a Decolonial IR," *Millennium* 45, no. 3 (2017): 293–311.

39. Bhambra, *Rethinking Modernity*, 70, emphasis added.

40. Kate Sullivan, "Exceptionalism in Indian Diplomacy: The Origins of India's Moral Leadership Aspirations," *South Asia: Journal of South Asian Studies* 37, no. 4 (October 2014): 640–55.

41. Mona Bhan and Purnima Bose, "Modi's Hubris: Hindu Exceptionalism and COVID-19," *Against the Current* (September/October 2021): 20–25.

42. Rajiv Malhotra, *Being Different: An Indian Challenge to Western Universalism* (New Delhi: HarperCollins India, 2013).

43. J. K. Gibson-Graham, *The End of Capitalism (As We Knew It): A Feminist Critique of Political Economy* (Minneapolis: University of Minnesota Press, 2006), ch. 6.

44. John Law, *After Method: Mess in Social Science Research* (Abingdon, England: Routledge, 2004).

45. Somdeep Sen, *Decolonizing Palestine: Hamas between the Anticolonial and the Postcolonial* (Ithaca, NY: Cornell University Press, 2020).

46. John Law and Wen-Yuan Lin, "Cultivating Disconcertment," *Sociological Review* 58 (2010): 135–53.

47. Law and Lin, "Cultivating Disconcertment," 141.

48. Dipesh Chakrabarty, *Provincializing Europe: Postcolonial Thought and Historical Difference* (Princeton, N.J.: Princeton University Press, 2000), 48.

49. Law and Lin, "Cultivating Disconcertment," 141.

50. Annemarie Mol, "Ontological Politics: A Word and Some Questions," in *Actor Network Theory and After*, ed. John Law and John Hassard (Oxford: Blackwell, 1999), 74–89; Marisol de la Cadena and Mario Blaser, *A World of Many Worlds* (Durham, N.C.: Duke University Press, 2018).

51. John Law, "What's Wrong with a One-World World?," *Distinktion: Journal of Social Theory* 16, no. 1 (2015): 126–39.

52. Lisa Stampnitzky, "Rethinking the 'Crisis of Expertise': A Relational Approach," *Theory and Society* 52 (March 2023): 1097–1124.

Chapter Six

1. "India Pursues Homeland Security Technologies," Wikileaks Public Library of U.S. Diplomacy, 16 October 2009, https://wikileaks.org/plusd/cables/09NEWDELHI2116_a.html.

2. "Securing Asia 2012 Event Guide: The Global Hub for Asian Homeland Security and Counter Terror," Security Watch India, June 2012.

3. Timothy Mitchell, *Colonising Egypt* (Berkeley: University of California Press, 1991).

4. For parallel historical and contemporary examples of this in the Indian context, see Stephen Legg, "Imperial Internationalism: The Round Table Conference and the Making of India in London, 1930–1932," *Humanity: An International Journal of Human Rights, Humanitarianism, and Development* 11, no. 1 (2020): 32–53; Ravinder Kaur, *Brand New Nation: Capitalist Dreams and Nationalist Designs in Twenty-First-Century India* (Stanford: Stanford University Press, 2020).

5. Christian Berndt and Marc Boeckler, "Performative Regional (Dis)Integration: Transnational Markets, Mobile Commodities, and Bordered North-South Differences," *Environment and Planning A: Economy and Space* 43, no. 5 (May 2011): 1057–78.

6. Timothy Mitchell, *Rule of Experts: Egypt, Techno-Politics, Modernity* (Berkeley: University of California Press, 2002).

7. Donald MacKenzie, Fabian Muniesa, and Lucia Siu, eds., "Introduction: Monetary Theory at Thirteen Thousand Feet," in *Do Economists Make Markets? On the Performativity of Economics* (Princeton, N.J.: Princeton University Press, 2007), 2–5.

8. Michel Callon, "What Does It Mean to Say That Economics Is Performative?," in *Do Economists Make Markets? On the Performativity of Economics*, ed. Donald MacKenzie, Fabian Muniesa, and Lucia Siu (Princeton, N.J.: Princeton University Press, 2007), 329, 335, 351.

9. Darryl Li, *The Universal Enemy: Jihad, Empire, and the Challenge of Solidarity* (Stanford: Stanford University Press, 2019), 14.

10. Mark Neocleous, *A Critical Theory of Police Power: The Fabrication of the Social Order* (London: Verso, 2021), 37–38.

11. Lisa Tilley and Robbie Shilliam, "Raced Markets: An Introduction," *New Political Economy* 23, no. 5 (2018): 534–43.

12. Sylvia Wynter, "Unsettling the Coloniality of Being/Power/Truth/Freedom: Towards the Human, After Man, Its Overrepresentation—An Argument," *CR: The New Centennial Review* 3, no. 3 (2003): 307.

13. Wynter, "Unsettling the Coloniality," 60.

14. KPMG-ASSOCHAM, "Homeland Security in India: An Overview," KPMG & Associated Chambers of Commerce and Industry of India, 2010, http://www.kpmg.com/IN/en/IssuesAndInsights/ThoughtLeadership/HomelandSecurityinIndia_ASSOCHAM.pdf; "Homeland Security Assessment—India: Expansion and Growth," Aviotech and Associated Chambers of Commerce and Industry (ASSOCHAM), June 2011; "Task Force on National Security and Terrorism," Federation of Indian Chambers of Commerce and Industry (FICCI), New Delhi, 2009.

15. "Task Force on National Security and Terrorism," 7–10.

16. KPMG-ASSOCHAM, "Homeland Security in India," 15.

17. KPMG-ASSOCHAM, "Homeland Security in India," 17.

18. "Task Force on National Security and Terrorism," 6.

19. "Task Force on National Security and Terrorism," 6.

20. KPMG-ASSOCHAM, "Homeland Security in India," 13.

21. KPMG-ASSOCHAM, "Homeland Security in India," 13.

22. "Task Force on National Security and Terrorism," 12.

23. KPMG-ASSOCHAM, "Homeland Security in India," 13–15.

24. "IFSEC & Homeland Security India-Post Show Report 2012," International Fire and Security Exhibition and Conference (IFSEC), 2012.

25. "IFSEC & Homeland Security India-Post Show Report 2012," International Fire and Security Exhibition and Conference (IFSEC), 2012.

26. "Security Watch India Homepage," accessed 8 July 2014, http://securitywatchindia.org.in/About_SWI.aspx, emphasis added.

27. "Securing Asia 2012 Event Guide: The Global Hub for Asian Homeland Security and Counter Terror." Security Watch India, June 2012.

28. See also Ravinder Kaur, *Brand New Nation: Capitalist Dreams and Nationalist Designs in Twenty-First-Century India* (Stanford: Stanford University Press, 2020), 43.

29. "Citizens' Action Group (in Association with Bombay First) (Formed under G.R. No. Mumbai Vikas 2004/C.R. No 12/2004/Special Projects 'White Paper on Crisis Management in Mumbai,'" Bombay First, February 2009. Bombay First later changed its title to Mumbai First.

30. "Citizens" Action Group."

31. "India Risk Survey 2012," Pinkerton Consulting & Investigations (India) Pvt. Ltd and Federation of Indian Chambers of Commerce and Industry (FICCI), 2012.

32. KPMG-ASSOCHAM, "Homeland Security in India: An Overview," KPMG & Associated Chambers of Commerce and Industry of India, 2010.

33. "Security Watch India."

34. "Security Watch India."

35. "Securing Asia 2012 Event Guide: The Global Hub for Asian Homeland Security and Counter Terror," Security Watch India, June 2012.

36. KPMG-ASSOCHAM, "Homeland Security in India," 15.

37. In the United States in the 1980s, publications like the *Security Awareness Bulletin* seem to have been central to such projects. See, for instance, Defense Security Institute, *Security Awareness in the 1980s: Featured Articles from the Security Awareness Bulletin, 1981–1989* (Richmond, Va.: Defense Security Institute, 1992). Critical scholars have also explored security awareness to some extent. See, for instance, Bradley S. Klein, "Conclusion: Every Month Is 'Security Awareness Month,'" in *Critical Security Studies: Concepts and Strategies*, ed. Keith Krause and Michael C. Williams (London: Routledge, 1997), 359–68. This imperative of awareness-raising and education has also been cited as a key element of efforts to continuously build the U.S. homeland security state and its surrounding industries by cultivating the necessary subjects, subjectivities and skills required to sustain them within the United States. Nicole Nguyen, *A Curriculum of Fear: Homeland Security in U.S. Public Schools* (Minneapolis: University of Minnesota Press, 2016). Within longer histories of U.S. empire, Aziz Rana has explored how the project of constitutional veneration overlaps with parallel efforts to develop publics' veneration of the emergent U.S. national security state by focusing on such groups as National Security League and the American Defense Society. Aziz Rana, *The Constitutional Bind: How Americans Came to Idolize a Document That Fails Them* (Chicago: University of Chicago Press, 2024), chapter 6.

38. GTC, "Are We Security Conscious?," *United Services Institution Journal*, no. January-March (1971): 52.

39. "Task Force on National Security and Terrorism," Federation of Indian Chambers of Commerce and Industry (FICCI), New Delhi, 2009, 7.

40. "Securing Asia 2012 Event Guide."

41. Kate Sullivan, "Exceptionalism in Indian Diplomacy: The Origins of India"s Moral Leadership Aspirations," *South Asia: Journal of South Asian Studies* 37, no. 4 (October 2014): 651.

42. Kirpal Dhillon, *Police and Politics in India—Colonial Concepts, Democratic Compulsions: Indian Police 1947–2002* (New Delhi: Manohar Publishers, 2005), 286.

43. Kaur, *Brand New Nation*, 9; Sankaran Krishna, *Postcolonial Insecurities: India, Sri Lanka, and the Question of Nationhood* (Minneapolis: University of Minnesota Press, 1999).

44. See for example: George K. Tanham, "Indian Strategic Thought: An Interpretive Essay," RAND Corporation, 1 January 1992.

45. GTC, "Are We Security Conscious?," 48.

46. Sanjay Seth, "'Once Was Blind but Now Can See': Modernity and the Social Sciences," *International Political Sociology* 7, no. 2 (June 2013): 136–51.

47. Michel Callon, "What Does It Mean to Say That Economics Is Performative?," in *Do Economists Make Markets? On the Performativity of Economics*, ed. Donald MacKenzie, Fabian Muniesa, and Lucia Siu (Princeton, N.J.: Princeton University Press, 2007), 323.

48. Elida K. U. Jacobsen, "Unique Identification: Inclusion and Surveillance in the Indian Biometric Assemblage," *Security Dialogue* 43, no. 5 (2012): 457–74; Reetika Khera, "The UID Project and Welfare Schemes," *Economic and Political Weekly* 46, no. 9 (2011): 38–43.

49. Christophe Jaffrelot and Ingrid Therwath, "The Sangh Parivar and the Hindu Diaspora in the West: What Kind of 'Long-Distance Nationalism'?," *International Political Sociology* 1, no. 3 (September 2007): 278–95; Arvind Rajagopal, "Hindu Nationalism in the U.S.: Changing Configurations of Political Practice," *Ethnic and Racial Studies* 23, no. 3 (January 2000): 467–96.

50. Thomas Birtchnell, "Jugaad as Systemic Risk and Disruptive Innovation in India," *Contemporary South Asia* 19, no. 4 (December 2011): 357–72; Beatrice Jauregui, "Provisional Agency in India: Jugaad and Legitimation of Corruption," *American Ethnologist* 41, no. 1 (2014): 83.

51. Itty Abraham, "Segurança/Security in Brazil and the United States," in *Words in Motion: Toward a Global Lexicon*, ed. Carol Gluck and Anna Lowenhaupt Tsing (Durham, N.C.: Duke University Press, 2009), 21–39; Pinar Bilgin, "Security in the Arab World and Turkey: Differently Different," in *Thinking International Relations Differently*, ed. Arlene B. Tickner and David L. Blaney (Abingdon, England: Routledge, 2012), 27–47; Holger Stritzel, "Securitization, Power, Intertextuality: Discourse Theory and the Translations of Organized Crime," *Security Dialogue* 43, no. 6 (2012): 549–67.

52. Sanjay Seth, *Subject Lessons: The Western Education of Colonial India* (Durham, N.C.:Duke University Press, 2007), 186.

53. Seth, *Subject Lessons,* 45.

54. Seth, *Subject Lessons,* 45.

55. Swapna Banerjee-Guha, "Post–September 11 Indo-U.S. Strategic Ties: Locating Power and Hegemony," *Geographical Journal* 177, no. 3 (September 2011): 223–27; Achin Vanaik, ed., *Masks of Empire* (New Delhi: Tulika Books, 2007).

56. Partha Chatterjee, *The Nation and Its Fragments* (Princeton, N.J.: Princeton University Press, 1993), xi.

57. "Securing Asia 2013 Event Guide: The Asian Homeland Security and Counter Terror Summit-Bringing Asia to Your Doorstep," Security Watch India, June 2013.

58. Seth, *Subject Lessons*, 59.

59. David L. Blaney and Arlene B. Tickner, "Worlding, Ontological Politics, and the Possibility of a Decolonial IR," *Millennium* 45, no. 3 (2017): 293–311.

60. Lisa Tilley and Robbie Shilliam, "Raced Markets: An Introduction," *New Political Economy* 23, no. 5 (2018): 534–43.

61. Timothy Mitchell, "The Properties of Markets," in *Do Economists Make Markets? On the Performativity of Economics*, ed. Donald MacKenzie, Fabian Muniesa, and Lucia Siu (Princeton, N.J.: Princeton University Press, 2007), 268.

62. Stritzel, "Securitization, Power, Intertextuality"; Holger Stritzel, *Security in Translation: Securitization Theory and the Localization of Threat*, New Security Challenges Series (London: Palgrave Macmillan, 2014).

63. Bilgin, "Security in the Arab World and Turkey: Differently Different"; Pinar Bilgin, "Inquiring into Others' Conceptions of the International and Security," *PS: Political Science and Politics* 50, no. 3 (July 2017): 652–55.

64. Chris Rossdale, "Enclosing Critique: The Limits of Ontological Security," *International Political Sociology* 9, no. 4 (December 2015): 369–86.

65. Mark Neocleous, *A Critical Theory of Police Power: The Fabrication of the Social Order* (London: Verso 2021), 60.

66. John Law, "What's Wrong with a One-World World?," *Distinktion: Journal of Social Theory* 16, no. 1 (2015): 126–39.

67. Ankit Gupta, "The Indian Homeland Security Industry," *Salute India*, 2020.

68. Mona Bhan and Purnima Bose, "Modi's Hubris: Hindu Exceptionalism and COVID-19," *Against the Current* (September/October 2021): 20–25.

69. "India's Defence Exports at Record Rs 13,000 Crore, 70% from Private Sector," *Times of India*, 9 July 2022.

70. Peter Robb, "The Ordering of Rural India: The Policing of Nineteenth-Century Bengal and Bihar," in *Policing the Empire: Government, Authority, and Control, 1830–1940*, ed. David M. Anderson and David Killingray (Manchester: Manchester University Press, 1991), 147.

71. Bruno Latour, *We Have Never Been Modern*, trans. Catherine Porter (Cambridge, Mass.: Harvard University Press, 1993).

Conclusion

1. Arundhati Roy, "9 Is Not 11," *Outlook Magazine*, 22 December 2008.

2. Anand Patwardhan, "Terror: Aftermath," November 2008, http://patwardhan.com/?page_id=668.

3. Vappala Balachandran, "Intelligence, Not Foreign Trips, Will Curb Terrorism," *The Sunday Guardian*, 2011.

4. Naresh Fernandes, "What Mumbai Spirit?" *The New Yorker* (blog), 14 July 2011. http://www.newyorker.com/online/blogs/newsdesk/2011/07/bombing-in-mumbai.html.

5. Ganesh Nadar, "'Corruption Is a Bigger Threat than Terrorism,'" *Rediff*, 27 November 2012.

6. "India Risk Survey 2019," Pinkerton Consulting & Investigations (India) Pvt. Ltd and Federation of Indian Chambers of Commerce and Industry (FICCI), 2019.

7. Kirpal Dhillon, *Police and Politics in India—Colonial Concepts, Democratic Compulsions: Indian Police 1947–2002* (New Delhi: Manohar Publishers, 2005), 23, 286.

8. Colin Gonzalves, "Our Politicians Are Still Not Listening," *Mail Today*, 20 December 2008.

9. Jinee Lokaneeta, *The Truth Machines: Policing, Violence, and Scientific Interrogations in India* (Ann Arbor: University of Michigan Press, 2020); Gagan Preet Singh, "Police–Public Relations in Colonial India," *History Compass* 17, no. 11 (2019): e12595.

10. Stuart Schrader, "To Protect and Serve Themselves: Police in U.S. Politics since the 1960s," *Public Culture* 31, no. 3 (September 2019): 601–23.

11. Manisha Sethi, *Kafkaland: Prejudice, Law, and Counterterrorism in India* (Gurgaon, India: Three Essays Collective, 2014).

12. Nileena M. S., "How the NIA Lost the Opportunity to Become India's Only Professional Investigative Agency," *The Caravan*, 30 June 2022.

13. Arvind Narrain, *India's Undeclared Emergency: Constitutionalism and the Politics of Resistance* (Chennai: Context, 2021), 80.

14. Amy Kaplan, "Homeland Insecurities: Some Reflections on Language and Space," *Radical History Review* 85, no. 1 (2003): 90.

15. Brendan McQuade, *Pacifying the Homeland: Intelligence Fusion and Mass Supervision* (Berkeley: University of California Press, 2019).

16. Donna J. Haraway, *Staying with the Trouble: Making Kin in the Chthulucene* (Durham, N.C.: Duke University Press, 2016).

17. Anna Lowenhaupt Tsing, *The Mushroom at the End of the World: On the Possibility of Life in Capitalist Ruins* (Princeton, N.J.: Princeton University Press, 2015), 17.

18. Nadav Morag, *Comparative Homeland Security: Global Lessons* (Hoboken, N.J.: John Wiley & Sons, 2011), 9.

19. Roland Barthes, *Mythologies*, trans. Jonathan Cape (London: Vintage, 1972), 149.

20. Jodi Dean, "Anticipating Homeland Security," *Communication and Critical/Cultural Studies* 4, no. 2 (June 2007): 209, emphasis added.

21. Dean, "Anticipating Homeland Security," 209–10.

22. KPMG-ASSOCHAM, "Homeland Security in India: An Overview," KPMG & Associated Chambers of Commerce and Industry of India, 2010, 16.

23. W. E. B. DuBois, "Worlds of Color," *Foreign Affairs* 3, no. 3 (1925): 423–44.

24. John Law, "What's Wrong with a One-World World?," *Distinktion: Journal of Social Theory* 16, no. 1 (2015): 126–39.

25. Marisol de la Cadena and Mario Blaser, *A World of Many Worlds* (Durham, N.C.: Duke University Press, 2018); Cristina Rojas, "Contesting the Colonial Logics of the International: Toward a Relational Politics for the Pluriverse," *International Political Sociology* 10, no. 4 (December 2016): 369–82.

26. R. S. McGregor, ed., *The Oxford Hindi-English Dictionary* (New Delhi: Oxford University Press, 2002).

27. *Glossary of Administrative Terms (English-Hindi)* (New Delhi: Government of India, 1968).

28. McGregor, ed., *Oxford Hindi-English Dictionary*, 657.

29. George S. Rigakos, *Security/Capital: A General Theory of Pacification* (Edinburgh: Edinburgh University Press, 2016); Mark Neocleous and George S. Rigakos, eds., "Anti-Security: A Declaration," in *Anti-Security* (Ottawa: Red Quill Books, 2011), 15–21.

30. Mark Neocleous, *The Universal Adversary: Security, Capital, and "The Enemies of All Mankind"* (Abingdon, England: Routledge, 2016), 11.

31. Samar Al-Bulushi, Sahana Ghosh, and Inderpal Grewal, "Security from the South: Postcolonial and Imperial Entanglements," *Social Text* 40, no. 3 (152) (September 2022): 1–15.

32. Stuart Schrader, *Badges Without Borders: How Global Counterinsurgency Transformed American Policing* (Oakland: University of California Press, 2019), 273.

Epilogue

1. Azad Essa, *Hostile Homelands: The New Alliance Between India and Israel* (London: Pluto Press, 2023), 60.

2. 'Israel-India Military Relations: Ideological Paradigms of Security' (BDS India/People's Dispatch/Newsclick.in, 22 January 2020), https://peoplesdispatch.org/tag/israel-india-military-relations/.

3. "Israelising India: The Hindutva Fantasy That Is Realising Itself," Indian Cultural Forum, 20 August 2019, https://archive.indianculturalforum.in/2019/08/20/israelising-india-the-hindutva-fantasy-that-is-realising-itself/. See also Vinod Mubayi, "Why

Modi and Hindutva Love Israeli Settler-Colonialism and See It as a Model for Kashmir," *The Wire*, 9 July 2021.

4. Essa, *Hostile Homelands*, 56.

5. Essa, *Hostile Homelands*, 56.

6. "IPS Officers Visit Israel to Learn Best Policing Practices," *The Economic Times*, 19 August 2015.

7. "Israeli Firm Planning Security Academy in Gujarat," *The Times of India*, 12 January 2018.

8. Essa, *Hostile Homelands*, 71.

9. Ladeeda Farzana, "India House Demolitions: Another Israeli-Style War Crime against Muslims," *Middle East Eye*, 24 June 2022.

BIBLIOGRAPHY

Abraham, Itty. "Segurança/Security in Brazil and the United States." In *Words in Motion: Toward a Global Lexicon*, edited by Carol Gluck and Anna Lowenhaupt Tsing, 21–39. Durham, N.C.: Duke University Press, 2009.

"After 26/11, R. R. Patil Returns as Home Minister," NDTV, 9 November 2009.

"After Mumbai." *Mideast Mirror*, 1 December 2008.

Agarwal, Sapna. "No Consensus on Security Plan Even a Month after Mumbai Attacks." *Business Standard*, 27 December 2008.

Al-Bulushi, Samar, Sahana Ghosh, and Inderpal Grewal. "Security from the South: Postcolonial and Imperial Entanglements." *Social Text* 40, no. 3 (152) (September 2022): 1–15.

Alam, M. Shahid. *Israeli Exceptionalism: The Destabilizing Logic of Zionism*. New York: Palgrave Macmillan, 2009.

Ali, Sharib. "Politics of Terror: The Mecca Masjid Blast Case." *Economic and Political Weekly* 48, no. 34 (2013): 36–46.

Althusser, Louis. *On Ideology*. London: Verso, 2008.

Amar, Paul. *The Security Archipelago: Human-Security States, Sexuality Politics, and the End of Neoliberalism*. Durham, N.C.: Duke University Press, 2013.

"America's New War: Terrorist Attacks Cause Gridlock; President Encourages CIA." *The Point with Greta van Susteren*. CNN, 26 September 2001.

Anderson, Perry. *The Indian Ideology*. 2nd ed. London: Verso, 2021.

Ansari, Moin. "Mumbai: Israel Calls Indian Forces Lackadaisical, Unprofessional, Incompetent, Untrained, Slow, Confused and Inefficient." *Rupee News*, 30 November 2008.

Ansari, Rehnan. "Mumbai NGOs Urge India to Snap Ties with Israel." TwoCircles.net, 15 May 2012.

"Antulay Raises Doubts over Karkare's Killing." *Economic Times*, 17 December 2008.

Appadurai, Arjun. *Fear of Small Numbers: An Essay on the Geography of Anger*. Durham, N.C.: Duke University Press, 2006.

———. "Spectral Housing and Urban Cleansing: Notes on Millennial Mumbai." *Public Culture* 12, no. 3 (2000): 627–51.

Aradau, Claudia. "Assembling (Non)Knowledge: Security, Law, and Surveillance in a Digital World." *International Political Sociology* 11, no. 4 (2017): 327–42.

Aradau, Claudia, and Rens Van Munster. *Politics of Catastrophe: Genealogies of the Unknown*. Abingdon, England: Routledge, 2011.

Arnold, David. *Police Power and Colonial Rule: Madras, 1859–1947*. New Delhi: Oxford University Press, 1986.

Asad, Talal. “Thinking about Terrorism and Just War.” *Cambridge Review of International Affairs* 23, no. 1 (2010): 3–24.

Ayyub, Rana. “‘Gafoor Was Promoted, Not Transferred.’” *Tehelka*, 27 June 2009.

———. “In the Eye of the Storm.” *Tehelka*, 12 December 2009.

Bachmann, Jan, Coleen Bell, and Caroline Holmqvist, eds. *War, Police, and Assemblages of Intervention*. London: Routledge, 2015.

Bakhtin, Mikhail M. *The Dialogic Imagination: Four Essays*. Translated by Caryl Emerson and Michael Holquist. Austin: University of Texas Press, 1981.

Balachandran, Vappala. “Dealing with Aftermath of Attacks: Lessons from Mumbai and Elsewhere on What to Do and What Not to Do.” St. Antony’s College, Oxford University, 2010.

———. “An Essay on Mossad.” *The Pioneer*, 18 March 2007.

———. “Intelligence, Not Foreign Trips, Will Curb Terrorism.” *The Sunday Guardian*, 2011.

Balmer, Brian, and Brian Rappert, eds. *Absence in Science, Security and Policy: From Research Agendas to Global Strategy*. Basingstoke: Palgrave Macmillan, 2016.

Banerjee, Sikata. *Gender, Nation, and Popular Film in India: Globalizing Muscular Nationalism*. London: Routledge, 2016.

———. “Warriors in Politics: Religious Nationalism, Masculine Hinduism, and the Shiv Sena in Bombay.” *Women and Politics* 20, no. 3 (September 1999): 1–26.

Banerjee-Guha, Swapna. “Post–September 11 Indo-U.S. Strategic Ties: Locating Power and Hegemony.” *Geographical Journal* 177, no. 3 (September 2011): 223–27.

Barak, Oren, and Gabriel Sheffer. “Israel’s ‘Security Network’ and Its Impact: An Exploration of a New Approach.” *International Journal of Middle East Studies* 38, no. 2 (2006): 235–61.

Barnard-Wills, David, and Cerwyn Moore. “The Terrorism of the Other: Towards a Contrapuntal Reading of Terrorism in India.” *Critical Studies on Terrorism* 3, no. 3 (2010): 383–402.

Barry, Andrew. “Political Situations: Knowledge Controversies in Transnational Governance.” *Critical Policy Studies* 6, no. 3 (October 2012): 324–36.

———. “The Politics of Contingency: Events, Travelling Models, and Situations.” Gefördert von der DFG, 2016.

Barthes, Roland. *Mythologies*. Translated by Jonathan Cape. London: Vintage, 1972.

Bass, Warren. *Support Any Friend: Kennedy’s Middle East and the Making of the U.S.-Israel Alliance*. New York: Oxford University Press, 2003.

Baweja, Harinder. “Slaughter House Files.” *Tehelka*, 13 June 2009.

———. “Why Can’t You See The 26/11 Report?” *Tehelka*, 22 August 2009.

Bayley, David H. *The Police and Political Development in India*. Princeton: Princeton University Press, 1969.

Bedi, Rahul, and Damien McElroy. “India Asks for Foreign Help to Hit Terrorists.” *The Daily Telegraph* (London), 3 December 2008.

Beit-Hallahmi, Benjamin. *The Israeli Connection: Who Israel Arms and Why*. 1st ed. New York: Pantheon Books, 1987.

Belur, Jyoti. “Police Stop and Search in India: Mumbai Nakabandi.” *Policing and Society* 21, no. 4 (2011): 420–31.

———. "Police Use of Deadly Force: Police Perceptions of a Culture of Approval." *Journal of Contemporary Criminal Justice* 25, no. 2 (May 2009): 237–52.

Berda, Yael. *Colonial Bureaucracy and Contemporary Citizenship*. Cambridge: Cambridge University Press, 2022.

———. *Living Emergency: Israel's Permit Regime in the Occupied West Bank*. Stanford: Stanford University Press, 2017.

———. "Managing "Dangerous Populations: How Colonial Emergency Laws Shape Citizenship." *Security Dialogue* 51, no. 6 (2020): 557–78.

Berenschot, Ward. *Riot Politics: India's Hindu-Muslim Violence and the Everyday Mediation of the State*. London: Hurst & Co, 2011.

Berndt, Christian, and Marc Boeckler. "Performative Regional (Dis)Integration: Transnational Markets, Mobile Commodities, and Bordered North–South Differences." *Environment and Planning A: Economy and Space* 43, no. 5 (May 2011): 1057–78.

Bhabha, Homi K. *The Location of Culture*. London: Routledge, 1994.

Bhambra, Gurminder K. *Rethinking Modernity: Postcolonialism and the Sociological Imagination*. Houndmills, England: Palgrave Macmillan, 2007.

Bhan, Mona, and Purnima Bose. "Modi's Hubris: Hindu Exceptionalism & COVID-19." *Against the Current* (September/October 2021): 20–25.

Bhan, Ramesh. "Indian, US Officials Discuss Security, Prevention of Terrorism." *United News of India*, 28 September 2008.

Bhattacharyya, Gargi. "Globalizing Racism and Myths of the Other in the 'War on Terror.'" In *Thinking Palestine*, edited by Ronit Lentin, 46–62. New York: Zed Books, 2008.

Bigo, Didier. "Liaison Officers in Europe: New Officers in the European Security Field." In *Issues in Transnational Policing*, edited by James Sheptycki, 67–99. London: Routledge, 2000.

———. "The Möbius Ribbon of Internal and External Security(ies)." In *Identities, Borders, Orders: Rethinking International Relations Theory*, edited by Mathias Albert, David Jacobson, and Yosef Lapid, 91–116. Minneapolis: University of Minnesota Press, 2001.

Bilgin, Pinar. "Inquiring into Others' Conceptions of the International and Security." *PS: Political Science and Politics* 50, no. 3 (July 2017): 652–55.

———. "Security in the Arab World and Turkey: Differently Different." In *Thinking International Relations Differently*, edited by Arlene B. Tickner and David L. Blaney, 27–47. Abingdon, England: Routledge, 2012.

Birtchnell, Thomas. "Jugaad as Systemic Risk and Disruptive Innovation in India." *Contemporary South Asia* 19, no. 4 (December 2011): 357–72.

Blaney, David L., and Arlene B. Tickner. "Worlding, Ontological Politics and the Possibility of a Decolonial IR." *Millennium* 45, no. 3 (2017): 293–311.

Blankfield, Keren. "Hollywood Heavyweight." *Forbes*, 29 March 2010.

Blarel, Nicolas. *The Evolution of India's Israel Policy: Continuity, Change, and Compromise since 1922*. New Delhi: Oxford University Press, 2014.

Blitz, James. "Israelis Critical of India's Response to Attacks." *Financial Times*, 29 November 2008.

Blom Hansen, Thomas. "Governance and State Mythologies in Mumbai." In *States of Imagination: Ethnographic Explorations of the Postcolonial State*, edited by Thomas Blom Hansen and Finn Stepputat, 221–57. Durham, N.C.: Duke University Press, 2001.

———. *The Law of Force: The Violent Heart of Indian Politics*. New Delhi: Aleph Book Company, 2021.

———. *The Saffron Wave: Democracy and Hindu Nationalism in Modern India*. Princeton, N.J.: Princeton University Press, 1999.

———. *Wages of Violence: Naming and Identity in Postcolonial Bombay*. Princeton, N.J.: Princeton University Press, 2001.

Blom Hansen, Thomas, and Finn Stepputat. "Introduction." In *Sovereign Bodies: Citizens, Migrants, and States in the Postcolonial World*, edited by Thomas Blom Hansen and Finn Stepputat, 1–38. Princeton, N.J.: Princeton University Press, 2005.

———. "Introduction: States of Imagination." In *States of Imagination: Ethnographic Explorations of the Postcolonial State*, edited by Thomas Blom Hansen and Finn Stepputat, 1–40. Durham, N.C.: Duke University Press, 2001.

Boon, Kia Meng. "'The Only Thing Is You Have to Know Them First': Protest Policing and Malaysia's BERSIH Protests (2011–2016)." *Small Wars and Insurgencies* 33, no. 4–5 (July 2022): 868–901.

Boose, Lynda. "Techno-Muscularity and the 'Boy Eternal': From the Quagmire to the Gulf." In *Cultures of United States Imperialism*, edited by Susan Jeffords and Donald E. Pease, 581–615. Durham, N.C.: Duke University Press, 1993.

Boudreaux, Richard. "How Mumbai Attack on Jews Unfolded." *Los Angeles Times*, 3 December 2008.

Boukalas, Christos. *Homeland Security, Its Law, and Its State: A Design of Power for the Twenty-First Century*. Abingdon, England: Routledge, 2014.

Brass, Paul R. *Theft of an Idol: Text and Context in the Representation of Collective Violence*. Princeton, N.J.: Princeton University Press, 1997.

Bresheeth-Zabner, Haim. *An Army Like No Other: How the Israel Defense Forces Made a Nation*. London: Verso, 2020.

Brucato, Ben. "Fabricating the Color Line in a White Democracy: From Slave Catchers to Petty Sovereigns." *Theoria* 61, no. 141 (December 2014): 30–54.

———. "Policing Race and Racing Police: The Origin of U.S. Police in Slave Patrols." *Social Justice* 47, no. 3/4 (161/162) (2020): 115–36.

Brulin, Remi. "Compartmentalization, Contexts of Speech, and the Israeli Origins of the American Discourse on 'Terrorism.'" *Dialectical Anthropology* 39, no. 1 (March 2015): 69–119.

Buck, Tobias. "Israel Offers Assistance to End Mumbai Siege." *Financial Times*, 28 November 2008.

Cadena, Marisol de la, and Mario Blaser. *A World of Many Worlds*. Durham, N.C.: Duke University Press, 2018.

Cahill, Richard Andrew. "'Going Beserk': 'Black and Tans' in Palestine." *Jerusalem Quarterly* 38 (January 2009): 59–66.

Caldeira, Teresa P. R. *City of Walls: Crime, Segregation, and Citizenship in São Paulo*. Berkeley: University of California Press, 2000.

Callon, Michel. "Some Elements of a Sociology of Translation: Domestication of the Scallops and the Fishermen of St. Brieuc Bay." *Sociological Review* 32, no. 1 Suppl (1984): 196–233.

———. "What Does It Mean to Say That Economics Is Performative?" In *Do Economists Make Markets? On the Performativity of Economics*, edited by Donald MacKenzie, Fabian Muniesa, and Lucia Siu, 331–57. Princeton, N.J.: Princeton University Press, 2007.

Callon, Michel, and Bruno Latour. "Unscrewing the Big Leviathan: How Actors Macro-Structure Reality and How Sociologists Help Them to Do So." In *Advances in Social Theory and Methodology: Toward an Integration of Micro-and Macro-Sociologies*, edited by Karin Knorr-Cetina and Aaron V. Cicourel, 277–303. London: Routledge, 1981.

Camp, Jordan T., and Christina Heatherton, eds. *Policing the Planet: Why the Policing Crisis Led to Black Lives Matter.* London: Verso, 2016.

Chakrabarty, Dipesh. "The Difference-Deferral of (a) Colonial Modernity: Public Debates on Domesticity in British Bengal." *History Workshop Journal* 36 (1993): 1–34.

———. *Provincializing Europe: Postcolonial Thought and Historical Difference.* Princeton, N.J.: Princeton University Press, 2000.

Chatterjee, Partha. *Lineages of Political Society: Studies in Postcolonial Democracy.* New York: Columbia University Press, 2011.

———. *The Nation and Its Fragments.* Princeton, N.J.: Princeton University Press, 1993.

———. *Nationalist Thought and the Colonial World: A Derivative Discourse.* London: Zed Books, 1993.

———. *The Politics of the Governed: Reflections on Popular Politics in Most of the World.* New York: Columbia University Press, 2004.

Chatterji, Angana P., Thomas Blom Hansen, and Christophe Jaffrelot, eds. *Majoritarian State: How Hindu Nationalism Is Changing India.* Oxford: Oxford University Press, 2019.

Chaudhary, Roy Dipanjan. "Israel Ambassador Hails India for Job Well Done." *India Today*, 1 December 2008.

Chaudhuri, Pramit Pal, and Aloke Tikku. "Homeland Security: Who Is in Charge Here?" 3 December 2008.

Chengappa, Bidanda M. "Indo-Israeli Relations: The Great Leap Forward." *Indian Defence Review* 8, no. 3 (July 1993): 107–8.

Cheyfitz, Eric. "The Force of Exceptionalist Narratives in the Israeli-Palestinian Conflict." *Journal of the Native American and Indigenous Studies Association* 1, no. 2 (2014): 107–24.

Chomsky, Noam. *Fateful Triangle: The United States, Israel, and the Palestinians.* London: Pluto Press, 1999.

Chowdhury, Sagnik. "Security Tips from Tel Aviv and High-End Training." *Indian Express*, 26 July 2009.

"Citizens' Action Group (in Association with Bombay First) (Formed under G.R. No. Mumbai Vikas 2004/C.R. No 12/2004/Special Projects 'White Paper on Crisis Management in Mumbai.'" *Bombay First,* February 2009.

Closs Stephens, A., and N. Vaughan-Williams, eds. *Terrorism and the Politics of Response.* Abingdon, England: Routledge, 2009.

Coaffee, Jon. "Rings of Steel, Rings of Concrete, and Rings of Confidence: Designing out Terrorism in Central London Pre and Post September 11." *International Journal of Urban and Regional Research* 28, no. 1 (2004): 201–11.

———. *Terrorism, Risk, and the City: The Making of a Contemporary Urban Landscape.* Aldershot, England: Ashgate, 2003.

Coaffee, Jon, and David Murakami Wood. "Security Is Coming Home: Rethinking Scale and Constructing Resilience in the Global Urban Response to Terrorist Risk." *International Relations* 20, no. 4 (2006): 503–17.

Coaffee, Jon, and Peter Rogers. "Rebordering the City for New Security Challenges: From Counter-Terrorism to Community Resilience." *Space and Polity* 12, no. 1 (2008): 101–18.

Coleman, Mat. "State Power in Blue." *Political Geography* 51 (2016): 76–86.

Collier, Stephen J., and Andrew Lakoff. "Distributed Preparedness: The Spatial Logic of Domestic Security in the United States." *Environment and Planning D: Society and Space* 26, no. 1 (2008): 7–28.

Connolly, William E. "The Evangelical-Capitalist Resonance Machine." *Political Theory* 33, no. 6 (2005): 105–28.

Coward, Martin. "Network-Centric Violence, Critical Infrastructure, and the Urbanization of Security." *Security Dialogue* 40, no. 4–5 (2009): 399–418.

———. *Urbicide: The Politics of Urban Destruction.* London: Routledge, 2008.

Cowen, Deborah. "Militarism? A Mini Forum." *Society and Space,* 5 September 2012.

Cowen, Deborah, and Neil Smith. "'Martial Law in the Streets of Toronto': G20 Security and State Violence." *Human Geography* 3, no. 3 (2010): 29–49.

Dallek, Matthew. *Defenseless Under the Night: The Roosevelt Years and the Origins of Homeland Security.* New York: Oxford University Press, 2016.

Dana, Tariq. "Israel's Big Business of War." The Political Economy Project, 9 January 2017.

Daniel, Vaihayasi P. "Mossad's Ex-Chief on the Lessons of 26/11." *rediff,* 25 November 2009.

Das, Veena. *Critical Events: An Anthropological Perspective on Contemporary India.* Oxford: Oxford University Press, 1996.

Das, Veena, and Deborah Poole, eds. *Anthropology in the Margins of the State.* Oxford: Oxford University Press, 2004.

Davis, Mike. *City of Quartz: Excavating the Future in Los Angeles.* London: Verso, 1990.

Dean, Jodi. "Anticipating Homeland Security." *Communication and Critical/Cultural Studies* 4, no. 2 (June 2007): 205–10.

Defense Security Institute. *Security Awareness in the 1980s: Featured Articles from the Security Awareness Bulletin, 1981–1989.* Richmond, Va.: Defense Security Institute, 1992.

Delehanty, Casey. "Police with Lots of Military Gear Kill Civilians More Often than Less-Militarized Officers." Homeland Security Newswire, 2 July 2020.

Denes, Nick. "From Tanks to Wheelchairs: Unmanned Aerial Vehicles, Zionist Battlefield Experiments, and the Transparence of the Civilian." In *Surveillance and Control in Israel/Palestine: Population, Territory and Power*, edited by Elia Zureik, David Lyon, and Yasmeen Abu-Laban, 171–96. London: Routledge, 2011.

Denyer Willis, Graham. *The Killing Consensus: Police, Organized Crime, and the Regulation of Life and Death in Urban Brazil.* Berkeley: University of California Press, 2015.

Dey, J. "Taking the Wind out of Mumbai's Sails." *Mid Day*, 18 March 2011.

Dhillon, Kirpal. *Police and Politics in India—Colonial Concepts, Democratic Compulsions: Indian Police 1947–2002.* New Delhi: Manohar Publishers, 2005.

Dixit, Nikhil S. "On 26/11, Cops Had 247 AK-47s, but They Stayed under Lock and Key." *Daily News and Analysis*, 24 December 2009.

Doval, Ajit. "Terror Tactics Change, but Do We?" *Hindustan Times*, 10 September 2007.

Du Bois, W. E. B. "Worlds of Color." *Foreign Affairs* 3, no. 3 (1925): 423–44.

Dubber, Markus Dirk. *The Police Power: Patriarchy and the Foundations of American Government.*" New York: Columbia University Press, 2005.

Dubber, Markus Dirk, and Mariana Valverde, eds. *The New Police Science: The Police Power in Domestic and International Governance.* Stanford: Stanford University Press, 2006.

Dunbar-Ortiz, Roxanne. *Loaded: A Disarming History of the Second Amendment.* San Francisco: City Lights Books, 2018.

Dunn Cavelty, Myriam Anna, and Kristian Søby Kristensen, eds. *Securing "the Homeland": Critical Infrastructure, Risk, and (In)Security.* Abingdon, England: Routledge, 2008.

Eastwood, James. *Ethics as a Weapon of War: Militarism and Morality in Israel.* Cambridge: Cambridge University Press, 2017.

Eckert, Julia M. *The Charisma of Direct Action: Power, Politics, and the Shiv Sena.* New Delhi: Oxford University Press, 2003.

El Rifai, Yasid, Dima Yaser, and Adele Jarrar. "Tegart's Modern Legacy: The Reproduction of Power, a Timeless Paradox." *Jerusalem Quarterly*, no. 69 (2017): 78.

Elden, Stuart. *Terror and Territory: The Spatial Extent of Sovereignty.* Minneapolis: University of Minnesota Press, 2009.

Erakat, Noura. *Justice for Some: Law and the Question of Palestine.* Stanford: Stanford University Press, 2019.

Ericson, Richard V. "Patrolling the Facts: Secrecy and Publicity in Police Work." *British Journal of Sociology* 40, no. 2 (1989): 205–26.

Erlenbusch, Verena. "How (Not) to Study Terrorism." *Critical Review of International Social and Political Philosophy* 17, no. 4 (2014): 470–91.

Essa, Azad. *Hostile Homelands: The New Alliance Between India and Israel.* London: Pluto Press, 2023.

Eyal, Gil. *The Disenchantment of the Orient: Expertise in Arab Affairs and the Israeli State.* Stanford: Stanford University Press, 2006.

Farzana, Ladeeda. "India House Demolitions: Another Israeli-Style War Crime against Muslims." *Middle East Eye*, 24 June 2022.

Feldman, Allen. "Securocratic Wars of Public Safety." *Interventions* 6, no. 3 (2004): 330–50.

Feldman, Keith P. *A Shadow over Palestine: The Imperial Life of Race in America*. Minneapolis: University of Minnesota Press, 2015.

Fernandes, Naresh. "What Mumbai Spirit?" *The New Yorker* (blog). 14 July 2011. http://www.newyorker.com/online/blogs/newsdesk/2011/07/bombing-in-mumbai.html.

Finkelstein, Norman G. *Beyond Chutzpah: On the Misuse of Anti-Semitism and the Abuse of History*. Berkeley: University of California Press, 2005.

———. *The Holocaust Industry: Reflections on the Exploitation of Jewish Suffering*. Ebook. London: Verso, 2003.

"First India-Israel Homeland Security Forum Next Month." *India Today*, 24 February 2009. http://indiatoday.intoday.in/story/First+India-.

Foont, Brian E. "Shooting Down Civilian Aircraft: Is There an International Law?." *Journal of Air Law and Commerce* 72, no. 3 (2007): 695–725.

"Force One, State-of-Art Guns to Guard Mumbai." *Telegraph India*, 18 December 2008.

Foucault, Michel. *Security, Territory, Population: Lectures at the College de France 1977–1978*. Edited by Michel Senellart. Translated by Graham Burchell. New York: Picador, 2007.

Franklin, Sarah. *Dolly Mixtures: The Remaking of Genealogy*. Durham, N.C.: Duke University Press, 2007.

Fregonese, Sara. *War and the City: Urban Geopolitics in Lebanon*. London: I. B. Tauris, 2019.

Friedman, Robert I. "Selling Israel to America." *Journal of Palestine Studies* 16, no. 4 (1987): 169–79.

Gangan, Surendra. "Speedboats Guzzle Fuel Worth Rs60 Crore, Maharashtra Grapples for Funds." *Daily News and Analysis*, 11 October 2011.

Gayer, Laurent, and Christophe Jaffrelot. "Introduction: Muslims of the Indian City: From Centrality to Marginality." In *Muslims in Indian Cities: Trajectories of Marginalisation*, edited by Laurent Gayer and Christophe Jaffrelot, 1–22. New Delhi: HaperCollins India, 2012.

George, Varghese K. "'Can't Give up War on Terror.'" *Hindustan Times*, 28 September 2008.

Getzoff, Joseph F. "Start-up Nationalism: The Rationalities of Neoliberal Zionism." *Environment and Planning D: Society and Space* 38, no. 5 (October 2020): 811–28.

Gill, K.P.S. "Terrorism, Institutional Collapse, and Emergency Response Protocols." In *Terror and Containment: Perspectives on India's Internal Security*, edited by K.P.S. Gill and Ajai Sahni, 251–94. New Delhi: Gyan Publishing House, 2000.

Gilmore, Craig. "Foreword (Foreword) to the Second Edition." In *Police: A Field Guide.*, edited by David Correia and Tyler Wall, ix–xiv. London: Verso, 2022.

Gilmore, Ruth Wilson. "Fatal Couplings of Power and Difference: Notes on Racism and Geography." *Professional Geographer* 54, no. 1 (February 2002): 15–24.

———. *Golden Gulag: Prisons, Surplus, Crisis, and Opposition in Globalizing California*. Berkeley: University of California Press, 2007.

———. "Race, Prisons, and War: Scenes from the Gilmore History of U.S. Violence." *Socialist Register* 45 (March 2009).

Gilmore, Ruth Wilson, and Craig Gilmore. "Beyond Bratton." In *Policing the Planet: Why the Policing Crisis Led to Black Lives Matter*, edited by Jordan T. Camp and Christina Heatherton, 173–200. London: Verso, 2016.

Giroux, Henry A. "War on Terror: The Militarising of Public Space and Culture in the United States." *Third Text* 18, no. 4 (2004): 211–21.

Glossary of Administrative Terms (English-Hindi). New Delhi: Government of India, 1968.

Glück, Zoltán. "Security Urbanism and the Counterterror State in Kenya." *Anthropological Theory* 17, no. 3 (2017): 297–321.

Goede, Marieke de. "The Chain of Security." *Review of International Studies* 44, no. 1 (January 2018): 24–42.

Gonzalves, Colin. "Our Politicians Are Still Not Listening." *Mail Today*, 20 November 2008.

Gopal, Priyamvada. *Insurgent Empire: Anticolonial Resistance and British Dissent.* London: Verso, 2019.

Gordon, Neve. "Israel's Emergence as a Homeland Security Capital." In *Surveillance and Control in Israel/Palestine: Population, Territory, and Power*, edited by David Lyon, Elia Zureik, and Yasmeen Abu-Laban, 134–53. New York: Routledge, 2011.

———. "The Political Economy of Israel's Homeland Security/Surveillance Industry." Working Paper III, *The New Transparency: Surveillance and Social Sorting*, 2009.

Graham, Stephen. "Cities and the 'War on Terror.'" *International Journal of Urban and Regional Research* 30, no. 2 (2006): 255–76.

———. *Cities Under Siege: The New Military Urbanism*. New York: Verso, 2010.

———, ed. *Cities, War, and Terrorism: Towards an Urban Geopolitics*. Oxford: Blackwell, 2004.

———. "'Homeland' Insecurities? Katrina and the Politics of 'Security' in Metropolitan America." *Space and Culture* 9, no. 1 (2006): 63–67.

———. "Laboratories of War: United States-Israeli Collaboration in Urban War and Securitization the Urbanizing Middle East." *Brown Journal of World Affairs* 17, no. 1 (2010): 35–52.

Graham, Stephen, and Alexander Baker. "Laboratories of Pacification and Permanent War: Israeli-U.S. Collaboration in the Global Making of Policing." In *The Global Making of Policing*, edited by Jana Hönke and Michael-Marcus Müller, 40–58. Abingdon, England: Routledge, 2016.

Grassiani, Erella. "Commercialised Occupation Skills: Israeli Security Experience as an International Brand." In *Security/Mobility: Politics of Movement*, edited by Matthias Leese and Stef Wittendorp, 37–56. Manchester: Manchester University Press, 2017.

———. "Performing Politics at the Israeli Security Fair." *Policing and Society* 34, no. 1–2 (June 2022): 1–17.

Gregory, Derek. *The Colonial Present: Afghanistan, Palestine, Iraq*. Malden, Mass.: Blackwell, 2004.

Grewal, S. S., and B. K. Khanna. "Low Intensity Conflict in the Indian Context." *Pratividrohi* (September 1993): 14–27.

GTC. "Are We Security Conscious?" *United Services Institution Journal* 101, no. 422–25 (January–December 1971): 48–52.

Guha, Ranajit. "The Prose of Counter-Insurgency." In *The Small Voice of History*, edited by Partha Chatterjee, 194–238. Ranikhet, India: Orient BlackSwan, 2009.

Gupta, Ankit. "The Indian Homeland Security Industry." *Salute India*, 2020.

Hagmann, Jonas. "Security in the Society of Control: The Politics and Practices of Securing Urban Spaces." *International Political Sociology* 11, no. 4 (December 2017): 418–38.

Hagmann, Jonas, Hendrik Hegemann, and Andrew Neal. "The Politicisation of Security: Controversy, Mobilisation, Arena Shifting." *European Review of International Studies* 5, no. 3 (2018): 3–29.

Hajjar, Lisa. "International Humanitarian Law and 'Wars on Terror': A Comparative Analysis of Israeli and American Doctrines and Policies." *Journal of Palestine Studies* 36, no. 1 (2006): 21–42.

———. "Israel as Innovator in the Mainstreaming of Extreme Violence." *Middle East Report*, Summer 2016.

Hall, Stuart, Chas Critcher, Tony Jefferson, John Clarke, and Brian Roberts. *Policing the Crisis: Mugging, the State, and Law and Order*. 2nd ed. Houndmills, England: Palgrave Macmillan, 2014.

Halper, Jeff. *War Against the People: Israel, the Palestinians, and Global Pacification*. London: Pluto Press, 2015.

Hameed, Abdul. "Mumbai Attack: Terrorists Spoke Marathi?" *TwoCircles.Net* (blog), 29 November 2008.

Hameed, Sayeed. "What Are We Learning from Israeli Security Experts?" *The Milli Gazette*, 2 August 2010.

Hansa, Raveena. "India's Terror Dossier: Further Evidence of A Conspiracy." *Countercurrents.org*, 9 February 2009. https://countercurrents.org/hansa050209.htm.

———. "The Mumbai Terror Attacks: Need for a Thorough Investigation." In *Mumbai Post 26/11: An Alternative Perspective*, edited by Ram Puniyani and Shabnam Hashmi. New Delhi: SAGE Publications India, 2010.

Harcourt, Bernard E. *The Counterrevolution: How Our Government Went to War Against Its Own Citizens*. New York: Basic Books, 2018.

Haraway, Donna J. *Simians, Cyborgs, and Women: The Reinvention of Nature*. London: Free Association Books, 1991.

———. *Staying with the Trouble: Making Kin in the Chthulucene*. Durham, N.C.,: Duke University Press, 2016.

Harding, Sandra, ed. *The Postcolonial Science and Technology Studies Reader*. Durham, N.C.: Duke University Press, 2011.

Harel, Amos. "India Declines Israeli Offer of Aid Delegation to Mumbai." *Haaretz*, 28 November 2008.

———. "Israeli Experts: Slow Operation Meant 'No Chance' for Hostages at Mumbai Chabad House." *Haaretz*, 30 November 2008.

Hawkins, Richard. "The 'Irish Model' and the Empire: A Case for Reassessment." In *Policing the Empire: Government, Authority, and Control, 1830–1940*, edited by David M. Anderson and David Killingray, 18–32. Manchester: Manchester University Press, 1991.

Heath, Deana. *Colonial Terror: Torture and State Violence in Colonial India*. Oxford: Oxford University Press, 2021.

Herbert, Steve. "The Normative Ordering of Police Territoriality: Making and Marking Space with the Los Angeles Police Department." *Annals of the Association of American Geographers* 86, no. 3 (1996): 567–82.

———. *Policing Space: Territoriality and the Los Angeles Police Department*. Minneapolis: University of Minnesota Press, 1997.

Herman, Edward, and Gerry O'Sullivan. *The "Terrorism" Industry: The Experts and Institutions That Shape Our View of Terror*. New York: Pantheon Books, 1989.

Herzl, Theodor. *The Complete Diaries of Theodor Herzl*. Edited by Raphael Patai. Translated by Harry Zohn. Vol. 1. New York: Thomas Yoselof, 1960.

Hever, Shir. *The Privatization of Israeli Security*. London: Pluto Press, 2018.

Hockstader, Lee. "Israelis Say U.S. Could Learn from Their Tactics." *Washington Post*, 13 September 2001.

"Homeland Security Assessment—India: Expansion and Growth." Aviotech and Associated Chambers of Commerce and Industry (ASSOCHAM), June 2011.

"Homeland Security Budget," *Costs of War*, June 2021. https://watson.brown.edu/costsofwar/costs/economic/budget/dhs.

"HomeLand Security Industry: Born of Necessity. Matured by Reality." Israel Export and International Cooperation Institute (IEICI), n.d.

Howard, Michael, and Robert Hunter. "Israel and the Arab World: The Crisis of 1967." *Adelphi Papers* 7, no. 41 (October 1967).

Howell, Alison. "Forget 'Militarization': Race, Disability and the 'Martial Politics' of the Police and of the University." *International Feminist Journal of Politics* 20, no. 2 (2018): 117–36.

Hughes, Matthew. *Britain's Pacification of Palestine: The British Army, the Colonial State, and the Arab Revolt, 1936–1939*. Cambridge: Cambridge University Press, 2019.

Hughes, Sara Salazar. "Unbounded Territoriality: Territorial Control, Settler Colonialism, and Israel/Palestine." *Settler Colonial Studies* 10, no. 2 (April 2020): 216–33.

"IFSEC and Homeland Security India-Post Show Report 2012." International Fire and Security Exhibition and Conference (IFSEC), 2012.

Inbar, Efraim. "The Indian-Israeli Entente." *Orbis* 48, no. 1 (2004): 89–104.

"India Pursues Homeland Security Technologies." Wikileaks Public Library of U.S. Diplomacy. India New Delhi, 16 October 2009. https://wikileaks.org/plusd/cables/09NEWDELHI2116_a.html.

"India Risk Survey 2012." Pinkerton Consulting and Investigations (India) Pvt. Ltd and Federation of Indian Chambers of Commerce and Industry (FICCI), 2012.

"India Risk Survey 2019." Pinkerton Consulting and Investigations (India) Pvt. Ltd and Federation of Indian Chambers of Commerce and Industry (FICCI), 2019.

"Indian and Israeli Firms to Jointly Provide Advanced Security Systems." *Hindustan Times*, 22 December 2008.

"Indian Forces May Have Killed Some Hostages: Report." *Hindustan Times,* 2 December 2008.

"Indian Intelligence Agencies Lack Coordination: Experts." Indo-Asian News Service, 20 October 2004.

"India's Defence Exports at Record Rs 13,000 Crore, 70% from Private Sector." *Times of India*, 9 July 2022.

"India's Rescue Efforts 'Premature and Badly Planned,' Says Israel." *Hindustan Times*, 27 November 2008.

International Security and Defense Systems Ltd. Corporate Brochure. International Security and Defense Systems Ltd. (ISDS).

"IPS Officers Visit Israel to Learn Best Policing Practices." *Economic Times*, 19 August 2015.

"Israel Calls Indian Troops Handling of Mumbai Terror Siege 'Risky and Premature.'" *Hindustan Times*, 28 November 2008.

"Israel for Sharing Technology with India." *Assam Tribune,* 14 October 2006.

"Israel HomeLand Security Industry." Israel Export and International Cooperation Institute, 2010.

"Israel-India Military Relations: Ideological Paradigms of Security." BDS India/People's Dispatch/Newsclick.in, 22 January 2020.

"Israel Says Mumbai Terrorists Targeted Its Citizens." *Bharat Chronicle,* 29 November 2008.

"Israeli Consulate's Mumbai Security Chief Arrested En Route to Chabad House Rescue." *Jerusalem Post*, 30 November 2008.

"Israeli Firm Planning Security Academy in Gujarat." *Times of India*, 12 January 2018.

"Israeli Media Calls India's Reaction 'Slow, Confused.'" *News18*, 28 November 2008.

"Israelising India: The Hindutva Fantasy That Is Realising Itself." Indian Cultural Forum, 20 August 2019.

"Israel's Innovative Homeland Security Solutions." *Indo-Israeli Business*, September–November 2010.

Jabotinsky, Ze'ev (Vladimir). "The Iron Wall—We and the Arabs," 1923. http://www.marxists.de/middleast/ironwall/ironwall.htm.

Jacobsen, Elida K. U. "Unique Identification: Inclusion and Surveillance in the Indian Biometric Assemblage." *Security Dialogue* 43, no. 5 (2012): 457–74.

Jaffrelot, Christophe, ed. *Hindu Nationalism: A Reader.* Princeton: Princeton University Press, 2009.

———. "Hindu Nationalism: Strategic Syncretism in Ideology Building." *Economic and Political Weekly* 28, no. 12/13 (1993): 517–24.

———. *Modi's India: Hindu Nationalism and the Rise of Ethnic Democracy.* Translated by Cynthia Schoch. Princeton, N.J.: Princeton University Press, 2021.

Jaffrelot, Christophe, and Ingrid Therwath. "The Sangh Parivar and the Hindu Diaspora in the West: What Kind of 'Long-Distance Nationalism'?" *International Political Sociology* 1, no. 3 (September 2007): 278–95.

"Jagrut Mumbaikar—Joint Initiative on Citizens' Safety and Security: Fighting Bullets and Bombs with Your Ears and Eyes." *The Mumbai Protector: A Magazine for the Mumbai Police* 1, no. 1 (September/October 2009): 26.

Jansen, G. H. "A Study of Indian Reactions to Israel's Military 'Victory.'" *United Services Institution Journal* LXXXXIX, no. 417 (October 1969).

Jauregui, Beatrice. "Just War: The Metaphysics of Police Vigilantism in India." *Conflict and Society* 1, no. 1 (2015): 41–59.

———. "Provisional Agency in India: Jugaad and Legitimation of Corruption." *American Ethnologist* 41, no. 1 (2014): 76–91.

———. *Provisional Authority: Police, Order, and Security in India*. Chicago: University of Chicago Press, 2016.

Jazeel, Tariq. "Singularity: A Manifesto for Incomparable Geographies," *Singapore Journal of Tropical Geography* 40, no. 1 (2019): 5–21.

Jelly-Schapiro, Eli. *Security and Terror: American Culture and the Long History of Colonial Modernity*. Oakland: University of California Press, 2018.

Jha, Subhash K. "Israel Concerned about Rabbi Held Hostage, to Send Rescue Team." Indo-Asian News Service, 28 November 2008.

Jones, Craig. "Lawfare and the Juridification of Late Modern War." *Progress in Human Geography* 40, no. 2 (April 2016): 221–39.

———. *The War Lawyers: The United States, Israel, and Juridical Warfare*. Oxford: Oxford University Press, 2020.

Jones, Reece. *Border Walls: Security and the War on Terror in the United States, India, and Israel.* London: Zed Books, 2012.

———. "Geopolitical Boundary Narratives, the Global War on Terror and Border Fencing in India." *Transactions of the Institute of British Geographers* 34, no. 3 (July 2009): 290–304.

Joronen, Mikko. "Atmospheric Negations: Weaponising Breathing, Attuning Irreducible Bodies." *Environment and Planning D: Society and Space* 41, no. 5 (2023): 765–83.

Kamte, Vinita, and Vinita Deshmukh. *To the Last Bullet: The Inspiring Story of Braveheart Ashok Kamte*. 1st ed. Pune, India: Ameya Prakashan, 2009.

Kaplan, Amy. *The Anarchy of Empire in the Making of U.S. Culture*. Cambridge, Mass.: Harvard University Press, 2002.

———. "Homeland Insecurities: Some Reflections on Language and Space." *Radical History Review* 85, no. 1 (2003): 82–93.

———. *Our American Israel: The Story of an Entangled Alliance*. Cambridge, Mass.: Harvard University Press, 2018.

Kaplan, Caren. "The Biopolitics of Technoculture in the Mumbai Attacks." *Theory, Culture, and Society* 26, no. 7–8 (2009): 301–13.

Katz, Cindi. "Banal Terrorism." In *Violent Geographies: Fear, Terror, and Political Violence*, edited by Derek Gregory and Allan Pred, 349–62. New York: Routledge, 2007.

Katz, Yaakov. "Israel Closely Watching India's Investigation of Mumbai Attacks. Defense Industries Concerned That Israeli Criticism of India May Jeopardize Contracts." *Jerusalem Post*, 1 December 2008.

———. "Israeli Officials Say India Mishandled Hostage Situation. Israel Offers Aid, but Not Sending Commando Units to Mumbai." *Jerusalem Post*, 27 November 2008.

Kaur, Ravinder. *Brand New Nation: Capitalist Dreams and Nationalist Designs in Twenty-First-Century India*. Stanford: Stanford University Press, 2020.

Keinon, Herb. "Looking Past Mumbai." *Jerusalem Post*, 5 December 2008.

———. "State Angry at Zaka's Mumbai 'Meddling.'" *Jerusalem Post*, 2 December 2008.

Keinon, Herb, and Judy Siegel-Itzkovich. "MDA, ZAKA Dispatch Teams to Mumbai." *Jerusalem Post*, 27 November 2008.

Khalidi, Rashid. *Palestinian Identity: The Construction of Modern National Consciousness*. New York: Columbia University Press, 1997.

Khalili, Laleh. "The Location of Palestine in Global Counterinsurgencies." *International Journal of Middle East Studies* 42, no. 3 (2010): 413–33.

———. "The New (and Old) Classics of Counterinsurgency." *Middle East Report*, no. 255 (2010).

———. *Time in the Shadows: Confinement in Counterinsurgencies*. Stanford: Stanford University Press, 2013.

Khanduri, C. B. "Moshe Dayan: The Military Commander." *Defence Review Annual*, 1982, 59–61.

Khanikar, Santana. *State, Violence, and Legitimacy in India*. Oxford: Oxford University Press, 2018.

Khera, Reetika. "The UID Project and Welfare Schemes." *Economic and Political Weekly* 46, no. 9 (2011): 38–43.

Khilnani, Sunil. *The Idea of India*. London: Penguin Books, 2004.

Klein, Bradley S. "Conclusion: Every Month Is 'Security Awareness Month.'" In *Critical Security Studies: Concepts and Strategies*, edited by Keith Krause and Michael C. Williams, 359–68. London: Routledge, 1997.

Klein, Naomi. "Laboratory for a Fortressed World." *The Nation*, 14 June 2007.

———. *The Shock Doctrine: The Rise of Disaster Capitalism*. Toronto: Vintage Canada, 2007.

Kolben, Kevin. "Blowing an Opportunity with India." *Jerusalem Post*, 3 December 2008.

Kolinsky, Martin. "Reorganization of the Palestine Police after the Riots of 1929." *Journal of Israeli History* 10, no. 2 (1989): 155–73.

Kolås, Åshild. "The 2008 Mumbai Terror Attacks: (Re-)Constructing Indian (Counter-)Terrorism." *Critical Studies on Terrorism* 3, no. 1 (2010): 83–98.

Koutsoukis, Jason. "Israeli Military Will Not Intervene; Mumbai Massacre." *Sydney Morning Herald (Australia)*, 29 November 2008.

KPMG-ASSOCHAM. "Homeland Security in India: An Overview." KPMG and Associated Chambers of Commerce and Industry of India, 2010.

Kraska, Peter B., and Victor E. Kappeler. "Militarizing American Police: The Rise and Normalization of Paramilitary Units." *Social Problems* 44, no. 1 (1997): 1–18.

Krishna, Sankaran. *Postcolonial Insecurities: India, Sri Lanka, and the Question of Nationhood*. Minneapolis: University of Minnesota Press, 1999.

Kroizer, Gad. "From Dowbiggin to Tegart: Revolutionary Change in the Colonial Police in Palestine during the 1930s." *Journal of Imperial and Commonwealth History* 32, no. 2 (2004): 115–33.

Kumar, A. Vinod. "The Fidayeens Are Back, But We Aren't Ready." Indo-Asian News Service, 30 November 2008.

Kumar, Deepa. "Terrorcraft: Empire and the Making of the Racialised Terrorist Threat." *Race and Class* 62, no. 2 (October 2020): 34–60.

Kumar, Krishna. "Did Police Tweak 26/11 Sequence?" *Mail Today*, 6 June 2009.

Kumar, Radha. *Police Matters: The Everyday State and Caste Politics in South India, 1900–1975*. Ithaca, N.Y.: Cornell University Press, 2021.

Kumaraswamy, P. R. "India and Israel: Emerging Partnership." *Journal of Strategic Studies* 25 (2002): 192–206.

———. "Indo-Israeli Military Relations: Prospects and Limitations." *Indian Defence Review* 8, no. 3 (1993): 45–52.

———. *India's Israel Policy*. New York: Columbia University Press, 2010.

La, Fanga. "The Arab Israeli War." *United Services Institution Journal* LXXXXVII, no. 408 (July 1967): 213–29.

Lakshmi, Rama. "Official Quits Amid Public Anger at India's Leadership." *Washington Post*, 1 December 2008.

Lappin, Yaakov. "Zaka Head: Indian Forces May Have Killed Some Hostages." *Jerusalem Post*, 30 November 2008.

Latour, Bruno. *Pandora's Hope: Essays on the Reality of Science Studies*. Cambridge, Mass., and London: Harvard University Press, 1999.

———. *Science in Action: How to Follow Scientists and Engineers through Society*. Boston: Harvard University Press, 1987.

———. *We Have Never Been Modern*. Translated by Catherine Porter. Cambridge, Mass.: Harvard University Press, 1993.

Law, John. "After ANT: Complexity, Naming, Topology." In *Actor Network Theory and After*, edited by John Law and John Hassard, 1–14. Oxford: Blackwell, 1999.

———. *After Method: Mess in Social Science Research*. Abingdon, England: Routledge, 2004.

———. "What's Wrong with a One-World World?" *Distinktion: Journal of Social Theory* 16, no. 1 (2015): 126–39.

LeBrón, Marisol. *Policing Life and Death: Race, Violence, and Resistance in Puerto Rico*. Oakland: University of California Press, 2019.

Legg, Stephen. "Imperial Internationalism: The Round Table Conference and the Making of India in London, 1930–1932." *Humanity: An International Journal of Human Rights, Humanitarianism, and Development* 11, no. 1 (2020): 32–53.

Li, Darryl. "Lies, Damned Lies, and Plagiarizing 'Experts.'" *Middle East Report*, no. 260 (2011): 5.

———. *The Universal Enemy: Jihad, Empire, and the Challenge of Solidarity*. Stanford: Stanford University Press, 2019.

Lokaneeta, Jinee. *Transnational Torture: Law, Violence, and State Power in the United States and India*. New York: New York University Press, 2011.

———. *The Truth Machines: Policing, Violence, and Scientific Interrogations in India*. Ann Arbor: University of Michigan Press, 2020.

Lowenstein, Antony. *The Palestine Laboratory: How Israel Exports the Technology of Occupation around the World*. London: Verso, 2023.

Lubin, Alex. "From Home Rule to Homeland: Counterterrorism as a Way of Life." *American Quarterly* 74, no. 3 (2022): 556–62.

———. *Never-Ending War on Terror. Never-Ending War on Terror.* Berkeley: University of California Press, 2020.

———. "'We Are All Israelis': The Politics of Colonial Comparisons." *South Atlantic Quarterly* 107, no. 4 (October 2008): 671–90.

M. S., Nileena. "How the NIA Lost the Opportunity to Become India's Only Professional Investigative Agency." *The Caravan*, 30 June 2022.

Machold, Rhys. "India's Counterinsurgency Knowledge: Theorizing Global Position in Wars on Terror." *Small Wars and Insurgencies* 33, no. 4–5 (July 2022): 796–818.

———. "Policing Reality: Urban Disorder, Failure, and Expert Undoings." *International Political Sociology* 14, no. 1 (2020): 22–39.

———. "Reconsidering the Laboratory Thesis: Palestine/Israel and the Geopolitics of Representation." *Political Geography* 65 (2018): 88–97.

———. "Staying with the Failures: Iron Dome and Zionist Security 'Innovation.'" In *Encounters with Colonial Power: Emergent Spaces of Violence and Struggle in Palestine*, edited by Mikko Joronen and Mark Griffiths, 122–48. Lincoln: University of Nebraska Press, 2023.

Machold, Rhys, and Catherine Chiniara Charrett. "Beyond Ambivalence: Locating the Whiteness of Security." *Security Dialogue* 52, no. 1 Suppl (November 2021): 38–48.

MacKay, Joseph. *The Counterinsurgent Imagination: A New Intellectual History*. Cambridge: Cambridge University Press, 2023.

MacKenzie, Donald A. *Inventing Accuracy: A Historical Sociology of Nuclear Missile Guidance*. Boston: MIT Press, 1990.

MacKenzie, Donald, Fabian Muniesa, and Lucia Siu. "Introduction: Monetary Theory at Thirteen Thousand Feet." In *Do Economists Make Markets? On the Performativity of Economics*, edited by Donald MacKenzie, Fabian Muniesa, and Lucia Siu, 1–18. Princeton, N.J.: Princeton University Press, 2007.

"Maha's Elite Counter Terror Unit Force One Becomes Operational." *Business Standard*, 25 November 2009.

Manchanda, Nivi, and Sharri Plonski. "Between Mobile Corridors and Immobilizing Borders: Race, Fixity, and Friction in Palestine/Israel." *International Affairs* 98, no. 1 (January 2022): 183–207.

Marwecki, Daniel. *Germany and Israel: Whitewashing and Statebuilding*. Oxford: Oxford University Press, 2020.

Marx, Karl. "6: On the Jewish Question." In *Karl Marx: Selected Writings*, edited by David McLellan, 2nd ed. Oxford: Oxford University Press, 2000.

Masco, Joseph. *The Theater of Operations: National Security Affect from the Cold War to the War on Terror*. Durham, N.C.: Duke University Press, 2014.

Massad, Joseph A. *The Persistence of the Palestinian Question: Essays on Zionism and the Palestinians*. Abingdon, England: Routledge, 2006.

Mathew, Biju. "As the Fires Die: The Terror of the Aftermath." *Samar: South Asian Magazine for Action and Reflection*, 1 December 2008.

"Max Security Testimonials Page." Accessed 1 February 2014. https://www.max-security.com/testimonials/.

McAlister, Melani. *Epic Encounters: Culture, Media, and U.S. Interests in the Middle East since 1945*. Berkeley: University of California Press, 2001.

McCoy, Alfred W. *Policing America's Empire: The United States, the Philippines, and the Rise of the Surveillance State*. Madison: University of Wisconsin Press, 2009.

McElroy, Damian. "Mumbai Attacks: Foreign Governments Criticise India's Response." *The Telegraph*, 28 November 2008.

McGirk, Tim. "Israel Reacts to the Mumbai Massacre." *Time*, 28 November 2008.

McGoey, Linsey. "The Logic of Strategic Ignorance." *British Journal of Sociology* 63, no. 3 (2012): 533–76.

———. "Strategic Unknowns: Towards a Sociology of Ignorance." *Economy and Society* 41, no. 1 (2012): 1–16.

McGregor, R. S., ed. *The Oxford Hindi-English Dictionary*. Oxford: Oxford University Press, 2002.

McMichael, Christopher. "Pacification and Police: A Critique of the Police Militarization Thesis." *Capital and Class* 41, no. 1 (2017): 115–32.

McQuade, Brendan. *Pacifying the Homeland: Intelligence Fusion and Mass Supervision*. Berkeley: University of California Press, 2019.

McQuade, Joseph. *A Genealogy of Terrorism: Colonial Law and the Origins of an Idea*. Cambridge: Cambridge University Press, 2020.

Medzini, Ronen. "Mumbai Horror: Rescue Workers Shocked by Chabad Massacre Site." Ynetnews, 29 November 2008.

Mehta, Tejas. "Mumbai Ko Haath Lagana Mushkil Hi Nahin Namumkin Hain: Anti-Terror Chief Quotes 'Don.'" NDTV, 27 November 2014.

Menon, Meena. "A Smart Anti-Terror Force for Mumbai Now." *The Hindu*, 25 November 2009.

Merom, Gil. "Israel's National Security and the Myth of Exceptionalism." *Political Science Quarterly* 114, no. 3 (1999): 409–34.

Mignolo, Walter D. "The Geopolitics of Knowledge and the Colonial Difference." *South Atlantic Quarterly* 101, no. 1 (January 2002): 57–96.

Mignolo, Walter D., and Catherine E. Walsh. *On Decoloniality: Concepts, Analytics, Praxis*. Durham, N.C., and London: Duke University Press, 2018.

Misra, Neelesh. "Advantage Militants as Law Lacks Teeth." *Hindustan Times*, 1 January 2008.

Mitchell, Don. *The Right to the City: Social Justice and the Fight for Public Space*. New York: Guilford Press, 2003.

Mitchell, Timothy. *Carbon Democracy: Political Power in the Age of Oil*. London: Verso Books, 2011.

———. *Colonising Egypt*. Berkeley: University of California Press, 1991.

———. "The Properties of Markets." In *Do Economists Make Markets?: On the Performativity of Economics*, edited by Donald MacKenzie, Fabian Muniesa, and Lucia Siu, 244–75. Princeton, N.J.: Princeton University Press, 2007.

———. *Rule of Experts: Egypt, Techno-Politics, Modernity*. Berkeley: University of California Press, 2002.

———. "The Stage of Modernity." In *Questions of Modernity*, edited by Timothy Mitchell, 1–34. Minneapolis: University of Minnesota Press, 2000.

Mol, Annemarie. "Ontological Politics: A Word and Some Questions." In *Actor Network Theory and After*, edited by John Law and John Hassard, 74–89. Oxford: Blackwell, 1999.

Morag, Nadav. *Comparative Homeland Security: Global Lessons*. Hoboken, N.J.: John Wiley & Sons, 2011.

Mubayi, Vinod. "Why Modi and Hindutva Love Israeli Settler-Colonialism and See It as a Model for Kashmir." *The Wire*, 9 July 2021.

"Mumbai Attack Analysis." New York Police Department (NYPD) Intelligence Division, 4 December 2008.

Mushrif, S. M. *Who Killed Karkare? The Real Face of Terrorism in India*. 1st ed. Delhi: Pharos Media and Publishing, 2009.

Nadar, Ganesh. "'Corruption Is a Bigger Threat than Terrorism.'" *Rediff*, 27 November 2012.

Najeeb, Muhammad. "Hatred of Jews Spurred Nariman House Attack: Israel." Indo-Asian News Service, 30 November 2008.

Narrain, Arvind. *India's Undeclared Emergency: Constitutionalism and the Politics of Resistance*. Chennai: Context, 2021.

"A Nation That Cannot Afford to Sleep." *Hindustan Times*, 28 November 2008.

"National Strategy for Homeland Security." Office of Homeland Security, July 2002.

Nayar, Rahul. "India and Israel: A People to People Link." *Free Press Journal* (India), 18 January 2018.

Neal, Andrew W. "'Events Dear Boy, Events': Terrorism and Security from the Perspective of Politics." *Critical Studies on Terrorism* 5, no. 1 (April 2012): 107–20.

Neocleous, Mark. "'A Brighter and Nicer New Life': Security as Pacification." *Social and Legal Studies* 20, no. 2 (2011): 191–208.

———. *A Critical Theory of Police Power: The Fabrication of the Social Order*. London: Verso, 2021.

———. *Critique of Security*. Edinburgh: Edinburgh University Press, 2008.

———. *The Fabrication of Social Order: A Critical Theory of Police Power*. London: Pluto Press, 2000.

———. *The Universal Adversary: Security, Capital, and "The Enemies of All Mankind."* Abingdon, England, and New York: Routledge, 2016.

———. *War Power, Police Power*. Edinburgh: Edinburgh University Press, 2014.

Neocleous, Mark, and George S. Rigakos, eds. "Anti-Security: A Declaration." In *Anti-Security*, 15–21. Ottawa: Red Quill Books, 2011.

Neocleous, Mark, George Rigakos, and Tyler Wall. "On Pacification: Introduction to the Special Issue." *Socialist Studies/Études Socialistes* 9, no. 2 (2013).

Nguyen, Nicole. *A Curriculum of Fear: Homeland Security in U.S. Public Schools*. Minneapolis: University of Minnesota Press, 2016.

———. *Suspect Communities: Anti-Muslim Racism and the Domestic War on Terror*. Minneapolis: University of Minnesota Press, 2019.

Ninan, Sevanti. "Do We Deserve This?" *The Hindu*, 7 December 2008.

Nolan, Tom. "Militarization Has Fostered a Policing Culture That Sets Up Protesters as 'The Enemy.'" *Homeland Security Newswire*, 3 June 2020.

Ochs, Juliana. *Security and Suspicion: An Ethnography of Everyday Life in Israel*. Philadelphia: University of Pennsylvania Press, 2010.

"Olmert: No Doubt Mumbai Attack Targeted Jewish Institutions." *Haaretz*, 30 November 2008.

Owens, Patricia. *Economy of Force: Counterinsurgency and the Historical Rise of the Social*. Cambridge: Cambridge University Press, 2015.

Oza, Rupal. "Contrapuntal Geographies of Threat and Security: The United States, India, and Israel." *Environment and Planning D: Society and Space* 25, no. 1 (2007): 9–32.

———. "The Geography of Hindu Right-Wing Violence in India." In *Violent Geographies: Fear, Terror, and Political Violence*, edited by Derek Gregory and Allan Pred, 153–74. Routledge: New York, 2007.

———. "India's Relations with Israel and Palestine: Tracing a Tectonic Shift." *Society and Space Open Site*, September 18, 2014.

Pai, Aditi, and Swati Mathur. "Lame Duck Committee to Investigate 26/11." *India Today*, 31 December 2008.

Palshikar, Suhas. "In the Shadow of Terror: Anti-Politician or Anti-Politics?" *Economic and Political Weekly* 43, no. 50 (2008): 10–11.

Pant, Harsh V. "India and Israel: A Bond Is Forged." *Jerusalem Post*, 9 January 2009.

Pappé, Ilan. *The Idea of Israel: A History of Power and Knowledge*. Ebook. London: Verso, 2014.

Patwardhan, Anand. "Free of All Zealots." *Hindustan Times*, 10 December 2008.

———. "Terror: Aftermath," November 2008. http://patwardhan.com/?page_id=668.

Pease, Donald E. "The Global Homeland State: Bush's Biopolitical Settlement." *Boundary 2* 30, no. 3 (2003): 1–18.

Pedahzur, Ami. "From Munich to Mumbai." *New York Times*, 20 December 2008.

Pepper, Daniel. "Breaking of Mumbai Siege Turns into Street Theatre." *The Guardian*, 28 November 2008.

Peraino, Kevin. "Why Israel Isn't Angry." *The Daily Beast*, 3 December 2008.

Peretz, Martin. "Counting." *The New Republic*, 24 September 2001.

Peretz, Sapir. "A Partner in Need; Officials in Israel Believe India Is Likely to Step Up Demand for Israeli Products, Services, and Know-How Related to Homeland Security." *Globes*, 3 December 2008.

Pfeffer, Anshel. "9 Dead in Mumbai Chabad House Attack; Israel to Help Identify Bodies." *Haaretz*, 28 November 2008.

Poets, Desirée. "The Securitization of Citizenship in a 'Segregated City': A Reflection on Rio's Pacifying Police Units." *Urbe. Revista Brasileira de Gestão Urbana* 7 (May 2015): 182–94.

Pradhan, Ram, and Vappala Balachandran. "Report of the High Level Enquiry Committee (HLEC) on 26/11 (Appointed by the Maharashtra Government Vide GAD GR No: Raasua.2008/C.R.34/29-A, 30th Dec 2008)," 2009.

Prakash, Prem. "Anger against Politicians Is Justified: We Need Accountability." *Hindustan Times*, 19 December 2008.

Prashad, Vijay. *Namaste Sharon: Hindutva and Sharonism under U.S. Hegemony*. New Delhi: LeftWord Books, 2003.

"Probe Points at Violation in Bomb Suits Purchase in Mumbai." *Daily News and Analysis*, 6 February 2012.

Puar, Jasbir K. *Terrorist Assemblages: Homonationalism in Queer Times*. Durham, N.C.: Duke University Press, 2007.

Quijano, Aníbal. "Coloniality and Modernity/Rationality." *Cultural Studies* 21, no. 2–3 (2007): 168–78.

———. "Coloniality of Power and Eurocentrism in Latin America." *International Sociology* 15, no. 2 (2000): 215–32.

Rajagopal, Arvind. "Hindu Nationalism in the U.S.: Changing Configurations of Political Practice." *Ethnic and Racial Studies* 23, no. 3 (January 2000): 467–96.

Ramadan, A. "Destroying Nahr El-Bared: Sovereignty and Urbicide in the Space of Exception." *Political Geography* 28, no. 3 (2009): 153–63.

Raman, B. "The Anti-Israeli Angle." *Outlook India*, 4 December 2008.

———. "My Jerusalem Diary." *Indian Defence Review* 18, no. 3 (September 2003): 8–12.

Rana, Aziz. *The Constitutional Bind: How Americans Came to Idolize a Document That Fails Them*. Chicago: University of Chicago Press, 2024.

———. "Settler Wars and the National Security State." *Settler Colonial Studies* 4, no. 2 (April 2014): 171–75.

Rao, Vyjayanthi. "How to Read a Bomb: Scenes from Bombay's Black Friday." *Public Culture* 19, no. 3 (2007): 567.

Reeves, Joshua. "If You See Something, Say Something: Lateral Surveillance and the Uses of Responsibility." *Surveillance and Society* 10, nos. 3/4 (2012): 235–48.

Rifkin, Mark. "Settler Common Sense." *Settler Colonial Studies* 3, no. 3–04 (November 2013): 322–40.

Rigakos, George S. *Security/Capital: A General Theory of Pacification*. Edinburgh: Edinburgh University Press, 2016.

Robb, Peter. "The Ordering of Rural India: The Policing of Nineteenth-Century Bengal and Bihar." In *Policing the Empire: Government, Authority, and Control, 1830–1940*, edited by David M. Anderson and David Killingray, 126–50. Manchester: Manchester University Press, 1991.

Robinson, Cedric J. *Black Marxism: The Making of the Black Radical Tradition*. Chapel Hill: University of North Carolina Press, 2000.

Rojas, Cristina. "Contesting the Colonial Logics of the International: Toward a Relational Politics for the Pluriverse." *International Political Sociology* 10, no. 4 (December 2016): 369–82.

Rossdale, Chris. "Enclosing Critique: The Limits of Ontological Security." *International Political Sociology* 9, no. 4 (December 2015): 369–86.

Roy, Arundhati. "9 Is Not 11." *Outlook Magazine*, 22 December 2008.

Roy, Tania. "'India's 9/11': Accidents of a Moveable Metaphor." *Theory, Culture, and Society* 26, no. 7–8 (2009): 314–28.

Rubin, Barry. "India and Israel: The Parallels." *Jerusalem Post*, 1 December 2008.

Sabbagh-Khoury, Areej. "Memory for Forgetfulness: Conceptualizing a Memory Practice of Settler Colonial Disavowal." *Theory and Society*, 7 July 2022.

Sa'di, Ahmad H. "The Borders of Colonial Encounter: The Case of Israel's Wall." *Asian Journal of Social Science* 38, no. 1 (2010): 46–59.

———. "Israel's Settler-Colonialism as a Global Security Paradigm." *Race and Class* 63, no. 2 (April 2021): 21–37.

Sahni, Ajai. "Counter-Terrorism: The Architecture of Failure." *Eurasia Review*, 28 February 2012.

———. "A Triumph of Form over Content." *Seminar*, 2009.

Said, Edward W. "The Essential Terrorist." *Arab Studies Quarterly* 9, no. 2 (1987): 195–203.

———. "An Ideology of Difference." *Critical Inquiry* 12, no. 1 (1985): 38–58.

———. *The Question of Palestine*. London: Vintage, 1992.

Salaita, Steven. *Inter/Nationalism: Decolonizing Native America and Palestine*. Minneapolis: University of Minnesota Press, 2016.

———. *Israel's Dead Soul*. Philadelphia: Temple University Press, 2011.

Sarin, Ritu. "From Israel, Lessons on Fighting Terror." *Indian Express*, 21 July 2009.

———. "No 26/11 Repeat: Maharashtra Shops for Israeli Solutions." *Indian Express*, 13 July 2009.

Schedler, Andreas. "Introduction: Antipolitics—Closing and Colonizing the Public Sphere." In *The End of Politics? Explorations into Modern Antipolitics*, edited by Andreas Schedler, 1–20. London: Macmillan Press, 1997.

Schrader, Stuart. *Badges Without Borders: How Global Counterinsurgency Transformed American Policing*. Oakland: University of California Press, 2019.

———. "Cops at War: How World War II Transformed U.S. Policing." *Modern American History* 4, no. 2 (July 2021): 159–79.

———. "To Protect and Serve Themselves: Police in U.S. Politics since the 1960s." *Public Culture* 31, no. 3 (September 2019): 601–23.

———. "To Secure the Global Great Society: Participation in Pacification." *Humanity: An International Journal of Human Rights, Humanitarianism, and Development* 7, no. 2 (2016): 225–53.

"Securing Asia 2012 Event Guide: The Global Hub for Asian Homeland Security and Counter Terror." Security Watch India, June 2012.

"Securing Asia 2013 Event Guide: The Asian Homeland Security and Counter Terror Summit-Bringing Asia to Your Doorstep." Security Watch India, June 2013.

"Security Watch India Homepage." Accessed 8 July 2014. http://securitywatchindia.org.in/About_SWI.aspx.

Seigel, Micol. "Always Already Military: Police, Public Safety, and State Violence." *American Quarterly* 71, no. 2 (July 2019): 519–39.

———. "Beyond Compare: Comparative Method after the Transnational Turn." *Radical History Review* 2005, no. 91 (2005): 62–90.

———. *Violence Work: State Power and the Limits of Police*. Durham, N.C.: Duke University Press, 2018.

Sen, Arjun. "Raytheon Eyes $1-Bn Indian Civilian Business by 2018." Indo-Asian News Service, 21 November 2008.

Sen, Somdeep. "Antagonistic Landscapes." *Environment and Planning C: Politics and Space* 39, no. 4 (June 2021): 705–21.

———. *Decolonizing Palestine: Hamas between the Anticolonial and the Postcolonial*. Ithaca, N.Y.: Cornell University Press, 2020.

Sen, Somdeep, and John Collins, eds. *Globalizing Collateral Language: From 9/11 to Endless War*. Athens: University of Georgia Press, 2021.

Sen, Somit. "Once in the Army, Now in Force One." *Times of India*, 19 December 2008.

Senor, Dan, and Saul Singer. *Start-Up Nation: The Story of Israel's Economic Miracle*. Toronto: McClelland & Stewart, 2009.

Seri, Guillermina. *Seguridad: Crime, Police Power, and Democracy in Argentina*. New York: Continuum, 2012.

Seth, Sanjay. "'Once Was Blind but Now Can See': Modernity and the Social Sciences." *International Political Sociology* 7, no. 2 (June 2013): 136–51.

———. *Subject Lessons: The Western Education of Colonial India*. Durham, N.C.: Duke University Press, 2007.

Sethi, Manisha. *Kafkaland: Prejudice, Law, and Counterterrorism in India*. Gurgaon, India: Three Essays Collective, 2014.

Shaban, Abdul. "Ethnic Politics, Muslims, and Space in Contemporary Mumbai." In *Lives of Muslims in India*, edited by Abdul Shaban, 209–23. London: Routledge, 2018.

———. "Ghettoisation, Crime, and Punishment in Mumbai." *Economic and Political Weekly* 43, no. 33 (2008): 68–73.

Shaikh, Abdul Wahid. *Innocent Prisoners*. New Delhi: Pharos, 2017.

Shalhoub-Kevorkian, Nadera. *Security Theology, Surveillance, and the Politics of Fear*. Cambridge: Cambridge University Press, 2015.

Sharma, Kalpana. "Governance Failures and the Anti-Political Fallout." *Economic and Political Weekly* 43, no. 49 (June 2008): 13–15.

Sharma, Ritu. "Eight, Including Jewish Centre Rabbi, Stuck in Nariman House." Indo-Asian News Service, 28 November 2008.

Sikand, Yoginder. "Mossad-CIA Connection to Mumbai Terror Attacks? *Countercurrents*, 29 November 2008.

Sinclair, Georgina. "'Get into a Crack Force and Earn £20 a Month and All Found . . .': The Influence of the Palestine Police upon Colonial Policing, 1922–1948." *European Review of History/Revue Européenne d'histoire* 13, no. 1 (March 2006): 49–65.

Singh, Gagan Preet. "Police-Public Relations in Colonial India." *History Compass* 17, no. 11 (2019): e12595.

———. "Property's Guardians, People's Terror: Police Avoidance in Colonial North India." *Radical History Review* 2020, no. 137 (May 2020): 54–74.

Singh, Nikhil Pal. *Race and America's Long War*. Oakland: University of California Press, 2017.

———. "Racial Formation in an Age of Permanent War." In *Racial Formation in the Twenty-First Century*, edited by Daniel HoSang, Oneka LaBennett, and Laura Pulido, 276–301. Berkeley: University of California Press, 2012.

Singh, Shailza. "The 'Homeland Security Moment' in International Politics: Implications for the Third World." *International Studies* 58, no. 3 (July 2021): 380–96.

Singha, Radhika. "'Providential' Circumstances: The Thuggee Campaign of the 1830s and Legal Innovation." *Modern Asian Studies* 27, no. 1 (February 1993): 83–146.

———. "Settle, Mobilize, Verify: Identification Practices in Colonial India." *Studies in History* 16, no. 2 (August 2000): 151–98.

Sivanandhan, D. "Tackling Terrorism: My First Priority." *The Mumbai Protector: A Magazine for the Mumbai Police* 1, no. 1 (September–October 2009): 9–15.

———. "View from the Top." *The Mumbai Protector: A Magazine for the Mumbai Police* 1, no. 2 (November-December 2009): 6.

Smith, Terence. "Israelis Down a Libyan Airliner in the Sinai, Killing at Least 74; Say It Ignored Warnings to Land." *New York Times*, 22 February 1973.

Sorkin, Michael, ed. *Indefensible Space: The Architecture of the National Insecurity State*. New York: Routledge, 2008.

Stampnitzky, Lisa. "Can Terrorism Be Defined?" In *Constructions of Terrorism: An Interdisciplinary Approach to Research and Policy*, edited by Michael Stohl, Richard Burchill, and Scott Howard Englund, 11–20. Berkeley: University of California Press, 2017.

———. *Disciplining Terror: How Experts Invented "Terrorism."* Cambridge: Cambridge University Press, 2013.

———. "Rethinking the 'Crisis of Expertise': A Relational Approach." *Theory and Society* 52 (March 2023): 1097–1124.

"Stay Fit, East Healthy Diet." *The Mumbai Protector: A Magazine for the Mumbai Police* 1, no. 2 (November–December 2009): 84–86.

Stockmarr, Leila. "Seeing Is Striking: Selling Israeli Warfare." *Jadaliyya*, 18 January 2014.

Stoler, Ann Laura. *Duress: Imperial Durabilities in Our Times*. Durham, N.C.: Duke University Press, 2016.

Stoler, Ann Laura, and Carole McGranahan. "Refiguring Imperial Terrains." *Ab Imperio* 2006, no. 2 (2006): 17–58.

Stritzel, Holger. "Securitization, Power, Intertextuality: Discourse Theory and the Translations of Organized Crime." *Security Dialogue* 43, no. 6 (2012): 549–67.

———. 2011. "Security as Translation: Threats, Discourse, and the Politics of Localisation." *Review of International Studies* 37, no. 5 (2011): 2491–2517.

———. *Security in Translation: Securitization Theory and the Localization of Threat*. New Security Challenges Series. London: Palgrave Macmillan, 2014.

Subramanian, K. S. *Political Violence and the Police in India*. New Delhi: SAGE Publications India, 2007.

Sullivan, Kate. "Exceptionalism in Indian Diplomacy: The Origins of India's Moral Leadership Aspirations." *South Asia: Journal of South Asian Studies* 37, no. 4 (October 2014): 640–55.

Swami, Praveen. "Mumbai Police Modernisation Generates Controversy." *The Hindu*, 8 April 2009.

———. "Mumbai Siege Turns Spotlight on Crisis within NSG." *The Hindu*, 12 December 2008.

"Syrian Airliner Seized by Israel: Plane, 10 Aboard, Is Forced Down—Damascus Sees Tie to Soldiers' Capture." *New York Times*, 13 December 1954.

Tanham, George K. "Indian Strategic Thought: An Interpretive Essay." RAND Corporation, 1 January 1992.

Tarvainen, Antti. "The Modern/Colonial Hell of Innovation Economy: Future as a Return to Colonial Mythologies," *Globalizations*, 21 March 2022, 1–23.

"Task Force on National Security and Terrorism." New Delhi: Federation of Indian Chambers of Commerce and Industry (FICCI), 2009.

Thapan, Arjun. "The Arab-Israeli Conflict June 1967 and Its Origins." *United Services Institution Journal* LXXXXVIII, no. 412 (July 1968): 282–308.

Tilley, Lisa, and Robbie Shilliam. "Raced Markets: An Introduction." *New Political Economy* 23, no. 5 (2018): 534–43.

Tilly, Charles. "Terror, Terrorism, Terrorists." *Sociological Theory* 22, no. 1 (2004): 5–13.

Tiwary, Deeptiman. "Cops Get Israeli Answers for Terror." *Mumbai Mirror*, 12 July 2009.

———. "Mumbai Cops to Take Lessons from Israel." *Mumbai Mirror*, 11 July 2009.

Townshend, Charles. "The Defence of Palestine: Insurrection and Public Security, 1936–1939." *English Historical Review* 103, no. 409 (1988): 917–49.

Tsing, Anna Lowenhaupt. *Friction: An Ethnography of Global Connection*. Princeton, N.J.: Princeton University Press, 2005.

———. *The Mushroom at the End of the World: On the Possibility of Life in Capitalist Ruins*. Princeton, N.J.: Princeton University Press, 2015.

Tyner, James A. "Population Geography III: Precarity, Dead Peasants, and Truncated Life." *Progress in Human Geography* 40, no. 2 (April 2016): 275–89.

Unnikrishnan, C., and Sanjeev Shivadekar. "Anti-Corruption Bureau Starts Inquiry into Speed Boat Row." *Times of India*, 27 August 2012.

Unnithan, Sandeep. "Mumbai Terror Attacks Similar to Savoy Hotel Attack: Israeli Terror Expert." *India Today*, 1 December 2008.

Unnithan, Sandeep, and Bhavna Vij-Aurora. "India Doesn't Learn: Four Years after 26/11, Intelligence Wars within and Ill-Equipped Security Paint a Frightening Picture of Unpreparedness." *India Today*, 16 November 2012.

Valverde, Mariana. *Chronotopes of Law: Jurisdiction, Scale, and Governance*. Oxford and New York: Routledge, 2015.

Vanaik, Achin, ed. *Masks of Empire*. New Delhi: Tulika Books, 2007.

———. *The Painful Transition: Bourgeois Democracy in India*. London: Verso, 1990.

———. *The Rise of Hindi Authoritarianism: Secular Claims, Communal Realities*. London: Verso, 2017.

Vine, David. *The United States of War: A Global History of America's Endless Conflicts, from Columbus to the Islamic State*. Oakland: University of California Press, 2020.

Visvak. "Anand Patwardhan on His Latest Film, 'Vivek.'" *The Caravan*, 6 April 2019. https://caravanmagazine.in/culture/anand-patwardhan-film-vivek-right-wing-rationality.

Vitale, Alex S. *City of Disorder: How the Quality of Life Campaign Transformed New York Politics*. New York: NYU Press, 2008.

Wagner, Kim A. "Savage Warfare: Violence and the Rule of Colonial Difference in Early British Counterinsurgency." *History Workshop Journal* 85 (April 2018): 217–37.

Wahl, Rachel. *Just Violence: Torture and Human Rights in the Eyes of the Police*. Stanford: Stanford University Press, 2017.

Wall, Tyler, and Travis Linnemann. "No Chance: The Secret of Police, or the Violence of Discretion." *Social Justice* 47, no. 4–5 (2020): 19.

Walters, William. "Editor's Introduction: Anti-Policy and Anti-Politics: Critical Reflections on Certain Schemes to Govern Bad Things." *European Journal of Cultural Studies* 11, no. 3 (2008): 267–88.

———. "Rezoning the Global: Technological Zones, Technological Work, and the (Un-)Making of Biometric Borders." In *The Contested Politics of Mobility:*

Borderzones and Irregularity, edited by Vicki Squire, 51–73. Abingdon, England: Routledge, 2011.

———. "Secrecy, Publicity, and the Milieu of Security." *Dialogues in Human Geography* 5, no. 3 (2015): 287–90.

Waseem, Zoha. *Insecure Guardians: Enforcement, Encounters, and Everyday Policing in Postcolonial Karachi*. London: Hurst Publishers, 2022.

"We Pledge to Keep Mumbai Safe and Secure." *The Mumbai Protector: A Magazine for the Mumbai Police*, 2009.

Weisburd, David, Thomas Feucht, Idit Hakimi, Lois Mock, and Simon Perry, eds. *To Protect and Serve: Policing in an Age of Terrorism*. London: Springer, 2009.

Weisburd, David, Tal Jonathan, and Simon Perry. "The Israeli Model for Policing Terrorism: Goals, Strategies, and Open Questions." *Criminal Justice and Behavior* 36 (2009): 1259–78.

Weizman, Eyal. *Hollow Land: Israel's Architecture of Occupation*. London: Verso, 2007.

———. *The Worst of All Possible Evils: Humanitarian Violence from Arendt to Gaza*. London: Verso, 2012.

"'Why Did No Backup Arrive for My Husband?'" *Hindustan Times*, 15 January 2009.

Wind, Maya. *Towers of Ivory and Steel: How Israeli Universities Deny Palestinian Freedom*. New York: Verso, 2024.

"Wives of Kamte, Karkare Question Clean Chit," *Indian Express*, 28 May 2009.

Wolfe, Patrick. "Purchase by Other Means: The Palestine Nakba and Zionism's Conquest of Economics." *Settler Colonial Studies* 2, no. 1 (2012): 133–71.

———. "Settler Colonialism and the Elimination of the Native." *Journal of Genocide Research* 8, no. 4 (2006): 387–409.

"World Rallies Behind India in Anti-Terror Fight." Indo-Asian News Service, 27 November 2008.

Wynter, Sylvia. "Unsettling the Coloniality of Being/Power/Truth/Freedom: Towards the Human, After Man, Its Overrepresentation—An Argument." *CR: The New Centennial Review* 3, no. 3 (2003): 257–337.

Yacobi, Haim. *Israel and Africa: A Genealogy of Moral Geography*. New York: Routledge, 2016.

Yadhav, Vijay Kumar. "Anti-Terrorism Cell Is Mumbai Police's Best Kept Secret." *Hindustan Times*, 15 November 2018.

Yonucu, Deniz. *Police, Provocation, Politics: Counterinsurgency in Istanbul*. Ithaca, N.Y.: Cornell University Press, 2022.

———. "Urban Vigilantism: A Study of Anti-Terror Law, Politics and Policing in Istanbul." *International Journal of Urban and Regional Research* 42, no. 3 (2018): 408–22.

Yousif, Elias. "Factsheet: U.S. Arms Sales and Security Assistance to Israel." securityassistance.org, April 2021. https://securityassistance.org/publications/factsheet-us-arms-sales-and-security-assistance-to-israel/.

"ZAKA Is Not a Trustworthy Source for Allegations of Sexual Violence on October 7." Mondoweiss, 30 December 2023. https://mondoweiss.net/2023/12/zaka-is-not-a-trustworthy-source-for-allegations-of-sexual-violence-on-october-7/.

"Zicom & IMI, Israel Ties up with Security Training & Education Academy." 9 January 2009. www.derivatives.capitaline.com.

INDEX

Note: Page numbers in italics indicate figures.

actor-network theory (ANT), 3, 17, 60–61, 200, 223, 257n11. *See also* enrollment
Aditya (pseudonym), 178, 179, 181, 189
Afghanistan, 3, 40, 232
Africa, 12, 66, 87, 88, 89. *See also* Operation Entebbe
Al-Qaeda, 2, 46, 126
Althusser, Louis, 35, 120
ANT (actor-network theory), 3, 17, 60–61, 200, 223, 257n11. *See also* enrollment
Anti-Terrorism Squad (ATS), 99–100, 112, 144, *144*, 150, 177. *See also* Karkare, Hemant
Appadurai, Arjun, 152
Arabic, 82, 243
Arabs: accused of propaganda, 70; anti-Arab incitement, 70; Arab-Israeli conflict in general, 68, 93–96, 165; French colonialism and, 66; Indian military analysis of, 94; India's contradictory posture and, 96, 167; IOF undercover as, 77; Israel as western empire and, 67; Israeli claims of knowing, 82; Israeli expertise as limited to, 85; stereotyped, 179. See also *individual countries*
Ari (pseudonym), 78, 79, 80, 87, 184, 188, 190, 195
Arnold, David, 15–16
Arzi, David, 47
Associated Chambers of Commerce and Industry of India (ASSOCHAM), 202, 203, 205, 214, 216, 242
Athena Security Implementations, 81, 186. *See also* Noam (pseudonym)
ATS (Anti-Terrorism Squad), 99–100, 112, 144, *144*, 150, 177. *See also* Karkare, Hemant
authoritarianism: Indian police apparatus and, 10, 100, 161, 237; India's turn to, 27, 101, 102, 125, 135, 245; populism and, 30, 101, 128. *See also* legitimacy, crises of
authority: difference and, 169; global, 5, 86–90
authority, Indian state, 102; policing crises of, 29–30, 106, 122, 123, 125, 128–29
authority, Israeli, 51, 58, 175, 192–93; as a brand, 78, 86–88, 91, 112, 191; challenges to/refusal of, 24, 30, 180, 181, 189–90, 193–94, 195–96; comparison and, 51–52, 54–55, 74, 81–82, 85–86; foreign enrollment in, 88–89; as universal, 85
authority, Israeli performance of, 39, 48, 52–53, 54, 56; and enrolling networks, 50–51; production of controversy and, 35, 45, 50, 51, 53–54 (*see also* Israel, positioning post-26/11); by security firms, 87, 88–89, 90
Avi (pseudonym), 77, 78, 79–80, 85, 86, 181, 188–89, 191
awareness, Indian homeland security and, 198–99, 213–16; education efforts and, 30, 196, 201, 214–15, 285n37; Israeli perception as lacking,

awareness (*continued*)
187; police modernization and, 102, 120–21; as a process of time, 222–23; the security industry and, 205, 206, 209, 213–16, *215*, 222, 242; security messaging and, 26, 142, 143. *See also* security messaging; 26/11 as security turning point
awareness, Israeli model of, 18, 79, 80, 102, 120–21, 213, 285n37
Azmi, Shahid, 156–57

backwardness, 8, 48–49, 52, 192, 201; framing Israeli security sales failures with, 24, 168, 180, 186, 188, 189, 194; the "Indian mind" and, 216, 222, 236
Balachandran, Vappala, 103, 104; access to police logs, 127; critique of police modernization, 124; police modernization lobbyists and, 108; preference of DHS model, 124–25, 273n94; on public confidence, 148–49; questioning delegation to London, 233; questioning delegation to Palestine/Israel, 124, 125; skepticism of Israeli model, 124, 166. *See also* HLEC
Banerjee, Sikita, 122
Barak, Ehud, 36, 39, 40, 41, 46, 53
Barry, Andrew, 35, 50
Barthes, Roland, 240
Beit-Hallahmi, Benjamin, 58
Ben-Gurion, David, 64, 66, 78
Ben-Israel, Isaac, 73–74, 265n97
Berda, Yael, 70
BG Ilanit Gates and Urban Elements Ltd. (BGI), 137, *137–38*, 163, *164*, 183, *207*
Bhabha, Homi, 169
Bhambra, Gurminder, 192, 282n37
Bharatiya Janata Party (BJP), 7, 27, 99, 112–23, 125, 235, 245–46, 247. *See also* Modi, Narendra
Bhujbal, Chhagan, 104–5, 235
Bin, Uriel, 184–85, 187, 190–91, 192
BJP (Bharatiya Janata Party), 7, 27, 99, 112–23, 125, 235, 245–46, 247. *See also* Modi, Narendra
bollards, 25, 163, 182, 185, 197, 241; as materialized homeland security, 135–37, *136*, *137–38*, 163, *164*, 183, *207*
Bombay Stock Exchange (BSE), 137, 142–43, 159, 162, 163
bourgeoisie, Indian, 16, 230; India Inc. and, 99, 121, 236; security concerns of, 99, 102, 110, 128, 233. *See also* class, socioeconomic
bourgeoisie, western, 30, 202
British Mandate for Palestine, 14–15, 61, 62–63, 64. *See also* Palestine/Israel
Brokenshire, James, 210, 227
BSE (Bombay Stock Exchange), 137, 142–43, 159, 162, 163
Bush, George W., 3, 71

CAA (Citizenship Amendment Act), 162, 163, 279n85
Callon, Michel, 200
Cama Hospital, 99, 126, 270n34. *See also* Karkare, Hemant
capital, 196; collusion with the security state, 13; comparative geopolitics and, 52, 167; difference and, 167, 170, 280n11; fabricating social order for, 16, 244. *See also* homeland security industry, the
capital, Indian, 30, 202, 203, 205, 235, 244. *See also* trade shows
capitalism, 12; claim to universality, 191–92; difference and, 280n11; disaster capitalism, 55, 199, 204–5, 235; empire and, 14, 17, 52, 167, 170, 196, 240; Israel and, 67; race-making and, 14, 201; racial, 201; social class and, 160; social order under, 13–14, 16, 244. *See also* economics; homeland security industry, the
caste, 8, 15, 153–54. *See also* class, socioeconomic (Indian)

CCTV cameras, 18, 25–26, 224; British use of, 223, 233; images allegedly from, 126; installation in Maharashtra/Mumbai, 109, 135, 145, 146, 162, 163, 174, 223; Israeli use of, 114; rejection of, 124; sales of, 47, 205, 209. *See also* surveillance
Chakrabarty, Dipesh, 58, 168, 280n11
Challenges for India's Homeland Security, 206, 209, 225
changing same, the, 30, 129, 134, 140–45, 159–60, 161
Chatterjee, Partha, 168, 280n12
Chavan, Ashok, 111–12, 115, 123
Chhatrapati Shivaji Terminus (CST): as different from Palestine/Israel, 179; as impossible to secure, 137–38, 179; Marksman jeeps stationed at, 135, *136*; metal detectors installed in, 137–38, *139*, 162; physical fortification of, 138, 159, 162; 26/11 attack on, 126
Chibber, Vivek, 282n37
China, 111, 187–88, 190–91, 199
Chomsky, Noam, 267n121
Churchgate station, 137, 142, 162
Citizenship Amendment Act (CAA), 162, 163, 279n85
civilization, 167, 219; counterinsurgency as enforcing, 12; Indian, 111–12, 220–21, 225 (*see also* Hindutva ideology); Israeli/Zionist rhetoric of, 52, 64, 70, 82, 85, 90, 194; security as political technology of, 14, 227; western, 90, 193, 220
class, socioeconomic (Indian): bureaucratic, 237; capitalist, 160; dangerous, 152, 160; educated, 222; elite, 16, 99, 157, 222, 223, 226, 236; formation of, 14; middle, 99, 120, 157; political, 3, 16, 99, 236, 237; upper, 120; and urban fragmentation, 153–54. *See also* bourgeoisie; caste
CNN, 1, 5, 97
Cold War, the, 71, 97, 282n35. *See also* Soviet Union, the
colonialism: anticolonialism and, 16, 65–66, 194; British Mandate for Palestine, 14–15, 61, 62–63, 64; colonial policing and, 8, 15–16, 62–63, 86, 89, 140, 166; definitions of terrorism and, 27–28; education and, 226–27, 228; grammars of, 35; homeland security as, 13; imbricated with security, 14, 221–22; in Kashmir, 282n37; long history of, 12, 91, 160, 228–29, 280n12; pacification and, 14–15, 58, 91, 229–30; security training and, 8; universality of governance and, 280n12. *See also* Man-as-human; postcolonial theory; race: hierarchies of; settler colonialism; U. K., the
colonialism, difference and, 226, 227; Israeli perception of India and, 52, 175, 181, 187; Othering and, 168, 181; politics of, 169, 193, 196; racialized hierarchy and, 97, 169–70, 187, 192, 196, 200–201, 228, 242; rule of, 168, 202
colonialism, policing and, 8, 62–63, 86, 89; history in India, 14–17, 140, 161, 230; inheritance of, 16, 27–28, 166, 230, 234, 237, 238, 242
coloniality, 35, 161, 234, 238
commando units, 110, 114; Israeli, 39, 48, 110, 165 (*see also* Operation Entebbe); NSG Nariman House raid and, 38–39, 40. *See also* Force One
comparison: empire and, 83–84; mobilized by Indian officials, 122–23; politics and, 35, 83–84. *See also* difference; geopolitics, comparative
comparison, Indo-Israeli post-26/11, 43, 48–49, 53–54; Israeli claims of terrorism expertise and, 51–52, 54–55, 74, 81–82, 85–86. *See also* difference, Indo-Israeli interactions and
confidence: in the local state, 106, 114; in the police, 106, 119–20, 121, 135, 142, 148–49, 159; of the police, 122, 177; of the state, 102, 129, 230–31 (*see also* legitimacy, crises of)

consulting: consultancy reports, 22, 30, 216; Indian firms offering, 178, 188, 212, 213, 221, 235 (*see also* Rajiv); Indian individuals offering, 235, 241; Indian subsidiaries offering, 202; Israeli experience and, 76; Israeli firms offering, 42, 76, 81, 87, 184, 186, 247; marketing of, 73, 184, 186, 247
corruption, 156; *jugaad* and, 101, 145, 161; Benjamin Netanyahu and, 281n21; post-26/11 actions and, 145, 146, 161, 238; post-26/11 critique and, 8, 10, 100, 101
counterinsurgency: British, 14–15, 61–62, 63, 83; as civilizing, 12; India as model of, 97; Israel as exemplar of, 2–3, 59, 246; legitimation of, 14; ongoing, 13, 129, 239; pretexts of, 129; self-declared campaigns of, 14; U.S., 2–3, 63, 249n2
counterterrorism: foreign models in general, 6, 8, 33–34, 110, 112, 132–33, 176, 233; India's credentials in, 96, 97, 110–11, 151, 177; law and order vs. counterterrorism/security policing, 15, 149, 150, 151, 162, 237; legitimating systemic mistreatment, 238; moral frame of, 28, 65; police station embedding and, 162. *See also* HLEC; terrorism
counterterrorism, Indo-Israeli cooperation/collaboration and: calls for, 47, 165; early stages of, 6; gendered marketing of, 172; impediments to, 165–67, 175, 177–78, 179–80; increase under Modi, 245–47; Israeli lack of engagement in, 97; pledges of, 11, 46, 53–54; skepticism of, 54–55, 179, 181–82. *See also* Maharashtra delegation to Palestine/Israel; training
counterterrorism, Israeli: approach contrast with India, 38, 43, 45, 46, 51–52; assassination policy of, 71; calls to emulate, 46, 48, 54–55, 251n36; materiel and, 44–45; as modern/innovative, 29, 34, 52, 71, 96, 193; Mossad and, 42–43, 113, 155; Operation Entebbe and, 43, 68, 70, 74, 95; *Sayeret Matkal* and, 42, 43; skepticism of, 34, 233; as unsuited to India, 165–66; U.S. embrace of, 2–3, 71; Yamam and, 41–42, 77, 110, 120
counterterrorism, Israeli expertise in, 42, 51–52, 193; Force One training and, 112; post-9/11 positioning and, 5, 71, 73, 74; pre-26/11 belief in, 55–56; valorization of, 43, 47–48, 58–59, 68–69, 112; worldly credentials of, 90
CST (Chhatrapati Shivaji Terminus): as different from Palestine/Israel, 179; as impossible to secure, 137–38, 179; Marksman jeeps stationed at, 135, *136*; metal detectors installed in, 137–38, *139*, 162; physical fortification of, 138, 159, 162; 26/11 attack on, 126

Das, Veena, 11
Davis, Mike, 133
Dayan, Moshe, 96
Dean, Jodi, 240–42
death squads, 63, 88
democracy, Indian, 16, 96, 101, 125–26, 166; antidemocratic objectives and, 106, 123, 125, 238
Denes, Nick, 84
Dhaul, Harry, 198–99, 201, 206, 211, 219, 231. *See also* Securing Asia; SWI
Dhillon, Kirpal, 237
DHS (United States Department of Homeland Security): budgetary spending on, 12, 242; creation of, 3; as draconian, 9; emulation of, 8, 142, 241–42; India perceived as needing equivalent, 7–8, 9, 10, 124–25; Israel's expertise as outstripping, 11, 73; mandate of, 4; official Indian meetings with, 9; as security exemplar, 33; SWI and, 218, *218*; unlikelihood in India, 241–42

difference: as backwardness, 201; capitalism and, 280n11; destabilizing universality, 192; elision of, 31; flattening, 257n11; framing, 166–67, 222, 226–27; ideology of, 64, 168 (*see also* Hindutva ideology); negotiation and, 19, 170, 199, 212–13, 240, 242–43; neoliberalism and, 229; Othering of, 168, 180, 181, 194, 201; politics of, 168, 169, 228; postcolonial theory and, 168, 169, 191–92, 282n37

difference, colonial: avoiding, 226, 227; Israeli perception of India and, 52, 175, 181, 187; Othering and, 168, 181; politics of, 169, 193, 196; racialized hierarchy and, 97, 169–70, 187, 192, 196, 200–201, 228, 242; rule of, 168, 202

difference, Indo-Israeli interactions and: colonial hierarchy and, 97, 196; contingency and, 194; differences in security realities, 55, 124, 149–50, 179, 181; disconcertment and, 194–95; Leo Gleser on, 179–80, 181, 185, 188–89, 190; Hindu nationalism and, 168–69; as impediment to homeland security sales, 183–90, 282n35; as impediment to Israeli universality, 175, 176, 177–78, 179, 192, 193; Indian perceptions of security approaches and, 151, 177–82, 192; Indian vs. Palestinian/Israeli publics, 165–66, 174; Israeli perception of India and, 5, 52, 166–67, 175, 181, 194 (*see also* racism: Israeli). *See also* comparison, Israel-India post-26/11

difference, overcoming/transcending, 200–201, 227; failure of, 195, 224; through common concerns, 221; through (re)education, 192, 199, 213, 220, 228–29; through universalism, 85, 191. *See also* universality of homeland security

difference, postcolonial, 168, 169, 193, 196

Doval, Ajit, 8, 10

Du Bois, W. E. B., 242

Dunbar-Ortiz, Roxanne, 92

economics: defining, 200; economic exceptionalism, 76; neoliberal reasoning of, 204, 227; performativity of, 200, 223, 230. *See also* capitalism

economy, the: calculating the state of, 188, 204, 222, 246; globalized, 11, 198; the making of, 20, 200; political, 12, 242; processes of, 14; ties of, 13; vulnerabilities of, 154, 204; of war, 63

education, colonial, 226–27, 228

education, security: awareness and, 30, 196, 199, 201, 214–15, 285n37; "educating the market" concept, 30, 205–6, 209, 210, 214–15, 216, 222, 235; enrolled networks and, 200, 201; *homo securitas* and, 201–2, 223, 226, 230; the "Indian mind" and, 216–23, *217–18*, 225, 242; as not feasible or possible, 188, 189, 190; as overcoming/transcending difference, 192, 199, 213, 220, 228–29; purported need for (re)education and, 81, 216–17, 222, 223, 225, 228–29, 242; as route to superiority, 80; vendors educated on Indian/Asian culture, 211–12, 213, 215–16. *See also* trade shows; training

efficiency: Indian, 52, 110, 173, 179, 181, 204, 236, 239; Israeli, 52, 65, 76, 112, 173; western, 169

Egypt, 66, 67, 68, 95

Eisenhower, Dwight, 66

empire: British, 62, 70, 86, 140, 210, 228, 231, 280n12 (*see also* British Mandate for Palestine; colonialism); capital and, 14, 17, 240; contemporary, 5, 12–13, 89, 201, 239; durability of, 20; exceptionalism and, 12, 60, 83–84, 175, 192, 193; fragmentation and, 26, 145; grammars of, 35, 60, 61, 83, 90, 192, 200; historical, 14, 83, 134, 194, 227, 229, 234, 239; history in Palestine, 60, 62–63, 69–70 (*see

empire (*continued*)
also British Mandate for Palestine); India as buffer against, 5; Israeli, 52, 67–68, 167, 175–76, 192 (*see also* settler colonialism, Zionist); metropoles of, 134; models of, 83–84; race-making and, 14, 182, 201 (*see also* hierarchy). *See also* difference; geopolitics, comparative; pacification; policing; universality of homeland security

empire, U.S.: India's imbrication in, 6, 167, 227; Israel's image to, 93; security awareness and, 285n37; U.S. exceptionalism and, 83; Vietnam's damage to, 122

enrollment, 35, 49–50, 200–201, 210. *See also* ANT

enrollment, Israeli: creating reality, 48–49, 50, 53; failure of, 25, 89; international, 61, 70–71, 72, 88–89, 90, 91–92; reliance on, 86; translation and, 60–61, 70–71, 72

Entebbe. *See* Operation Entebbe

epistemology: epistemic violence, 19; of Man-as-human, 30, 201–2, 226, 228, 230; market education and, 223, 228, 242; of modernity, 226; privilege and, 228; standpoint, 76. *See also* ontology

Erakat, Noura, 63

Essa, Azad, 5, 6, 166

Europe: aid to Israel, 65–66, 91; companies in India, 185; experience with terrorism, 77, 82, 85; Indian exceptionalism and, 220–21; Israel identified with, 58, 59, 64, 65, 91; Israeli security firms and, 82, 89, 90, 191; monitoring Muslims in, 82, 90; origin of Man-as-human in, 201; perception of Israel in, 65, 88; training approach of, 82; Zionists from, 62. *See also* colonialism; West, the; *individual countries*

exceptionality/exceptionalism: American, 4, 65, 83; blurred with the everyday, 133; of histories of violence, 61; in homeland security marketing, 209–10 (*see also* homeland security, Israel as exemplar of); in law and order vs. counterterrorism, 149, 150, 151; refusal of, 180–81; tension with universality, 4–5, 83–84, 86, 88, 90; 26/11 as exceptional event, 149, 150, 224–25, 233–34. *See also* Other, the

exceptionality/exceptionalism, Indian/Hindu, 193; as alternative to western universalism, 225; as counterterrorism leader, 96, 97, 225; democracy and, 96, 166; "Make in India" campaign and, 230; moral leadership and, 220–21; security approach as, 149, 238. *See also* Hindutva ideology

exceptionality/exceptionalism, Israeli/Jewish/Zionist, 60; as contingent, 54, 61, 65, 91–92; democracy and, 166; Israel as extension of European power and, 65–66; Israeli homeland security experience and, 59, 76–80, 90, 91, 113–14, 174–75, 234; Israeli homeland security innovation and, 29, 34, 59, 71, 174, 192; legitimating violence, 64, 65, 69, 78, 92; need for, 91; as othering, 64; outside claims of, 90, 113–14; refusal of, 92, 180–81, 182, 193, 239; settler colonialism and, 63, 64, 69, 76, 78, 80, 92, 239; specificity of security approach and, 83, 85, 88, 173, 174–75, 176, 179, 195; start-up discourse and, 76, 188; technology and, 76, 175–76; theological, 64, 92. *See also* comparison, Indo-Israeli post-26/11; geopolitics, comparative; homeland security, Israel as exemplar of

Eyal (pseudonym), 77, 81–83, 86, 89, 90, 184, 191

Federation of Indian Chambers of Commerce (FICCI), 49, 202, 230, 260n85; FICCI-Pinkerton India Risk Survey,

214, 224–25, 236; homeland security education and, 216–17; new security threats and, 203, 204, 214, 224–25, 236
fences, 18, 64; manufacturers of, 21, 76, 87, 89, 182, 184, 188, 205; *nakabandi*, 139–40, 143, *143*, 162. *See also* bollards
Fernandes, Naresh, 233
FICCI (Federation of Indian Chambers of Commerce), 49, 202, 230, 260n85; FICCI-Pinkerton India Risk Survey, 214, 224–25, 236; homeland security education and, 216–17; new security threats and, 203, 204, 214, 224–25, 236
Fighel, Jonathan, 45–46
Finkelstein, Norm, 66, 67, 91
Force One: army staffing of, 110; foreign models and, 110, 148, 178–79; as Indian vs. as Israeli model, 177, 178–79; infrastructure for, 110–11; as inspiring confidence, 148; Israeli security technology and, 183; law and order vs. counterterrorism and, 150; modernized materiel as for, 110, 149; NSG and, 110, 115, 150; post-26/11 creation of, 109; public showcasing of, 115; training and, 110, 111, 112, 181, 281n32. *See also* Jaganathan, S.
France: Air France, 43, 68–69, 95 (*see also* Operation Entebbe); collaboration with Israel, 66; homeland security industry in, 209–10; homeland security lessons from, 4; view of Israel as European extension, 65–66

Gadkari, Nitin, 125
Gafoor, Hasan, 99, 104, 107, 110, 123
Gateway of India, 138, 140, *141–42*, 162
Gaza, 70, 94
gender: effeminacy and, 52, 168, 179; Hindu nationalism and, 122; marketing materials and, 172; masculinity and, 52, 120, 121–22, 194; national essences and, 52, 168, 179; "penetration" of the Indian market and, 24, 192–94; police image and, 120, 121–22
geography: of authority, 24, 87–88, 91; as contested, 92; difference and, 169–70, 195, 205; of homeland security, 4, 5, 18, 29, 229 (*see also* homeland security, fabrication of; transnationality); imaginations of, 51, 56, 113, 152, 153, 154–55, 167; of myth, 240; translation across, 60, 229, 280n9
geopolitics: destabilization of India and, 99; homeland security as basis of ties, 12–13; India's position within, 95, 96, 97, 155; Indo-Israeli-American triad, 6, 167, 280n9; Israeli lens of, 38; U.K. and French support of Israel and, 65–66; U.S.-Israel "special relationship," 66
geopolitics, comparative, 29, 167, 192, 257n11; classification and, 52, 54; exceptionalism and, 60, 72, 92, 96, 97, 192; Hindutva ideology and, 122–23, 193, 220–21; knowledge generation and, 35. *See also* comparison, Indo-Israeli post-26/11; difference, Indo-Israeli interactions and
Germany, 4, 43, 65–66, 68, 108, 114
Getzoff, Joe, 76
Gill, Kanwar Pal Singh (K.P.S.), 1–2, 6, 97, 176, 217, 237
Gilmore, Ruth Wilson, 134, 161
Gleser, Leo, 24; on Indian difference, 179–80, 181, 185, 188–89, 190; ISDS's foreign work and, 88–89, 177, 179; on the Israeli brand, 87; on Israeli exceptionalism, 79; on Israeli marketing flexibility, 84; on Israel's security experience, 74, 78; SWI and, 218, *218*. *See also* ISDS
Global North, the: homeland security approaches from, 3, 8, 102, 132–33, 199, 201 (*see also* Israel, homeland security of); interaction with the Global South, 228; as normative, 16;

Global North (*continued*)
police professionalism in, 132, 160; special operations clothing in, 148; state legitimacy in, 102; view of India's strategic thinking, 222. *See also* West, the
Global South, the: as antithesis of normalized North, 16; Israel's relations with, 58, 81, 88, 168; racialization of, 228; replication of homeland security in, 12, 133
Golan, Amos, 74–75, 77, 79, 83
Golwarkar, M. S., 112
Gonzalves, Colin, 237
Gordon, Neve, 76
governance: failure of, 52, 98, 105, 106, 222, 236; homeland security as technology/model of, 13, 18, 134, 202, 213, 214, 216; regimes of, 23, 29, 35, 60, 166, 280n12; solutions to, 198, 204, 221–22; transnational, 50, 192. *See also* legitimacy, crises of; pacification; policing
Guha, Ranajit, 14

Hall, Stuart, 28, 101–2
Halper, Jeff, 59
Hansen, Thomas Blom, 152
Haraway, Donna, 240
Hawkins, Richard, 86
Headley, David, 23, 255n102
Herzl, Theodor, 64
hierarchy: Indo-Israeli interactions and, 97, 196; racial, 97, 187, 192, 196, 200–201, 227, 228, 242
High-Level Enquiry Commission (HLEC), 102–6, 123–24; accusations of coverup, 125, 127; classifying of the report, 105–6, 125, 270n29; criticism for absolving police deaths, 126; lack of adequate materiel and, 104–5, 146, 235; limited mandate of, 103–4; Mumbai police and, 103–4, 124, 125, 235; policy and, 23, 103, 105, 123–24; transnational influences, 104. *See also* Balachandran, Vappala; Pradhan, Ram
hijackings: Air France, 43, 68–69, 95 (*see also* Operation Entebbe); Indian Airlines flight IC-814, 1, 2, 8; by Israel, 69; Israeli claims of plots, 69, 74, 267n128; Israeli training against, 250n16; maritime, 32. *See also* 9/11
Hindutva groups: implication in Karkare murder, 100; Shiv Sena, 100, 113, 122; violence against Muslims and, 7, 100, 152, 245–46. *See also* BJP; Karkare, Hemant
Hindutva ideology, 225; anti-Muslim thought and, 111–12; disavowal of violence and, 92, 97, 133–34; geographical imaginaries of, 113, 153, 245–46; globalizing ambitions of, 92; Narendra Modi and, 245–47; strategic syncretism of, 122–23, 169, 193, 220–21. *See also* exceptionality/exceptionalism, Indian/Hindu
HLEC (High-Level Enquiry Commission), 102–6, 123–24; accusations of coverup, 125, 127; classifying of the report, 105–6, 125, 270n29; criticism for absolving police deaths, 126; lack of adequate materiel and, 104–5, 146, 235; limited mandate of, 103–4; Mumbai police and, 103–4, 124, 125, 235; policy and, 23, 103, 105, 123–24; transnational influences, 104. *See also* Balachandran, Vappala; Pradhan, Ram
homeland, 12, 239
homeland security: as alien, 240; as all-encompassing approach, 151; Asia as uniquely in need of, 198, 199; as category of practice, 17; coining of term, 3, 11, 71, 73, 75, 240; as complete entity, 24; cross-border travel of, 26; as domestic and transnational, 4, 151; exporting, 12; fabric of,

22, 26, 160; geography of, 4, 5; Indian skepticism of replicating, 193, 223–27 (*see also* homeland security, Israel as exemplar (skepticism of)); investment in, 30; as model of policing, 3, 13, 19; as pacification, 14, 17; post-26/11 rise in references to, 33–34; replication of model, 11–12, 90; as in service to capital, 13; strategic syncretism of, 122–23, 193, 220–21; as transnational project, 3, 4–5, 18–19, 28, 60, 167; as uniquely American, 4; as universalizing, 3, 4–5, 14, 31, 192, 200, 205, 206; the U.S. security state and, 8 (*see also* DHS); western models of, 33, 132 (*see also* Israel, homeland security of); as western/modern, 200, 209, 214, 222. See also *homo securitas*; India, materialized homeland security of; pacification; policing; security; transnationality; world-making, homeland security as

homeland security, fabrication of, 17–21, 29, 35, 52, 92, 167; as artifactual, 20, 21; as both national and transnational, 4, 199–201, 220 (*see also* trade shows); as commodity fetish, 18 (*see also* homeland security industry, the); as constant making, 5, 18, 20, 230; as creation of models, 19, 61, 65, 234; as forming fabrics, 19–20, 22, 26, 102, 160, 238–39; as fragmentary, 21–27, 160, 240; Israeli in India, 52, 167, 192, 234 (*see also* homeland security, Israel as exemplar of); military aesthetics and, 30, 134; networking and, 210–13, 219; as performative process, 200, 230 (*see also* police modernization); as racial project, 228 (*see also* difference); resistance to, 223; Safe City projects and, 19, 74–75, 170–71, 172; sandbags as, 19, 139, 159, 163 (*see also* India, materialized homeland security of); strategic syncretism and, 220–21; transnational, 60, 167, 196 (*see also* Israel, homeland security industry of; Maharashtra delegation to Palestine/Israel); as universalist project, 19, 20, 199–200, 227. *See also* education, security; Israel, positioning post-26/11; settler colonialism; surveillance; world-making, homeland security as

homeland security, Indian, 26, 55, 101, 237; as ad-hoc, 10, 101, 205, 235 (see also *jugaad*); budget and procurement, 204, 205, 242 (*see also* police modernization: procurement); bureaucracy as impediment to, 8, 198, 205, 215, 225, 237, 270n35; CCTV and, 135, 162, 174; corruption as lack of modernization and, 101; critique post-26/11, 10, 27, 33, 34, 41; display of, 135–45, *136*, *137*, *138*, *139*, *140–42*, *143*, *144*, 162–63; domestic marketing to, 202–3, 206, 209, 214, 216; emulation of Israel and, 3, 6, 45, 54–55, 165, 251n36 (*see also* comparison, Indo-Israeli post-26/11; homeland security, Israel as model to be emulated); emulation of the West/Global North and, 3, 8, 102, 160, 220, 222, 223–27; Indo-Israeli comparison post-26/11, 43, 48–49, 51–52, 53–54, 179; intelligence and, 41, 42–43; lack of materiel and, 104–5; mindset and, 221–22 (*see also* education, security); need for DHS equivalent and, 7–8, 9, 10, 124–25; in private spaces, 135, *136*, 137, *137*; retaining preexisting infrastructure and, 29–30, 129, 134, 140–45, 159–60; selective adaptation of Israeli approach, 178–79. *See also* HLEC; homeland security, lack of modern; lobbyists; police modernization; preparedness, solutions to India's lack of; trade shows homeland security, Indian (materialized), 138–39, 159–60, 183; bollards, 135–37, *136*, *137–38*, 163, *164*, 183, *207*; metal detectors, 137–38, *139*, 162; *nakabandi*, 139–40, 143, *143*, 162; sandbags, 139, *140*, 143, 159, 163; security messaging attached to, 142–43, *143*

homeland security, Israel as exemplar of, 3, 58–59, 72; Hindutva ideology and, 113; the Israeli approach and, 80–86; Israeli experience and, 68–69, 70, 74, 76–80, 95; Israeli primacy and, 73–75; "killer instinct" and, 111, 112, 130; post-9/11 positioning and, 2; post-26/11 comparison and, 11, 33, 43, 48–49, 51–52, 53–54 (*see also* Israel, positioning post-26/11); proactiveness and, 73–74, 79, 80, 92; the Six-Day War and, 67–68, 93–95; as specifically anti-Muslim, 112, 155; as work in progress, 54, 72–73. *See also* authority, Israeli; enrollment; exceptionality/exceptionalism, Israeli/Jewish/Zionist; Maharashtra delegation to Palestine/Israel

homeland security, Israel as exemplar (skepticism of), 66; difference and, 124, 165–66, 174–75, 178–82, 193, 232 (*see also* difference, Indo-Israeli interactions and); post-Munich Olympics bombings and, 68; strategic affairs analysis and, 93–96

homeland security, Israel as model to be emulated, 67–69; as contingent, 72, 91 (*see also* enrollment); disavowing violence and, 69, 70–71, 72, 91–92, 111; experience and, 76–80, 112; in Latin America, 267n121; as political project, 65; primacy and, 73–75; proactiveness and, 73–74, 79, 80, 92; rejection of, 124, 165–66, 174–75, 178–79, 193; scholarly citation of, 58–59; the Six-Day War and, 67, 93; skepticism of, 6, 68, 93–96, 182, 193; success story narrative and, 91–92; unique approach and, 80–86 (*see also* awareness; exceptionality/exceptionalism, Israeli/Jewish/Zionist); as universalist project, 29 (*see also* universality of homeland security); by the U.S., 2–3; western media coverage and, 68–69. *See also* authority, Israeli; enrollment, Israeli; Israel, positioning post-26/11; Maharashtra delegation to Palestine/Israel; world-making, homeland security as

homeland security, lack of modern, 52–53, 121, 193; adoption of Global North approaches and, 3, 8, 10, 129–30, 132; as cultural issue, 48–49, 52, 177, 179, 189, 228–29; lack of expertise and, 45, 48–49; post-26/11 solidifying, 33, 34, 50–52, 123, 128, 193, 200; root causes of, 101, 146–47, 148; solutions to, 34, 52–53, 123, 173–74, 200 (*see also* education, security; homeland security industry, the; police modernization)

homeland security as global mission, 4, 5, 12, 19, 20, 23, 24, 234. *See also* universality of homeland security; world-making, homeland security as

homeland security industry, Israeli, 5, 29; arms sales and, 6, 46, 47, 56, 59, 64, 75, 156, 180; attempts to "penetrate" the Indian market, 24, 182–91; awareness and, 18, 79, 80, 102, 120–21, 213, 285n37; bollard sales, *136*, 137, *137–38*, 163, *164*, 183, *207*; claims of unique experience, 73–74, 76–80, 90, 91 (*see also* exceptionality/exceptionalism, Israeli/Jewish/Zionist); contingent power of, 30, 54, 56, 170, 196; CornerShot and, 75, 79, 183; disaster capitalism and, 55; early presence in India, 8–9, 12–13; early trade events post-26/11, 49; failure in India, 6, 23–24, 47, 97, 183–90, 194; foreign success and, 88, 89, 90; implications for Indian

Muslims, 154–55; Israeli primacy and, 73–75; joint ventures in India, 47–48, 49; local Indian connections to, 47–48, 156, 183; post-26/11 lobbying by, 108; precursors to, 62–64; predictions post-26/11, 47, 55, 183; private intelligence companies, 46, 81, 182, 209; private security and, 49, 64; Safe City projects and, 19, 74–75, 170–71, 172; SIBAT and, 86; as solution to terrorism "problem," 34, 47, 113, 171, 186, 193, 232; start-up discourse and, 76, 188; success in India, 182–83, 188, 190, 245–47; third party sales and, 88, 188; trade show presence, 205, *208*, 209. *See also* Gleser, Leo; IEICI; Maharashtra delegation to Palestine/Israel; technology, Israeli

homeland security industry, Israeli (firms): Athena Security Implementations, 81, 186; BG Ilanit Gates and Urban Elements Ltd. (BGI), 137, *137–38*, 163, *164*, 183, *207*; ISDS, 74, 88–89, 179, 180, 191; Orad, 87, 88, 185; risk management and, 78, 80, 81, 182–83, 184, 186

homeland security industry, Israeli (informants): Ari (pseudonym), 78, 79, 80, 87, 184, 188, 190, 195; Avi (pseudonym), 77, 78, 79–80, 85, 86, 181, 188–89, 191; Eyal (pseudonym) and, 77, 81–83, 86, 89, 90, 184, 191; Moshe (pseudonym), 185–86, 190; Noam (pseudonym), 81, 83, 84, 186, 189

homeland security industry, Israeli (marketing/promotion), 73, 86–88, 91, 272n67; brochures, 74, 90; marketing representatives, 74, 83, 87, 88, 184, 188, 191 (*see also* Ari); media coverage of Israeli industry, 8–9, 47–48, 113–14, 156, 176, 246; press releases, 49; video, 89, 172; websites and, 81, 82, 86, 88, 89, 90, 191. *See also* enrollment, Israeli; exceptionality/exceptionalism, Israeli/Jewish/Zionist; Israel, national branding of

homeland security industry, Israeli (training), 30, 130, 154, 176–78, 281n32; attempts to secure, 24, 49, 87, 182–83, 192, 246, 247; claim of unique approach, 82, 180; as explicitly anti-Muslim, 155; firms offering, 48 (*see also* Ari; Avi; Eyal); foreign credentials and, 89, 90, 191; foreign governments as clients, 86, 88; as incompatible with Indian reality, 177–78, 179, 181–82, 189; intensification under Modi, 245–46; Israeli distaste for, 181–82, 184, 185, 191; justification for, 111, 112, 155–56; *Krav Maga* and, 81, 177; private clients, 281n21. *See also* Maharashtra delegation to Palestine/Israel; training, Indo-Israeli partnerships in

homeland security industry, the, 3, 18–19, 34–35; early presence in India, 8, 9; financial outlays to, 12, 55, 59, 183, 204 (*see also* police modernization, procurement and); networking events and, 24 (*see also* policy conferences; trade shows); secrecy and, 26. *See also* CCTV cameras; fences; Israel, homeland security industry of; lobbyists

homeland security industry, Indian: attempts to build the market, 30, 49, 215–16 (*see also* trade shows); as brokers for foreign goods, 146; Mahindra Marksman jeeps and, 109, 135, 137, 148, 162–63; "Make in India" campaign and, 230

homeland security industry, U.S., 3, 9, 12–13, 232; arms sales to India, 114, 197, 221

homo securitas, 201–2, 223, 226, 228, 230, 241. *See also* Man-as-human

hostages: Indian attempts to rescue, 38–39, 42; Israeli expertise and, 34,

hostages (*continued*)
37, 39, 42, 68–69, 177; killed, 33, 38–39, 68; 1972 Olympics and, 44, 68
Howell, Alison, 134
human rights activists, 101, 155, 237

IB (Intelligence Bureau), 104, 126, 274n110
ideology, 194, 196, 282n37; difference and, 170; French-Israeli linkages of, 66; of homeland security, 18, 19, 22; of policing, 13, 149, 150, 161, 242; recruitment and, 120; recycled, 53, 57; of security, 132–33, 243, 244; uniquely Israeli, 59; of universalist projects, 196; western, 228; Zionist, 60, 64, 78, 168
ideology, Hindutva: anti-Muslim sentiment and, 111–12, 134, 153; disavowal of violence and, 97, 133–34; geographical imaginaries of, 113, 153; the idea of India and, 92; Indian exceptionalism and, 97, 193, 225; Narendra Modi and, 245–47; strategic syncretism of, 122–23, 169, 193, 220–21
IEICI (Israel Export and International Cooperation Institute), 75, 86; Israeli exceptionalism and, 78–79; post-26/11 statements, 47; protecting western civilization and, 90; sales failure in India and, 188; trade delegations and, 49, 86 (*see also* Maharashtra delegation to Palestine/Israel). *See also* Israel, homeland security industry of; Zuri, Guy
IFSEC (International Fire and Security Exhibition and Conference), 183, 202; IFSEC and Homeland Security India, 205–6, *206*, *207–8*, 216, 221, 224
Inbar, Efraim, 55
incompetence: HLEC report as glossing over, 127; Israeli accusations of, 38, 40, 42, 45, 51, 52; police modernization as response to, 9–10, 107, 114; as systemic mythology, 146, 238
India: analysis of Israeli military pre-26/11, 93–97; caste in, 8, 15, 153–54; counterterrorism credentials of, 1–2, 5, 96, 97, 110–11, 151, 177; historic anti-Zionist stance, 6, 96, 167; inter-ethnic/religious harmony in, 96–97, 101; Kashmir and, 48, 165, 245, 282n37; Ministry of Home Affairs (MHA), 104, 156, 202, 203, 260n85; Prevention of Terrorism Act (POTA), 7, 154, 250n24; as primitive, 44, 51, 52, 220, 228 (*see also* backwardness); right-wing violence in, 7, 125–26; security collaboration with the U.S., 7, 270n25; stereotypes of, 24, 54, 188–89, 194–95, 212; Unlawful Activities Prevention Act (UAPA), 7, 10–11, 166. *See also* Hindutva groups; Maharashtra; Mumbai; Singh, Manmohan
India, British colonialism in, 204, 280n12; as attempt to remake India, 226, 231; education and, 228; Mumbai's connection to, 140, 160 (*see also* policing, infrastructure of); as Palestine model, 62–63. *See also* colonialism, policing and; difference, colonial
India, homeland security industry of: attempts to build the market, 30, 49, 215–16 (*see also* trade shows); as brokers for foreign goods, 146; Mahindra Marksman jeeps and, 109, 135, 137, 148, 162–63; "Make in India" campaign and, 230
India, homeland security of, 26, 55, 101, 237; as ad-hoc, 10, 101, 205, 235 (see also *jugaad*); budget and procurement, 204, 205, 242 (*see also* police modernization: procurement); bureaucracy as impediment to, 8, 198, 205, 215, 225, 237, 270n35; CCTV and, 135, 162, 174; corruption as lack

of modernization and, 101; critique post-26/11, 10, 27, 33, 34, 41; display of, 135–45, *136*, *137*, *138*, *139*, *140–42*, *143*, *144*, 162–63; domestic marketing to, 202–3, 206, 209, 214, 216; emulation of Israel and, 3, 6, 45, 54–55, 165, 251n36 (*see also* comparison, Indo-Israeli post-26/11; homeland security, Israel as model to be emulated); emulation of the West/Global North and, 3, 8, 102, 160, 220, 222, 223–27; Indo-Israeli comparison post-26/11, 43, 48–49, 51–52, 53–54, 179; intelligence and, 41, 42–43; lack of materiel and, 104–5; mindset and, 221–22 (*see also* education, security); need for DHS equivalent and, 7–8, 9, 10, 124–25; in private spaces, 135, *136*, 137, *137*; retaining preexisting infrastructure and, 29–30, 129, 134, 140–45, 159–60; selective adaptation of Israeli approach, 178–79. *See also* HLEC; homeland security, lack of modern; lobbyists; police modernization; preparedness, solutions to India's lack of; trade shows

India, materialized homeland security of, 138–39, 159–60, 183; bollards, 135–37, *136*, *137–38*, 163, *164*, 183, *207*; metal detectors, 137–38, *139*, 162; *nakabandi*, 139–40, 143, *143*, 162; sandbags, 139, *140*, 143, 159, 163; security messaging attached to, 142–43, *143*

India, Muslim demonization in: Bajrang Dal and, 7; blame for 26/11 and, 38, 127, 259n41; Citizenship Amendment Act (CAA) and, 162, 163, 279n85; as common ground with Israel, 113, 172–74, 175–76, 280n9; disavowal of, 238; Hindutva ideology and, 111–12, 134, 153; Hindutva violence against, 7, 152, 157, 166, 280n9; housing demolition and, 246; Israeli training of police and, 154–56; labeled as riot threat, 152 (*see also* Mumbai, history of violence in); "Muslim-sympathizer" as epithet, 100; policing and, 144, *144*, 152–59, *158–59*, 161, 175; political marginalization and, 152, 153, 157; Prevention of Terrorism Act (POTA) and, 7, 154, 250n24; SIMI as threat, 7, 153; stereotyped as terrorists, 6–7, 155 (*see also* terrorism as global "Islamic" threat); Unlawful Activities Prevention Act (UAPA) and, 7, 10–11, 166

Indian Army, the: Israeli arms sales to, 183, 187; police training by, 178; question of use in homeland security, 251n36; training in Israel, 250n16. *See also* Force One

"Indian mind," the, 280n12; Securing Asia and, 211–13, *212*, 215–16, 219–20, 221; security education and, 216–23, *217–18*, 225, 228–29, 242

Indo-Israeli cooperation/collaboration: calls for, 47, 165; early stages of, 6; gendered marketing of, 172; impediments to, 165–66, 175, 177–78, 179–80; increase under Modi, 245–47; Israeli lack of engagement in, 97; pledges of, 11, 46, 53–54; skepticism of, 54–55. *See also* Maharashtra delegation to Palestine/Israel; training

Indo-Israeli relations, 27; ambivalence to the western Other and, 176; Israeli accusations post-26/11, 37–38; Israeli arms sales to India and, 6, 46, 47, 56, 64, 167, 180, 245; promotion of, 21, 272n67 (*see also* Israel, homeland security industry of (marketing/promotion)); rebuffed 26/11 aid offers and, 39, 40, 44, 51, 53, 56; relations pre-26/11, 5–6, 56–57, 96; skepticism of post-26/11 collaboration, 54–55, 179, 181–82; strengthening under Modi, 245–47; tensions post-26/11, 44, 45, 46, 50, 51, 53, 56–57. *See also* difference, Indo-Israeli interactions and

information, suppressing, 101, 103, 105–6, 125, 127, 128
intelligence: centralized, 151; cooperation of, 46; DHS and, 7, 105; FICCI and, 260n85; Indian failure of, 41–43, 46, 52–53, 104, 105; Israel-India comparison of, 45, 51, 52–53, 96–97, 151; new schemes post-26/11, 109; sharing, 3, 46; U.K. in India, 37; U.S. in India, 37, 270n25. *See also* Balachandran, Vappala; Doval, Ajit
intelligence, Israeli, 165; critique of 26/11 and, 37, 39, 41, 48; expertise in gathering, 48, 51; intelligence officers in Mumbai, 37; intelligence-sharing and, 3; justification of violence and, 69, 74; private, 46, 81, 209; private firms, 46, 81, 182, 209; surveillance in Palestine/Israel, 3, 25, 113–14
Intelligence Bureau (IB), 104, 126, 274n110
International Fire and Security Exhibition and Conference (IFSEC), 183, 202; IFSEC and Homeland Security India, 205–6, *206*, *207–8*, 216, 221, 224
International Security and Defense Systems Ltd. (ISDS), 74, 88–89, 179, 180, 191. *See also* Gleser, Leo
interventions, Israeli, 29, 34, 50–57, 72. *See also* Israel, positioning post-26/11
IOF (Israel Occupation Forces), 25, 63–64, 67, 74–75, 77, 241, 255n104
Iran, 36, 88
Iraq, 3, 84, 219
ISDS (International Security and Defense Systems Ltd.), 74, 88–89, 179, 180, 191. *See also* Gleser, Leo
Islam: as anti-Western, 41; claimed Israeli knowledge of, 82; Hindutva ambivalence toward, 169. *See also* Muslims; terrorism as global "Islamic" threat
Israel: the Arab-Israeli War and, 68; attacks on commercial flights, 69; capitalism and, 67; civilizational rhetoric of, 52, 64, 70, 82, 85, 90, 194; early political isolation of, 66; emulation of the U.S., 65; Foreign Ministry of, 37, 39, 45, 46; foreign policy of, 36; fortification and, 3, 25; France and 65, 66, 66; Germany and, 43, 65–66, 68; idea of, 29, 60, 72, 80; ideology of, 59, 66; intelligence-gathering expertise, 48, 51; intelligence officers in Mumbai, 37; intelligence-sharing and, 3; Israelis as indigenous, 67; Magen David Adom (MDA) and, 37, 55, 234, 258n22; military aid to, 64, 65–66, 67; military budget of, 59, 95; as moral force, 65, 67; Munich Olympics and, 43, 68; as planning to destabilize India, 99; policing model of, 6, 51, 91, 112, 124, 193, 245; pre-state Zionist history, 61–63; propaganda/publicity campaigns (*hasbara*), 60, 70–71, 95, 258n23; relations with the Global South, 58, 81, 88, 168; retaliatory violence and, 68; Shin Bet, 37, 53; the Six-Day War and, 67–68, 93–95; state officials of, 34, 36–37, 39, 41, 44 (*see also* Barak, Ehud; Olmert, Ehud); the Suez War and, 66; surveillance within, 3, 25, 114; as threat to all Muslims, 154–55; Vietnam failures and, 66, 67, 94, 122; as western, 52, 91; western fetishization of, 65, 68, 70, 91, 96. *See also* media, Israeli; Palestine/Israel
Israel, counterterrorism approach of: approach contrast with India, 38, 43, 45, 46, 51–52; assassination policy of, 71; calls to emulate, 46, 48, 54–55, 251n36; materiel and, 44–45; as modern/innovative, 29, 34, 52, 71, 96, 193; Mossad and, 42–43, 113, 155; Operation Entebbe and, 43, 68, 70, 74, 95; *Sayeret Matkal* and, 42, 43; skepticism of, 34, 233; as unsuited to India, 165–66; U.S. embrace of, 71; Yamam and, 41–42, 77, 110, 120

Israel, counterterrorism expertise in, 42, 51–52, 193; Force One training and, 112; post-9/11 positioning and, 5, 71, 73, 74; pre-26/11 belief in, 55–56; valorization of, 43, 47–48, 58–59, 68–69, 112; worldly credentials of, 90

Israel, homeland security industry of, 5, 29; arms sales and, 6, 46, 47, 56, 59, 64, 75, 156, 180; attempts to "penetrate" the Indian market, 24, 182–91; awareness and, 18, 79, 80, 102, 120–21, 213, 285n37; bollard sales, *136*, 137, *137–38*, 163, *164*, 183, *207*; claims of unique experience, 73–74, 76–80, 90, 91 (*see also* exceptionality/exceptionalism, Israeli/Jewish/Zionist); contingent power of, 30, 54, 56, 170, 196; CornerShot and, 75, 79, 183; disaster capitalism and, 55; early presence in India, 8–9, 12–13; early trade events post-26/11, 49; failure in India, 6, 23–24, 47, 97, 183–90, 194; foreign success and, 88, 89, 90; implications for Indian Muslims, 154–55; Israeli primacy and, 73–75; joint ventures in India, 47–48, 49; local Indian connections to, 47–48, 156, 183; post-26/11 lobbying by, 108; precursors to, 62–64; predictions post-26/11, 47, 55, 183; private intelligence companies, 46, 81, 182, 209; private security and, 49, 64; Safe City projects and, 19, 74–75, 170–71, 172; SIBAT and, 86; as solution to terrorism "problem," 34, 47, 113, 171, 186, 193, 232; start-up discourse and, 76, 188; success in India, 182–83, 188, 190, 245–47; third party sales and, 88, 188; trade show presence, 205, *208*, 209. *See also* Gleser, Leo; IEICI; Maharashtra delegation to Palestine/Israel; technology, Israeli

Israel, homeland security industry of (firms): Athena Security Implementations, 81, 186; BG Ilanit Gates and Urban Elements Ltd. (BGI), 137, *137–38*, 163, *164*, 183, *207*; ISDS, 74, 88–89, 179, 180, 191; Orad, 87, 88, 185; risk management and, 78, 80, 81, 182–83, 184, 186

Israel, homeland security industry of (informants): Ari (pseudonym), 78, 79, 80, 87, 184, 188, 190, 195; Avi (pseudonym), 77, 78, 79–80, 85, 86, 181, 188–89, 191; Eyal (pseudonym) and, 77, 81–83, 86, 89, 90, 184, 191; Moshe (pseudonym), 185–86, 190; Noam (pseudonym), 81, 83, 84, 186, 189

Israel, homeland security industry of (marketing/promotion), 73, 86–88, 91, 272n67; brochures, 74, 90; marketing representatives, 74, 83, 87, 88, 184, 188, 191 (*see also* Ari); media coverage of Israeli industry, 8–9, 47–48, 113–14, 156, 176, 246; press releases, 49; video, 89, 172; websites and, 81, 82, 86, 88, 89, 90, 191. *See also* enrollment, Israeli; exceptionality/exceptionalism, Israeli/Jewish/Zionist; Israel, national branding of

Israel, homeland security industry of (training), 30, 130, 154, 176–78, 281n32; attempts to secure, 24, 49, 87, 182–83, 192, 246, 247; claim of unique approach, 82, 180; as explicitly anti-Muslim, 155; firms offering, 48 (*see also* Ari; Avi; Eyal); foreign credentials and, 89, 90, 191; foreign governments as clients, 86, 88; as incompatible with Indian reality, 177–78, 179, 181–82, 189; intensification under Modi, 245–46; Israeli distaste for, 181–82, 184, 185, 191; justification for, 111, 112, 155–56; *Krav Maga* and, 81, 177; private clients, 281n21. *See also* Maharashtra delegation to Palestine/Israel; training, Indo-Israeli partnerships in

Israel, homeland security of: approach to, 80–86, 151, 171, 179, 195; development

Israel (*continued*)
prior to term, 3, 71, 73–75; as modern, 51, 52, 193; roots in British rule, 14–15, 62, 63, 89; as solution to India's vulnerabilities, 29, 48, 49–50, 51–52, 54, 55–56. *See also* homeland security, Israel as exemplar of; interventions; violence, Israeli/Zionist
Israel, national branding of, 4, 60; as authority, 78, 86–88, 91, 112, 191; homeland security sales and, 78–79, 80, 86–88, 91
Israel, pacification model of: British roots of, 63; as exceptional, 72, 75, 234; French use of, 66; hegemony of, 91; as idea of Israel, 60; as incompatible in India, 124, 165; Israeli technology and, 58–59, 73, 75, 113; as security innovation, 75, 80–86; as universalist project, 29, 58–59, 61, 65, 89, 196
Israel, positioning post-26/11, 11, 36, 45, 49, 72; centering Israeli viewpoints, 41, 42, 44, 51, 53, 97; as enrollment, 48, 49–50, 53–54, 55–56; hostage response critique, 33, 37, 38–39, 41, 42, 44–45, 50–51; Israel as having unique insights, 34, 36, 37–38, 43, 48, 50, 55–56; tempering of criticism and, 41–42, 43–46, 50, 53, 56–57
Israel, presence in response to 26/11, 37, 39–40, 50, 234, 258n21; Magen David Adom (MDA), 37, 55, 234, 258n22. *See also* ZAKA
Israel, terrorism expertise and, 24, 55–56, 67, 278n75; contingency and, 192–93, 194–95, 196; establishing comparisons and, 51–52, 54–55, 74, 81–82; as exceptional, 43, 59, 76–77, 81, 82; experience and, 2, 37–38, 76–80, 84 (*see also* terrorism, Israel's experience with); Indian unsettling of, 177–82, 189–90; the Israeli approach and, 80–86; offers of 26/11 help and, 36, 39, 40, 44, 51, 53, 56; primacy and, 2, 73–75; promoted by Indian sources, 11, 47–48, 96, 112–13, 177; 26/11 Nariman House response and, 39–40, 41; ZAKA critique of Nariman House response, 42, 43, 44, 45, 46, 53, 55–56, 234. *See also* authority, Israeli
Israel Export and International Cooperation Institute (IEICI), 47, 75, 86, 188; Israeli exceptionalism and, 78–79; protecting western civilization and, 90; trade delegations and, 49, 86 (*see also* Maharashtra delegation to Palestine/Israel). *See also* Zuri, Guy
Israel Occupation Forces (IOF), 25, 63–64, 67, 74–75, 77, 241, 255n104
Iyengar, Chandra, 111, 113–14, 123, 170

Jaffrelot, Christoffe, 122, 169
Jagannathan, S., 111, 123, 170
Jain, P. K., 111, 170
Jauregui, Beatrice, 145–46
jugaad: association with corruption, 101, 145, 161; celebration of, 92, 225; as improvisation and provisionality, 145–46, 160, 161, 163, 235; multivalence of, 101, 145. *See also* police modernization

Kahlberg, Marc, 76, 79, 81, 83
Kamte, Ashok, 99, 100, 105
Kamte, Vinita, 100, 106, 125, 127, 128–29; *To the Last Bullet*, 126–27
Kaplan, Amy, 12, 83, 239
Karkare, Hemant, 99–100, 101, 105, 125–27
Karkare, Kavita, 125
Kasab, Ajmal Mohammed Amir, 33, 106, 126, 270n34
Kashmir, 48, 165, 245, 282n37. *See also* Pakistan
Kelly, Raymond, 104, 105
Kennedy, John F., 66
Khalidi, Rashid, 62, 263n39
Klein, Naomi, 55
knowledge: anti-knowledge and, 123; conflicts of, 103; controversies of, 103; direct, 21; geopolitics of, 35,

52; monopolized, 28; official, 105; restriction of, 106, 123, 128–29; security as global form of, 19; sources of, 53; travel of, 18, 29; as world-making, 4
knowledge, production of, 35, 57, 60; about Israeli terror expertise, 51, 54, 70–71, 171; the post-26/11 security crisis and, 128. *See also* geopolitics, comparative
KPMG, 202, 203, 205, 214, 242
Krishna, Sankaran, 120
Kumar, Radha, 16

landscape, urban, 135–45; ghettoization of, 153–54; militarization of, 11, 30, 132, 133; political violence and, 131 (*see also* violence, Mumbai's history of); social order in, 150, 152, 157, 172, 175–76, 193; warfare in, 58–59, 110, 115, 119, 147–48, 177. *See also* India, materialized homeland security of
law: British colonial, 27–28, 62, 70, 166; Citizenship Amendment Act (CAA), 162, 163, 279n85; defense/human rights law, 156–57, 237; Indian policing and, 16, 100, 103, 154, 237 (*see also* police); Indian precolonial, 15; Indo-Israeli commonalities, 166; international, 71, 94; Jewish religious, 258n23; preventing Israeli approach, 83
law, anti-terror, 152, 154, 162, 166; Prevention of Terrorism Act (POTA), 7, 154, 250n24; Unlawful Activities Prevention Act (UAPA), 7, 10–11, 166
Law, John, 194
Leary, John Patrick, 32
Lebanon, 68
legitimacy, crises of, 29, 100, 120, 122; policing, 29–30, 101–2, 106, 122, 123, 125, 128
Leopold Café, 32, 131
Li, Darryl, 28, 85
liberalism: justification of Israeli violence and, 65; order and, 14, 276n19; security's modern roots in, 13; tropes of cooperation and, 219; vision of security as universal, 229, 243–44. *See also* neoliberalism
Libya, 69, 72–74, 92
Lin, Wen-Yuan, 194
Livni, Tzipi, 38, 39, 41
lobbyists, 34, 49, 50, 55, 108, 156, 210–11, 234; Bombay First, 108, 213–14; The Israel Project, 38; SWI, 197, 198, *203*, 206–7, 209, 214–15, *215*, 217, *217*, 230–31
Lokaneeta, Jinee, 150
Lotan, Lior, 42

Magen David Adom (MDA), 37, 55, 234, 258n22
Maharashtra: attempts to police legitimacy crisis, 29–30, 101–2, 106, 122, 123, 125, 128–29; funding of police modernization, 107, 108, 110; Home Ministry, 23, 104, 107, 108, 139; official handling of HLEC, 104, 105–6, 124, 233; Palestine/Israel agricultural delegation and, 271n50; as preserving the status quo, 134; promises of materiel purchases, 109, 223; U.K. trade delegation and, 211; violent interpellation and, 121. *See also* HLEC; Mumbai; police, Maharashtra; police modernization
Maharashtra delegation to Palestine/Israel, 170–76, 271n50; initial response to, 113–14; Israel as initiating, 108; justification for, 111; questioning of, 124, 125; tempered response to, 130
Man-as-human, 30, 201–2, 226, 228, 230. See also *homo securitas*
Maria, Rakesh, 106, 125, 127, 129
Marshall, Samuel, 156, 278n75
martial arts training, 18, 80–81, 89, 177
Marx, Karl, 13, 244, 280n11

McAlister, Melani, 68
McGranahan, Carole, 35, 83
McMichael, Christopher, 133
McQuade, Brendan, 240
MDA (Magen David Adom), 37, 55, 234, 258n22
media: analysis of Israeli military and, 93–95, 96; calls for violent action in, 46; desire for homeland security and, 19, 33, 48, 146–47, 216, 232, 246; Indian delegations to Israel and, 88–89, 114–15; Indian homeland security industry and, 214; Israeli domestic security and, 48, 96–97, 165; Israeli homeland security industry and, 8–9, 47–48, 113–14, 156, 176, 246, 278n75, 281n32; killing of Hemant Karkare and, 100, 129, 274n110; 9/11 and, 1–2; police corruption and, 101; police modernization and, 110, 115, 123, 147 (see also *The Mumbai Protector*); police public relations and, 115, 123, 129, 176; resignation of Shivraj Patil and, 43; security attention pre-26/11, 7, 9; security awareness and, 7, 216, 222; 2011 Mumbai attacks and, 233; Urdu, 127, 155, 156; U.S. homeland security industry and, 9
media coverage of 26/11: framing 26/11 and, 128, 129; live commentary and, 36; questioning official events and, 270n31; spike in homeland security references, 10, 11, 33, 49; timeline of events and, 32–33; use in *Who Killed Karkare?* (Mushrif), 126; world reaction and, 36
media coverage of 26/11, critique of response and: comparison to Israel and, 43; critique of NSG, 269n22; critique of police resources, 100, 146–47; critique of political status quo, 8; as failure of governance, 98; as failure of local capacity, 123; lack of modernity and, 33; repetition of Israeli statements and, 37, 38–39, 41, 53–54. *See also* media, Israeli positioning post-26/11 and
media, Israeli: advocacy of the Israeli model in, 45, 48, 187, 192; on benefit of 26/11 for industry, 47; critique of India's 26/11 response and, 37, 39, 42; pushback on critique of India, 41–42, 44, 46
media, Israeli positioning post-26/11 and, 11, 36, 45, 49, 72; centering Israeli viewpoints and, 41, 42, 44, 51, 53, 97; as enrollment, 48, 49–50, 53–54, 55–56; hostage response critique and, 33, 37, 38–39, 41, 42, 44–45, 50–51; Israel as having unique insights and, 34, 37–38, 43, 48, 50, 55–56; tempering of criticism and, 41–42, 43–46, 50, 53, 56–57
media, Urdu, 127, 155, 156
Meir, Golda, 66, 69
Meshi-Zahav, Yehuda, 37, 258n23. *See also* ZAKA
metal detectors, 137–38, *139*, 162, 197
methodology, 4, 21–27, 29–31, 35, 60–61, 81, 233; actor-network theory (ANT), 3, 17, 35, 60–61, 200, 223, 257n11
MHA (Ministry of Home Affairs), 104, 156, 202, 203, 260n85
Mignolo, Walter, 35, 52
militarization: as commonsense, 133; as counterterror response, 132–33; of domestic spaces, 11, 30; Israel as epitome of, 59; martial politics and, 143, 160; merged with policing, 133, 140, 145, 160; of urban spaces, 11, 30, 132, 133, 140, 145. *See also* police modernization
military aesthetics, 30, 133, 134, 160, 161
Ministry of Home Affairs (MHA), 104, 156, 202, 203, 260n85
Mitchell, Tim, 20, 200, 229

Mizrahi, Jennifer Laszlo, 38
models: DHS as, 7–8, 9, 10, 124–25, 142, 241–42; foreignness of, 6, 32–34, 58, 83, 178–79, 193, 236–37 (*see also* homeland security, Israel as exemplar (skepticism of)); homeland security as new category, 3, 11–12, 18 (*see also* homeland security, fabrication of); as imperial convention, 175–76, 193, 196 (*see also* world-making, homeland security as); of security in general, 5, 6, 7–8, 18, 19, 33, 219–20, 224; translations in implementing, 15, 60–61, 72, 178, 221, 229, 243–44; transnationality and, 5. *See also* awareness, Israeli model of; homeland security, Israel as model to be emulated; pacification, Israeli/Zionist model of; violence, Israeli/Zionist: as global model
modernity, 59; bourgeois rule as, 230; embrace of, 282n37; epistemology of, 226; framing, 231; homeland security as, 200, 209, 214, 222; Israeli models and, 29, 34, 51, 52, 71, 96, 192, 193–94; lack of, 33, 189, 192, 193, 228–29 (*see also* homeland security, lack of modern); subjectivity and, 226–27
modernity, western, 96, 168, 191–92, 200, 225, 226, 228
Modi, Narendra, 27, 193; homeland security industry and, 230, 245–47; repression of critics, 157, 246. *See also* BJP (Bharatiya Janata Party)
Mol, Annemarie, 17, 195
Morag, Nadav, 4–5
Moshe (pseudonym), 185–86, 190
Mossad: as alleged 26/11 assailants, 126; Israeli counterterrorism and, 42–43, 113, 155; Mumbai police training and, 155, 156; Danny Yatom and, 42–43, 156
Mumbai, *xix*; arguments as safe city, 149; Bombay Stock Exchange, 137, 142–43, 159, 162, 163; bombings in, 112, 113, 233 (*see also* 26/11); as fortified city, 140; Muslims as perceived threat in, 144, *144*, 152–59, *158–59*, 161, 173, 175; protest in, 99, 157, 162, 163; rail danger in, 157–59, *158–59*; security infrastructure in, 25–26, 30, 135–45, *136*, *137–38*, *139*, *140*, *141–42*, *143*, *144*, 162–63, 234; as unique security challenge, 224, 233. *See also* Maharashtra delegation to Palestine/Israel; police, Mumbai; police modernization
Mumbai, history of violence in: bombings, 100, 112, 113, 154, 233; colonial occupation and, 140; riots, 113, 122, 133, 152. *See also* 26/11
The Mumbai Protector, 115–20, *116–19*, 121, 127, 129–30, 142, 147, *147*, 213
Mushrif, S. M.: *26/11 Probe: Why Judiciary Also Failed?*, 274n110; *Who Killed Karkare?*, 125–26, 127, 129, 273n97, 274n110
Muslims: displaced, 166; imprisonment in India, 1; incitement to violence against, 70; Israeli "expertise" in, 82, 85, 172; outside view of treatment in Israel, 96
Muslims, demonization of in India: Bajrang Dal and, 7; blame for 26/11 and, 38, 127, 259n41; Citizenship Amendment Act (CAA) and, 162, 163, 279n85; as common ground with Israel, 113, 172–74, 175–76, 280n9; disavowal of, 238; Hindutva ideology and, 111–12, 134, 153; Hindutva violence against, 7, 152, 157, 166, 280n9; housing demolition and, 246; Israeli training of police and, 154–56; labeled as riot threat, 152 (*see also* Mumbai, history of violence in); "Muslim-sympathizer" as epithet, 100; policing and, 144, *144*, 152–59, *158–59*, 161, 175; political marginalization and, 152, 153, 157; Prevention

Muslims (*continued*)
of Terrorism Act (POTA) and, 7, 154, 250n24; SIMI as threat, 7, 153; stereotyped as terrorists, 6–7, 155 (*see also* terrorism as global "Islamic" threat); Unlawful Activities Prevention Act (UAPA) and, 7, 10–11, 166

Nariman House, 32–33, 37, 38–41, 126, 235, 258n21; critique of response, 42–43, 44, 45, 46, 53, 55–56, 234; left abandoned, 131, *132*; reports of odd occurrences at, 99; turned into memorial, 162; ZAKA operations at, 40, 41, 269n24
National Investigative Agency (NIA), 10–11, 239
nationalism, anticolonial, 65–66
nationalism, Hindu: ambivalent relation to western modernity, 96, 225; idea of India and, 92; Rambo as icon of, 122; strategic syncretism and, 122–23, 169, 193, 220–21. *See also* Hindutva ideology
National Security Guard (NSG), 33, 162, 178; Force One and, 110, 115, 150; former members in private practice, 235, 241; HLEC report and, 104; hostage rescue attempts, 38–40, 42, 235, 241, 269n22; Mumbai hub, 109
Neocleous, Mark, 13
neoliberalism: difference and, 229; disaster capitalism and, 55, 198–99 204; economic reasoning of, 204, 227; excesses of, 133; private sector security and, 198–99. See also *homo securitas*; liberalism
Netanyahu, Benjamin, 70
networks: actor-network theory and, 3, 17, 60–61, 200, 223, 257n11 (*see also* enrollment); homeland security industry and, 48, 50, 86, 210–13, 219; *khabri* (spy) surveillance and, 153, 154; social, 24
New York Police Department (NYPD), 104, 105, 151, 256n1
9/11: effect on Indian anti-Muslim prejudice, 6–7; hijacking similar to flight IC-814, 1, 2; Indian responders to, 108; insecurity and, 11; Israeli claims of prior plots, 74; Israeli positioning after, 2–3, 4, 5, 71, 72–73; justification for U.S. intervention and, 12; as origination of "homeland security," 75; 26/11 parallels to, 9–10, 31, 49–50, 232, 234. *See also* US Department of Homeland Security
Noam (pseudonym), 81, 83, 84, 186, 189
NSG (National Security Guard), 33, 162, 178; Force One and, 110, 115, 150; former members in private practice, 235, 241; HLEC report and, 104; hostage rescue attempts, 38–40, 42, 235, 241, 269n22; Mumbai hub, 109
Nurieli, Nitzan, 41
NYPD (New York Police Department), 104, 105, 151, 256n1

Olmert, Ehud, 11, 42, 43–44, 45, 46
ontology: ontological politics, 17, 102, 195, 242; ontological security, 229; policing the terms of, 30, 102, 125, 128. *See also* difference; epistemology
Operation Entebbe, 43, 68–69, 70, 74, 95
order: fabrication of, 5, 13, 151, 238, 276n19; law and order vs. counterterrorism, 15, 149, 150, 151, 162, 237; political technologies of, 14; regulation of, 13, 237, 238; restored sense of, 114, 119
order, social: breakdowns in, 150; difference and, 168, 191; fabrication of, 5, 13, 16, 28, 134; incommensurable, 168, 169, 191, 280n11 (*see also* difference); multiple iterations of, 240; regulation of, 13, 129, 238; restoration of, 102, 120, 149
orientalism, 60, 82, 194. *See also* racism
Other, the: the colonized as, 168; exceptional, 168; extrajudicial violence and, 16; mimesis and, 122–23, 169; Muslims as, 113, 153–54, 173–74;

Palestinians as, 71; policing focus on, 152–54; as racialized/racial, 166, 167, 173, 201; resistance of, 169; the West as, 169, 176. *See also* Man-as-human
Othering, 180, 181, 194, 201
Oza, Rupal, 7, 167, 280n9

pacification, 14, 17, 20, 61, 122, 240; colonialism and, 14–15, 58, 61, 62–63, 66, 239, 242; global infrastructure/regimes of, 58–59, 65, 89, 90, 168, 170, 196, 242; policing as, 14, 15; recruitment to participate in, 102, 120, 121; regimes in Palestine/Israel, 59, 74, 83, 165; security as, 14, 229–30, 243–44. *See also* counterinsurgency; counterterrorism; policing; security subjects, creating/interpellating new
pacification, Israeli/Zionist model of: British roots of, 63; as exceptional, 72, 75, 234; French use of, 66; hegemony of, 91; as idea of Israel, 60; as incompatible in India, 124, 165 (*see also* homeland security, Israel as exemplar (skepticism of)); Israeli technology and, 58–59, 73, 75, 113; as security innovation, 75, 80–86; as universalist project, 29, 58–59, 61, 65, 89, 196
Pakistan, 111; calls to strike, 46; Inter-Services Intelligence of, 126, 259n41; Kashmir and, 48, 165, 245, 282n37; Lashkar-e-Taiba and, 126, 255n102, 259n41; as term for Muslim-majority districts, 153; 26/11 attacks as originating from, 32, 40, 99
Palestine: British Mandate for, 14–15, 61, 62–63, 64; Gaza, 70, 94; Israeli assemblage of control methods in, 15, 58–59, 165, 234, 246, 255n104, 265n97; Israeli forms of governance in, 29, 60; land title in, 61; Munich Olympics and, 43, 68; Operation Entebbe and, 43, 68–69, 95; Palestine Liberation Organization (PLO), 44; Palestinian Revolt, 62–63; pre-Israel infrastructures of violence in, 61–63; U.S. "shadow" over, 66–67, 71; West Bank, 25, 70, 94. *See also* settler colonialism, Zionist; violence, Israeli/Zionist
Palestine/Israel: continuation of British rule and, 63, 70–71; delegations pre-26/11, 271n50; delegations under Modi, 246; Indian perspective on pre-26/11, 93–97; Indian police training in, 246; Israeli comparisons and expertise, 74, 77, 78, 83, 84, 166–67, 175–76, 184; Israeli experience outside of, 64, 85, 87, 88, 90, 195; pacification regimes and, 59, 74, 83, 165; production of knowledge about, 59–60; surveillance within, 3, 25. *See also* Maharashtra delegation to Palestine/Israel; terrorism, Israel's experience with; violence, Israeli/Zionist
Palestinians: Al-Aqsa Intifada and, 76; changing frame of danger from, 71; contested geography and, 92; criminalization of, 64–65; displacement and dispossession of, 60, 61, 72–73, 76, 80 (*see also* violence, Israeli/Zionist); ethnic cleansing/genocide of, 12, 61, 64–65, 72, 80, 84, 85; increased resistance pre-Israel, 62–63; Indian support for, 6, 96, 167; protests by, 25, 62; as quintessential terrorists, 69, 71, 96; racialization of, 64–65
Pant, Harsh V., 48, 165–66, 167, 171, 182
Pappé, Ilan, 60
Patil, Jayant, 106, 107, 110, 112, 123, 150, 160
Patil, R. R., 44, 99, 233, 234–35, 259n59
Patil, Shivraj, 43, 44, 99
Patwardhan, Anand, 232–33, 234
Pawar, Sharad, 6, 271n50
Pedahzur, Ami, 54–55
Peres, Shimon, 36

performance: economics and, 200, 223, 230; enactment of reals and, 228, 230; fabricating Indian homeland security and, 200, 228; of Israeli domination, 29, 60; police modernization and, 120 (*see also* spectacle)
performance of Israeli authority, 39, 48, 52–53, 54, 56; and enrolling networks, 50–51; production of controversy and, 35, 45, 50, 51, 53–54 (*see also* media, Israeli positioning post-26/11 and); by security firms, 87, 88–89, 90 (*see also* Israel, homeland security industry of)
perimeter security, 76, 87, 136, 139, 163; bollards, 25, 135–37, *136*, *137–38*, 163, *164*, 182, 183, 185, 197, 241; *nakabandi*, 139–40, 143, *143*, 162
Photonis, 209–10
Pinkerton, 202, 214, 224, 236
police: anti-terrorism units, 26, 109, 135, *136*, 148, 149 (*see also* Force One); broadened power of, 231, 239; as the concept of security, 13; corruption and, 10, 100, 145, 146, 156, 161; infrastructure of, 29–30, 129, 160; Israeli, 41, 63, 76, 171; legitimacy of, 16; politicization of, 10, 100, 101, 161, 238; professionalization of, 10, 16, 43, 100, 132, 160, 237 (*see also* police modernization); provisional/contingent power of, 102, 134, 145–46, 150–51, 161, 242; Punjabi, 1, 246; quick response teams (QRTs), 109, 135, *136*, 148, 149; uniforms and, 18, 107, 109, 115, 122, 135, 145
police, Maharashtra, 22, 191; Aditya (pseudonym), 178, 179, 181, 189; HLEC and, 103–4; longstanding presence in Mumbai, 140; physical fortification of stations, 138; skepticism of Israeli model, 178, 179, 180–82, 193. *See also* HLEC; Maharashtra delegation to Palestine/Israel; police modernization
police, Mumbai: anti-Muslim bias of, 152–53, 154–55, 156; antiterror cells at police stations, 162; case against Ajmal Kasab, 106, 270n34; HLEC report and, 103–4, 124, 125, 235; increased use of *nakabandi*, 139–40, 143, *143*, 162; Israeli connections, 154–56, 191; longstanding presence in Mumbai, 140; Maharashtra coordination with, 112; Marksman jeeps for, 109, 135, 137, 148, 162–63; Mossad training and, 155, 156; *The Mumbai Protector* and, 115–20, *116–19*, 121, 127, 129–30, 142, 147, *147*, 213; new units post-26/11, 109 (*see also* Force One); public confidence in, 119–20; quick response teams (QRTs), 109, 115, 135, 148, 149; 26/11 actions, 38, 99, 100, 148–49. *See also* HLEC; Karkare, Hemant; Maharashtra delegation to Palestine/Israel; Maria, Rakesh; Salaskar, Vijay; Sivanandan, Dhanushkodi (D.)
police modernization: as bricolage, 30, 138–39, 145, 160, 235; as the changing same, 30, 129, 134, 140–45, 159–60, 161; differences in types of policing and, 149–50; domestic marketing to, 108–9, 203; emulation of Israel and, 114, 123, 130; emulation of the western approach, 122, 123, 130, 132, 236–37; foreign engagement in, 110–14; HLEC and, 124–25; Israeli marketing to, 108, 203, 204; Marksman jeeps and, 109, 135, 137, 148, 162–63; as militarization, 132–33; *The Mumbai Protector* and, 115–20, *116–19*, 121, 127, 129–30, 142, 147, *147*, 213; Muslim perception of Israeli connection, 154–56; in national media, 123, 125; new unit creation and, 109; as pacification, 128; physical manifestations of, 135, 142, 145, 159–60; in police media, 115–19, *116–19*, 127; as policing ontology,

125–27; pre-26/11 initiatives, 107, 108, 270n35; questioning/critique of, 148, 151; Rambo as model and, 109, 122; showcasing of, 114–21, *116–19*, 159–60; skepticism of Israeli model, 178, 179, 180–82, 193; as spectacle, 114–15, 120, 121, 123, 127, 128, 154; as strictly counterterror, 149, 150; training and, 24, 110, 111, 176–77, 178, 191; in the U.K., 223. *See also* Force One; *jugaad*

police modernization, political focus post-26/11, 98, 124, 128, 135, 157, 234; to build public confidence, 106, 108, 114, 115, 120–21, 122, 129–30, 135, 148; as the changing same, 30, 134, 161; to displace conflict, 127; global scrutiny and, 101; lack of well-defined agenda, 231; to pacify local anti-politician backlash, 107, 114, 123, 129, 160, 234–35; policing the legitimacy crisis and, 29–30, 102, 106, 122, 123, 125, 128–29; to satisfy demands for security, 148. *See also* HLEC

police modernization, procurement and, 107–10, 122, 139, 182–83, 187, 225; action absent of HLEC's recommendations, 123–24; bureaucratic impediments and, 104–5, 235, 270n35; changes in focus post-26/11, 108–9; questioned priorities of, 146–48. *See also* Maharashtra delegation to Palestine/Israel

policing: borders of, 134, 149–51; critique of, 10, 15, 33, 48, 51, 100, 224, 237–38; demonization of Muslims in India and, 144, *144*, 152–59, *158–59*, 161; as generating disorder, 129; law and order vs. counterterrorism, 15, 149, 150, 151, 162, 237; of the legitimacy crisis, 29–30, 101–2, 106, 122, 123, 125, 128; modern, 33, 192; priorities of, 224–25; reform of, 63, 134, 160, 161, 186, 237 (*see also* HLEC); technology of, 23, 133, 162; transnationality of, 1, 5, 17. *See also* homeland security; pacification; spectacle

policing, colonial, 8, 62–63, 86, 89; colonial inheritance of, 16, 161, 166, 230, 237, 238, 242; history in India, 14–17, 140, 161, 230

policing, infrastructure of, 20, 48, 154, 224, 225, 236; *jugaad* and, 101, 145, 161; retaining preexisting, 29–30, 129, 134, 140–45, 154, 159–60. *See also* India, materialized homeland security of

policing, Israeli model of, 6, 51, 91, 112, 124, 193, 245; in pre-Israel Palestine, 62, 63

policy, 161, 214; HLEC and, 102–3, 105, 123–24; Israeli, 6, 36, 71, 95, 165, 174; militarization as 26/11 response, 30, 113, 132–33, 134, 173 (*see also* police modernization); Jayant Patil and, 150; reforms of, 12, 50, 102–3; responses to 9/11 and, 1, 2–3; unopposable measures of, 112. *See also* Pant, Harsh V.

policy conferences, 22, 23, 202, 210–11, 221, 255n101. *See also* Securing Asia

political situations, 35, 50, 257n11

politics: anti-political strategies and, 101–2, 205; of (post)colonial difference, 169–70, 193, 196; comparison and, 35, 83–84; martial, 134, 276n19; multiple forms of, 20; radical, 129; of response, 29, 35; of responsibility, 105; sanitizing, 133–34; of truth, 30, 128; typical crisis responses and, 103; warlike qualities and, 134. *See also* authoritarianism; geopolitics

politics, ontological, 17, 102, 195, 242

postcolonial cities, 160

postcolonial states, 16, 102, 120, 204, 222, 227

postcolonial theory, 3, 161, 194; difference and, 168, 169, 191–92, 282n37; knowledge production and, 59. *See also* colonialism

POTA (Prevention of Terrorism Act), 7, 154, 250n24
power, state: hyper-visible, 102, 120, 238 (*see also* spectacle); new forms of, 12; pre-existing, 61; social order and, 13; stand-ins for, 110. *See also* policing
Pradhan, Rajesh, 111, 170
Pradhan, Ram, 103, 233; access to police logs, 127; call to release HLEC report, 125; police modernization lobbyists and, 108; questioning delegation to Palestine/Israel, 124; ties to Congress Party, 104. *See also* HLEC
preparedness: HLEC and, 103; India's lack compared to DHS, 8, 10, 33, 105; Israel as exemplar of, 2, 33, 111, 123, 174, 177; root cause of India's lack of, 101; statements of, 115, 119, 177
preparedness, solutions to lack of: Global North approaches and, 8–9; homeland security as, 34, 123; Israeli homeland security and, 29, 34, 47, 50, 51–52, 123, 180 (*see also* Maharashtra delegation to Palestine/Israel); as process over time, 177, 224. *See also* police modernization
Prevention of Terrorism Act (POTA), 7, 154, 250n24
Punjab, 1–2, 246
Puri, Anil, 48–49

QRTs (quick response teams), 109, 135, *136*, 148, 149
quick response teams (QRTs), 109, 135, *136*, 148, 149

race: categorizing, 18; hierarchies of, 97, 187, 192, 196, 200–201, 227, 228, 242; homeland as term of racial purity, 12; racial violence, 28, 276n19; Zionism and, 12, 85
race-making, 12; capitalism and, 14, 201, 228; imbricated with security, 14
racialization: of civilization, 64, 82, 85; colonial, 200–201, 257n11 (*see also* difference, colonial); of the Global South, 228; of markets, 228; the Other and, 64, 166, 167, 168, 173, 201; of Palestinians, 64–65; in policing, 101, 153, 276n19; tropes of, 85
racism: British legacy of, 166, 226, 227–28; Israeli, 24, 166, 168, 179–80, 181–82, 184–85, 187, 188–89
Rahul (pseudonym), 172, 173–75, 176, 177, 180–81
Rajiv (pseudonym), 221–22, 223, 228
Raman, B., 96–97, 176
Rana, Aziz, 285n37
Rao, Nirupama, 1, 2
rationality, 168, 200, 201, 227–28, 229–30
realities, new: challenging, 55; critical events and, 11, 29; emergence from knowledge, 35; enrollment and, 48, 49, 53, 56; temporary, 130. *See also* world-making, homeland security as
reality: disavowal of creation of, 78; enrollment creating, 48, 49–50, 52–53, 80; as multiple, 17–18, 102; policing the terms of, 30, 102, 129; transnational production of, 60
reals: incommensurable, 169, 242; negotiation of, 169–70, 194–95, 239, 242; nondominant, 19; staging, 60, 228
Roy, A. N., 99, 104
Roy, Arundhati, 232, 233, 234, 235
Roy, Himanshu, 119
Rubin, David, 2

Sahni, Ajai, 109, 122, 151, 236–37, 238
Said, Edward, 59–60, 64, 65, 70, 79, 167
Salaita, Steven, 92
Salaskar, Vijay, 99, 100, 105
Sangh Parivar. *See* Hindutva groups
Sanjeev (pseudonym), 108–9, 114, 210
Schrader, Stuart, 14
Securing Asia, 197–201; as bringing East to West, 199, 200, 209, 210, 227–28; as educating the market, 199, 200, 201, 209; the "Indian mind" and, 211–13, *212*, 215–16, 219–20, 221;

rebranding and folding, 231. *See also* Dhaul, Harry
securitization, 11, 132–33, 229
security: models of, 5, 6, 7–8, 18, 19, 33, 219–20, 224 (*see also* homeland security; homeland security, Israel as exemplar of; settler colonialism, Zionist); police as embodiment of, 13, 16 (*see also* policing); as political technology, 14; rescaling of, 11; vs. safety, 81, 149, 151, 243; universality of, 31, 222–23, 226, 229, 243–44. *See also* homeland security, fabrication of; order, social; pacification; preparedness
security, Indian: bourgeois concerns of, 99, 102, 110, 128, 233, 236; deficiencies of approach, 48–49, 148–51, 186–88, 213–14, 220, 224, 236–37 (*see also* homeland security, Indian; *jugaad*; police modernization; preparedness); as exposing fabrication, 242; need to transform existing norms, 221, 225 (*see also* awareness, Indian homeland security and); as process over time, 177, 224; reform of, 8, 134, 186, 271n50 (*see also* police modernization); understanding/perception of as different, 213–14, 221–22, 226, 236–38, 243 (*see also* awareness; difference, Indo-Israeli interactions and). *See also* India, homeland security of
security, Indian (26/11 as turning point), 28, 98, 192, 232; as bringing India and Israel closer together, 47; challenge to, 225, 241; as creating a new reality, 11, 29, 34, 48, 50, 54; as crisis of security, 29–30, 44, 100, 101–2, 106, 122, 123, 125, 128; earlier discussions of security and, 33–34; immediate aftereffects and, 3, 9–10, 27; in security education, 216–17; trade show/conference positioning and, 199, 202–5, 211, 224–25, 227; as world-making trope, 227. *See also* India, materialized homeland security of; police modernization, political focus post-26/11
security, Indian (private), 149; Indian providers, 178, 241; Israeli providers, 49, 87, 183, 186, 188, 190; Israeli training and, 281n21; luxury real estate and, 188, 190–91
security, private (Israeli), 186, 188, 190; Blue Sky International, 49; Hashmira Security Technologies Ltd./G4S, 62, 64; Orad, 87. *See also* BG Ilanit Gates and Urban Elements Ltd.
security education: awareness and, 30, 196, 199, 201, 214–15, 285n37; "educating the market" concept, 30, 205–6, 209, 210, 214–15, 216, 222, 235; enrolled networks and, 200, 201; *homo securitas* and, 201–2, 223, 226, 230; the "Indian mind" and, 216–23, *217–18*, 225, 242; as not feasible or possible, 188, 189, 190; as overcoming/transcending difference, 192, 199, 213, 220, 228–29; purported need for (re)education and, 81, 216–17, 222, 223, 225, 228–29, 242; as route to superiority, 80; vendors educated on Indian/Asian culture, 211–12, 213, 215–16. *See also* trade shows; training
security experts, 33; international, 48, 50–51, 62, 219; Israeli, 34, 43, 46, 55, 193–94, 234 (*see also* Gleser, Leo; Israel, homeland security industry of (informants))
security experts, Indian, 43, 48, 235; K.P.S. Gill, 1–2, 6, 97, 176, 217, 237; Harsh V. Pant, 48, 165–66, 167, 171, 182
security infrastructures, 10; awareness raising and, 18, 79, 80, 102, 120–21, 213, 285n37; global, 89; martial arts training as, 18, 80–81, 89, 177; police uniforms as, 18, 107, 109, 115, 122, 135, 145; retaining pre-26/11, 29–30, 129, 134, 160. *See also* CCTV cameras;

security infrastructures (*continued*) fences; India, materialized homeland security of; surveillance
security messaging, 26, 142–44, *143*, *144*. *See also* awareness, Indian homeland security and
security state, Indian: refashioning, 10–11; violent interpellation and, 121, 159–60
security state, the, 12; collusion with capital, 13; excesses of, 133; Israel as exemplar of, 54; making of, 18; racial violence and, 28; secrecy and, 26; U.S., 3, 8, 285n37 (*see also* US Department of Homeland Security). *See also* homeland security industry; policing; surveillance
security subjects: education of, 216; Indians as unwilling to become, 24, 226, 229, 241
security subjects, creating/interpellating new, 30, 102, 120–21, 127, 142, 159–60; refusal of, 226, 240–41; security trade shows and, 201, 226. *see also* awareness
security training, 18, 48, 78, 281n21
Security Watch India (SWI), 197, 198, *203*, 206–7, 209, 214–15, *215*, 217, *217–18*, 230–31
Security Watch U.K. (SWUK), 197, 198
September 11. *See* 9/11
Setalvad, Teesta, 155, 157
Seth, Sanjay, 4, 19, 226–27
Sethi, Manisha, 99, 238
settler colonialism: disavowal of, 60, 85, 91; legitimation of, 60, 64–65, 92; long history of, 12, 239. *See also* colonialism
settler colonialism, Zionist, 29, 58, 59–60, 61–62; British collaboration with, 63; British legal structure and, 70; disavowal and, 78, 85; ethnic cleansing/genocide and, 12, 61, 64–65, 72, 80, 84, 85; exceptionalism and, 76, 78, 80, 84, 92; as inspiration/model, 66, 67, 70, 79, 92, 234, 246; as marketable experience, 76, 85; praise for, 67; theology of, 64–65, 85, 91; as unending war, 91; as universal experience/global knowledge, 60, 73, 84, 85; as worldview, 80, 91. *See also* exceptionality/exceptionalism, Israeli/Jewish/Zionist
Shaban, Abdul, 153–54
Shalhoub-Kevorkian, Nadera, 64–65, 91
Sharan, Devi, 1, 2
Shilliam, Robbie, 228
Shin Bet, 37, 53
Shiv Sena, 100, 113, 122. *See also* Hindutva groups
SIBAT (International Defense Cooperation Directorate), 86
SIMI (Students' Islamic Movement of India), 7, 153
Singh, Manmohan, 9, 11, 41, 46
Singha, Radhika, 15
Sivanandan, Dhanushkodi (D.), 127; accused of corruption, 146, 156; advocacy for Israeli solutions, 111–12, 114, 123, 156, 174; on corruption as bigger threat, 235–36; implication in Israeli arms deal, 156; *The Mumbai Protector* and, 115, 119–20; post-26/11 backlash and, 98; procurement post-26/11 and, 107, 114; response to questions of Israeli involvement, 155–56; retirement and consultancy, 178; skepticism of Israeli solutions, 130, 174–75. *see also* Maharashtra delegation to Palestine/Israel
Six-Day War, the, 67–68, 93–95
Sofer, Mark, 44, 47
Soviet Union, the, 67, 71, 272n35. *See also* Cold War, the
spectacle: police modernization as, 102, 114–15, 120, 121, 123, 127, 128, 154, 236; 26/11 as, 33, 122
staging: of 26/11, 202–3; of homeland security, 3, 19; of homeland security markets, 199, 209 (*see also* trade

shows); Israeli military prowess, 61, 72; of reals, 60; of the world, 5, 20; of Zionist settler colonialism, 29, 60, 91
Stampnitsky, Lisa, 71
state power: colonial, 61; forms of, 12; social order and, 13; violence and, 7, 92, 129, 154–55, 156–57, 161, 237; visibility of, 102, 110, 120, 238. *See also* police modernization; policing; surveillance
Stoler, Ann Laura, 20, 35, 83
Students' Islamic Movement of India (SIMI), 7, 153
subjectivity, 213–14, 226–27, 229, 239, 285n37
Subrahmanyam, K., 7, 8
Sullivan, Kate, 221–22
surveillance, 18; centralized, 151; facial recognition, 162; *khabri* (spy) networks and, 153, 154; marketing of, 73, 74, 182, 205, 209, 211, 247; of Muslims in Europe, 82, 90; of Muslims in India, 152, 154; in Palestine/Israel, 3, 25, 113–14; permanent counterinsurgency and, 238–39, 246; as for public benefit, 142; skepticism of, 224; in the U.K., 223, 233; within the U.S., 3. *See also* CCTV cameras
surveillance, implementation post-26/11, 25–26, 142, 162, 163; police modernization and, 106, 132, 145. *See also* CCTV cameras
surveillance, technologies of, 19, 26, 182; cell phone surveillance, 209, 246; military, 133. *See also* CCTV cameras
SWI (Security Watch India), 197, 198, *203*, 206–7, 209, 214–15, *215*, 217, *217–18*, 230–31
SWUK (Security Watch U.K.), 197, 198
Syria, 67–68, 69, 95

Taj Hotel, 40–41, 49, 232; critique of handling, 37, 235; physical security post-26/11, 135, *136*, 137, *141*, 162–63, 241; protests at, 99; theories surrounding attack of, 126
Taliban, the, 1, 126
Tamboli, Nisar, 111, 170
technology, 11; Hindu nationalism and, 122, 169; imagery of, 115–19, *116–19*; incompatibility/unfeasibility of, 23, 83, 224; legitimacy and, 120; making the homeland security state and, 18, 25, 33, 128, 132–33, 153; marketing, 197, 199 (*see also* trade shows); new grafted onto existing, 30, 134, 135, 138–40, *140–42*, 145, 160, 235; as peripheral pre-26/11, 33–34.; privileging of, 132–33; science and technology studies (STS), 3; showcasing, 115–19, *116–19*; skepticism of, 224, 225; violent sources of, 25. *See also* police modernization; surveillance, technologies of
technology, Israeli: cell phone surveillance and, 209, 246; centrality in global pacification, 58–59, 73, 75, 113; CornerShot, 75, 79, 183; emulating, 6, 113, 192; exceptionalism of, 76, 175–76; Indian partnerships in, 47–48, 49; Indian skepticism of, 193; the Israeli model and, 59, 83; pre-Israel roots of, 62, 63–64; research and development, 75, 77; sales of, 64, 75, 178, 182–83, 185, 246–47, 278n75 (*see also* Israel, homeland security industry of)
technology, Israeli (marketing of): enrollment and, 24–25, 89; foreign experience and, 191; gendered terminology and, 172, 192–93; the Israeli brand and, 87–88, 91; Israeli trade delegations and, 8–9; media coverage of Israeli homeland security industry, 8–9, 47–48, 113–14, 156, 176, 246; as part of integrated solution, 186; SIBAT and, 86; trade shows and, 205, *207–8*, 209. *See also* IEICI; Israel, positioning

technology (*continued*)
post-26/11; Maharashtra delegation to Palestine/Israel
terrorism: charges of, 1, 7, 156, 239, 255n102; defining the "problem" of, 34, 71; as economic threat, 204; false accusations of, 69, 72–74, 92, 267n128; framing the term, 27–28; Hindutva, 155; Indian government cooperation on, 7; Israeli conferences on, 70; Israeli/Zionist, 54–55, 64, 255n104; knowledge restriction and, 28; law and order vs. counterterrorism, 15, 149, 150, 151, 162, 237; Maoist, 152, 203; Prevention of Terrorism Act (POTA), 7, 154, 250n24; reality of preparing for, 235–36; state-complicit, 126; state-sponsored, 7; Unlawful Activities Prevention Act (UAPA), 7, 10–11, 166. *See also* awareness; counterterrorism; DHS; preparedness; war on terror, the
terrorism, India's experience with: Bombay bombings, 100, 112, 113, 154, 233 (*see also* 26/11); as common ground with Israel, 34, 51, 97, 171 (*see also* Israel, positioning post-26/11); counter-terrorism exceptionality and, 96, 97; homeland security as out of proportion to, 241; as increasing, 8, 9, 112, 204; Indian Airlines flight IC-814, 1, 2, 8. *See also* Indo-Israeli cooperation/collaboration; police modernization; preparedness
terrorism, Israel's experience with, 76–80, 91; colonial roots of, 63; Entebbe and, 68–69; Indian evaluation of Israeli policy on, 6; as marketable, 47, 71, 76–80, 85, 96–97, 112; primacy and, 73–75; as quintessential victim, 69; 26/11 as parallel to, 34, 37–38, 41, 43, 44, 47, 48, 50–51, 53–54; as universal knowledge, 85. *See also* counterterrorism, Israeli; homeland security, Israel as exemplar of; Israel, positioning post-26/11; Maharashtra delegation to Palestine/Israel
terrorism as global ("Islamic") threat, 10, 98; as common enemy, 6, 167, 280n9; "international terrorism" and, 47, 58, 69, 70–71; Israel as first to experience, 2, 38; Israeli shift of focus to, 71; as reinforcing anti-Muslim sentiment, 155; 26/11 as new reality and, 34, 36, 187, 192 (*see also* 26/11 as security turning point); as against the West, 34, 51. *See also* Indo-Israeli cooperation/collaboration; preparedness; terrorism, Israel's experience with; 26/11 as security turning point
terrorists: Israelis/Zionists as, 54–55, 64, 255n104; Maoist, 152, 203; Palestinians as, 69, 71, 96–97; stereotype of Muslims in India as, 6–7, 112, 152–53. *See also* violence
Tilley, Lisa, 228
To the Last Bullet (V. Kamte), 126–27
tourism, 204; 26/11 attack and, 32, 131; in Israel, 76
trade shows, 22, 30, 86, 183, 198–99, 202, 210; Challenges for India's Homeland Security, 206, 209, 225; government officials at, 209; Homeland Security India, 183, 199, 205–6, *206–8*, 216, 221, 224, 255n101; India-Israel Homeland Security Cooperation Forum as, 49. *See also* IFSEC (International Fire and Security Exhibition and Conference)
training: by the Indian Army, 178; the Israeli approach to, 81–82, 180; marketing of, 73, 77, 78, 86, 89, 90, 247; martial arts and, 18, 80–81, 89, 177; by the NSG, 178; similarity of, 180; of state terror forces, 88
training, Indo-Israeli partnerships in, 191; facilitation of, 49 (*see also* Maharashtra delegation to Palestine/Israel); Force One and, 112, 181, 281n32; under Modi, 245–46; Mumbai police

and, 155, 156; private security and, 281n21; skepticism of, 177–79, 192–93
transnationality: of business, 210–11; collaboration and, 50, 211 (*see also* Indo-Israeli cooperation/collaboration); colonial, 16–17, 62–63; encounters of, 5, 29, 60, 65–72 (*see also* Israel, positioning post-26/11); the making of homeland security and, 3, 4–5, 18–19, 28, 60, 167; the mission of homeland security as, 4, 17–18; multiplication of homeland security and, 12, 104, 105, 155, 168 (*see also* homeland security, Israel as exemplar of; settler colonialism, Zionist: as inspiration/model); of policing, 14, 17, 104, 134, 155; and production of reality, 60; of security models, 5, 14, 61, 88, 104, 105, 167; social order and, 28. *See also* homeland security, fabrication of; universality of homeland security
Tsing, Anna, 26, 240
26/11, *xix*, 3, 32–33; anti-politician anger after, 3, 96, 99 (*see also* police modernization, political focus post-26/11); casualties, 33, 38, 41, 256n1 (*see also* Karkare, Hemant); contested narratives of, 99, 100, 106, 123, 127, 129, 270n34 (see also *To the Last Bullet* (V. Kamte); *Who Killed Karkare?* (Mushrif)); crisis of legitimacy following, 29–30, 44, 100, 101–2, 106, 122, 123, 125, 128; death of Hemant Karkare and, 99–100, 101, 105, 125–27; as emasculating, 122; as exceptional, 149, 150, 224–25, 233–34; focus on homeland security after, 9–11, 27 (*see also* police modernization); greater security awareness after, 98, 102; as intelligence failure, 41–43, 46, 52–53, 104, 105; lack of homeland security and, 9–10; later Israeli marketing and, 87, 182–83, 187; media coverage of, 32, 33, 135, 146–47; memorials and reminders, 131–32, *132*, 162; parallels to 9/11, 9–10, 31, 49–50, 232; perception of inept/untruthful authority and, 51, 105, 127 (see also *To the Last Bullet* (V. Kamte); *Who Killed Karkare?* (Mushrif)); planning of, 46; as spectacle, 33, 122; whether preventable with technology, 224. *See also* Maria, Rakesh
26/11, alleged assailants, 46, 105, 273n97; Al-Qaeda, 46, 126; Shahid Azmi's defense of, 156–57; Brahmanist conspiracy and, 126, 129; David Headley, 23, 255n102; IB, 126; Ajmal Kasab, 33, 106, 126, 270n34; Lashkar-e-Taiba/Inter-Services Intelligence, 126, 259n41; Mossad/pro-Zionist groups, 126; Wahid Shaikh, 154
26/11, critique of handling of attacks, 98, 106; anti-politician anger after, 100, 106, 128, 129, 234; BJP calls for dismissals, 99; calls for political reform and, 99; forced resignations after, 43, 99, 234–35, 259n59; Israeli critique of hostage response, 33, 37, 38–39, 40, 41, 42, 44–45, 50–51; by Vinita Kamte, 100. *See also* HLEC
26/11, Israeli positioning and, 11, 36, 45, 49, 72; centering Israeli viewpoints, 41, 42, 44, 51, 53; as enrollment, 48, 49–50, 53–54, 55–56; hostage response critique, 33, 37, 38–39, 40, 41, 42, 44–45, 50–51; indifference to Indian experience, 97; Israel as having unique insights, 34, 37–38, 43, 48, 50, 55–56; tempering of criticism and, 41–42, 43–46, 50, 53, 56–57
26/11, Israeli presence in response to, 37, 39–40, 50, 234, 258n21; Magen David Adom (MDA), 37, 55, 234, 258n22. *See also* ZAKA
26/11 as security turning point, 28, 98, 192, 232; as bringing India and Israel closer together, 47; challenge to, 225, 241; as creating a new reality, 11, 29, 34, 48, 50, 54; earlier discussion

26/11 as security turning point (*continued*) of security, 33–34; immediate effect after and, 3, 9–10, 27; in security education, 216–17; trade show/conference positioning and, 199, 202–5, 211, 224–25, 227; as world-making trope, 227. *See also* India, materialized homeland security of; police modernization, political focus post-26/11
Tzur, David, 41–42

UAPA (Unlawful Activities Prevention Act), 7, 10–11, 166
Uganda, 43, 68–69, 70, 74, 95
U.K., the: British Mandate for Palestine, 14–15, 61, 62–63, 64; collaboration with India, 66, 210–11; collaboration with Israel, 66; colonial education and, 226–27, 228; colonial emergency law, 70; colonial policing and, 15, 86, 89, 140, 166; geostrategic partnership with India, 155, 210; homeland security lessons from, 4, 10, 33, 224; pacification in Palestine and, 62–63; police modernization consultation and, 108, 233; Securing Asia and Indo-British ties, 197, 219, 220, 221; trade delegation to India, 211; training approach, 82, 180; use of CCTV, 223, 233; view of Israel as European extension, 65–66. *See also* IFSEC
uniqueness: of Asia's challenges, 198; concept of homeland security and, 4; of Israeli experience, 36, 38, 43, 76–81, 82, 83, 90, 266n107 (*see also* homeland security, Israel as exemplar of; Israel, positioning post-26/11); of the Israeli model, 59, 81 (*see also* Israel, pacification model of); 9/11's lack of, 1–2, 74; training lack of, 180, 181. *See also* exceptionality/exceptionalism
United States, the: counterterrorism model of, 6, 251n36 (*see also* United States Department of Homeland Security); diplomatic ties with India, 6, 7, 155, 167, 280n9; downing of Iranian passenger plane, 88; enrolled in Israeli propaganda, 70–71; exceptionalism of, 65, 83; K.P.S. Gill and, 97; hegemonic masculinity of, 109, 122; homeland security concept and, 4, 12, 75; Israel as emulating, 65; Israel as model for counterinsurgency, 2–3; Israeli-American casualties on 26/11, 33, 38, 41; Israeli exceptionalism and, 2–3, 65; the Israeli homeland security industry and, 88, 90; Jewish regard of Israel in, 66; military aid to Israel, 64, 66, 67; as planning to destabilize India, 99; policing models of, 91, 105, 110, 120; security collaboration with India, 270n25; security model of, 6, 81; training by, 81–82, 180, 249n2; 26/11 aid, 37; 26/11 lessons, 104, 105, 270n25; as unprepared, 2, 74; Vietnam and, 67, 94, 122. *See also* 9/11
United States Department of Homeland Security (DHS): budgetary spending on, 12, 242; creation of, 3; as draconian, 9; emulation of, 8, 142, 241–42; India perceived as needing equivalent, 7–8, 9, 10, 124–25; Israel's expertise as outstripping, 11, 73; mandate of, 4; official Indian meetings with, 9; as security exemplar, 33; SWI and, 218, *218*; unlikelihood in India, 241–42
United States, homeland security industry of, 3, 9, 12–13, 232; arms sales to India, 114, 197, 221
universality: capitalism's claim to, 191–92; challenging, 227; Israeli authority claimed as, 84, 85, 90, 182, 189; liberalism's vision of security as, 229, 243–44; of modern power, 280n12; refusing Israeli authority as, 175, 176, 182, 194, 196 (*see also* difference, Indo-Israeli interactions and); of subjectivity, 170, 199–200, 227; tension with exceptionality, 4–5, 83–84,

86, 88, 90, 200; universalism and, 85, 191, 193, 196, 225, 244 (*see also* difference); the West and, 120, 193, 225, 229; western modernity and, 168, 200; worldmaking and, 17, 199–200, 229–30; Zionist settler colonialism as, 29, 60, 73, 84, 85

universality of homeland security, 206, 229–30; colonial racism and, 227–28; Israeli claims to, 61, 192; limits of, 26; tension with exceptionality, 4–5, 200; as transnational project, 3, 227 (*see also* world-making, homeland security as)

universality of homeland security, unsettling, 31, 205, 239–44; as colonizing modality, 13, 14, 229, 280n12; difference and, 192, 229; the "Indian mind" and, 222–23; Indian skepticism and, 226; Man-as-human episteme and, 202

Unlawful Activities Prevention Act (UAPA), 7, 10–11, 166

urban spaces, 19, 25, 135–45, 153, 159–60; militarization of, 11, 30, 132, 133; political violence and, 131 (*see also* India, materialized homeland security of; 26/11: memorials and reminders); social order in, 150, 152, 157, 172, 175–76, 193; warfare in, 58–59, 110, 115, 119, 147–48, 177. *see also* India, materialized homeland security of; Mumbai

Vanaik, Achin, 16, 129, 160

Van Susteren, Greta, 1, 5, 97

Verran, Helen, 194

Vietnam, 66, 67, 94, 122

violence: condemnation of, 36, 94; of contemporary empire, 5; disavowal/legitimation of, 19, 92, 97, 280n9 (*see also* violence, Israeli/Zionist: disavowal/legitimation of); domination and, 29, 60, 92, 134, 228, 282n37; extrajudicial, 16, 100; as foundational to homeland security, 19; Hindutva, 112, 113, 125–26, 129, 155, 157; historical narratives of, 61, 92, 134; inciting, 7, 70, 113, 157; as inevitable, 79; the IOF and, 25; Israel as having unique insight on, 36, 38, 78 (*see also* terrorism, Israel's experience with); lack of state monopoly on, 102; military, 140, 142; naming of, 73; origins of, 99; Palestinian, 76, 96, 97; political, 28, 33, 35, 61, 97, 129, 131, 133–34 (*see also* India, materialized homeland security of; terrorism; 26/11: memorials and reminders); as political crisis, 35, 101; politics as antithetical to, 133–34; professionalization of, 82–83; racial, 28; Rambo and, 122; structural reliance on, 160; suicide bombings, 76, 96; systemic, 133, 239. *See also* pacification; policing; terrorism; 26/11

violence, British imperial/colonial, 15–16, 62, 63, 161; legacy of, 14–15, 16, 61, 63, 140, 161, 238. *See also* colonialism, policing and

violence, Israeli/Zionist: as begetting more violence, 95; British legacy and, 61, 63; death squads, 63; differential treatment of, 65; disavowal/legitimation of, 64, 69–70, 72, 78, 79, 80, 92; emulation of, 65; ethnic cleansing/genocide, 12, 61, 64–65, 72, 80, 84, 85; as exceptional, 65, 80; framed as anti-violence, 79, 82–83; as global model, 58–59, 61, 64, 65, 72, 79 (*see also* homeland security, Israel as exemplar of); the idea of Israel justifying, 59–60; IDF as euphemism for, 263n39; Israeli claims of unique experience, 73–74, 76–81, 92; material infrastructures of, 61–62, 63–64; repression of protest and, 25; as terrorism, 64

violence, Mumbai's history of, 140; Bombay bombings, 100, 112, 113, 154, 233; Bombay riots, 113, 122, 133, 152; colonial occupation and, 140 violence, state-sponsored/complicit, 156–57, 166; as British legacy, 238; death squads, 63, 88; disavowal/legitimation of, 92, 237, 280n9; Israel as model of, 58, 154–55; legislation and, 7; shoot to kill orders, 152; silencing critique and, 156–57; usefulness to the existing order, 129, 160, 161, 238; as visible state power, 102. *See also* pacification; policing; violence, Israeli/Zionist

war: of conquest, 14; historical imbrication with, 160; police association with, 115, 122, 132–33, 140; small, 62–63; as unending, 12, 91, 174, 239

warfare, urban, 58–59, 110, 115, 119, 147–48, 177

war on terror, the: beginnings of, 7, 72–73, 240–41; critical literature on, 14, 31, 167; deepening Indo-Israeli ties and, 6; as global project, 18, 242; homeland security as cornerstone of, 3, 18; homeland security as new category and, 19; Indian position within, 97, 132–33, 227, 242, 249n2; Israeli counterterrorism marketing and, 71, 73, 74; militarized response and, 132–33 (*see also* police modernization); U.S. lead in, 3, 6, 227, 249n2 (*see also* DHS)

Waseem, Zoha, 161

Weingarten, Haim, 42

West, the: conception of Man-as-human and, 30, 201–2, 226, 228, 230; global terrorism as against, 34, 38, 51; Hindutva ambivalence toward, 169, 193, 220, 226; India remade in image of, 200; India/the East brought to, 199, 200, 209, 210, 211; Israeli disavowal of support from, 91; Israeli framing of, 41; Israel merging with, 65, 90; security myths of, 219; as universal, 120, 193

West Bank, the, 25, 70, 94

Who Killed Karkare? (Mushrif), 125–26, 127, 129, 274n110

world-making, homeland security as, 3–4, 26–27; erasing the nondominant and, 19; masking contingency and, 20; remaking the world and, 18, 19, 80, 228, 240, 242–43; as self-conscious endeavor, 5, 240; universal/rational pretenses of, 4–5, 11–12, 14, 17, 199–200, 229–30

world-making, homeland security as remaking India and, 3, 230–31, 235, 239; in Israel's image, 52, 167, 192; in the West's image, 199–200, 220, 226, 227

Wynter, Sylvia, 201, 228

Yaron, Amos, 55

Yatom, Danny, 42–43, 156

Yonucu, Deniz, 121

ZAKA, 37, 234, 258n23; critique of Nariman House response, 42, 43, 44, 45, 46, 53, 55–56, 234; Israeli government distancing from, 45, 46; operations at Nariman House, 40, 41, 269n24

Zionism, 59; civilizational rhetoric of, 64; early Indian support for, 5–6; ideology of, 60, 64, 78, 168; propaganda/publicity (*hasbara*) and, 95; racial purity and, 12, 61, 64, 72, 80, 84, 85; settler colonialism and, 29, 58–60; western origins of, 91. *See also* exceptionality, Israeli/Jewish/Zionist; settler colonialism, Zionist

Zuri, Guy, 278n75; flexibility of Israeli model and, 84; homeland security term and, 75; Israeli homeland security brand and, 78, 87; marketing to India and, 171–73, 188, 189; particularity of Israeli model and, 83, 84, 184. *See also* IEICI

ALSO PUBLISHED IN THE SOUTH ASIA IN MOTION SERIES

Resistance as Negotiation: Making States and Tribes in the Margins of Modern India
Uday Chandra (2024)

Fragile Hope: Seeking Justice for Hate Crimes in India
Sandhya Fuchs (2024)

Breathless: Tuberculosis, Inequality, and Care in Rural India
Andrew McDowell (2024)

Labors of Division: Global Capitalism and the Emergence of the Peasant in Colonial Panjab
Navyug Gill (2024)

The Political Outsider: Indian Democracy and the Lineages of Populism
Srirupa Roy (2024)

Qaum, Mulk, Sultanat: Citizenship and National Belonging in Pakistan
Ali Usman Qasmi (2023)

Boats in a Storm: Law, Migration, and Decolonization in South and Southeast Asia, 1942–1962
Kalyani Ramnath (2023)

Life Beyond Waste: Work and Infrastructure in Urban Pakistan
Waqas Butt (2023)

Colonizing Kashmir: State-building under Indian Occupation
Hafsa Kanjwal (2023)

Dust on the Throne: The Search for Buddhism in Modern India
Douglas Ober (2023)

Mother Cow, Mother India: A Multispecies Politics of Dairy in India
Yamini Narayanan (2023)

The Vulgarity of Caste: Dalits, Sexuality, and Humanity in Modern India
Shailaja Paik (2022)

Delhi Reborn: Partition and Nation Building in India's Capital
Rotem Geva (2022)

The Right to Be Counted: The Urban Poor and the Politics of Resettlement in Delhi
Sanjeev Routray (2022)

Protestant Textuality and the Tamil Modern: Political Oratory and the Social Imaginary in South Asia
Bernard Bate, Edited by E. Annamalai, Francis Cody, Malarvizhi Jayanth, and Constantine V. Nakassis (2021)

Special Treatment: Student Doctors at the All India Institute of Medical Sciences
Anna Ruddock (2021)

From Raj to Republic: Sovereignty, Violence, and Democracy in India
Sunil Purushotham (2021)

The Greater India Experiment: Hindutva Becoming and the Northeast
Arkotong Longkumer (2020)

Nobody's People: Hierarchy as Hope in a Society of Thieves
Anastasia Piliavsky (2020)

Brand New Nation: Capitalist Dreams and Nationalist Designs in Twenty-First-Century India
Ravinder Kaur (2020)

Partisan Aesthetics: Modern Art and India's Long Decolonization
Sanjukta Sunderason (2020)

For a complete listing of titles in this series, visit the Stanford University Press website, www.sup.org.